Contemporary Product Development

Contemporary Product Development

A FOCUS ON INNOVATION

First Edition

Keith Edmund Ferguson, John Sztykiel, and Moss Ingram

Florida State University • Michigan State University • Grand Rapids Community College

cognella® SAN DIEGO

Bassim Hamadeh, CEO and Publisher
Jennifer Codner, Senior Field Acquisitions Editor
Michelle Piehl, Senior Project Editor
Christian Berk, Production Editor
Emely Villavicencio, Senior Graphic Designer
Alexa Lucido, Licensing Manager
Natalie Piccotti, Director of Marketing
Kassie Graves, Vice President of Editorial
Jamie Giganti, Director of Academic Publishing

Cover image: Copyright © 2016 iStockphoto LP/chinaface.

Printed in the United States of America.

3970 Sorrento Valley Blvd., Ste. 500, San Diego, CA 92121

As I reflect on this two-year process of writing this text, I would like to dedicate it to my family, my wife Maureen for her support and patience. Many days and nights were spent in the office away from her and she never complained, only encouraged me.

I also dedicate this to my children, Lauren and Delainey, and son-in-law Michael. Your thoughts and encouragement were motivating toward the completion of this text.

Finally, I dedicate this text to my late brother Kevin. I know he would have been proud, and I miss him every day. He was one of the most innovative people I have known!

—Keith E. Ferguson

Pablo Picasso once said, "Every child is born an artist, the challenge is to remain an artist as one gets older." My wife, Joni, is an artist, innovator, and creator. Not only has she inspired me since the day I first met her, but she has challenged me every day to do my best. I strive every day to not only remain creative, and innovative, but to grow, and in growing, help solve the world's issues. Joni believes that any issue can be solved as long we think differently and are not afraid to be creative. An artist who sees the world for what it should be, and asks questions, begins to paint a picture of a better world. Through innovation and creativity that picture can become a reality, a better world. For these reasons, and many more, I dedicate this book to my wife Joni, a far better person than me.

—John Sztykiel

I dedicate this book to my dear friend Liz McCormick, without whom innovation and human-centered design would not be such an important part of so many people's daily practice, including my own. What a journey—through thick and thin, from cacophony to crickets, to the preferred futures near and far.

Thank you, Liz. I appreciate you so.

—Moss Ingram

Contents

Foreword

Over the past 35 years I have led design and innovation teams that have developed products for Fortune 500 companies, serving industries as wide ranging as automotive to medical, and through it all I have basically learned two things. First, all industries, companies, and the people who work for them evolve over time by responding to a myriad of influences (both good and bad), and as a result, people develop new skills, processes, and competencies. The second is that over time, as people are constantly bombarded by this myriad of influences, many will eventually succumb to doubt, fear, and confusion; however, there is a core set of activities that, if done well, can lead a product development team from the nascent germination of a meaningful idea to the creation of meaningful value, repeatedly. In other words, there is a path forward for product developers and their teams when they are purposeful in developing and improving their product development competencies, and this text is a guidebook for those who are just becoming aware of their journey to create innovative products and services. What's more, the path provided by the authors of this text is proven.

As indicated by its title, this text is *contemporary* because it addresses the very current realities of business. Specifically, the authors have sifted through the noise associated with today's ever-changing influences that impede the success of the product development processes upon which so many businesses depend. They have also identified a core set of timeless, trend-proof activities, such as how to:

- Empathize with your customers' wants and needs and ensure that your product will become influential and integral in their lives
- Identify significant and meaningful problems to solve in order to substantially benefit customers
- Identify the best way to provide your product to your customers
- Motivate others to adopt your product and increase your customer base
- Test and retest the idea early and often during both "pre" and "post" launch phases to ensure the product and the product's support mechanisms provide all of the elements of a winning customer experience

These activities will not only increase your potential for success but will also boost your confidence to create additional products with greater ease and success as you continue to evolve as a product designer, innovator, and developer.

The other word from the title that stands out for me is *innovation*. Many companies struggle to define "innovation," much less create and refine the processes that allow the influence of innovation to contribute positively to their business. While there are many theories as to why so many companies never realize the desired return on their innovation investment, I think the main reason is that the road to realizing value from a new idea is long and complex, and quite frankly, when you consider all of the required activities for success, it is daunting, even when you have the backing of a large corporate budget. Yet, in this book you will learn that the word "innovation" implies that your great idea has not only reached its intended customers but that customers are using the product because it is providing them with new value—which also means that the product is providing value to your company. Additionally, despite the glamor and mystique often associated with developing and launching a new successful product to the market, product development requires a lot of hard work, and this text does not flinch in describing the work required for success. Whether you are an entrepreneur, an inventor, or a business person, the journey from an idea to value creation is a relentless pursuit of relevant knowledge and decision making. It cannot be overstated: developing and launching an innovation is a lot of work.

In order to streamline this work and increase the efficacy of the material, the authors have also leveraged the research and writings of thought leaders such as Simon Sinek (*Start with Why*), Daniel Coyle (*The Talent Code*), and Mihaly Csikszentmihalyi (*Finding Flow*) to structure the text in a way that reflects how the brain works, which also serves to reinforce both how to best approach the product development process as well as support how we learn. As anyone sets out to attain new knowledge or learn a new skill in a particular subject area, it is helpful to understand the big picture of *why* the topic exists and *why* it is worth your time and effort to study. In this text, you will learn that understanding the *why* of product development is your starting point, for a multitude of reasons, as your initial efforts must focus on understanding the reasons *why* your customers' problem exists and *why* it has evolved into its current form. Then, you will learn *how* to best respond in order to build the foundation of a differentiated approach that aligns with both the mission and vision of your company while also addressing the needs of your customer. This process finally leads to determining *what* the actual solution will be in the form of products, services, business models, and industry ecosystems. Additionally, this text will help you practice creating value for your customer by successfully addressing the original and ever-relevant question of *why* through repeated validation.

Keep in mind that relative to the work associated with answering the *why* and the *how*, the *what* is almost always the easiest to answer. In part, this is because resources are so much easier to acquire than ever before. Talent, technology, partners—now more than ever, there is a global pool of easily accessible assets and resources just waiting to help you create new value. The trick is knowing *who* and *what* you need, *how* and *when* you will put your resources to work, but most importantly *why* you are expending your time and resources toward these efforts in the first place. Ironically, *why* this is important is because all of this ever-increasing abundance of resources creates a cacophony of noise that makes the work of the product developer all the more challenging.

Therefore, the keys to benefiting from this text is to understand the sequence and depth of study required of each phase in the journey of developing a product and to experience why and how each phase of input results in progress. What's more, the authors have identified a subset of tools and methods to encourage rigor and evidence-based decision making. You will discover that the more you practice using these structured, serial work activities, the more you will understand which tools and methods will be most productive for you. As a result of your dedicated practice, you will naturally develop an intuition that will help you modify these methods and perhaps even invent your own.

I recommend you study this book in three waves. Wave one: Focus on understanding the "never-changing" tasks associated with making progress toward creating new value with your idea. In addition to becoming familiar with the high-level concepts that are supported by the tools and methods provided by the authors, analyze the necessity of each activity in order to best arrive at why all of these things are timeless to product developers in the first place. Wave two: understand each area of work and study these areas as they harbor key activities that, when done in the appropriate sequence, best inform your journey and support the successful launch of a new product. Wave three: engage in "deep practice" with these tools and methods so that you can first become proficient, but do it with the intent of mastering them.

As our problems on Earth grow greater and more complex every day, we need more innovators who are willing to identify meaningful problems, so they can create meaningful solutions that in turn will create meaningful and sustainable value. This text will introduce you to what you need to know to begin this work, and more importantly, it will introduce you to what you need to *do* since creating an innovation is both physically and mentally taxing. In other words, this text can be considered a playbook that is designed to promote continuous progress and success; therefore, you should also know that no one can do this work alone. It is rare to find people who possess the knowledge and skills to cover all the phases and activities of product development, hence the reason for three authors of this text rather than one.

Lastly, take this opportunity to dig deep into the areas you enjoy most, and over time. you will inherently gain mastery through your continued practice. Your confidence will motivate you to facilitate and enhance these methods for your teams, and you will become known for your mastery, as well as for your refined intuition for developing and launching successful products. Celebrate this moment as one that marks your first step on a journey toward attaining innovation wisdom. Each subsequent step forward (including some necessary steps backward too) will compel organizations and talented teams to seek you out because of the progress you started this very moment. All you need to do now is turn the page to celebrate another step toward your future success, and if the noise and distraction from the myriad of influences inherent in this work ever overwhelms you or your team, reach for this book to reenergize and refocus on the proven and timeless truths that will always underlie successful product development.

—Bill Fluharty
Director of Industrial Design
Stryker, Medical Division

Introduction to the Text

Welcome to *Contemporary Product Development: A Focus on Innovation*! We are excited to share the information we have prepared for you, especially our Go-To Market Aura Plan (GT-MAP) framework, which will help you understand what product innovation is, as well as understand the steps involved in designing, developing, marketing, launching, and measuring the success of your future product innovation.

The words "Go-To Market Aura Plan," as well as the acronym, GT-MAP, carry multiple meanings. First, GT is an acronym commonly used by the automobile industry, which stands for Gran Turismo. The meaning implies high performance and that a GT car meets strict specifications for racing, while at the same time providing "grand comfort" while touring. In this text, we will stress the importance of speed, and we will provide you with the concepts and practices by which you will learn the skills necessary to develop product innovation quickly and confidently. What's more, you will learn about high-performance product innovation, psychologically as well as biologically. Therefore, the first three words, Go-To Market, coupled with GT, mean to Go-To Market by means of high performance, as fast as possible, as comfortably as possible.

Second, the word "Plan" accurately indicates that we will follow a controlled, proven methodology, while the letters MAP indicate a structure or framework by which a product idea will progress through the myriad steps necessary to transform it into an innovation. The "MAP" in this text includes topics such as talent acquisition, identification of ideal markets, gauging the value that the product will provide to consumers (as well as society at large), measuring and analyzing collected data to predict if the product and its market are viable and if so identifying what type of innovation would be most effective, and much, much more.

In the middle of the "MAP," if you will, is the letter "A," which represents the concept of aura and how we recommend a dual approach to product development as we also want to simultaneously tease the market to build interest among consumers with proven techniques that gain attention, build excitement, and then transform that excitement into interest that creates demand for the product, long before it is available for purchase.

We hope that the knowledge and skills that you develop while learning from this text, and engaging with your peers in your business course, will set you on a course for repeated success in the field of product innovation!

Leveraging Emotions in Product Development

CHAPTER ONE

Discovering Contemporary Product Development through the Lens of Innovation

INTRODUCTION

There are three universal truths inherent in nearly every organization; and this first truth also serves as a primary, fundamental goal of most organizations, regardless of whether the organization is for profit or nonprofit, and it can be expressed in one word: growth. Most organizations desire growth more than anything else, and because organizations are not content with providing the same product and/or services to their same customers with the same sales, revenue, or grant funding year over year, leveraging this knowledge, coupled with what you will learn throughout this text, will provide you with a distinct advantage during an interview or product proposal.

The second truth manifests as a commonly shared experience within all organizations; again, it is true, regardless if the organization is for profit or nonprofit, and it can also be summarized in one word: pain. The third truth is that whenever someone is experiencing pain, he or she is undergoing an emotional experience to a problem. The interplay of these three truths (growth, pain, and problems) is that problems are what prevent organizations from growing, especially as problems prevent the organizations from designing and developing the most innovative products that consumers will appreciate, and in the middle of it all is pain. Therefore, as you think, learn, and practice how to design and develop new products, we urge you to consistently consider your product in the context of consumer pain.

If you interview consumers about the products they appreciate most, the root of their answers will reveal how their favorite products either reduce or eliminate pain, or conversely, increase or create joy. In other words, products that consumers appreciate most are ones that most effectively satisfy their wants or needs, and this is a key purpose of this text: to help you identify new opportunities and introduce you to the concepts and methods that designers and developers use to create and launch new products that consumers appreciate and love so that your organization can continually grow. The way this text accomplishes this is through demystifying the product innovation process and by presenting a new framework we call the Go-To Market Aura Plan, or GT-MAP, which we will introduce in the next chapter.

As we begin this journey together, there are a few other realities to keep in mind. In the world of product innovation, there are only two kinds of problems: those that you know exist and those that you don't. (We will expound on this concept later in this chapter.) Additionally, when you're attempting to solve difficult or "wicked" problems, be wary of easy answers. If you and your team arrive at an answer too easily, it's probably not a viable solution as someone else would have likely implemented it already if it was. Lastly, innovators are not born, they are grown, and starting with this chapter, you will begin learning about and practicing some of the very habits of the world's most innovative people who are responsible for creating some of the most important innovations of today and tomorrow.

Learning Objectives

In this chapter students will learn about the following:

- How to define what a product is
- The importance of value in regard to an innovation
- The difference between an innovation and an invention
- The most positive and negative ways to communicate during an ideation phase
- Maslow's hierarchy of needs in eight stages and how they relate to the human condition
- The structure of the human brain and how it correlates to Simon Sinek's golden circle
- Different methods used by industry, such as 5W2H and the five why's to learn more about the wants and needs of consumers
- The importance of problem statements when trying to understand, empathize, and solve consumer problems

Learning Outcomes

By the end of this chapter students will be able to do the following:

- Explain the difference between an innovation and an invention
- Explain why the metric of adoption is critical to the success of a product
- Explain how Maslow's hierarchy of needs can be used as a product design and development tool
- Describe the necessary steps to take in order to understand a consumer problem
- Write an effective and succinct problem statement

Key Terms

Product: A thing produced by labor, which includes things that are grown or raised through farming and are not limited to something physical; products can also be virtual or in "cyber form" such as software or a website

Value: Something of worth that uniquely satisfies a consumer's want and/or need

Innovation: A product, service, or process that provides new value to a group of people, and because it provides new value, it is adopted

Invention: Something that has never been made before; not all inventions are major advances as many are simply alterations to older technologies

Adoption: A way of measuring success of an innovation by the number of consumers who are using the product because of the value that the new product is providing (real or perceived) to its users

Maslow's hierarchy of needs: Provides designers and product developers with a valuable tool that depicts a spectrum of user needs, from survival to fulfillment

WIIFM or "What's in it for me": Widely regarded as the most important acronym in marketing and sales as it relates to how customers feel about whether they will purchase or use a product

5W2H: A popular method used to learn more about a consumer's problem by asking who, why, what, where, when, and how

Five why's: A method used to ask various stakeholders "why" several times over as that is the usual number of times required for a stakeholder to answer in a way that provides meaningful, actionable insights

Empathy: The ability to understand how someone else feels

Problem statement: A method defining who is experiencing a problem, then describing what the problem is and why it is a problem for the user

Design Charette: Common way of referring to a formal brainstorming session

THE UBIQUITY OF PRODUCTS

Before this day ends, every human alive on Earth will receive a positive benefit from using at least one product, regardless of their race, ethnicity, gender, age, religion, sexual orientation, education, geographic location, socioeconomic condition, political affiliation, or physical or mental health (including any human with a disability or even those who are completely incapacitated, e.g., in a coma). And it happens every day, without fail. Each of us benefits from using products every single day. It happened yesterday, and as long as there is at least one human alive by tomorrow, it will happen each and every day henceforth, guaranteed.

Why? Because humans and products are inseparable and have been, not just for thousands of years, but for millions and millions of years. In other words, humans are as inseparable from products as we are from our wants and needs, and that is why we have products.

Products Exist to Fulfill Our Wants and Needs

Look around. You are surrounded by products. (Even if you are consuming this text in a remarkably desolate place, you are most likely wearing some form of clothing; therefore, you are quite literally covered in products.) The most remote tribes on this planet also benefit from products every day, including the uncontacted tribe of the Sentinelese located on the North Sentinel Island of India's Andaman Islands, arguably the most isolated tribe in the world. Even they use products as part of their daily life, but let's not forget another very small, remote tribe of people who are currently living 200 miles above the Earth's surface on the International

Space Station; they would not survive without a plethora of products allowing them to simply do what many people take for granted, like breathe, much less all of the other products that they use to conduct research while circling the globe every 90 minutes at roughly 17,500 mph.

Extreme circumstances aside, you have benefited from a wide array of products ever since the very moment you were born, and you have never known life without products. As conveyed in this text's title, the subject of products is a primary topic in this book, coupled with how to design and develop products that will be successful in the marketplace. And while there are several definitions associated with the noun, product, our working definition for this text is a ***product*** is "a thing produced by labor,"[1] which includes things that are grown or raised through farming.[2] What's more, we also want to specify that a thing produced by labor is not limited to something physical; products can also be virtual or in "cyber form," such as software or a website, respectively.[3]

Lastly, in relation to our physical bodies, products are not limited to external uses. Have you ever received a vaccine or taken medicine of any kind? How about a multi-vitamin? How about the most recent meal you ate? In each of these instances, by definition, you have literally consumed a variety of products. Consider Ötzi, the mummified Similaun man who was discovered in the Alps in 1991. The ibex meat and wheat grains discovered in his stomach did not appear there on their own; either he or someone he knew provided him with a meal, which we will, from now on in this text, regard as another form of product. What about the arrow that scientists found that had cracked Ötzi's scapula and likely led to his death? That is another product. What about the 61 tattoos that were found all over his body? Those are also products, as they were made by labor, not to mention his clothing, shoes, quiver, his axe that was smelted from copper, or any number of his other belongings, each made by labor.

Now that we've identified what was in Özti's stomach at the time of his death, let's return our focus to posit what is likely in yours, right now. Can you be certain everything you've consumed today was 100-percent free of GMOs, hormones, herbicides, pesticides, or any other type of chemical (you know, all the ones that were made by labor)? Ötzi could, but can you? Each of those things, whether you like it or not, are coursing through your body right now, and each are different and unique human-made products.

What about the air you've breathed today? Have you breathed in any toxins, noxious particulate matter, fumes, or pollutants made by labor? Of course you have, and you've likely breathed an assortment of those things all day, just like yesterday, just like you will tomorrow. We all have, do, and will continue to. And it is these types of questions that expose a whole other level in which humans are inseparable from products and that will hopefully inspire you to join the growing ranks of product designers, developers, and innovators who are deeply concerned about the moral and ethical consequences intrinsically associated with this work: to be more responsible about the products we make and apply a systems thinking approach

---

1   "Product," https://www.dictionary.com/browse/product.

2   "Product," https://dictionary.cambridge.org/us/dictionary/english/product.

3   "Definition of 'product,'" https://economictimes.indiatimes.com/definition/product

to better understand the implications as well as the short-term and long-term adverse effects many of these products impose on living organisms and our environment, great and small.

Products are Not Only Ubiquitous Outside of Us, But Inside Us Too

Now that we have a better understanding of how pervasive, and in some cases, unwantedly intrusive, products are in our lives, we need to question the intended longevity of these products, which certainly seem to have a way of lasting a very long time, certainly long after a consumer's wants and needs are satisfied. In the case of Özti, that timeframe is around 5,300 years. In the case of products unearthed from the shores of Lake Turkana in Kenya, those products (specifically manifest as stone tools) are 3.3 million years old. Think about this in terms of the amount of plastic we currently produce every year, and that each year we make more plastic than the year before. How much plastic will be in our environment in fifty to one hundred years, notwithstanding 5,300 years? What will be the outcome of continuously increasing the amount of carbon we are emitting into the air in fifty to one hundred years, notwithstanding 5,300 years or even 3.3 million years?

Considering issues such as these, we must work harder to design, develop, and manufacture products that not only benefit consumers when they want and need them, but that ensure that the products do not cause harm from the labor of sourcing the materials, or from the making of the product, or while the consumer is using it, or especially after the consumer no longer wants or needs it. May this tenet serve as a guiding principle throughout this text and inform your future work, in whatever capacity.

There is powerful information in this text, and we hope that you will use it to benefit others rather than cause harm, however unintentional, and hopefully one day this viewpoint will not be considered "contemporary," as it is in reference to the title of this book. Instead, may it be adopted as the new normal and forever improved on by new thinking, practices, and technology. Be responsible for the impact you have when designing, developing, manufacturing, or marketing the products made through your labor, and hold others accountable for the impact of their practices as well.

Imagine if ancient cultures had produced the kinds of products we are manufacturing today, at the rate at which we are making them, and disposed of them in same way that we are today. What would the world be like, keeping in mind that plastic was only invented just over 150 years ago, interestingly around the same time as the world's oldest oil refineries came into being?[4] And while the road to mass-produced, cheap plastic was paved with the good intention of saving elephants from being killed for the sake of producing billiard balls (thankfully elephants did not become extinct due to human want for ivory billiard balls as the *New York Times* posited would likely happen back in the 1880s), instead we now have a different crisis of unintended consequences in the twenty-first century as swimming in the ocean in many places around the world is to swim in a sea of garbage, much of it plastic.

---

4   Susan Freinkel, "A Brief History of Plastic's Conquest of the World," Scientific American, May 29, 2011, https://www.scientificamerican.com/article/a-brief-history-of-plastic-world-conquest/

HOW CAN WE DEVELOP PRODUCTS WITH A *"FOCUS ON INNOVATION"*?

Innovation is probably one of the most overly misused words of the twenty-first century, so let's first provide some clarity regarding what innovation *actually* means, as well as the process by which you can make it real. Unfortunately, dictionaries and encyclopedias are not as helpful as one would hope when defining what an innovation is, and we will defend a strong opinion about how innovation should be defined, which thankfully aligns well with how many other thought leaders define innovation. In short, there are four explicit qualities that must be true in order for something to be called an innovation.

1. An innovation must be a product, service, and/or process.
2. The innovation must be new. (We understand the word *new* may be problematic, but we will provide more clarity on this.)
3. In addition to the innovation's "newness," it must provide unique value to a group of people, regardless of the group's size or whether the group is an intended or unintended market for the innovation, and this group must never have had access to this particular type of value before the innovation became available. In the context of innovation, *value* is something of worth that uniquely satisfies a consumer's want and/or need.
4. The innovation must be adopted and used by a group of people, again, regardless of the group's size or whether the group is an intended or unintended market for the innovation.

That's it. Or, more succinctly, an ***innovation*** is a product, service, or process that provides new value to a group of people, and because it provides new value, it is adopted. Moreover, the success of the innovation has less to do with what it is and more to do with the amount of value it provides, coupled with the size of the group or market who is using it. This is worth repeating because so many companies miss the mark on this and waste precious resources focusing on the product, service, or process itself. And that is a huge mistake, but oh how companies love to fawn over their nifty, clever, beautiful, sheik designs, or fascinate themselves over some marvel of complexity or intricacy of a service they've developed, or some new whizbang process.

Do not fall into this trap. Your product, service, or process needs to only meet one criterion, and that is this: be the ideal vehicle for providing new value to your user. Remember, new value is what is most deserving of your focus and efforts, and it must be of the highest priority to maximize success, rather than the product, service, or process.

The Importance of Providing New Value

If you'd like to carve out a successful career as an innovation consultant, help companies focus their efforts and resources on providing new, substantial value rather than the result of creating a product. This is an area where many companies are in need of desperate guidance, which will prevent them from losing millions of dollars, simply by refocusing their efforts on the new value they are providing to a group of users while secondarily designing the ideal vehicle (product, service, or process) to deliver that new value, rather than what usually happens: Most or all of the firm's attention is focused on some neato-whatever that doesn't deliver any new measurable or perceivable value for anybody. Another way to think about this is to help teams focus on the value the consumer experience rather than the product's gadgetry.

The Innovation Process, Simplified

Now that we have defined what an innovation is, let's identify the three steps required for any product, service, or process to reach the hallowed status of an innovation, along with a few additional, unique criteria that are true of all innovations. We choose to take this approach because developing innovations are not usually simple or straightforward, so we believe there is a great advantage to understanding how an innovation is developed by outlining the process first through simplicity rather than its usual complexity. The following chapters will address the inherent complexity of innovation.

First, every innovation begins with a process that engages creativity. It is impossible to release a new product, service, or process to the market without someone, somewhere being creative, yet it is astounding how leadership of some firms seem to believe that innovations are sourced from somewhere other than creativity. Therefore, in order to ensure that you and your team produce as many highly valuable ideas as possible, you must practice being creative and playful with solving problems through idea creation. Without creativity, there is no innovation. Ideally, a firm should nurture an environment in which employees feel inspired to create and explore all kinds of ideas; tinker with all kinds of notions regarding materials, processes, functions, and new consumer groups; but most of all, create value that a group of consumers will care about and adopt.

One of the most powerful ways innovation and design teams can begin this work is to preface their questions with "How might we … ?" How might we create new value? How might we provide new value to a different consumer group or demographic? How might we reduce the cost associated with making this product while increasing consumer value simultaneously?[5]

A few examples of the worst kinds of statements that can harm any potential innovation during an early stage of creativity are "That will never happen"; "Prove it"; or anything that is typically prefaced with "Not to be the devil's advocate, but … " In order to nurture a new mind-set amongst your team, consider practicing the "Yes, and" exercise, which is often used to highlight how much more productive positivity is when generating great ideas and creating community among innovation and design teams, especially when there are new members on the team who may not have experience being charged with creating a

---

5 "How Might We Questions," Project Fellows, https://dschool.stanford.edu/resources/how-might-we-questions.

new innovation.[6] Ironically, in order to capitalize on the power of the "Yes, and" method, it is recommended to begin by demonstrating the opposite through negativity: "No, but."

To begin, choose two people from the team and pick a topic of conversation between the two of them; one person's role will be to support the original idea being discussed while the other's role will be to relentlessly negate the idea and criticize it from as many different angles as possible by using logic. For instance, the first person could start with saying, "I'm thinking about taking my first cruise this year. What do you think?" Then the second person's response must begin with "That's a horrible idea, and here's why … " followed by a logical reason. Then the first person's response must begin with "But … " followed by the second person responding with, "No … " and coupled with another negative reason. Let this exercise play out for a few minutes. Take note of how uncomfortable it may feel, not just for the two people role-playing the negative conversation, but for everyone else on the team. Hopefully your team will experience some humor in this tragedy of an exercise while also noting how little to no progress is made in helping the first person determine how he or she should spend his or her vacation.

Now, ask the same two people to behave the opposite through the "Yes, and" exercise while using the same topic. After the first person says something like, "I'm thinking about taking my first cruise this year. What do you think?" the second person's response must be "I think that's a great idea, and … " followed by a helpful, positive suggestion. Then the first person must respond with, "Yes, and … " while building on the second person's statement. Again, let this exercise play out for a few minutes. Take note of the enthusiasm, not just for the two people who are role-playing, but for the entire team. Also note how the original idea morphed into something else entirely from where the two team members started their conversation. While criticism is a crucial part of creating an innovation, this is not the appropriate stage to practice it as criticism often prevents new ideas from being generated, except for the weakest, most conservative milquetoast ideas.

Second, every innovation must manifest as an invention, no matter if it is a product, service, or process. The earliest stage of this, especially as the purpose of this text is to focus on developing products, is to create at least one physical prototype. Teams should purposely facilitate "Yes, and" conversations regarding the prototype in order to uncover and explore new uses or purposes for the product, as well as identify a new market that might want to use the product, all while focusing on the new value the product will or could provide.

The purpose of this second stage is to arrive at an ***invention***, which means that what your team has created must be considered "something that has never been made before[7] while also remembering that "not all new inventions are major advances; many are simply alterations to older technologies."[8] Ideally, your team should create many different prototypes, recognizing

---

6   Hugh Hart, "Yes, And … 5 More Lessons In Improving Collaboration And Creativity From Second City," Fast Company, February 26, 2015, https://www.fastcompany.com/3042080/yes-and-5-more-lessons-in-improv-ing-collaboration-and-creativity-from-second-city

7   "Invention," https://dictionary.cambridge.org/us/dictionary/english/invention

8   Ibid.

all of their advantages and disadvantages and varying levels of value they provide to their target markets.

The last part of the invention stage is when the product is made available to the market via a launch event, which is the primary purpose and value of this text: to help you and your team launch your new product with great success, made possible by using the GT-MAP, the Go To Market Aura Plan that is outlined in chapter 2.

While the overwhelming majority of this book focuses on the intricacies of these first two stages of the simplified innovation process (creativity through invention to launch), it is important to identify *the third and final stage that your new product must reach in order to achieve the status of an innovation, and that is adoption.* The *adoption* stage begins immediately after a launch event and is a way of measuring success, not through typical metrics such as units sold, but by the number of consumers who are using the product and the value that the new product is providing (real or perceived) to its users. The formula for success is this: The greater value the product provides, the greater likelihood more people will adopt the product to benefit from its increased value over any other product of its kind in the market.

May this formula serve as a target for your team as you create new ideas and uncover new value, as well as develop a variety of prototypes. Again, focus on maximizing the value that the product will provide rather than the product itself. Remember, anything else is likely a trap that will capture and squander your firm's time and resources without providing a meaningful return on investment.

Adoption is the most critical stage as it determines the impact of your product's success, but the ever-important, underlying reason for adoption is none other than value. Simply put, no value, no adoption. Therefore, no adoption, no innovation, no matter how unique or spectacular. If people are not adopting the product, the product cannot be referred to as an innovation. And this concept leads to another unique and important aspect of innovation: Your product is not for you to call an innovation.

Customers Decide Which Products are Innovations

The only people who truly have the right to call your product an innovation are your customers. Imagine if your favorite artist repeatedly announced to the world, "I'm the most talented, unique, and successful artist!"—that's not likely to sit well with that artist's audience. Remember, the reason why that person is your favorite artist is because of how *you* feel about his or her art, not how *he or she* feels about his or her own art. A product is determined an innovation because of how its users feel or measure the value the product provides, not how you or your company feel or measure the value it provides. There is an enormous difference between the two.

Metrics for Measuring an Innovation's Success

What's more, we want to be abundantly clear about how measuring the value that the product provides its users and its adoption in the market are the only metrics that are applicable in determining an innovation's success. Economic terms such as *money, profit, revenue, returns,* or the like have no bearing on how successful an innovation is. This is one of the greatest and most problematic myths associated with innovation. Innovations are not required to make money, and how much money the product or service makes for a company doesn't matter in the least in determining the success of an innovation.

This will be difficult for many of your managers and peers to understand as they will want to use any number of other metrics, such as number of units sold, to determine the success of your firm's new product, and that is all well and good, just as long as they are not using that data to gauge the success of an innovation. Using the common metric of number of units sold as an example, the metric should be associated with real-time analytics of usage, which is far more valuable a metric than number of units sold. Why? Because real-time analytics of usage ensures that after consumers have presumably exchanged money for your product, they are still receiving value from using it, rather than it being shelved next to all sorts of other products associated with extraordinary number of units sold, like Kodak or Polaroid cameras, tape cassettes, VCRs, rotary phones, and the list goes on.

While companies should still care about metrics, such as number of units sold, they should realize that those data are not nearly as valuable as data regarding real-time analytics of usage, and here's why: Speed matters, and we emphasize this concept throughout the text. For example, if Google wants to learn how successful their Nest thermostats are right now, or Amazon with Alexa, or FitBit with one of their fitness watches, they can leverage data regarding real-time analytics of usage much more than units sold because it allows those firms to detect a drop-off in actual usage of their products, which in turn often serves as a warning for an imminent drop-off in units sold. This provides an important and unique opportunity to use that information to quickly to make adjustments, which will allow the firm to address whatever issues its active customers are encountering, rather than learning after its consumers have begun abandoning the product, spreading word to other consumers that the product is not as valuable as once perceived.

It is worth noting that when a product is designed well and consumers continue to experience increased value from using the device, this information will be reflected in data associated with real-time analytics of usage, which allows the firm to communicate to its manufacturers and distribution channels to anticipate a continued rise in orders and sales. In short, measurements associated with consumer value and adoption allow firms and all of their partners to be much more responsive to fluctuations in consumer demand.

Innovation Exists in All Economies, for All Reasons, Not Just For-Profit

Another myth about innovation is that it must be associated with capitalistic mechanisms and/or capitalistic motivations, such as the buying or selling of a product in a for-profit context, and this is not true. Many innovations are developed in socialist economies, just as many innovations are designed and developed as highly valuable products or services by nonprofit organizations, and every year in the US there are awards ceremonies to specifically recognize the innovations that nonprofits contribute annually, including the Drucker Prize, named after one of the most prominent thought leaders on innovation, Peter Drucker. For instance, the State of Minnesota has declared that they have nearly ended homelessness due to implementing a series of innovations across multiple agencies across the state.[9]

The Innovation Clock is Always Ticking

Another important quality to an innovation is that it has a timestamp. In other words, an innovation will not to be considered an innovation forever. Think of it this way: In the 1980s, the personal computer was widely regarded by the market as an innovation, and rightly so. Moreover, PCs were held in such high regard as an innovation that even PC users were regarded as "innovative" by non-users. But who today would regard a PC as a current innovation? And who would regard a PC user as someone who is innovative just because he or she uses a PC? While the PC once was an innovation, and the people who used PCs when they were new were innovative for using them, neither of these things are true anymore. Today, the PC is just an invention, and PC users are nearly as common as employees.

The same holds true for planes, trains, and automobiles. Each of those modes of transportation, when they were new and unique, were considered innovations by the people who used them, yet while there are some caveats today, this is overwhelmingly no longer true. For instance, one could argue that electric vehicles are still new enough that they could be considered an innovation and the people who own them are perhaps being somewhat innovative by driving them (even though we've had electric-powered cars since mid-1800s); however, it is the advent of autonomous vehicles that are very likely to become a disruptive innovation (as they have yet to be made widely available to the average consumer), and when they do, autonomous vehicles will be considered an innovation until they become the normal, everyday expectation of how all vehicles navigate from point A to point B. Then autonomous vehicles will simply be regarded as an invention, and this highlights a significant difference between innovation and invention, which is while innovations have a timestamp, inventions are timeless.

Consider the millions of filings at the US Patent Office, many of which were deemed worthy of a patent because it represented something that had not been invented before. Yet, how many of them became innovations? The answer is hardly any, even though every single one of them is by definition an invention, will remain so until the end of time.

Timing an Innovation

The next important difference between an invention versus an innovation, which is also related to time, is the timing of the product launch and its availability to the market. Again, inventions are allowed a great deal of latitude; the only criterion an invention must meet is to be first. While that may be easier said than done, it is nothing in comparison to the criteria an innovation must satisfy. Not only must the innovation be first, but it must be perfectly timed

---

9 "Series of Innovations Has Virtually Ended Homelessness among Veterans in Minnesota, *CBS News*, April 6, 2019, https://www.cbsnews.com/news/minnesota-program-aims-to-end-veteran-homelessness/

and targeted to a market that is ready and willing to adopt it, and that market must experience the increased value it receives from using it. This is no small feat.

The last important differentiator that we will discuss regarding inventions versus innovations focuses on the fundamental requirement of an innovation's purpose. While an invention is only required to be first and be different (or at least different enough) from anything else preceding it, an invention is not required to solve a problem, whereas all innovations, without exception, must solve a problem (the more problems solved, the better, and the more significant the problem that is solved, the better) for a group of people, however large or small, regardless if the group of people recognizes that they have a problem or not.

For instance, prior to the launch of the iPhone in 2007, smartphone users did not recognize that they had a problem that only the iPhone could solve by integrating a logical keyboard into the screen instead of including a physical QWERTY keyboard. Conversely, a few years ago Apple introduced a butterfly-mechanism keyboard in their MacBook, MacBook Pro, and MacBook Air models, which was intended to improve the user's typing experience. Instead, this unnecessary, over-engineered butterfly mechanism has caused enormous problems for users, and rather than solving a problem, which we would argue never existed in the first place, it is now causing such significant issues that people are now avoiding the purchase any of those three models from Apple.

What's even more troubling is that Apple has not been able to solved the issue, even with its third-generation keyboard redesign because they will not abandon their faulty butterfly mechanism, which is the original root of the problem.[10]

The obvious questions is, "Did MacBook users have a problem with their keyboards prior to the introduction of the butterfly mechanism?" From our vantage point, they didn't seem to; however, they certainly do now. (And how is it that in the twenty-first century, any computer user should harbor concern about the reliability of their computer's keyboard?) Moreover, while the butterfly mechanism is an invention, it is the antithesis of innovation, especially as Apple's invention is actively driving customers away, whereas the purpose of an innovation is to inspire increased adoption through the way in which it uniquely solves a real problem and provides significant value.[11] In this outlandish example, Apple has attempted to fix a problem that wasn't there, and has attempted to accomplish this bizarre exercise, of their own making, three times over, unsuccessfully. This is the very type of brazen behavior that sinks newer companies, albeit with much less capital in their coffers.

---

10 Samuel Axon, "Apple Apologizes yet Again: The Failures may be Uncommon, but the Third Time Isn't the Charm with This Design," *Ars Technica*, March 28, 2019, https://arstechnica.com/gadgets/2019/03/apple-apologizes-for-failing-macbook-keyboards-yet-again/?ref=hvper.com.

11 Antonio Villas-Boas, "Prominent Apple Bloggers Call the MacBook's Butterfly Keyboard the 'Worst Products in Apple History'," *Business Insider*, March 27, 2019, https://www.businessinsider.com/macbook-butterfly-keyboard-called-worst-product-in-apple-history-2019-3.

IN A WORLD OF PROBLEMS, INNOVATORS ONLY SEE OPPORTUNITY

While there are thousands of ways to solve problems and thousands of proven methods and tools from which to choose, we will focus on a select few that we believe will be most effective in introducing you to design and innovation work, as we also want to build your confidence, efficacy, and agency, so that in the future, you will likely feel more comfortable and well positioned to join or lead other teams, experience personal and professional growth by adopting other methods and practices of problem solving, and explore new tools.

As the famed psychologist Abraham Maslow wrote, "[I]t is tempting, if the only tool you ever have is a hammer, to treat everything as if it were a nail,"[12] yet our world and its problems are far more complex and nuanced than how many people act, as if one method, system, philosophy or political viewpoint is capable of solving all problems. If only that were true. Instead, let's introduce a few different methods, practices, and tools in an effort to begin developing your fluency in using them.

Maslow's Hierarchy of Needs in Relation to Innovation

Abraham Maslow was a psychologist who noticed a failing within his profession: Most of his colleagues were intensely focused on studying the negative manifestations of human psychology, so he purposefully set forth to identify and study positive, healthy qualities from a psychological perspective, and after his paper, "A Theory of Human Motivation," was published in the *Psychological Review* in 1943, he set forth to solidify a new framework of understanding our wants and needs. Despite the ongoing criticism his work receives in academia, *Maslow's hierarchy of Needs* provides designers and product developers with a valuable tool.[13]

Maslow's original framework was presented as a five-stage pyramid but was later updated in the 1970s to portray eight stages, which is the model we prefer when designing and developing new products. The eight stages are as follows:

1. *Biological and physiological needs*: Air, food, drink, shelter, warmth, sex, sleep, etc.
2. *Safety needs*: Protection from elements, security, order, law, stability, etc.
3. *Love and belongingness needs*: Friendship, intimacy, trust, and acceptance, receiving and giving affection and love. Affiliating, being part of a group (family, friends, work)
4. *Esteem needs*: Maslow classified into two categories: (i) esteem for oneself (dignity, achievement, mastery, independence) and (ii) the desire for reputation or respect from others (e.g., status, prestige)

---

12   "The Law of the Instrument," Wikipedia, https://en.wikipedia.org/wiki/Law_of_the_instrument.

13   "Maslow's Hierarchy of Needs," Wikipedia, https://en.wikipedia.org/wiki/Maslow's_hierarchy_of_needs.

5. *Cognitive needs*: Knowledge and understanding, curiosity, exploration, need for meaning and predictability
6. *Aesthetic needs*: Appreciation and search for beauty, balance, form, etc.
7. *Self-actualization needs*: Realizing personal potential, self-fulfillment, seeking personal growth and peak experiences
8. *Transcendence needs*: A person is motivated by values that transcend beyond the personal self (e.g., mystical experiences and certain experiences with nature, aesthetic experiences, sexual experiences, service to others, the pursuit of science, religious faith, etc.)[14]

Leveraging Maslow's Hierarchy of Needs to Ensure a Product's Future Success

Maslow's hierarchy of needs is a valuable foil when designing and developing a product as it can help inform and, in some instances, even reveal new value that the product could or should provide. What's more, it can also serve to determine a product's success in the market. Let's explore how.

First, write down the names of five of your favorite products and compare the value that each provides you against Maslow's eight-stage list. Take the time to note how each of your favorite products is likely providing either enormous value from one stage or value from multiple stages. Now consider five other products you use, but those for which you do not hold any particular affinity. Again, take the time to note how most or all of these products are providing some limited value to you, and likely only from one stage.

In first-world countries, the sweet spot for products is often found in the middle stages as the lower stages tend to be commoditized since an average citizen's basic needs are typically being met. However, in third-world countries, the lower stages are some of the most important with the most immediate needs as citizens in these parts of the world have basic needs that are not being met. In both cases, the market for the upper stages of the list tends to be dominated by religious institutions, graduate schools, and doctoral programs. Will this always be the case?

LEVERAGING THE STRUCTURE OF THE HUMAN BRAIN

Humans are creatures of emotions and feelings much more than we are creatures of cognition or thinking, and the anatomy of our brains is responsible for this. All attempts to negate or remove our emotions from how we approach problems, design and develop products, and communicate the new value our products to prospective customers is an enormous mistake.

---

14   Sean McLeod, "Maslow's Hierarchy of Needs," Simply Psychology, 2018, https://www.simplypsychology.org/maslow.html.

Instead, we should accept that humans are emotion-based, feeling creatures—you, everyone on your team, your fellow employees, all of the stakeholders who you strive to satisfy, and especially your customers—and you should leverage this reality to your advantage in order to increase your product's success in providing new value, which will propel your product forward in the market toward the great goal of adoption.

As Simon Sinek wrote in his *New York Times* bestselling book, *Start with Why: How Great Leaders Inspire Everyone to Take Action*, the most advantageous way to communicate with anyone is to do so at an emotional level first, then at the behavioral level, and finally at a cognitive level.[15] He describes this as the golden circle, which "correspond[s] precisely with the three major levels of the brain," and he recommends this as a way of understanding effective communication.[16] When you communicate *why* first, then *how,* you are speaking directly to the oldest, most central part of the human brain, otherwise known as the limbic brain, which Sinek writes, "is responsible for all our feelings, such as trust and loyalty. It is also responsible for all human behavior and all our decision-making."[17] And this is why those who ignore human emotions and feelings, especially when communicating with others, do so to their own detriment. Facts and figures, or as Sinek labels the *what* part of our communication, actually garners the least amount of our attention and consideration. It's all about how we feel, including how we feel about all those facts and figures. And if something doesn't feel right, no matter what data we are presented, we are likely to go with our "gut" or our "heart," which is actually our limbic brain.

Invariably, we predict there are a few readers who are disputing this right now. Some of those readers are likely saying to themselves, "That's not right. That's not what *I* do. *I* use cold hard data; nothing but facts and figures influence *my* decisions." And where is that response coming from? It's coming from your limbic brain as your dispute is an emotional response—*Hey, that doesn't feel right*—which, ironically, just further supports the point. Remember, *all* of your behavior and decisions are made in your limbic brain, and this is based in biology. Later the in the book we will further discuss this concept in the chapter that describes the importance of being "intuitive-wise" and "data-informed."

Everything Communicates

When you listen to a song for the first time, how long does it take for you to determine if you like it and if you will continue listening? How about when you visit a website for the first time? How long does it take for you to determine if you will continue spending time on the site? According to the Nielson Norman Group, "[U]sers often leave Web pages in 10-20 seconds."

---

15   Simon, Sinek. *Start with why: How great leaders inspire everyone to take action*. Penguin, 2009.

16   Ibid., 55.

17   Ibid., 56.

And why? It has everything to do with whether the user receives communication of a "clear value proposition within 10 seconds."[18]

This immediate emotional-then-behavioral response is so common it has its own acronym: *WIIFM*, which stands for "*What's in it for me?*" and it is widely regarded as the most important acronym in marketing and sales.[19] As Sinek writes about the effect that Martin Luther King Jr. had on a pre-civil rights America, "People followed him not because of his idea of a changed America. People followed him because of *their* idea of a changed America."[20] And while Dr. King' s "I Have A Dream" speech aligned with what so many others wanted and needed to change in America, what mattered most was that it aligned more with *why* they wanted it. A quarter of a million people who arrived to listen to him speak in the summer of 1963 from the steps of the Lincoln Memorial didn't show up for him; "[t]hey showed up for themselves." As Sinek writes, "It was what *they* believed."[21] In other words, people followed him for what it meant to them, or to put it more bluntly, WIIFM.

To further highlight the importance of this structure of communication, as you design, develop, and collaborate over your new product, it is precisely how scenes are structured in any well-written story or novel. In Dwight V. Swain's book, *Techniques of the Selling Writer*, he exposes how to construct a character's response in a way that makes perfect sense to all readers, and to be successful, it must be executed in the "strict[est] chronological order": (1) feeling, (2) action, (3) speech, which directly translates to the order that our brains process information, the *why,* then *how* in the limbic brain, followed by *what* in the neocortex, which correlates perfectly the order of how we experience life: first through emotions, second through behaviors, and then last, through our thoughts.[22]

How This Text is Organized

Consequently, we have organized the first half or first three sections of this text to correlate with the structure and relationship between your limbic brain and your neocortex. The first section is called "Leveraging Emotions in Product Development," the second section is called "Understanding the Dynamics of Consumer Behavior," and the third section is called "Thinking through the Details Before Launch." The second half or last three sections of the book continue with "Disciplined Preparation: Communication, Presentation, and Validation," then "Launch," followed by "Assessing the Product's Performance and Applying Adjustments to Increase Success."

---

18   Jakob Nielson, "How Long Do Users Stay on Web Pages?" Nielson Norman Group, September 12, 2011, https://www.nngroup.com/articles/how-long-do-users-stay-on-web-pages/

19   Ben Sobieck, "The Most Important Marketing Acronym: WIIFM," Writers Digest, June 9, 2010, https://www.writersdigest.com/editor-blogs/there-are-no-rules/general/the-most-important-marketing-acronym-wiifm

20   Sinek, 129.

21   Ibid.

22   Swain, Dwight V. *Techniques of the selling writer.* University of Oklahoma Press, 1981, 55.

THE WORK BEGINS WITH A PROBLEM: WHO IS IMPACTED AND WHY?

To determine how innovation begins, we must first identify the problem stakeholders face and ask who is impacted and why? The following section will identify ways to discover the root cause of the problem by gaining insights and information from the stakeholder through an empathetic lens. Next, innovators learn to use the 5W2H technique to gain a deeper appreciation for the problem, the stakeholder's pain, and how to innovate to correct it. In addition, writing a succinct problem statement can help to define the problem in a way that is best to leverage a design charette in order to devise ways to overcome the problem. Finally, these techniques are vital to innovators as a starting point for innovation and finding ways to gain an advantage by satisfying unmet or future needs of the stakeholder.

Interview, Observe, and Empathize with Stakeholders' Problems and Their Pain

As you identify all of the stakeholders who are experiencing what you and your team identify as a problem, interview as many of them as possible to learn how they feel, behave, and think about the problem you are attempting to solve. You must also coordinate time to observe the stakeholders as they experience the problem. Note everything possible about their emotions, behaviors, and actions. We recommend that you do this until you feel as though your stakeholders' problem is your problem, and you come to believe that you feel as they feel, which is most likely to experience some form of pain. Then, and only then, will you be prepared to truly define the problem in a holistic sense and begin to ideate ways in which the problem may be solved.

5W2H

A popular method used to help define problem statements and develop an action plan is the **5W2H**. The name is derived from the questions that you and your team will ask, and the following is the order that we believe yields the greatest results:

- *Who*: Who is involved or impacted by the problem?
- *Why*: Why is it a problem? Why do we care?
- *What*: What is happening that causes the problem to occur?
- *Where*: Where is the problem happening? Where is the problem occurring in Maslow's hierarchy of needs?
- *When*: When is the problem happening? When did the problem begin?
- *How*: How does the problem happen (in regard to process)? How do we know it's a problem?
- *How*: How can the problem be defined quantitatively? How frequently does the problem occur? How much of a problem is it? How many stakeholders are affected? How many factors are involved?

As each problem will have its own nuances and idiosyncrasies, you and your team should customize the most applicable and appropriate questions to learn as much as possible about the problem from your stakeholders.

The Five Why's, and Why the Five Why's Are Necessary

The *five why's* is a common, proven method used in the design community to ask various stakeholders "why" several times over as that is the usual number of times required for a stakeholder to answer in a way that provides meaningful, actionable insights that you and your team can leverage or integrate into the design of your innovation. As Sinek's book illustrates, your interviewee may have a difficult time putting to words what you are asking about the emotions and feelings because "[the limbic brain] has no capacity for language."[23]

Additionally, be prepared when asking someone about a problem he or she is having that his or her response will likely exhibit one or more self-defense mechanisms. Be empathetic in your approach. Consider how you would feel if someone asked you to explain why you experience pain in regard to a particular problem, because that is in fact what you are doing. (And if you're tackling a problem where none of the stakeholders seem to experience significant pain or difficult obstacles, then we suggest finding a different problem to solve because solving this problem probably won't make much difference or yield meaningful results to anyone, and one of the worst things you can do as an innovator is solve a problem to which your users respond by shrugging their shoulders. "Meh. Whatever. Who cares?")

Be thoughtful about how you use the five why's. Be sure to ask your series of questions in a way that conveys to your interviewee that you care about his or her pain, that you seek to better understand his or her experience through *empathy*, which is the ability to understand how someone else feels, and that you want to help find a unique and powerful solution that will dramatically improve his or her situation. In other words, the idea is not be like an annoying three-year old relentlessly asking "why," which will likely cause an emotional response (as you've likely witnessed a three-year old pester an adult), but it will not likely be productive or act as a gateway toward a greater insight about his or her problem.

Integrating the Five Why's with 5W2H

The technique of merging the five why's with the process of using the 5W2H tool is a proven method toward uncovering valuable insights; however, this technique is not intended nor recommended as a substitute for pointedly asking the five why's, but rather used in addition to asking the five why's when it is deemed useful.

Writing a Succinct Problem Statement

Once you and your team feel that you understand the problem and fully empathize with your stakeholders, it is critical to write an effective problem statement from which your team will

---

23   Sinek, 56.

base all of your design and innovation efforts. While there are many approaches to writing a *problem statement*, we recommend that you start defining who is experiencing the problem, then describe what the problem is and why it is a problem for the user. Use the following as a template:

[Who] *X* is experiencing [a problem with] *Y* because [of] *Z*.

Note that your problem statement should not contain a solution to the problem, just an identification of who is having the problem, what the problem is, and why it is a problem. We recommend that any time you hear or read the word *problem* you immediately associate that word with *pain*. Whenever someone is experiencing pain, you and your team must first do everything possible to best understand, research, and empathize with the people who are experiencing pain and why.

Be prepared to revise this statement several times throughout your work. In fact, if you are not revising and tweaking this statement as you begin your work, you are likely engaging in assumptions and biases and will be more inclined to leap to presumed solutions. Unless the problem is your own, you should be learning new information, uncovering new insights, and analyzing new data, all of which should influence your problem statement.

Consider Creating a Design Charette

No innovation was ever the product of one person's efforts. In order to leverage the passion and talent of your team, consider conducting a *design charette*, otherwise known as a brainstorming session. Design charettes should purposefully be inclusive and diverse. There is little to no value to a team populated with members who all feel, behave, and think more alike than different.

In the future, as objectively as you can, truly assess the strengths of each member of your design team. If they all have the similar talents, knowledge, skills, and abilities, you will likely develop product that will be similar to the products that your team developed before. This is no way to create an innovation, especially today. Small, diverse teams, inclusive of wildly different people with wildly different backgrounds, experiences, and passions are the best way to maximize creative problem solving and innovative product development.

Framing and Reframing Your Design Challenge

The way in which you "look" at your design challenge influences the way in you approach your work in a myriad of ways, most of which we are likely not even aware. This is due to all of our assumptions, biases, and presumed solutions our brains are so eager to validate, not to mention our inherent feelings about the problem. You must also take into account any design constraints that will affect how you and your team proceed with the work of solving your stakeholders' problem. Also, be prepared to rewrite your problem statement, perhaps several times over as you and your team question its accuracy. As you do so, you should also "reframe" your design challenge.

Throughout this text, we will often refer to your product in development as an innovation, and while this may be presumptuous of us, we believe that if you follow the steps herein, your product will have the greatest opportunity to be deemed an innovation by your customers. And now that we've defined what products and innovations are, along with outlining a basic roadmap that must be followed in order for your product to be considered an innovation, it's time to introduce the most significant concept of this text, the GT-MAP or Go-To Market Aura Plan in the next chapter.

Review Questions

1. Which of the following are not products, if any: a movie, video game, YouTube video, TV show, bestselling novel, short story, news article, online interview, or a poem?
2. How is a landline phone different from a smartphone? Which is an innovation and which is an invention? Why?
3. Who ultimately decides whether a product is an innovation?
4. What primary metric is used to determine whether a product is a successful innovation?
5. Are innovations applicable to nonprofit organizations? Why or why not?
6. Which part of your brain is responsible for all of your feelings and decision making?
7. Besides interviewing and observing consumers, what practice is most important to understand how a consumer feels?
8. What are the basic elements in a problem statement, and what should never be included in a problem statement?

Discussion Questions

1. How many inventions do you use on a daily basis in comparison to innovations?
2. How long has humanity made inventions in comparison to innovations?
3. Who in your life is the best at practicing empathy? How much of an effect has that person had on your life? How much of their effect on you had to do with their ability to practice empathy?
4. At what stage of Maslow's hierarchy of needs does a person's "needs" transition to being more about "wants" rather than what is truly needed for survival?

Extension Activity

Visit the website challenges.openideo.com/challenge to view IDEO's "open innovation platform" to view a wide range of global design challenges. Pick three that you find most interesting and write a problem statement for each.

BIBLIOGRAPHY

"Product," https://www.dictionary.com/browse/product.

"Product," https://dictionary.cambridge.org/us/dictionary/english/product.

"Definition of 'product,'" https://economictimes.indiatimes.com/definition/product

Freinkel, Susan. "A Brief History of Plastic's Conquest of the World," *Scientific American,* May 29, 2011, https://www.scientificamerican.com/article/a-brief-history-of-plastic-world-conquest/

"How Might We Questions," Project Fellows, https://dschool.stanford.edu/resources/how-might-we-questions.

Hugh Hart, "Yes, And ... 5 More Lessons In Improving Collaboration And Creativity From Second City," Fast Company, February 26, 2015, https://www.fastcompany.com/3042080/yes-and-5-more-lessons-in-improving-collaboration-and-creativity-from-second-city

"Invention," https://dictionary.cambridge.org/us/dictionary/english/invention

"Series of Innovations Has Virtually Ended Homelessness among Veterans in Minnesota, *CBS N News,* April 6, 2019, https://www.cbsnews.com/news/minnesota-program-aims-to-end-veteran-homelessness/

Axon, Samuel. "Apple Apologizes yet Again: The Failures may be Uncommon, but the Third Time Isn't the Charm with This Design," Ars Technica, March 28, 2019, https://arstechnica.com/gadgets/2019/03/apple-apologizes-for-failing-macbook-keyboards-yet-again/?ref=hvper.com.

Villas-Boas, Antonio. "Prominent Apple Bloggers Call the MacBook's Butterfly Keyboard 'the Worst Products in Apple History'," *Business Insider,* March 27, 2019, https://www.businessinsider.com/macbook-butterfly-keyboard-called-worst-product-in-apple-history-2019-3.

"The Law of the Instrument," Wikipedia, https://en.wikipedia.org/wiki/Law_of_the_instrument.

"Maslow's Hierarchy of Needs," Wikipedia, https://en.wikipedia.org/wiki/Maslow's_hierarchy_of_needs.

McLeod, Sean. "Maslow's Hierarchy of Needs," Simply Psychology, 2018, https://www.simplypsychology.org/maslow.html.

Sinek, Simon. *Start with why: How great leaders inspire everyone to take action.* Penguin, 2009.

Nielson, Jakob. "How Long Do Users Stay on Web Pages?" Nielson Norman Group, September 12, 2011, https://www.nngroup.com/articles/how-long-do-users-stay-on-web-pages/

Sobieck, Ben. "The Most Important Marketing Acronym: WIIFM," Writers Digest, June 9, 2010, https://www.writersdigest.com/editor-blogs/there-are-no-rules/general/the-most-important-marketing-acronym-wiifm

Swain, Dwight V. *Techniques of the selling writer.* University of Oklahoma Press, 1981, 55.

CHAPTER TWO

Go-To Market Aura Plan (GT-MAP)

DESIGNING OPTIMAL EXPERIENCES

INTRODUCTION

The GT (Go-To) MAP (Market Aura Plan) is a comprehensive framework designed to cultivate high performance innovations. By leveraging the knowledge associated with the GT-MAP and engaging in the recommended processes and tools herein, you will increase the success of your product innovation, especially as it will help you understand the market for which your innovation is intended, identify what optimal experiences your market wants or needs, and thereby attract attention or aura for your product.

There is a symbiotic relationship between anything regarded as high performance and aura. Consumers from all walks of life, athletes to zoologists, are drawn to anything associated with high performance, and the natural byproduct of a consumer's interest in high performance is aura. The symbiosis of this relationship occurs when someone or an organization is the subject of aura; it often inspires that individual or organization to increase their performance, just as when a child receives praise, that child is more likely to seek repeating the action for which he or she received praise while at the same striving to perform the action better than before; therefore, leveraging this relationship of high performance and aura is an effective method to accelerate the development of a new product, or even an entire organization, from good to great, to singularly outstanding.

This is important as businesses today face increasing complex challenges in the global market. Firms must adopt new methods of communicating with consumers beyond the traditional means of marketing and attune themselves to an increasingly dynamic, ever-changing landscape. Amongst several topics, this chapter will examine the pros and cons of various outlets to reach the market and which media sources might be best suited for particular situations while avoiding conflicts that can harm or distract consumers from receiving a firm's messaging, as the first challenge is always to gain customers' attention in a positive way.

Learning Objectives

In this chapter students will learn the following:
- To understand what the GT-MAP is
- To understand the difference between performance and high performance
- Understand the importance of GT (high performance) MAP (Market Aura Plan) in today's world
- Understand the flywheel effect as proposed by Jim Collins
- Why firms fail today
- Why marketing is changing today
- The different avenues to utilize
- What media source alignment and conflict are
- "Aura" and its value today

Learning Outcomes

By the end of this chapter students will be able to do the following:
- Apply the GT-MAP to business strategy to achieve success
- Understand why winning is second nature to humans and how it can help firm success
- Explain the difference between performance and high performance and give examples of each
- Share why aura is important to innovation and firm success
- Explain how the flywheel effect brings firms and people from good to great
- Share reasons why firms fail and how the GT-MAP can overcome this failure
- Apply ways to address the changing world of marketing as we go global
- Explain how to determine which media sources are best and how to devise an advertising strategy
- Tell the difference between a real and scripted firm
- Understand why media source conflict occurs and ways to avoid them

Key Terms

Gran turismo: Describes something that meets a very high level of specifications, usually associated with automobiles

Go-To Market Aura Plan (GT-MAP): Comprehensive framework for innovation that stresses the importance of speed to market, knowing your customer, creating an aura around the innovation to gain attention, and developing a plan to succeed

Performance: Level of execution

High performance: Better, faster, and operates more efficiently than normal performance

Clarity: The ability to have a clear vision of what is to be accomplished

Energy: Inner-drive that provides the power to keep one going to achieve a goal

Courage: Mental fortitude needed to overcome fear and to succeed

Productivity: Using the time allotted to achieve maximum results

Influence: Direct or indirect power one has creating action

Aura: Distinctive attention that surrounds a person, place, or thing due to a committed and interested audience for a sustained period of time

Flywheel effect: How businesses transform from good to great not by one fell swoop, but by continually striving to achieve greatness by leveraging their momentum

Fluidity: The ability of an object to move and change its shape without being separated from its associated mass

Real firm: One that speaks from the heart and has empathy and compassion for its mission and customers

Scripted firm: One that carefully addresses its target audience, but its real interest lies in profit maximization and forwarding their mission

Missionary selling: Indirect selling where a salesperson provides information to a buyer about products versus direct sales, which actively tries to sell products

Trade show: Typically an industry-wide sponsored event that allows manufacturers to showcase their newest products to channel intermediaries (wholesalers, retailers, brokers, etc.)

Staying power: The length of time the message is remembered or still present in the market

THE "WHY" BEHIND ADMIRATION AND APPRECIATION

Let's begin this chapter will a brief, three-step exercise. First, write down the names of three people who you admire most, but who you do not know personally. As you begin thinking about this list, these three people must be individuals who you hold in the highest regard, and for the purpose of this exercise, it does not matter if they are living or deceased.

Got it?

Second, write down the names of three products for which you have a great affinity, but they cannot be anything of sentimental value, such as an engagement ring or a gift from a late grandparent. Perhaps these are products that have significantly enriched your life, or maybe these are products that have benefited humanity in some profound way at one time or another, or maybe these are products that are astounding due to their uniqueness from anything else that has ever existed and that reflect marvelous ingenuity human creativity or engineering.

Lastly, next to the name of the people you admire and the products you love, write just one or two reasons *why*. (Now, unless you have spent time thinking about this before, you may find it difficult to put into words why you admire the three people you listed over everyone else available to choose as there are over seven billion people alive today, much less all of your other choices throughout the millions of years that constitute the history of humanity, and we know *why* this exercise may be difficult as this question is asking you to use language to identify your emotional admiration of other people and products, and that is likely difficult to answer because this particular request can only be answered by very part of your brain that has no control over language. So, unless you have previously wrestled with why you feel the way you do, ask yourself *what* have they done or *what* they do that you admire so much, maybe follow that up with *how* they did it and then *why* these things matter to you (this involves a considerable amount of communication, shuttling back and forth between your limbic brain and your neo cortex.) For instance, consider the following examples.

Regardless as to whether this exercise was challenging, we want to share with you the underlying reason for your reasons, or, if you will, the answer behind your answer, as it is a central purpose of this chapter and the book. And the answer that we will provide will be equally true for each of the people who you listed, regardless of if one of them is or was an entrepreneur or an athlete or a scientist or an inventor or a religious figure … you get the idea. In other words, our answer will be the same, no matter what, and the same goes for the products you listed.

This answer points to how you, and we, and everyone, have been judged or critiqued all of our lives, such as how your professors critique you as a student, how your manager assessed you as an employee, how well you did in high school, how many points you scored in "the big game," how fast your ran your first race, how many words you could read by kindergarten, how soon you were able to ride a bike without training wheels, and how old you were when you first began to walk. What are we talking about? We are talking about performance.

What's more, the reason *why* you listed the three people you did is because of their performance (and because their performance means something to you). The same is true of the products you listed. What you appreciate so much about those products over all the others in the world is their performance (and because each of those product's performance means something to you).

How we define **performance** matters greatly, and the definition we are using is "the action or process of carrying out or accomplishing an action, task, or function," along with two of its supporting or sub-definitions: "a task or operation seen in terms of how successfully it is performed," and in relation to the specific performance of a product, "the capabilities of a machine, product, or vehicle."[1]

Pick one of the three people that you chose and write down what they did that makes them so special to you. (Note *how* much easier it is to answer this *what* question than the *why* question earlier.) Look closely at what you wrote because it is recognition of their remarkable performance. Do the same for one of the products you chose. Again, your answer is a recognition of its remarkable performance.

Let's test this with the opposite exercise. List three people who you deeply despise, and then list three products you hate. Now answer this one question: *Why?* (Why do you despise each of the individuals, and why do you hate these three products?) While everyone's answer will be unique, the underlying reason to your responses are that each of those individuals or products performed poorly (or worse). This is why performance matters, and why we want to focus on the importance of high performance, because in consideration of the original lists of people and products you admire and appreciate, it is due to their high level of performance.

---

1   "Performance," https://en.oxforddictionaries.com/definition/performance.

High-performance people and products have a positive effect on us, and it should come as no surprise that companies desire to hire employees who they believe will be the highest performers, and consumers seek to purchase "high-performance" products, especially when those products provide an important value to the consumer relative to price. Our desire for you is to learn and practice the very methods that will increase your value to a "high-performance" status while simultaneously developing and launching high-performance products.

What is a High-Performance Product?

Each market judges or critiques what high-performance means based on that particular market's niche values, and what high performance means to one consumer is likely to be quite different from another if their interests are associated with different markets. As product designers and developers, we must avoid our own biases and assumptions about what a particular market values, how it measures that value, and why. Therefore, how we measure a high-performance product is how well it performs while being used by consumers' values, including hopes and expectations, of its particular market. This is a very important concept and is worthy of further explanation.

For instance, if you asked a consumer with minimal knowledge of motorcycles which maker of motorcycles is best known for high performance, he or she may not be able to answer the question; yet, if you asked a consumer who is knowledgeable about motorcycles the same question, he or she would likely answer with a name like "Ducati" or a few other manufacturers who are known for high-performance motorcycles, and herein lies the problem as it exposes biases and assumptions.

What are the biases and assumptions regarding high-performance motorcycles? Two common biased criteria are that they must be able to reach a top speed very quickly and they must be able to hug a tight corner, but what about a Harley-Davidson motorcycle, which is not known for its quick acceleration or its ability to hug a tight corner? The answer lies in what Harley-Davidson fans value, which is not to focus on quick acceleration or top speed, but rather the sound. No other motorcycle sounds like a Harley, and while the deep guttural rumble of a custom Harley makes Harley fans delirious, it makes fans of Moto GP and Superbikes roll their eyes. Again, this is why it is so important to empathize with consumers, interview them, observe them, and work to understand what they value, before rushing to devise something that they may neither want or need.

Criteria for Evaluating High-Performance Products in Three Stages

The criteria for judging if a market will agree about the high performance of a product is rather straightforward, which makes one wonder why so many companies do such a poor job at satisfying their customers with high-performance products. The first part is to understand the market and align the question of high performance with user expectations, and to do so with one to three words.

Stage 1: One-to-Three Word Alignment with User Value

What word might a team decide best aligns with Harley-Davidson fans' expectations? One word might be *authenticity*. What if we were focused on a product for fans of superbikes? A few words might be *racing*, *speed*, or *agility*.

Stage 2: Three Levels of Assurances to Satisfy User Expectation

The second part is to use this pairing of high performance with whatever values align with your users' expectations. Using the example of Harley fans and authenticity, you want to ensure that the new product design inspires the target user with positive

1. *emotions* that *feel* congruent with *authenticity,*
2. *actions* that *behave* congruent with *authenticity, and*
3. *thoughts* that are *cognitively* congruent with *authenticity.*

If you can satisfy users' wants or needs at each of these levels as they align with the three areas of your users' brains, you are likely to launch a product innovation, but there is one more stage to satisfy.

Stage 3: The Promise of an Optimal User Experience

The last stage in determining whether the product you and your team are designing for a desired market is whether it will provide the user with an optimal experience. People who want or need high performance expect the product to either provide or support the occasion of an optimal experience. If your product can ensure the user will have an optimal experience using the product, again using the example of Harley-Davidson, an optimal experience in authenticity, then your product is more likely to succeed.

Let's consider a different example, such as cleaning products in a professional context. One user group may want to use a high-performance industrial cleaner that will effectively remove a carpet stain, while another user group may want to use a high-performance eco-friendly cleaner that will also effectively remove a carpet stain. One product is likely to have ingredients that are harmful to the person who uses it improperly and are harmful to the environment as industrial cleaners often contain an assortment of toxic chemicals, yet these products are highly desirable because they make the process of removing a carpet stain easy and effective. Conversely, the other product is likely to have all-natural, perhaps even organic ingredients that may require a little more effort to use, but it is much less likely to harm the person using it or to the environment.

If we choose to use some of these aforementioned words for the first stage of aligning a new product design to an industrial cleaner, such as *effective*, *easy*, and perhaps *powerful*, and align a different product design to an eco-cleaner, such as *eco-friendly*, *organic*, and perhaps *safe*, the next stage of testing would look like this:

Does our new product design inspire our target user with positive

1. *emotions* that *feel* congruent with *effective, easy,* and *powerful?*
2. *actions* that *behave* congruent with *effective, easy,* and *powerful?*
3. *thoughts* that are *cognitively* congruent with *effective, easy,* and *powerful?*

Or in the case of the eco-friendly cleaner, does our new product design <u>inspire our target user with positive</u>

1. *emotions* that *feel* congruent with *eco-friendly, organic,* and *safe?*
2. *actions* that *behave* congruent with *eco-friendly, organic,* and *safe?*
3. *thoughts* that are *cognitively* congruent with *eco-friendly, organic,* and *safe?*

You and your team should do everything possible to ensure that you have accurately identified the very best one to three words that align with your target market's values and that you can answer yes to all three of these questions.

Lastly, you need to repeatedly test your product design to ensure that it will make good on the promise of an optimal experience as it aligns with the expectation of high performance. An optimal experience is a period of time when your consumer benefits from the high-performance design of your product.

OPTIMAL EXPERIENCES, AKA FLOW

In Mihaly Csikszentmihalyi's book *Finding Flow* he writes, "These exceptional moments are what I call flow experiences. The metaphor of 'flow' is one that many people have used to describe the sense of effortless action they feel in moments that stand out as the best in their lives."[2]

Our purpose for presenting information on flow and promoting its benefits are twofold. The first is that while you and your team are designing and developing your product, we highly recommend that you consistently consider how your product can either encourage or inspire flow for your user, or ensure that if nothing else, your product will not interrupt the opportunity for your user to experience flow.

The second is that high performance products perform better if they are designed, developed, and launched by high performance individuals and their teams. This does not mean that the only people who can or should design, develop, and launch a high-performance product are athletes or performing artists. That's nonsense. What it means is that your team's capability and capacity to design and develop a high-performance product will increase if your team understands what it means to engage in optimal experiences or flow.

---

2   Mihaly, Csikszentmihalyi. *Finding flow: The psychology of engagement with everyday life.* Basic Books, 1997, (29).

Criteria for Experiencing Flow

Csikszentmihalyi's research indicates that there are a few criteria for increasing the chance of experiencing flow. He writes, "Flow tends to occur when a person faces a clear set of goals that require appropriate responses. It is easy to enter flow in games such as chess, tennis, or poker, because they have goals and rules for action that make it possible for the player to act without questioning what should be done, and how … flow activities allow a person to focus on goals that are clear and compatible."[3]

How to Become a High Performer

This is why we have provided specific, defined activities for you: to design and develop your product innovation based on practicing empathy for your users; conducting interviews, observations, and research; as well as engaging in proven methods with the goal of writing an effective problem statement that will help direct your work and evaluate your product's high-performance design in order to provide your user with an optimal experience and extraordinary value. And in order to do this well, it will require a great deal of practice to develop these skills.

Skill level is a key aspect to experiencing flow when paired with a particular challenge or difficulty. Csikszentmihalyi writes, "[F]low tends to occur when a person's skills are fully involved in overcoming a challenge that is just about manageable. Optimal experiences usually involve a fine balance between one's ability to act, and the available opportunities for action."[4] As your skills increase in the aforementioned activities, you must seek out more and more challenging projects in order to re-experience flow, which is exactly how one becomes a high-performance individual.

Deep Practice Leads to Increased Skills, Speed, and Grace

Daniel Coyle writes further about this concept and how to achieve increased levels of high performance in his book, *The Talent Code.* His research points to an activity of deep practice to efficiently and effectively increase your skills so that you can tackle increased challenges. He writes, "Deep practice is built on a paradox: struggling in certain targeted ways—operating at the edges of your ability, where you make mistakes—makes you smarter. Or to put it a slightly different way, experiences where you're forced to slow down, make errors, and correct them—as you would if you were walking up an ice-covered hill, slipping and stumbling as you go—end up making you swift and graceful without your realizing it."[5]

And just as Sinek identified how different parts of the human brain support the correlation of feelings to *why,* actions to *how,* and cognition to *what,* Coyle discusses how and why deep practice affects the brain as we develop and refine a particular skill, and it is based on three biological facts:

---

3   Ibid., 30.

4   Ibid., 30.

5   Daniel, Coyle. *The talent code: Greatness isn't born, it's grown.* Random House, 2010, (18)

1. Every human movement, thought, or feeling is a precisely timed electric signal traveling through a chain of neurons—a circuit of nerve fibers.
2. Myelin is the insulation that wraps these nerve fibers and increases signal strength, speed, and accuracy.
3. The more we fire a particular circuit, the more myelin optimizes that circuit, and the stronger, faster, and more fluent our movements and thoughts become.[6]

As you continue through this text and its associated course, not only do we expect that you will struggle with developing the skills necessary for product innovation, but we want you to challenge yourself. As Coyle writes, "Struggle is not optional—it's neurologically required: in order to get your skill circuit to fire optimally, you must by definition fire the circuit suboptimally; you must make mistakes and pay attention to those mistakes; you must slowly teach your circuit—i.e., practicing—in order to keep myelin functioning properly."[7]

> *"If people knew how hard I had to work to gain my mastery, it would not seem so wonderful at all."*
>
> —Michelangelo

However, as much as we hope you will challenge yourself, and yes, struggle, with these concepts and practices, at the same time we also want to avoid you becoming overwhelmed to the point of disinterest. There are many reasons why most start-ups fail, new products flop, and giant corporations fall, and unfortunately the most common, fundamental reason why is because people chose not to do the hard work, much less understand what the hard work is by defining a problem statement.

Making Hard Work Easier through Deep Practice

According to Coyle's research, there are three rules to follow when facing great, and perhaps intimidating, challenges: (1) Chunk it up, (2) repeat it, and (3) learn to feel it. Coyle adds that there are three dimensions to the first rule, as he writes, "First, the participants look at the task as a whole—one big chunk, the megacircuit. Second, they divide it into its smallest possible chunks. Third, they play with time, slowing the action down, then speeding it up, to learn its inner architecture."[8]

Next, follow the second rule to make your hard work easier: Repeat it, over and over and over again. Anyone who is considered a high performer follows these two rules. Look at your original list of three names. Each one of them took a task that he or she initially experienced as daunting, absorbed the entirety of the work, then broke it up into smaller subtasks or

---

6 Ibid., 32.

7 Ibid., 43.

8 Ibid., 80.

subroutines and executed those smaller subroutines in a myriad of ways, and then he or she did that over and over again.

Lastly, discover, remind, and reinforce why you are engaging in this challenge. Answering this question, as difficult as answering a why question is, will give meaning to your efforts, and that is a form of reward in and of itself. Additionally, this will invariably cause you to experience new connections—feelings and emotions for this type of work. Developing and marketing a product innovation is not easy, but we're also not interested in making it any harder than need be.

High Performance Creates Aura

Aura is the distinctive atmosphere that surrounds a person, place, or thing and that elevates whatever is the subject of aura to an almost surreal status, and each aura is unique. Consider the aura associated with Ivy League or Big Ten schools, yet Harvard's aura is unique from Yale, which is unique from Princeton. This is also true of corporations, as Apple's aura is unique from Googles' aura, which is unique from Microsoft. Consider the aura of Martin Luther King, Jr., which is unique from Steve Jobs, which is unique from Mother Teresa. However, each of these examples are either institutions or individuals that have transcended whatever product or service they are known for providing due to their sustained high performance.

Building Employee Commitment through High Performance

As performance is a subjective term for action and is used to refer to a level of execution, not all levels of performance are desirable or acceptable. Think of the Olympics and the performance of the athletes. Was every athlete's performance rewarded with a gold medal? There were different levels of performance and only the best performances received a medal. Therefore, to achieve optimal performance, businesses need to clarify and train their employees on what level of performance is acceptable and strive to set standard to help everyone know what is expected.

While performance results can vary depending on the individual or organization, there is a great level of performance that adds higher efficiency, quality, and energy. This higher performance level is high performance. **High performance** is better and faster and operates more efficiently than normal performance. High performance is synonymous with GT in the context of innovation because the most successful firms are superior, quicker to ideate and launch, and more efficient that low performing companies. Again, in order to become a high performer, you must identify what actions are associated with high performance and develop habits that allow you to practice those actions over and over until they become skills of a second nature, which will produce outstanding results in an efficient manner as you will have performed them until the skill is perfected.

These are the five traits that are unique to high performers:

1. Clarity

2. Energy
3. Courage
4. Productivity
5. Influence

Clarity

Clarity is the ability to have a clear vision of what is to be accomplished. High performers are clear on three things. They know themselves, what they want to achieve, and how to interact with others. The possess excellent focus and due to their high levels of clarity, they are always striving to achieve their goals. Clarity also brings about long-term vision as high performers never lose track of their goal despite temporary setbacks.

Energy

Energy is the inner drive that provides the power to keep one moving closer toward achieving a goal. High performers generate high levels of energy, which help them to obtain their goals. They put in the extra time and accomplish the impossible because they have the energy to sustain themselves when others simply quit.

Courage

Courage is mental fortitude needed to overcome fear and succeed. High performers vocalize what they want and despite their fear take risks in order to achieve what they set out to accomplish. They possess an aura of confidence because they know they can be successful even when the path to success is laden with obstacles.

Productivity

Productivity is using the time available to achieve maximum results. High performers accomplish more than their counterparts because they are focused and efficient with their time. Their focus helps them to be critical thinkers and allows them to be more objective when evaluating how to move forward through challenging situations.

Influence

Influence is direct or indirect power one has to inspire action in others. High performers have excellent people skills, especially with active listening and practicing empathy. Because of this, others are naturally drawn to them as they are successful yet approachable. They also tend to be very kind and generous.[9]

Take a moment to reflect on these traits and compare them to your own. Think of someone you know who took steps to improve one or more of these traits. What specific steps did they he or she to accomplish his or her goal? Consider what steps you can take to accomplish your

---

9   Brendon Burchard, "What Is High Performance," Life, April 28, 2015, https://www.huffingtonpost.com/brendon-burchard/what-is-high-performance_b_7153652.html

goal. If one of these traits presents a challenge for you, consider writing a problem statement and begin designing your solution.

The Flywheel Effect: Good to Great!

In Jim Collins book *Good to Great: Why Some Companies Make the Leap. … and Others Don't* Collins uses the analogy of a heavy flywheel (a 5,000-pound metal disk that is 2 feet thick and 30 feet in diameter, attached to an axle) that an individual or firm is assigned to turn as fast as they can.[10] Collins describes how in the beginning, the individual who is assigned to turn the flywheel can barely move it, but with continued effort, it turns a little faster over time until it is spinning faster and faster, and the flywheel is able to turn for a sustained period of time due to its own momentum. Collins uses this example, which is called the *flywheel effect*, to depict how businesses go from good to great, not in one fell swoop, but through the continuous effort by a group of people who have focused their efforts to achieve greatness and feeding off of their team's energy and momentum to accomplish great things.

Firms that celebrate each little victory to create a high-performance community reap the benefits of sustained momentum and speed through their employees' commitment and alignment of goals. The community's own investment in their high-performance traits, clarity, courage, energy, productivity, and influence, create the momentum to rise from good to great.

WHY DO MOST FIRMS FAIL TODAY?

Business failure is an unfortunate reality. A big part of business failures is that most businesses in the U.S are small businesses. Specifically, 99.7 percent of all businesses in the US employee less than one hundred people classifying them as a small business or a "mom-and-pop" business. This equates to 28.8 million businesses.[11] The influence these small businesses have on the corporate landscape is profound, employing 48 percent of the workforce or 56.8 million people. However, their failure rate is as follows:

1. 20 percent in the first year
2. 34 percent by the second year
3. 50 percent by the fifth year
4. 70 percent by the tenth year

---

10   Jim Collins, *From Good to Great: Why Some Companies Make the Leap. … and Others Don't* (New York: Random House, 2001).

11   RoseLeadum," 5 Reasons Why Businesses Fail (Infographic)," Entrepreneur, July 1, 2017, https://www.entre-preneur.com/article/296491.

These numbers are staggering as only three of ten businesses will still exist ten years after they open their doors.[12]

Furthermore, the top five reasons why these small businesses are as follows:

1. 19 percent were outcompeted
2. 23 percent didn't have the right personnel in place
3. 29 percent went bankrupt
4. 42 percent couldn't identify the right markets to buy their products
5. 82 percent had cash flow issues

As you reflect on these top five reasons for small business failure, what are some of the key components that contributed to them going out of business?

1. The first is a clear example of not having the proper financial resources available. Small business owners typically underestimate the dollars required to be successful.
2. They didn't assemble the right team.
3. They failed to do market research to identify their competition and who would buy their products, along with the best methods to market and advertise to reach their target market.
4. They failed to plan.

The following list includes the GT-MAP's values, including a comparison for the reasons why businesses typically fail:

1. *GT (Go-To): Are you engaged in sustained optimal experiences delivering high performance results, akin to "gran turismo"?* It is paramount for firms to hire high performers with the ideal skills for creating products that provide customers with optimal experiences.
2. *Market: The "M" is your target audience or consumer, and it is critical that you not only know who they are, but understand their wants and needs as they relate to your product portfolio.* This element could have prevented being outcompeted and not identifying the right market to sell the products. It is essential to have this information to be more efficient.
3. *Aura: The atmosphere that surrounds the company, product, service.* The word *aura* was never mentioned, nor the concept. Creating an aura around the high-performance purpose of their firm helps avoid the early failures as people are drawn to products that provide optimal experiences, which establishes a strong cash flow with plenty of money to operate.

---

12   Ibid.

4. *Plan: A detailed proposal for doing or achieving something.* Firms that fail to plan expose the organization to undo risk. Planning is a key part to all aspects of life, especially to business.

What Firms Cannot Control

It is important to recognize that the aforementioned failures are largely within a business's locus of control, at least enough to influence a positive outcome; however, there are many factors that are not, such as the following:

- Macro-economic forces (i.e., external environmental factors)
- Competition
- Weather
- Government regulations
- Political-legal aspects

Avenues to Markets

The avenues to market tomorrow will have shifted slightly from yesterday's, and as time progresses, the avenues to market are becoming much more fluid. *Fluidity* is the ability of an object to move and change its shape without being separated from its associated mass. Firms must not rely on the traditional manners of addressing domestic markets as global markets require them to be fluid, which also happens to be from where most materials and finished goods are sourced. This is important to recognize as your firm must strive to be fluid in satisfying the needs of the market as it shifts in ways that can be difficult to predict, and your goal is to shift with it without separating from the mass of your consumer group.

Real versus Scripted

Today's consumer target audience is empowered and biased toward action as nearly everyone has access to immediate information through the internet, including digital media as well as one-to-one and one-to-many conversations. Consumers can easily discover whether a firm is "real" or "scripted." A *real firm* is one that speaks from the heart, practices empathy for others, and expresses compassion for its customers. A *scripted firm* is one that carefully addresses its target audience, but its real interest lies in maximizing its profits, pushing its mission and agenda forward without much regard for how others may feel or react. Most large, publicly traded firms in the US fall into this category.

THE CHANGING FACE OF MARKETING

McKinsey Quarterly published a piece identifying the future changes in marketing as we continue to morph into an increasingly interconnected a global economy.[13] There were five areas this text will focus on that address the new avenues to markets. These five areas include the following:

1. Customers dominating the markets
2. The increased role of marketing research
3. An ever-increasing role of computerization
4. The changing face of field selling
5. Developing improved ways to perform global market planning

Firms that fail to address these inevitable shifts will either go out of business or limit themselves to selling in local or regional markets; therefore, in order to ensure long-term viability, understanding a global perspective is a proactive reality to survival.

Customer-Dominated Markets

A world that is filled with homogenous customers is no longer the norm in business. A global economy is a market of consumers consisting of different origins and values, which can shift rather quickly due to reasons well beyond the locus of the firm's control. These shifting variables require firms to have greater market intelligence, which also causes them to increasingly rely on market research to understand who the target markets are and how they are trending in various countries. This means that firms must strive to maintain the current client base while adding new customers.

The Increased Role of Marketing Research

Discovering who global clients are and how to address them has placed a greater role on market research as part of the planning process. The days when market research focused on sales projections are long gone. Today market research analyzes such things as potential consumer buying behavior, the effect certain advertisements have, sales effectiveness, and other functions that give firms key indicators for global success. Market research will also help in the future to find effective and efficient distribution channels, evaluating sales person's compensation, and identifying consumer imagery of potential acquisition firms. As discussed in detail with the GT-MAP, knowing your market and planning new ways to meet its needs are key elements, and marketing research can help to provide invaluable data for both.

---

13   John D. Louth, "The Changing Face of Marketing," *McKinsey Quarterly*, September 1966, https://www.mckinsey.com/business-functions/marketing-and-sales/our-insights/the-changing-face-of-marketing.

An Ever-Increasing Role of Computerization

Historically, there has been reluctance on businesses to fully utilize electronic-data processing analysis. This can be the result either a lack of knowledge or experience on the part of decision makers, or not having the right equipment in place. In the future, firms will rely more on using electronic analysis to increase efficiencies and to discover new ways to compete globally.

The Changing Face of Field Selling

Traditional field selling typically involves a representative flying or driving to accounts and selling a firm's products; however, according to McKinsey, this will change, as they propose that the role of field selling will morph from creating sales volume to more of a profit-oriented or field marketing strategy. This means sales representatives will be involved in more than just selling products and instead will focus on performing market analysis, assisting with advertising campaigns and promotions, as well as consulting buyers on controlling their inventory. In addition, they will also offer suggestions on new target customers and profitability reports and assist with creating specialized offers and conduct missionary selling. *Missionary selling* is indirect selling where a salesperson provides information to a buyer about products versus direct sales, which actively tries to sell products.

Developing Improved Ways to Perform Global Market Planning

In a global marketplace, there are exchanges of ownership due to many factors including cheaper labor costs, easier access to raw materials, cheaper manufacturing and shipping costs, and reduced tax rates. This creates opportunities for firms to analyze their entry mode strategy to find the best one that will meet their needs. Marketing can help with this type of analysis by determining the market potential in the areas of interest and discovering if consumer buying behaviors match the firm's capabilities.

As innovations are sold both domestically and internationally, marketing will play an ever-increasing role to help determine which avenues are best to utilize in order to enter these new markets. As previously addressed, firms must be fluid in their approach to a global marketplace as traditional practices may not be effective outside the US. Competing in a global market requires firms to learn about new consumer buying behaviors and the needs of unfamiliar customers.

Media Sources: How to Reach an Elusive Customer

In the GT-MAP, again we focus on the M or market. Firms must understand the customer to be successful with the innovations. This requires identifying how to not only reach customers, but inspire them to trial the innovation, communicate the cost, and know where it can be purchased. Most often, this involves the use of media. While there are several media sources available to consumers, not every consumer segment uses the same one. The following are advantages and disadvantages of several media sources.

1. Print

There are certain disadvantages of *print*, as it can be expensive and time consuming, but there is one huge benefit: People hold onto it, place it on their computer desk, kitchen table, nightstand, or wherever, and as it is a physical object and therefore touched, that has its advantages over digital media.

TABLE 2.1   *Advantages and Disadvantages of Print*

ADVANTAGES	DISADVANTAGES
• You control the execution	• Not global
• Easy	• Could be very expensive
• Potentially large circulation	• Multiple layers of planning
• Can be very targeted	• Noise is the message getting lost with other pieces
• Speed, timing	• Expensive
	• No human-to-human connection, it is only one-way communication
	• Limited, single event that is expensive

2. Trade Shows: Industry

A *trade show* is typically an industry-wide sponsored event that allows manufacturers to showcase their newest products to channel intermediaries, such as wholesalers, retailers, and brokers.

TABLE 2.2   *Advantages and Disadvantages of Trade Shows*

ADVANTAGES	DISADVANTAGES
• Impressions, big splash, visual exposure	• Expensive
• Face to face, human to human, personal, two-way communication	• Limited to one to five days
• Direct sales	• Potentially low turnout
• Media opportunity	• Competitors are present
• Networking	• Other exhibitors may be distracting
• You control the execution	• Speed and timing are key factors at the trade shows

3. Distribution

Distribution is any method by which firms deliver their products to the final consumer. A popular option used by many firms is to sell the products to a wholesaler who then takes possession of a tangible good and resells it to a retailer to then sell the good to the final consumer. Services are unique as they are sold and consumed immediately by the final consumer. Whether the firm is providing the consumer with a good or service, firms should consider many options, including the best way to remain competitive or reduce costs by partnering wholesalers so that the desired price point is achieved to attract consumers to the value proposition.

TABLE 2.3   *Advantages and Disadvantages to Distribution*

ADVANTAGES	DISADVANTAGES
• Cost is born by the distribution network	• You give up revenue
• Connection to consumers, as they know the market and territory	• No longer can control
• Selling by writing an order	• Product focus is lost as the competition and you exhibit your goods and services
• Gives you human interaction and spurs creativity	• Speed/timing: Distribution determines its acceptance and rollout
• Partner in the process	
• Can be very focused and directed	
• You determine speed and timing	

4. Radio

In the early 1900s, Radio was the primary source of entertainment for Americans; however, the advent of television disrupted radio's effectiveness in regard to marketing. Today, radio continues to advance as an innovation as it has introduced satellite radio, thus increasing its the ability to reach a myriad of target markets.

TABLE 2.4   *Advantages and Disadvantages to Radio*

ADVANTAGES	DISADVANTAGES
• Broad coverage	• One-way non-interactive
• Speed/timing: Fast	• Cannot target the audience
• Multitasking/subliminal. People can do something else while listening	• No visual communication
• "Dream Effect": People will visually expand and dream within their own minds the message you are sending	• Very difficult to track results
• Flexibility: You choose where and when	

Note: In the US radio advertising is still a very popular medium, with just over $19.81 billion in advertising sales in 2017.[14]

5. Television

Television's impact on innovation has been tremendous. It provided a way for firms to show their innovations and to demonstrate how they are used. However, while television was once

---

14   "U.S. Radio Industry – Statistics and Facts," Statista, https://www.statista.com/topics/1330/radio/.

the dominant way to reach consumers, it has been replaced due to technology with Netflix, Hulu, and YouTube to reach our target audience.

TABLE 2.5 *Advantages and Disadvantages of Television*

ADVANTAGES	DISADVANTAGES
• Time is essential as people still spend an average of four hours/day (In the US) watching television. • Focused reach creates a large audience in a short time interval • Visually dynamic, portraying the message with visuals, sound, voice, and motion • Multi-tasking: Viewers can do other things during this time, so you get subliminal messages	• Expensive • One way and not interactive • Very little opportunity to adjust • Difficult to target • Speed/timing: Can be very time consuming to produce

6. Digital Media

What is digital media? We know it as Facebook, Instagram, Snapchat, Twitter, and email. Nothing has changed the world more than digital media. In 2018, Facebook boasted that 2.19 billion people interacted on Facebook in the first quarter.[15]

TABLE 2.6 *Advantages and Disadvantages of Digital Media*

ADVANTAGES	DISADVANTAGES
• Inexpensive • Visually dynamic • Broad coverage: The ability to pass on (or "share") • Flexibility: You choose everything • Interactive • Data analytics • Big splash • Personal/personal power • Time: Between television, tablets, smartphones, and computers, Americans spend an average of two hours per day, while teens spend nine hours per day using digital media. • Speed/timing: Nearly instantaneous	• Once started, out of your control • Cannot multitask • No dream effect

---

15   "Number of Monthly Active Facebook Users Worldwide as of First Quarter 2019 (in Millions)," Statista, https://www.statista.com/statistics/264810/number-of-monthly-active-facebook-users-worldwide/.

Media Source Alignment

To align your media sources with your target market, firms must practice the three P's, which are planning, preparation, and persistence. The three P's also align with the GT-MAP as firms must practice all three parts to be successful. There are several steps firms must follow to properly align their media sources to be effective.

First, firms must identify who their target market is. It is hard to sell products when you have no idea who will buy them. Marketing research can help with this task and should be utilized to avoid wasting valuable resources by trying to reach a market that has no interest in the product.

Second, firms must identify what media sources their target market utilize. Typically, consumers use many channels, but a more strategic approach could help to determine what the media mix should be and what are the long- and short-term objectives. Third, firms must devise a plan. Planning can include frequency of advertising, objectives of the advertising campaign, targeted return on investment, or increase in sales.

To be successful, the plan needs to be realistic, measurable, and attainable. Planning should also include a timeframe to measure the success. Will the company check for results in one week or one month, or three months to determine if they are on track?

Fourth, the company needs to devise a budget to determine the return on investment based on the media plan. If the budget is more than the expected return, the firm needs to determine other media sources or ways to reach the target market.

Fifth, firms need to implement the plan. The company must execute the plan and monitor its success to determine if it is reaching its goals. This also helps to determine if the message is being received in the manner the firm intended and there is no misconception with the offer or information being broadcast.

Sixth, firms must determine the level of success of their plan and if the media mix helped to reach their goals. Firms should use this time to reflect on what went well versus what went wrong and then benchmark which actions should become the firm's new best practices for future advertising.

Devising the right strategy for using various media sources is not easy, and firms want staying power with their advertising campaigns. *Staying power* is the length of time the message is remembered or still present in the market. Does your family have magnetic advertising on the refrigerator at home? If so, chances are it has been there awhile, likely holding a memorable picture to the door. This is an example of staying power. With the amount of advertising consumers are exposed to everyday, the message is often lost, so finding ways to lengthen the staying power of a message is key.

Media Source Conflict

Obviously, this is the opposite of alignment, but too often organizations will execute a plan that involves several media channels and rarely assess if the messages within each channel align and support each other. As a result, digital media is often focused in one direction while the print media focuses in another. Distribution is still another. Ultimately, the target market and the customer are confused. Conflict, in other words, is never positive in any organization's GT-MAP. Fluidity is the reality in today's marketplace, one that has no shape, with different mediums working at different times. There is not just one plan that works all the time or even a rule of thumb that can be applied for success.

MORE ON AURA

Aura, or "influence marketing" as others call it today is probably the biggest change from a marketing perspective since the advent of the smartphone in 2007. The iPhone was the start of the mobile revolution—visual imagery, information, and sound all at your fingertips, instantaneously.

It was this technology that enabled one person to become an ambassador and work to drive others and the marketplace in a different direction other than before. No longer did companies need to spend millions on marketing. They now could determine the right flavor of aura and who the right people were to develop and expand the aura and then unveil it for a particular group who is most likely eager to experience it.

Influence marketing is the process of identifying who the people are who "influence and impact the behavior" of the target market consumer. In the past, this was seen more as a role of celebrities, such as Bono of U2 in music, Lebron James in basketball, Tiger Woods in golf, Michael Jordan in basketball, and Matthew McConaughey in acting. However, in today's world, many consumers will be motivated or influenced by which companies will go out of their way to promote their product/service. Those individuals who are the "influencers" may still be compensated, but it is very little compared to a celebrity. Frequently, they are given free products instead, as what drives the marketing is the love for the product and company.

Seth Godin, author of *The Purple Cow*,[16] one of the best go-to market books since 2000, discusses the importance of the following:

- *"Purple cow"*: Differentiation
- *Hard to replicate*: Uniqueness
- *Word of mouth*: Physically and digitally (positive and negative)

Aura is the distinctive atmosphere or quality that surrounds a person, place, thing, or organization and inspires an audience to view whatever has aura as something larger than life. Aura is the "flywheel accelerator" of an effective go-to market plan, powered by a person or product that is high performance. The components of an effective aura plan are as follows:

- Interviews
- Articles
- Twitter
- Facebook

16   Seth, Godin. *Purple Cow, New Edition: Transform Your Business by Being Remarkable*. Penguin, 2009.

- LinkedIn
- YouTube
- Instagram

Review Questions

1. What does the term "go-to market aura plan" mean?
2. Why do people/firms like to win?
3. What is the difference between performance and high performance?
4. Name the five traits of high performance and explain each.
5. What is aura? Why is it important? Why is aura a flywheel accelerator?
6. What is the flywheel effect proposed by Jim Collins?
7. What are three ways firms fail? How can the GT-MAP help to prevent failure?
8. How is marketing fluid? What are ways marketing is changing in a global marketplace?
9. How can firms align media sources to gain success?
10. What are possible media channel conflicts?

Discussion Questions

1. Discuss with a classmate the importance of the go-to market aura plan and the benefits it provides to innovation and firm success.
2. Do you agree people like to win? Share with someone why winning is important for business and employees.
3. Talk with a classmate about the difference between performance and high performance. Which one is your school's football team? Why?
4. Compare yourself to the five traits of high performance. Which of these traits do you possess? If you lack some, how can you change to fulfill all five?
5. Discuss a company that has aura with someone. How does it help the company compete in the market?
6. Share a firm that has used the flywheel effect. What does it do that is better than its competition?
7. Talk about other reasons why firms fail. Does the GT-MAP provide guidance to help prevent this? Why?
8. Discuss other ways not mentioned in the text as to how marketing is changing as we become a global economy.
9. Compare the various media sources you utilize with a classmate. Why do you use them and how can firms better reach you?
10. Share three examples of real and scripted firms. Does the difference between them influence your buying behavior? Why?

Extension Activity

Think of a company that is not doing well. Apply the GT-MAP to the company and provide ways this framework could help it be more successful.

BIBLIOGRAPHY

"Performance," https://en.oxforddictionaries.com/definition/performance.

Csikszentmihalyi, Mihaly. *Finding flow: The psychology of engagement with everyday life.* Basic Books, 1997, (29).

Coyle, Daniel. *The talent code: Greatness isn't born, it's grown.* Random House, 2010, (18)

Burchard, Brendon, "What Is High Performance," Life, April 28, 2015, https://www.huffingtonpost.com/brendon-burchard/what-is-high-performance_b_7153652.html

Collins, Jim, *From Good to Great: Why Some Companies Make the Leap … and Others Don't (New York: Random House, 2001).*

Leadum,Rose. "5 Reasons Why Businesses Fail (Infographic)," Entrepreneur, July 1, 2017, https://www.entrepreneur.com/article/296491.

Louth, John D. "The Changing Face of Marketing," *McKinsey Quarterly*, September 1966, https://www.mckinsey.com/business-functions/marketing-and-sales/our-insights/the-changing-face-of-marketing.

"U.S. Radio Industry–Statistics and Facts," Statista, https://www.statista.com/topics/1330/radio/.

"Number of Monthly Active Facebook Users Worldwide as of First Quarter 2019 (in Millions),"

Statista, https://www.statista.com/statistics/264810/number-of-monthly-active-facebook-users-worldwide/.

Godin, Seth. *Purple Cow, New Edition: Transform Your Business by Being Remarkable.* Penguin, 2009.

CHAPTER THREE

Why is Speed Essential to Gain Momentum?

INTRODUCTION

Innovation centers around satisfying customers' needs as well as getting a product to market as quickly as possible, before the competition can copy it. Companies that are considered innovative should strive to develop products that are original to avoid being accused of copycat behavior. Additionally, companies must validate their resources using proper fit and timing, avoiding bias, acting quickly, and growing. When companies work to accomplish these objectives, success is practically imminent, and there is no better place to begin ensuring success than the company's business plan.

Every business plan must consist of eight key ingredients, including an executive summary, business description, market analysis, organization and management, estimation of sales, and financing requirements, as well as a list of potential risks and the company's counter measures with which to respond to the risks. These elements are essential in helping define why the company should exist and how well it should perform.

However, a company's innovation plan along with its ability follow through with its innovation plan is just as important. How will your company generate new ideas, identify new market opportunities, gauge consumer wants and needs, and determine which ideas to pursue? Additionally, how does the company develop a product plan that will positively affect its stakeholders? And finally, how will the company develop and launch the product to market with speed? In this chapter, speed is important to innovation because in a global economy, companies no longer have the luxury they once did, taking their time to develop and launch new products.

Learning Objectives

In this chapter students will learn about the following:
- How to be aware of the need to innovate with speed

49

- Using the five ways of product validation to innovate quickly
- How to develop a business plan
- Methods to devise a business plan quickly
- Ways to develop a product development plan
- Why keeping momentum is important when innovating

Learning Outcomes

By the end of this chapter students will be able to do the following:

- Prevent ways for competitors to copycat innovations
- Validate an innovation using the five steps provided
- Write a business plan
- Start a product develop plan
- Apply ways to keep momentum going for innovation by companies

Key Terms

Bottom-up approach: Studies the target markets from an empathic perspective to see how they can satisfy their needs

Top-down approach: Identifies if the target market wants or needs the product

Consumer insights: Evidence that is revealed regarding the marketplace and not focused on an individual's needs

Bias: A feeling, opinion, trend, or notion that is preconceived or without reason

Business plan: A document that describes in detail the goals of the organization and how to achieve them; the marketing, financial, and operational perspectives used to be successful

Executive summary: A concise document that sums up the overall business plan written in simple terms and with simple projections

Business description: Gives an overall description of the business in terms of its mission and vision, history, business model, and other information pertinent to stakeholders wishing to gain a deeper understanding of who a firm is

Market analysis: Describes elements of a market including factors that affect it, conditions present, and characteristics that distinguish it from other markets

Share of wallet: Marketing term that describes the amount of disposable income a firm can capture from the sales of its products to the market

Price skimming: A pricing strategy that starts out with a high unit price and reduces it over time

Pricing penetration: A price strategy that starts out low and raises over time. It is a good strategy to gain market share

Everyday low prices (EDLP): Offers consumers prices that are usually below the normal price paid at competitors

Psychological pricing: A pricing strategy that attempts to make the price seem less than it really is

Bundle pricing: A pricing strategy that bundles typically services at an initial low cost to get consumers to trial the products, influencing their purchase in the future

Financial projections: Used to show current and future revenue, plus expenses that will impact a company

Income statement: A financial statement measuring a company's financial performance over a specified period

Revenue: Funds that are earned for selling a company's products

Expenses: The costs (direct and general and administrative) incurred by a company

Total income: The income result when you subtract revenue minus expenses before income tax

Cash flow projection: A statement showing inflows and outflows of cash into a business over a specific period (usually one year)

Balance sheet: Shows a company's assets, liabilities, and shareholder equity at a specified point in time

Product development plan: A document that outlines the modification or creation of a new product on *the part of companies and sets in motion the parts needed to complete its development*

Idea generation: A process whereby ideas are thought out, concepts are innovated, processes are developed, and the idea is brought to existence to satisfy the needs of the target market

Risk: Exposure to danger, imperil, hazard, or threat

Countermeasure: An action taken to counteract a danger or threat

COPYCATS ARE READY TO POUNCE

Matthew and Mark McLachlan developed a product called a fidget cube through Kickerstarter.com. Kickstarter is a company that solicits for investors for product development, so the innovative ideas are available for public viewing. The fidget cube is a device that allows people to fidget using roller gears and a ball, a rotating dial, buttons that are both audible and non-audible, a joystick, and a flip switch. The McLachlan brothers had a patent pending on the fidget cube, so they thought they were protected from copycats. Therefore, they felt they had piece of mind to raise the needed capital and manufacture the fidget cube.

Jack, an entrepreneur from China, found manufacturers in China to copy the fidget cube and his version was called the stress cube. Jack was first to the market with the stress cube and in a little more than two months, he earned $345,000 selling his knock-off version.

You may be asking yourself, how could "Jack" do this with a patent pending? The answer lies in the fact that small companies don't have the resources to mount a full-scale legal battle with the copycat firm. Also, copycats will abandon the product if the legal pressure gets too high or sales start to drop. In other words, there is not long-term strategy with copycats; it is purely profit driven and once the sales for one item slow down, another item can be copied within two weeks and marketed.

Protecting Your Product
Nick Skillicorn, CEO of Improvides Innovation Consulting, suggests four ways to prevent your product from being copied.

1. *Make it obvious you are the original creator*: Consumers' value perceptions of original items are quite favorable in terms of quality and paying a higher price.
2. *Get to market ASAP!*: This entire chapter is based on this concept of speed to market, and it is not surprising that this is one of the aspects that helps prevent a firm's product idea from being copied by others. Since the fidget cube was open to the public for donations, it also allowed for others to see the innovation and thus get copied. Develop the product, test it, and launch it, then follow up. We will cover the term *adjust on the fly* in greater detail later, but for now, launch the product and fix it as you go. Be the first to market and realize first-mover advantages.
3. *Get your message and audience interaction right*: Copycat's strategy is short-term profits. They will not advertise their product because once sales slow, they move on. Therefore, as the original, be sure you have an effective message stating you are the original and why your product is superior. This will help you charge a premium price.
4. *Innovate outside the product*: Once you launch a product, you must continue to innovate. Don't get hung up that your one product is the only one you will ever produce. Launch the product, get feedback, and keep innovating.[1]

Product Validation

Product validation is not an exact science nor is it easy to accomplish. Many companies have missed their window of opportunity due to their slow validation process because by the time they launched their new product, the need no longer existed. So, what can a company do to improve and streamline its validation processes?

Dr. Greg Nyilasy of the University of Melbourne has developed five ways to validate your innovation based on research he and his team have conducted. These five ways include the following:

1. Fit
2. Time
3. De-bias
4. Act
5. Grow

Fit

Every innovator must evaluate how well the new product fits the needs of his or her target market. If the product does not satisfy a need, the product will be rejected, and as a result, the company will have wasted valuable resources. When evaluating fit, innovators must take

---

1   Nick Skillicorn, "Guy Makes Living Stealing People's Ideas," Idea to Value, 2017, https://www.ideatovalue.com/inno/nickskillicorn/2017/02/guy-makes-living-stealing-peoples-ideas/.

a bottom-up or a top-down approach to determine what will be most useful in evaluating how well the innovation will be accepted. A *bottom-up approach* studies the target market from an empathic perspective to see how the firm can satisfy their target market's needs. A *top-down approach* identifies if the target market wants or needs the product. This dual approach is effective in evaluating what is needed in the market and how well the innovation will be accepted. However, when developing new products, a bottom-up approach is the recommended course of action to determine how the company can satisfy the needs of its customers. Taking a top-down approach may not reveal enough insight, especially in a highly competitive market rife with new products being readied for launch, as a top-down approach is much better utilized when making small attribute changes or when utilizing continuous innovation to determine what changes customers would appreciate from existing products they already use.

Another approach when identifying fit is to seek out consumer insights regarding what kinds of product changes or the types of entirely new products consumers believe would be successful in the market. *Consumer insights* are an accumulation of evidence that reveals insights about the marketplace rather than focusing on an individual's needs. Since consumers usually will only identify what changes they would like to see in a new product that usually represents a very small interest group, consumer insights are intended to reveal broader perspectives on how an innovation can help society. This type of research is led by a facilitator who gathers these data from focus groups, and facilitators are trained to engage focus groups as needed to further pursue potentially valuable insights, which is an enormous advantage over using a survey.

Time

Fortunes have been won by being in the right place at the right time, but these types of successes are largely based on chance and luck, and while we need both chance and luck for innovation, we recommend a more calculated and deliberate approach in regard to how your company spends its time and times the launch of your new product. And since no one has a crystal ball, a common pitfall in innovation is missing the proper time to introduce a product or failing to identify the trends that indicate what consumers will likely want or need in the future.

Validating an innovation for development has several pitfalls that companies are guilty of following, such as waiting too long to launch a product, excessive product testing before launch, and failing to gauge whether the time is right to enter the market. So, how should you and your team time the validation process for your firm? As previously outlined, you should interview and observe your consumers to best understand their wants and needs so well that you will be able to effectively empathize with them. Only then will you be able to most accurately time the when the value proposition you are offering will likely be most be wanted or needed.

De-Bias

Bias is part of human nature. *Bias* is a feeling, opinion, trend, or notion that is preconceived without an objective or evidence-based reason, and it either positively or negatively influences the decisions we make, all too often automatically. We are all guilty of bias in our daily life. Innovation creates bias as well on the part of managers, innovators, and employees. Top managers may feel that a certain new product will not do well without sound data or knowledge to back up the way innovators often feel, which is that the new product will be the next big thing. So, what are a few ways that bias can be prevented or at least curbed? One way is to ask a series of critical questions, such as the following:

1. Why do you believe this is the best data on which to base our decisions?
2. Why do you believe your interviews accurately represent a sample of the target market?
3. What data might we be missing or overlooking that we might regret not realizing in the future?
4. If the report seems too good to be true, ask the analyst to demonstrate how the report was generated and discuss what other ways the data may be used to provide a more accurate and realistic view of how well the product will likely perform.

It is easier to ask the hard questions before prototypes are built and the product is launched rather than incurring a greater financial burden on the company.

Act

Innovators must act before the act, meaning an action plan must be in place to map out the way the process will proceed to bring a new product to market. For example, before you travel to a new place, you are sure to get the address, use the Internet to calculate the best route, enter the information into a navigation system either on your phone or car, and have the contact number of the party you are seeking to visit. These are all done prior to or just before the trip begins. Innovation is no different. Failure to plan often results in an unplanned failure.

When we seek to validate, the action plan is also needed. Who will you test? What approach will you take to collect and analyze data? And what are the goals for validating the product? Sound validation requires a measurement and learning plan be in place before the process begins in order for your team to understand how data will be collected, analyzed, and used to validate the innovation.

Grow

This may seem like an unnecessary subsection for an innovation text; however, too many product developers devise a first great product with nothing else in the pipeline to follow up with a second great product. While we have suggested some ways to continue to grow (monitor customer needs, know the best time to launch a product, and have a plan), several companies are either underfunded for the second launch or grow lazy and bank on their first hit sustaining the firm for a longer time period than is feasible. Therefore, it is recommended that companies adopt a policy of growth through innovation. Recall that the percentage of Fortune 500 companies that are still in business today since 1955 is only 12 percent.[2] What did these companies fail to do to become nonexistent? In many cases, the answer is they have either gone bankrupt, merged with another company, were bought by another company, or have fallen out of the top Fortune 500 company list due to falling revenues, but the lesson is this: It is important to follow the five steps to validate an innovation and to keep a steady stream of ideas in the pipeline. Staying focused on your target market will drive future innovation and keep your firm on a path of growth and profitability. All too often executives and other leaders in management take too much time to make a decision based on fear. Tomorrow becomes today every 24 hours, and before they know it, their competition has passed them by.

WHAT IS A BUSINESS PLAN AND WHY IS IT IMPORTANT?

A business plan gives stakeholders a view of how the business is run, its strategies, the leaders, financial projections, and much more. More specifically, a *business plan* is a document that describes in detail the goals of the organization and how to achieve them, the marketing, financial, and operational perspectives used to be successful. A business plan gives investors, lenders, and other stakeholders the ability to see past accomplishments of the organization and its future goals. A business plan is useful in innovation because it provides a roadmap, guiding the firm toward achieving its goals and driving the development of new products. Most business startups fail due to lack of a plan. Without a plan it is impossible to monitor what is working and what is not and make the necessary adjustments that all healthy businesses do on a regular basis.

A business plan is comprised of several sections, which help to drive the strategies and operations of the firm. These sections include the following:

- Executive summary
- Business description
- Market analysis
- Organization and management
- Sales strategies
- Funding requirements
- Financial projections
- Risks and counter measures

Each section is important to communicate what the business wishes to accomplish by thinking of each of the areas and doing projections to support the goals. As stated in previous

---

2   Marl J. Perry, "Fortune 500 Companies 1955 vs. 2016: Only 12% Remain Thanks to the Creative Destruction That Fuels Economic Prosperity," AEI, December 13, 2016, http://www.aei.org/publication/fortune-500-firms-1955-v-2016-only-12-remain-thanks-to-the-creative-destruction-that-fuels-economic-prosperity/.

chapters, it is important that the goals are measurable to get an accurate reading of if the company is being successful.

Another area where a business plan is useful is for borrowing money to support an innovation. Lenders want to see a business plan to assess if they believe the company is a good risk before drawing up a loan agreement. The lender will pay close attention to the financial projections, the current financial state of the company to determine the likelihood that they will be able to pay the loan back, marketing plans and projections, how the future products align with the company's mission and vision, and if the company can provide sound reasons why the innovations should be produced based on satisfying the needs of the target market and society.

Investors will also pay close attention to the business plan to assess the capability and business acumen of the top managers running the company, if they feel the company has a good product portfolio, and if they deem the company's proposed strategies and goals are realistic. Therefore, the business plan helps not only external stakeholders, but it also serves to remind the organization how they will innovate, the potential success of the plan, and what kind of resources are necessary to develop the product.

Executive Summary

The *executive summary* is a concise document that sums up the overall business plan, which is written in simple terms and with simple projections. It describes all the functional areas of the business plan, and while the length is debatable, this section is usually between one to five pages, or no more than 10 percent of the length of the entire plan. An executive summary is like an elevator pitch in that it presents the most essential information to help influence stakeholders.

Business Description

A *business description* gives an overall description of the business in terms of its mission, vision, history, business model, and other information pertinent to stakeholders seeking a deeper understanding of what purpose the firm serves and to whom. In addition, it provides the firm's address, information about the key managers, what legal structure the business follows (i.e., incorporated, partnership, and sole proprietor), what market opportunities the firm seeks, and information about its competitors. The business description also tells of the projected growth it hopes to achieve based on new innovations and future opportunities.

Market Analysis

A *market analysis* describes elements of a market including factors that affect it, present conditions, and characteristics that distinguish it from other markets. In a business plan, the market analysis will give stakeholders the ability to see a glimpse of what the company faces regarding competitors and how to increase the share of the consumer's wallet. A *share of wallet* is marketing term that describes the amount of disposable income a firm can capture from the sales of its products to the market. The market analysis also shows how the company fits into the market and its strengths versus its competition. A way for companies to see where they fit into the market is to create a perceptual map.

The market analysis also addresses such thing as trends in the industry and identifies who the target market is. The ability to discover trends is important to capitalize on future innovation ideas. The ability to know your target market and learn what it seeks in products is key to longevity and profitability. Companies must always analyze current and future trends and learn from past events, as history repeats itself in business and life. The market analysis thus serves as a tool to create both strategic (long-term) and tactical (short-term) plans to guide businesses' innovation agenda and operations.

Organization and Management

This section affords a company the opportunity to highlight its top managers and their accomplishments. A strong managerial team has been shown to influence stakeholder involvement more than the products the company offers. In addition to information about the company's top managers, this section also includes a highlight of the executives' previous employment, along with their accomplishments and qualifications, and it should provide a sense of where the company is going based on these criteria as leaders typically develop a management style that is forged by past success, and they often stay true to their established methods. The organization and management section also provides insights as to how the company will be run based on past success, which can either be viewed as positive or negative by stakeholders. It also serves as a way for investors to consider buying a share of the company based on the top managers.

Sales Strategies

Every company has unique sales strategies based on the markets they serve, customer preference, product type, and location. More specifically, companies reporting their sales strategies would include their pricing strategies, including the following:

- *Price skimming*: A pricing strategy that starts out with a high unit price and reduces it over time. This type of strategy is popular with electronics such as cell phones.
- *Pricing penetration*: A price strategy that starts out low and raises over time. It is a good strategy to gain market share. This strategy is popular with utilities and cable television. Consumers pay an initial low price and this price increases over time.
- *Everyday low prices (EDLP)*: This strategy offers consumers prices that are usually below the normal price paid at competitors. It is highly effective because consumers feel they can get the lowest prices in any market segment when companies use this. The reality is that not all products are low priced. This is a common strategy used for retailers such as Walmart.
- *Psychological pricing*: A pricing strategy that attempts to make the price seem less than it really is. Items sound cheaper at $2.99 than at $3.00, or buy one, get another for 50%

off. Consumers are very susceptible to these types of strategies because they make the offer sound so enticing that it is hard to not buy.

- *Bundle pricing*: A pricing strategy that bundles typically services at an initial low cost to get consumers to trial the products, influencing their purchase in the future. Examples of this strategy include cable television companies offering a low price for cable television, Internet, and phone. This is a very effective strategy to get people to try a variety of products simultaneously in hope they will continue at a higher price in the future.

In addition to these specific types of pricing methods, other pricing strategies should also include a discussion around the price points and the reasons why they exist. Also, it should address how pricing will incorporate social media as an effective way to advertise price to a targeted customer base. Moreover, additional sales strategies will include the use of public relations, other ways to increase brand awareness, and any other approaches the company intends to use to encourage customers to buy (adding urgency, special sales, loyalty programs, offering financing, etc.). It is also recommended that companies include information about how they will leverage search engine optimization and geolocation and how positive word of mouth will be supported by consumers using smartphones.

Funding Requirements

As discussed earlier, business plans can be used for lenders to determine if a company is worthy of borrowing money. Companies should use the funding requirements section to show how the borrowed money will be used. The amount can be a range (lowest amount to highest amount) or an exact dollar amount. The funding requirements should also show what the company is expected to yield for margins and costs (see the next section on financial projections). When reading through the funding stage, the risks and countermeasures are extremely important, and even though nothing is guaranteed, people want to be as informed as possible about the potential upside(s) versus the investment and what the risks are.

Financial Projections

Financial projections are used to show current and future revenue, plus expenses that will impact a company. Financial projections also consider market trends and how they will impact revenue streams. Financial projections incorporate many statements to help make sense of their current and future financial position (one-, three-, and five-year plans). Financial projections show stakeholders the income statement, cash flow projection, and balance sheet.

Income Statement

An *income statement is* a financial statement measuring a company's financial performance over a specified period. The income statement shows the revenue, expenses, total income, and net income for a firm. The *revenue is* the amount of money earned from selling a company's products. *Expenses* are the costs (direct and general and administrative) incurred by a company. *Total income* is the income resulting when you subtract revenue minus expenses before income tax. The income statement gives the company and stakeholders a view at the current and anticipated earnings the firms seek to achieve in a prescribed period.

Cash Flow Projection

A *cash flow projection* is a statement showing inflows and outflows of cash into a business over a specific period (usually one year). It helps to predict any shortcomings, which would require raising capital to meet the need to fund business operations. A key ingredient in business is to be able to estimate your financial status to ensure the business is run uninterrupted; therefore, it is important to provide an accurate cash flow projection to prevent any surprises in the company's operations.

Balance Sheet

A *balance sheet* shows a company's assets, liabilities, and shareholder equity at a specified point in time. The balance sheet is useful for determining the net worth of a company by viewing its assets and liabilities. It also gives investors the ability to gauge the current financial position of a company and how well its resources are managed.[3]

Risk and Countermeasures

Risks and countermeasures are not widely adopted in the United States but are common in Japan. Isuzu introduced Spartan Motors to this wise management process in 2011. *Risk* is exposure to danger, imperil, hazard, or threat, while a *countermeasure* is an action taken to counteract a danger or threat. Notice the word *action* in countermeasure. Without acting, a countermeasure will never be effective; therefore, companies must act to counter the threat present. This section provides an opportunity for the company's top leadership to demonstrate how they analyze risks and how they apply countermeasures to stop a threat. Remember, leadership is paid to predict and plan for the future in a way that ensures their plan will become reality.

HOW DO WE INNOVATE FAST AND PROMOTE THE BUSINESS PLAN?

Typically, others within the organization are aware of the innovation in progress. The first step is to inform people of the vision for the product. Next, it is important to communicate regular updates so that everyone is aware of any changes and of the current direction the innovation is going. Information regarding the market, features, benefits, finances, and risks should be discussed by the team to keep everyone apprised. Consider circulating a two-page executive summary as this will now enable people to be prepared for the discussion. A detailed

---

3 "A Step-by-Step Guide to Drafting a Business Plan," Quickbooks, https://quickbooks.intuit.com/r/business-planning/7-elements-business-plan.

business plan should only be done when the executive summary includes every component of a detailed business plan. In business, no one likes a surprise as even good surprises regarding sharp demand can have negative consequences, such as a shortage of product to sell.

What Steps Can We Take to Begin the Product Development Plan?

In addition to the business plan, companies should begin the process of developing a product development plan. A *product development plan i*s a document that outlines the company's process for modifying or creating a new product, and it defines what resources are required to complete the project. We have stressed several times in the text thus far that speed is critical in innovation. Companies must therefore begin the process early and perfect it when it comes to developing a new product. While this is a part of a great plan, the speed at which a company can innovate will determine everything, from when a product will launch, but it will also influence every subsequent launch. Any progress made in reducing the length of time needed for any part of the process to create, manufacture, and launch the company's next product will increase revenue for years to come; therefore, let's explore some ways to begin the new product development process.

While there are more steps in the new product development process, we will begin with the following to give you an idea of what is needed to develop a new product:

- **Idea generation**. *Idea generation* is a process whereby ideas are thought out, concepts are innovated, processes are developed, and the idea is brought to existence to satisfy the needs of the target market. It starts with an analysis that determines the strengths, weaknesses, opportunities, and threats facing a business (SWOT). The SWOT analysis serves to drive policies guiding the strategies of the company and innovation. A SWOT analysis looks at every area of the business to help it capitalize on strengths and opportunities while limiting the weaknesses and threats. Without an honest evaluation of what the company has and doesn't have to compete, it cannot be successful. Therefore, a SWOT analysis is a key component driving the marketing strategies of a resourceful company.
- **Screening the idea**. All ideas for innovation should be evaluated based on the four rules of product development. In addition, innovators must ask "How does my innovation compare to the competitor's product?" "How will consumers compare my innovation to my competitors?" We will discuss in future chapters ways to develop ideas, but to plant the seed, the functional team must evaluate its target market to find ways to satisfy its future needs and to evaluate several ideas to do so. Several ideas should be presented and a "go/no-go" decision must be made. Therefore, idea screening is an important step to consider when formulating the next innovation.
- **Product considerations**. As the team begins developing prototypes, other considerations should be taken into account, such as whether the firm should file a patent, what kind of market intelligence must be acquired before moving forward, and if there are any legalities the company must consider, as well as how to educate the consumer about

the innovation so that it will be adopted sooner and the team's level of certainty that the new product satisfies a need or want. This last point is related to creating the aura around the product to create excitement for its availability to consumers.

- **Developing business analytics**. Before the innovation is started, thoughts should be given to how the innovator will measure the success of the product. A system should be built to measure the progress of the development (input and output metrics) as well as marketing analytics such as what percent of the market the innovation will capture, profit margins, initial price, distribution, and advertising strategies, and so on. Above all, every part of the analytics must be measurable with realistic goals set in place. The key to business success is to be proactive and not reactive; therefore, developing realistic analytics will help to guide the innovation process by considering the variables before the process begins.

We will discuss these various points later in the text, but at this point, our goal is to introduce you to these initial phases of innovation and how they should unfold once the business plan is developed. Like any process, innovators must consider every facet of the development process so that the team can gain momentum in going to market. Often, there is a lot of momentum that is lost by poor planning and procrastination. It is best if every step of the innovation process is planned and measured to maximize success.

Developing the Product Development Plan

Developing a product development plan is similar to writing a business plan: It starts with the vision, a timeline, and a list of desired outcomes. Every business is different, so the following are some of the most common, key considerations:

1. What is the vision and how do we inspire people?
2. How can we seek input and alignment from stakeholders?
3. How can data alignment (market and financial) improve success?
4. What are the risks and countermeasures?
5. Focus, communicate, focus, communicate.

Hitting the Market with Momentum

Each step leads to a closer launch, and one of the most common mistakes teams make in writing their product development plan is that it does not include detailed steps the company will take to ensure the product's success in the market after it is launched. As a result, many companies will rush their product to market and then slow to a crawl, providing little to no support for the product once it is available, which often seals its lackluster fate; therefore, the product development plan should include what specific actions the company will take after the launch.

Review Questions

1. How might a copycat's products affect a company's reputation? Why?
2. What is a product you feel would fit the five ways to validate and why?
3. What biases do you have toward a product? Are they justified and why?
4. What business structure do you feel you would pursue if you were developing a product (corporation, sole proprietorship, etc.)? Why?
5. What sales strategies are most effective to get you to purchase products? Why?
6. Describe your ideal product idea. How does it fit with the four rules?

Discussion Questions

1. Of the five ways to validate an innovation, which do you feel is the most important and why?
2. Discuss an innovation that would make your life easier. Why?
3. Describe your perfect boss and their management style. Why is this style appealing to you?
4. Do you feel a corporation is better than a partnership when forming a business? Why?
5. How does market intelligence impact innovation?
6. Do you think carrying momentum of an innovation is important? Why?

Extension Activity

Be prepared to discuss in class the following questions:

1. What type of psychological pricing strategy do you feel is most effective for selling automobiles, restaurants, and legal haircuts? Why?
2. What product innovation do you feel would help your college's or university's parking situation? What metrics would you develop to test it?

BIBLIOGRAPHY

Skillicorn, Nick. "Guy Makes Living Stealing People's Ideas," Idea to Value, 2017, https://www.ide-atovalue.com/inno/nickskillicorn/2017/02/guy-makes-living-stealing-peoples ideas/.

Perry, J., Marl. "Fortune 500 Companies 1955 vs. 2016: Only 12% Remain Thanks to the Creative Destruction That Fuels Economic Prosperity," AEI, December 13, 2016, http://www.aei.org/publication/fortune-500-firms-1955-v-2016-only-12-remain-thanks-to-the-creative-destruction-that-fuels-economic-prosperity/.

"A Step-by-Step Guide to Drafting a Business Plan," Quickbooks, https://quickbooks.intuit.com/r/business-planning/7-elements-business-plan.

CHAPTER FOUR

Just Who Exactly is Us?

INTRODUCTION

Companies have the unique ability to improve the quality of life for their customers, better the world in which we live, and improve products and processes currently being used. These things are accomplished through innovation, seeking talent to accomplish the vision of the company while supporting the mission, and creating a community in which citizens of Earth live together. The importance of this chapter is to gain a sense of "us," how innovators and their stakeholders must interact together to better the world we live and create a community. Firms must also learn how to document the skills set they possess with their current employees and determine if they must go outside the firm to seek the talents they need.

Firms must also foster a way for groups to form and realize there may be many phases they go through while working together. Finally, firms must refine a sense of community by providing an orientation and training, seeking a consensus to support the mission and vision of the firm.

Learning Objectives

In this chapter students will learn the following:
- How to identify a company's vision
- The mission that we are to pursue
- Why fostering a sense of community over culture so important
- What we are trying to accomplish through innovation
- Analyzing if we have the talent to accomplish our mission and vision
- Identifying the reason for being in business

Learning Outcomes

By the end of this chapter students will be able to do the following:

- Craft an effective mission statement
- Craft an effective vision statement
- Describe why business has moved from a sense of culture to community
- Understand how to attract and retain talent
- Gain an understanding of why businesses exist

Key Terms

Mission: Describes the purpose of the company's existence and guides its actions and decisions

Mission statement: Communicates to the company's stakeholders the purpose of the organization and what it represents

Vision: Describes where the company is going and what it seeks to accomplish

Vision statement: A document meant to communicate what the company wishes to accomplish and how to sustain future growth

Community: A feeling of fellowship with others created by sharing interactions and relationships formed within the community

Culture: Learned behavior either by family or acclimation as you are exposed to different cultures

Continuous innovation: Innovation that typically involves attribute change and no change in consumer behavior

Incremental (dynamically continuous) innovation: Innovation that involves design changes to existing products and modifies consumer behavior

Disruptive (discontinuous) innovation: Innovation that requires significant change in consumer behavior and reshapes the dynamics of the industry. Also called new-to-the-world products

Internal candidates: Current employees of the company selected based on their experience, skill sets, and training

External (full-time or contract) candidates: Full-time is a permanent hire, while contact employees are brought in for a specified time

Joint venture: A business venture in which two or more parties agree to undertake a business venture and share in the profits and losses

Strategic alliance: One firm partners with another or several to develop a product without forming a separate company

Groupthink: Found in groups who reach a consensus without critical analyzing or evaluating consequences or alternatives

THINK ABOUT THIS!

How did CEO John Sztykiel use trends in the market to analyze a shift in future business? Did his actions benefit Spartan Motors, Inc.? Think of another company that shifted their business focus to ensure their survival?

While John Sztykiel was the CEO of Spartan Motors Inc. (Spartan), a manufacturer of specialty trucks based in Charlotte, Michigan, their product portfolio in 2009 was approximately 82 percent government dependent and the US was in a recession. When Sztykiel retired in 2015, less than 45 percent of Spartan's business was government dependent, sales were just over $500 million, they possessed very little debt, and they had over $24 million in cash on hand. These actions were taken due to changing trends that Sztykiel saw with the US adopting a strategy to ending the war in Iraq and finding other ways to do business without relying too heavily on government contracts.

HOW DO YOU TAKE THIS FROM THEORY TO PRACTICE?

Spartan's vision statement reads, "Increase the value of our company, expand our portfolio of brands, and enter new markets by exceeding customer expectations, becoming market leaders, and achieving quality excellence." Spartan accomplishes this by using trends to identify new products that benefit their stakeholders. A growing trend of Americans becoming obese led Spartan to install a hoist system on their ambulances to reduce injury to paramedics and provide a safe means of loading patients. Spartan also entered the delivery fleet market when it was realized that online ordering was on the rise, driving the demand for these types of vehicles. Finally, another way Spartan stays competitive is by concentrating on its core values.

WHAT IS A COMPANY'S MISSION?

The *mission* of the company describes the purpose of why the company is in existence and guides its actions and decisions. Having a long-term vision shapes the future of the organization, while the mission identifies the firm's present plans and what it seeks to accomplish. In a quote by Mark Zuckerberg, he says Facebook's mission is to allow for a more interconnected world through connectivity of its stakeholders. Think to yourself how easy it is to have a conversation with someone living in a different continent, where before Facebook or any other social media, it was very difficult and expensive. The mission of Facebook drives its ability to promote connectivity through innovation offering ways to achieve this goal in the present (e.g., connecting with people, instant messaging, posts, likes, calling features, etc.).

What is a Mission Statement?

Organizations broadcast their mission to their stakeholders through a mission statement. The *mission statement* communicates to the company's stakeholders the purpose of the organization and what it represents. The mission statement answers three questions:

1. *What* does the organization do?
2. *Who* does it do it for?
3. *How* does it accomplish its purpose?

The mission statement is written in a concise manner (one or two sentences) and represents a shorter period (one to two years) than the vision statement (two to ten years).[1]

WHAT IS A COMPANY'S VISION?

Before exploring how vision shapes the innovation process, we must first gain a better understanding of what vision is. The *vision* of a company identifies where the company is headed and what it seeks to accomplish. The vision is not to be confused with the strategic plans of the company. The strategic plans provide ways to accomplish the vision. Additionally, vision provides the ability to select which future opportunities the firm wishes to pursue, enabling it to sustain growth. Therefore, vision affects the people hired, the product portfolio, strategic partnerships, and profits and supports ethical behavior and the betterment of society. For example, Spartan has enacted core values and identified five focal points that guide its operational strategy. These five focal points include the following:

1. Turnaround the emergency response business.
2. Improve operational discipline and performance.
3. Increase the level of accountability.
4. Reduce quality and warranty expense.
5. Strengthen and develop the team.

Therefore, Spartan can support their vision focusing on these five focal points while creating opportunities, increasing value, and having an attitude striving for quality and excellence ,which will help to positively shape the company.[2]

---

1 Jenelle Evans, "Vision and Mission," *Psychology Today*, April 24, 2010, https://www.psychologytoday.com/blog/smartwork/201004/vision-and-mission.

2 "About Us," Spartan Motors, Inc., www.spartanmotors.com/about-us.

What Is a Vision Statement?

For firms to communicate their visions with stakeholders, they must be first devised and recorded. The *vision statement i*s document meant to communicate what the company wishes to accomplish to sustain growth (two to ten years). Writing a vision statement is not an easy task. It requires the ability to clearly think of what the vision will entail and then communicate it in a way anyone who reads it will understand. The following are some common pitfalls experienced when writing a vision statement:

1. *Lack of originality*: Companies have no idea what a vision statement is supposed to convey so they copy another firm. Each company's vision is unique; therefore, the vision must be original to have purpose and drive the company toward greatness.
2. *One author*: The vision statement should have the ability to be read by anyone and allow them to clearly understand the direction and purpose of the company. Having multiple authors ensures this will happen through reaching a consensus.
3. *Not concise*: Many vision statements are too wordy. Vision statements must be concise, meaning they should clearly communicate the exact meaning of companies' intentions.
4. *Too internally driven*: A vision statement must convey what the company intends to do not only for itself, but for its stakeholders. Spartan Motors' vision was both internal (increase the value of the company and expand brand portfolios) and external (enter new markets by exceeding customer expectations, becoming market leaders, and achieving quality excellence).[3]

Firms that can overcome these pitfalls of writing a vision statement will give employees, stakeholders, and management the means to provide long-term success by clearly communicating what it seeks to accomplish for years to come. The vision statement helps to formulate the strategic plans of the firm and acts as a vehicle that guides the future of the organization.

How Do We Write a Vision Statement?

Now that we have discussed the difficulties associated with writing a vision statement, let's focus on ways to communicate our corporate vision with the rest of the world. Capitalizing on the pitfalls of a poorly written vision statement, the following suggestions are for writing a useable vision statement:

1. *Assemble the authors*: Those involved in writing the vision statement should be the company's "C-suite" level of management in charge of implementing the strategies of the company (i.e., the chief executive officer (CEO), the chief operations officer (COO), the chief financial officer (CFO), the chief marketing officer (CMO), etc.). A

---

3   Kristen May, "What Makes Vision Statements Ineffective?" Chron, http://smallbusiness.chron.com/vision-statements-ineffective-35572.html.

recommended practice before writing the vision statement is to brainstorm what the company wishes to accomplish both internally and externally. Gather these ideas in a decision tree and then use the final version to write the vision statement.

2. *Be concise*: The vision statement must contain wording that accurately describes what the company wants to accomplish in as few words as possible. Do not add filler or be too wordy, as this will dilute the vision and cause confusion on the part of stakeholders trying to determine what the firm seeks to accomplish. The vision statement should be concise and should be written in a manner anyone could read and comprehend.

3. *Review the draft by the team and edit what is needed*: Sometimes it is easier to write the vision and then to table it for a short period of time. It is recommended to have the team read it again and then edit what does not fulfill the vision of the company.

4. *Seek a second opinion*: Once the final draft is written, seek the opinion of others to see if the vision statement clearly describes to others what the company seeks to do. If it does, then mission accomplished, but if not, make the necessary changes.

5. *Post the vision for the stakeholders to read*: Once the vision is agreed on, post the vision statement, allowing it to be seen by stakeholders. Another practice is to post the vision internally for employees to see. It is also recommended to preach the vision to employees, expressing what the company seeks to accomplish with their help. The vision should drive the actions, decisions, and innovations of the company. Only through clear understanding on the part of all stakeholders will this be accomplished.

Having a sound vision and mission statement benefits the organization in several ways. The following are a summary of these benefits:

1. They provide a common goal for all the employees.
2. They help in strategic and tactical planning by providing a clear focus.
3. They allow stakeholders to see the purpose and future growth potential of the company.
4. They drive innovation by aligning the development of goods and services with the mission and vision.

WHAT IS THE DIFFERENCE BETWEEN COMMUNITY AND CULTURE?

Most textbooks identify the concept of corporate culture and how this drives such things as organizational justice, values, ethics, and purpose, to name a few. We wish to extend this train of thought by introducing the term community. *Community* is a feeling of fellowship with others created by sharing interactions and relationships formed within the community. It involves sharing common attitudes, interests, behaviors, and goals. Community represents a choice an individual makes, and it does not change as people come and go, because it was already in existence before they arrived. Therefore, community strives to empower its members that they may get out what they put in.

Culture is learned behavior either by family or acclimation as you are exposed to different cultures (e.g., what would your behavior be like growing up in a farm community and then moving to a major city?). Culture is the sum of actions, beliefs, rules, customs, language, and attitudes. The description of culture in business is overused and is outdated. Based on the differences explained, community is a more accurate term describing how people interact with each other and how the firm motivates and nurtures their employees. Most employees hire into a firm where the community was already established, giving them the ability to get out what they put in. Once they leave, the community will continue as before and they will be part of a different community that was already in existence. While the difference between community and culture may seem confusing, a summary of the two shows how they differ.

TABLE 4.1   *Community versus Culture*

COMMUNITY	CULTURE
Interaction based, not learned	No interaction required
Empowers its members	Learned behavior
Binds it members through relationships	Taught by family or through acclimation
Shares common interests	Common language, customs, or rules

So, how does community affect today's workplace? Today's millennials desire four things in a career: say bye-bye to the traditional 9 to 5, be kept inspired, have a good work/life balance, and be made part of the solution. These requirements on the part of millennials are relationship and interaction focused and while they may seem simple to provide, most will only stay at a job less than three years.[4] In addition, friendly associations (interactions) with people who share similar interests draw us together. Today, most studies rank innovation, people/community, and unity as one and/or two of its biggest concerns. Therefore, we wish to introduce community as the new culture, as it allows firms to encourage interactions, empowers its members, promotes relationships, and is built on the common interests of its members.

---

4   Jeanne Meister, "The Future of Work: Job Hopping Is the 'New Normal' for Millennials," *Forbes*, August 14, 2012, https://www.forbes.com/sites/jeannemeister/2012/08/14/the-future-of-work-job-hopping-is-the-new-normal-for-millennials/#28effe5113b8.

WHAT ARE WE TRYING TO ACCOMPLISH THROUGH INNOVATION?

Now that we have a better understanding of the differences between mission and vision, and community and culture, let's ask the question "Why innovate?" Innovation allows for companies to achieve their vision (sustain growth) and mission (their purpose) by developing goods and services to accomplish both, plus satisfy the needs of their customers and sustain long-term existence. Before we proceed in learning about why we innovate, let's identify the three types of innovation that will be highlighted in this text:

1. *Continuous*: Innovation that requires very little change in consumer behavior to interact with the good or service, nor does it change the dynamics of an industry. This type of innovation usually includes attribute changes or upgrades in products. Examples include toothpaste with whitening, shampoo and body wash combination, or a new flavor of potato chip. This the most common type of innovation because it allows firms to build off existing brands, utilizes established wholesale and retail channels, and allows for firms to use existing manufacturing capabilities, thus reducing cost and risk.

2. *Incremental (dynamically continuous)*: Innovation that requires consumers to slightly modify their behavior or moderately changes an industry. It falls between continuous and disruptive innovation as consumers have previous experience with these types of products but will be required to learn a new method of using them. Examples include satellite television, ordering online, and hybrid vehicles.

3. *Disruptive (discontinuous)*: Innovation requiring significant change in consumer behavior and that reshapes the dynamics of the industry. This type of innovation is also called "new-to-the-world products" as they have never been seen or offered to consumers. Examples include the first smartphones, automobiles, laptops, and the Internet.

Other than supporting the mission and vision of the company, firms practice innovation for several other reasons:

1. *Survival*: There are many examples of companies who failed to innovate and went bankrupt or never recovered, including Blockbuster, Blackberry, Polaroid, Eastman Kodak, My Space, and Sears.[5] Innovative products provide firms with the ability to extend their existence in the product life cycle, build customer loyalty, increase the value of the product portfolio, provide long-term employment for employees, and better the world they interact with. It also allows for superior business performance by efficiency, quality, customer responsiveness, and speed.[6]

2. *Local or regional competition*: New start-up companies are threatening established firms due to their horizontal organizational structure, fast turnaround times of products, and responsiveness to the demands of the market. Established innovative firms must leverage their resources (i.e., economic, technical, and manufacturing) to combat these firms. Established firms have the benefit of benchmarking past innovation processes, which help them perfect the process. In other words, established firms have gotten through the learning curve where new start-up firms are just experiencing it. It is the responsibility of the established firm to capitalize on what it has learned and develop an innovation plan to perform better than its competition.

3. *Global competition*: Due to technology and a changing business climate, global competition is stronger than ever. Countries such as India, China, and others from Latin America threaten traditional companies. To compete, firms in the United States who for many decades enjoyed a competitive advantage to other firms worldwide must also compete and change the way they used to do business. Examples of this include strategic partnerships (SAIC-GMAC in China), moving manufacturing to countries with a lower labor rate (clothes made in Vietnam), and franchising (Starbucks in Europe).[7]

4. *Changing demographics*: As baby boomers are quickly being replaced in the market by millennials, product innovation is trying to keep up. Millennials will demand more products that allow them to use technology to work more efficiently. In addition, millennials will require products that are more focused on speed like grab-and-go

---

5   Rick Newman, "10 Great Companies That Lost Their Edge," *U.S. News and World Report*, April 19, 2010, http://money.usnews.com/money/blogs/flowchart/2010/08/19/10-great-companies-that-lost-their-edge.

6   Benn, Lawson and Danny, Samson, "Developing Innovation Capability in Organizations: A Dynamic Capabilities Approach," *Journal of Innovation Management* 5, no. 3 (2001): 377–400.

7   "General Motors Announces Growth Strategy for China, *General Motors*, March 21, 2016, https://media.gm.com/media/cn/en/gm/news.detail.html/content/Pages/news/cn/en/2016/Mar/0321_annoucement.html; Julie Jargon, "Starbucks Tries Franchising to Perk Up Europe Business," *Wall Street Journal*, November 29, 2013, https://www.wsj.com/articles/starbucks-tries-franchising-to-perk-up-europe-business-1385760998.

food items, renting versus buying a home due to rapid job change, travel, and energy drinks to name a few.[8]

5. *Innovation promotes innovation*: Companies that are good at innovation can increase market share, reduce costs, and increase corporate image due the introduction of new and efficient products that satisfy the needs of their target market. An example is Apple and the products they offer. While many feel Apple is a company that creates disruptive innovated products, they are really a successful innovator of continuous innovative products but use their marketing capabilities to promote the brand. As indicated, innovative firms learn what works best and continuously perfect this model to create a competitive advantage.

6. *Sustainability*: Consumers are increasingly demanding sustainable products. Companies who can innovative products that are good for the firm, society, and the environment will both address consumer wishes and be responsible to the stakeholders they serve. Examples include hybrid vehicles, organic foods, fair trade coffee, clothing not made by child labor, and construction products such as lumber that is grown and harvested using Forest Stewardship Council guidelines. While it was thought that producing sustainable meant lower profits, the opposite is being reported. Therefore, companies that can continue to answer the call of consumers to offer sustainable products will be rewarded.[9]

7. *Increased employee empowerment*: As discussed in the community section, employees who feel empowered have been shown to demonstrate more commitment and loyalty toward the firm. Innovation allows for employees to have an active part in the company's success and gives them a voice in the direction the firm seeks through participating in the innovation process. Empowerment also leads to great interaction by having employees work in cross-functional teams while the innovation process is progressing. This can result in greater empowerment and more interaction and can strengthen the community within the business.[10]

---

8   Brad Tuttle, "10 Things Millennials Buy More Than Any Other Generation," Money, July 31, 2015, http://money.com/money/3979425/millennials-consumers-boomers-gen-x/.

9   Ram, Nidumolu, Coimbatore, K,., Prahalad, and Madhavan R., Rangaswami, "Why Sustainability is Now the Key Driver of Innovation," *Harvard Business Review* 87, no. 9 (2009): 56–64.

10   Benn, Lawson and Danny, Samson, "Developing Innovation Capability in Organizations: A Dynamic Capabilities Approach," *Journal of Innovation Management* 5, no. 3 (2001): 377–400.

ANALYZING IF WE HAVE THE TALENT TO ACCOMPLISH OUR VISION AND MISSION

The title of this chapter is "Just Who Exactly Is Us?" which conveys the meaning that companies are not one person but a collection of many people bringing a variety of skills, talents, alternative ideas, and so on to form a community. The community assembled seeks to fulfill the vision and mission of the firm by utilizing the talents and skills of employees to drive innovation and product introduction today and in the future. One way to do this is by attracting the right people to our community and by encouraging interaction. This section identifies ways to determine if we have the right people in our community, if we need to hire additional employees, and how we can develop them to be innovators. We will focus on four ways to select the right people to construct an innovative community including the following:

1. *Internal candidates*: Current employees of the company selected based on their experience, skill sets, and training
2. *External (full-time or contract) candidates*: Full-time is a permanent hire, while contract employees are brought in for a specified time
3. *Joint venture*: A business venture in which two or more parties agree to undertake a business venture and share in the profits and losses
4. *Strategic alliance*: One firm partners with another or several to develop a product without forming a separate company

Do We Have the Right People?

Innovative managers must decide if the teams they manage have the right skill sets to successfully develop and launch the desired product. If they don't, human resources must seek outside talents to make the innovation a reality. Other options are to form a joint venture, which is a partnership characterized by ownership, or a strategic partnership which is two companies coming together without ownership. The following sections will explore and further define these options so that managers can make informed decisions.

Internal

Steps necessary for innovation can become standardized over time, but the process that is used is unique depending on what is being developed. It is important that before the innovation process begins, the human resource department has accurate records of skill sets, specialized training, and educational backgrounds of its employees. Also, it would be helpful if the human resource department had a record of previous participation in innovation projects and the evaluation of the employees involved.

Once top management determines the innovation to be developed, they must also assess if they have the talent currently within the company to succeed. A key point to assessing innovation teams is determining does the company has diversity. A common problem among innovation teams is the lack of diversity. A collection of people from similar backgrounds and thought processes tend to fall into groupthink. *Groupthink* is found in groups who reach a consensus without critically analyzing or evaluating consequences or alternatives. It is also characterized by a common desire among group members not to upset or cause conflict, thus leading to a lack of creativity and individuality.[11] While the concept of groupthink has been studied for more than forty years, proof of it has been debated by top management scholars for years. The consensus, however, believes that high levels of group diversity bring more perspectives and are a greater source of creativity and innovation.[12]

External

Once the internal talent, skill sets, and needed training have been evaluated, there may be a need to look to the external market to fill the talent and skill sets needed for the innovation team or process. Top management must work with human resources to provide the skills or training needed to fill the team. It is at this point that the company must determine if the external candidate who will be brought in is a full-time or contract (temporary) employee. Full-time employees tend to be more loyal and devoted due to their inclusion into the community. On the other hand, contract employees may feel little loyalty due to the fact they are hired on a temporary basis. One method companies use to increase the level of commitment on the part of contract employees is to let them know their performance on the project could lead to full-time employment. This scenario should only be given if it is sincere on the part of the company.

Hiring external candidates has advantages that may help companies meet the demands of being more innovative. External candidates bring in fresh perspectives, current knowledge of industry trends, reduce complacency, and overcome the lack of talent the current organization may have. Therefore, to meet the demands of a highly competitive marketplace, looking outside the organization has many benefits.

Joint Venture

A joint venture is a contractual agreement in which two or more parties form a single business unit combining property, money, efforts, and resources for the intent of gaining a profit. Joint ventures are not required to be equal in the percentage of ownership and the parties involve also share in the loss based on percentage owned.[13]

---

11   Will Kenton, "Groupthink," Investopedia, January 6, 2018, https://www.investopedia.com/terms/g/group-think.asp.

12   Gerben,S. Van der Vegt and Onne, Janssen, "Joint Impact of Interdependence and Group Diversity on Innovation," *Journal of Management* 29, no. 5 (2003): 729–751.

13   "Distinction between Joint Venture and Partnerships," U.S. Legal, https://jointventures.uslegal.com/distinction-between-joint-venture-and-partnerships/.

Strategic Alliance

Another option for assembling a team with all the skills and talents necessary for product development is to form a strategic alliance. A ***strategic alliance*** is two or more companies that form an alliance for working on a common objective. This differs from a joint venture is that there isn't the formation of a separate company, and when the work is complete, the parties may split.[14] The benefit of a strategic alliance is the people and processes that may be lacking to develop a product. Examples of strategic alliances include the following:

1. *Starbucks and Barnes and Noble*: Placing a coffeeshop inside a retail location, thus benefitting both retailers.
2. *Apple and Clearwell*: Jointly developed Clearwell's E-Discovery platform used in the iPad
3. *Eli Lily and Galapagos*: An American and Belgium company formed to develop osteoporosis medicine[15]

How Does an Effective Orientation Help New Employees Feel Like They are Part of the Community?

Once the candidates are hired, it is a good idea to give them an orientation to discuss company policy, expectations, and a tour of the facility; introduce them to members of the community; and emphasize the vision and mission of the company and whatever else is necessary to make them comfortable with the company, team, and what is expected of them. The main point of orientation is to develop a sense of community among the group members and for them to understand why the company exists and how they help make a difference. Unfortunately, when people become part of a group there are some dynamics that if not handled well by management could have negative consequences. Bruce Tuckman developed a model of what happens when groups form.[16] The stages of group development include the following:

1. *Forming*: The initial stage of group formation. This phase is characterized by polite conversation and getting to know one another. The group members tend to not express opinions or speak of sensitive topics as they do not know the others with whom they

---

14   "Strategic alliance," Business Dictionary, http://www.businessdictionary.com/definition/strategic-alliance.html.

15   Kimberlee Leonard, "Examples of Successful Strategic Alliances," Chron, February 4, 2019, https://small-business.chron.com/examples-successful-strategic-alliances-13859.html.

16   Bruce, W. Tuckman, "Development Sequence in Small Groups," *Psychological Bulleting* 63 (1965): 384–399; B. W. Tuckman and M. A. C. Jensen, "Stages of Small Group Development Revisited," *Group and Organization Studies* 2 (1977): 419–427.

will work. It is important for the company to encourage interaction and to develop relationships among group members (a key ingredient of community).

2. *Storming*: After the initial pleasantries, researchers have found that one or more group members usually seek leadership of the group. Top management must assert their authority to reinforce the goals, roles, and objectives of the group while allowing a hierarchy to be established.

3. *Norming*: Once the storming is over and a natural leader and team are defined, norms of what the group wants to accomplish are spelled out, and the project becomes the focus of the group. Managers can concentrate on balancing a work/life obligation and create a sense of interaction among the community of innovators.

4. *Performing*: Once the goal at hand is accomplished and the success of the team is shared among the team, management can organize a focus group to reveal what best practices were used and evaluate each team member's performance.

5. *Adjournment*: A point where the task is complete, and the group adjourns. This is marked by a period of anxiety as many members wonder what happens next. Management could have a celebration in which rewards are given or group members are assigned to their old task or a new one. It is important the management ensures the team members that their efforts will not negatively impact their employment as some employees may have been temporarily replaced while the participated in the innovation process. The ability to know what employees seek on the part of management regarding rewards is the key to a successful adjournment. Employees are either intrinsically (internally) motivated, extrinsically (external) motivated, or both in terms of rewards they seek. *Intrinsic rewards* are the feelings one gets by helping others not involving visible reward (e.g., sense of accomplish, the ability to help, a thank you, etc.). *Extrinsic rewards* are visible rewards (e.g., plaque, special party, employee-of-the-month parking spot, etc.).

The ability of management to benchmark best practices, document them, and evaluate group members' performance, is necessary for future innovation, promoting a sense of community, and living out the mission and vision of the firm.

Once We Have the Necessary Talent, How Do We Increase Commitment and Retention to Achieve the Mission and Vision?

Forbes offers additional ways to retain valuable members of the community:

1. *Communicate, communicate, communicate*: By communicating with employees, businesses strengthen the sense of community by providing a roadmap for employees to express where they wish to go and how the firm can help to get them there.

2. *Value individual contributions*: Perform a review of each employee's performance and reward those who support the mission and vision of the company and achieve the goals of the organization.

3. *Provide training*: As discussed earlier, provide training to show value to those employees who can help achieve the goals of the organization. Training also helps to deepen commitment to the firm and increase productivity.

4. *Mentor*: Similar to providing a quality orientation, match an experienced employee to help new hires for use as a reference, answering questions, and helping to develop them into great employees.

5. *Ask questions and listen to answers*: Employees can help top management solve problems when they listen to the answers they provide to make the company better. Another form of this is to provide a suggestion box and reward people for offering their input on topics that are important to the betterment of the firm.

6. *Engage employees to solve business problems*: Top management should never be afraid to listen to what employees feel can help improve the performance of the company. Engagement increases empowerment, which is a part of community. Employees are part of the community, so empower them to help make things better through their interaction.

7. *Recognize employees and praise effort*: As mentioned before, reward employees who contribute to the betterment of the company in a manner that satisfies their intrinsic or extrinsic needs.[17]

By determining ways to retain key employees, companies can use their skills to innovate more efficiently and cut costs. The cost to train a new employee and the loss of experience is insurmountable. Promoting within, providing training, rewarding effort, and so on are some of the ways to increase commitment and loyalty while retaining the valuable assets needed to effectively innovate to achieve the mission and vision.

Review Questions

1. Explain the difference between a mission and vision statement.
2. What is the difference between community and culture?
3. In your own words, describe each of the three types of innovation and provide two real-world examples that have not been already discussed in this chapter.
4. List each of the seven reasons why companies innovate and provide a real-world example of each.
5. Describe how companies fill the needs of the innovation team members.

---

17 Dianne M. Derkin, "How to Keep Employees Motivated," *Forbes*, September 16, 2010, https://www.forbes.com/2010/09/16/employees-motivation-business-forbes-woman-leadership-communication.html.

6. What are the five main stages of group formation? Relate a personal experience you have had joining a team using the five stages of group formation.

7. What are ways to retain employees? Give an example of each that has not been already discussed in this chapter.

Discussion Questions

1. Select two products from each type of innovation that have changed your life for the better or worse. Explain why.

2. Of the ways to retain employees discussed in the chapter, which do you feel are the most impactful and why?

3. If you have ever experienced the group dynamics stages as described by Tuckman, please share with the class.

4. Why do you feel innovation is important or unimportant to companies?

5. Name some companies not listed in the text that failed in their efforts to innovate and eventually cost them market share. What could they have done to prevent this?

Extension Activity

Be prepared to discuss this during class. Following are two questions that will help to see if you understand the concept of mission and vision.

1. Discuss your experience with culture (learned behavior) and community (interactions), and identify how they differ.

2. Select a major corporation whose mission and vision statement are available online. Do they follow these in the way they conduct their business?

3. The text discussed Spartan Motors' mission and vision statements. Give two examples from their website on how they fulfill their mission and vision. Do you feel they are accomplishing this? What would you change if you were the CEO? (www.spartan-motors.com/).

4. Rewrite Spartan Motors' mission and vision statements in a way that you believe their stakeholders would appreciate.

BIBLIOGRAPHY

Evans, Jenelle. "Vision and Mission," *Psychology Today*, April 24, 2010, https://www.psychologytoday.com/blog/smartwork/201004/vision-and-mission.

"About Us," Spartan Motors, Inc., www.spartanmotors.com/about-us.

May, Kristen. "What Makes Vision Statements Ineffective?" Chron, http://smallbusiness.chron.com/vision-statements-ineffective-35572.html.

Meister, Jeanne. "The Future of Work: Job Hopping Is the 'New Normal' for Millennials," *Forbes*, August 14, 2012, https://www.forbes.com/sites/jeannemeister/2012/08/14/the-future-of-work-job-hopping-is-the-new-normal-for-millennials/#28effe5113b8.

Newman, Rick. "10 Great Companies That Lost Their Edge," *U.S. News and World Report*, April 19, 2010, http://money.usnews.com/money/blogs/flowchart/2010/08/19/10-great-companies-that-lost-their-edge.

Lawson, Benn and Samson, Danny. "Developing Innovation Capability in Organizations: ADynamic Capabilities Approach," *Journal of Innovation Management* 5, no. 3 (2001): 377–400.

"General Motors Announces Growth Strategy for China, *General Motors*, March 21, 2016, https://media.gm.com/media/cn/en/gm/news.detail.html/content/Pages/news/cn/en/2016/Mar/0321_annoucement.html.

Julie Jargon, "Starbucks Tries Franchising to Perk Up Europe Business," *Wall Street Journal*, November 29, 2013, https://www.wsj.com/articles/starbucks-tries-franchising-to-perk-up-europe-business-1385760998.

Tuttle, Brad. "10 Things Millennials Buy More Than Any Other Generation," Money, July 31, 2015, http://money.com/money/3979425/millennials-consumers-boomers-gen-x/.

Nidumolu, Ram, Prahalad, Coimbatore, K., and Rangaswami, Madhavan, R. "Why Sustainability is Now the Key Driver of Innovation," *Harvard Business Review* 87, no. 9 (2009): 56–64.

Kenton, Will. "Groupthink," Investopedia, January 6, 2018, https://www.investopedia.com/terms/g/groupthink.asp.

Van der Vegt, Gerben.S. and Janssen, Onne. "Joint Impact of Interdependence and Group Diversity on Innovation," *Journal of Management* 29, no. 5 (2003): 729–751.

"Distinction between Joint Venture and Partnerships," U.S. Legal, https://jointventures.uslegal.com/distinction-between-joint-venture-and-partnerships/.

"Strategic alliance," Business Dictionary, http://www.businessdictionary.com/definition/strategic-alliance.html.

Leonard, Kimberlee. "Examples of Successful Strategic Alliances," Chron, February 4, 2019, https://smallbusiness.chron.com/examples-successful-strategic-alliances-13859.html.

Tuckman, Bruce, W. "Development Sequence in Small Groups," *Psychological Bulleting* 63 (1965): 384–399.

B. W. Tuckman and M. A. C. Jensen, "Stages of Small Group Development Revisited," *Group and Organization Studies* 2 (1977): 419–427.

Derkin, Dianne, M. "How to Keep Employees Motivated," *Forbes*, September 16, 2010, https://www.forbes.com/2010/09/16/employees-motivation-business-forbes-woman-leadership-communication.html.

Understanding the Dynamics of Consumer Behavior

CHAPTER FIVE

How Do We Rate Talent, Community, and Innovators?

INTRODUCTION

Community determines ways we need to rate the talent we have, seek ways to find the best talent, and then determine how the community assembled finds ways to improve itself to strengthen it. Just as innovation is a continuous process perfected on improvement, so is the ability to better our company by finding, developing, and supporting the talent and community that is part of it.

Innovators who seek to improve our community have certain characteristics that can improve the success for a company's innovation efforts. These characteristics include seeing things through a unique lens, having stamina and the right attitude, being conscientious, possessing the ability to maintain the long-term vision, and being a risk taker. While it is hard to hire someone with these qualities, it is important that companies look inward to find these people, or when it is evident this talent does not exist, then search externally. Innovative employees will drive the company and lead them to success.

It is important to build the right innovative network within the company. Top managers must look for employees who have the capabilities, can perform, provide leadership, and are driven. Many times, this talent comes not only from within, but globally. Therefore, managers must be aware of the talents they have available. This can be done by creating an environment that encourages innovation, builds rapport, and provides guidelines to support innovative employees.

Learning Objectives

In this chapter students will learn about the following:
- Characteristic traits of innovative people
- How innovators can maintain vision and drive to be successful
- How hiring practices have changed in the twenty-first century

- What it takes and how to build an innovative workforce
- Why global talent should be considered
- The advantages of hiring within an organization

Learning Outcomes

By the end of this chapter students will be able to do the following:
- Understand how innovator's characteristics shape organizations
- Understand the value of seeing the world differently as compared to others
- Know how a good attitude and being accurate in work is important
- Know the items needed to maintain a long-term vision
- Know how Generations X and Y have changed hiring practices
- Know the reasons why a global economy has changed hiring employees
- Understand why developing talent within an organization is important
- Know the role top managers play to make innovation a part of the strategic plan

Key Terms

Stamina: The strength to persevere in the face of difficulty

Attitude: The feelings one has toward an object or organization

Leaders: Motivate teams of employees to accomplish the mission, vision, and purpose of the task at hand

Internal and external networks: Groups of stakeholders that are found inside and outside the organization that provide the opportunity to succeed

Differentiated capabilities: The collective skills, abilities, and expertise that allow one company a superior advantage over its competitors

Performance acceleration: The ability to attract the right talent to improve the workforce

Leadership development: The right leadership in place and being developed

Talent culture: The right culture in place to attract a diverse workforce

WHO MAKES UP THE COMMUNITY?

A common response to change is fear. Innovators look at the world through a different lens as they see opportunities and a myriad of ways improve existing products, services, and processes. Henry Ford envisioned building cars from an assembly line versus building them one at a time to reduce costs. Thomas Edison had 2332 international patents and 1093 US patents, including the lightbulb, phonograph, alkaline batteries, and electronic locomotion. Steve Jobs, a renowned innovator, helped facilitate the introduction of products such as the Macintosh, iPod, iPhone, and MacBook. The common thread between these innovators throughout the past one hundred years is the ability to identify a problem they want solved, which we recommend doing by writing a succinct problem statement, and then work hard to identify the best solution to implement. In other words, innovators continuously cultivate a dynamic solution-focused mind-set rather than a static problem-focused mind-set.

Innovators possess unique characteristics that human resources should identify to gain the knowledge and drive to move their company in the right direction. The characteristics include the following:

1. Innovative people can look at the world around them and see connections in ways not seen by others. This ability is difficult as most people see the world from a conformist view to accept what is present in their life as normal. Who could imagine using a light-bulb to illuminate a room versus a candle or replacing a telephone with a cell phone?
2. Stamina is an important trait for innovative people. Stamina is the strength to persevere in the face of difficulty. It hinges on two fronts:

   • Attitude is important, as most people will disagree with your thought process. One must keep the right attitude and fight through negativity. Attitude is the feelings one has toward an object or organization. Innovative people always a have a bit of a "Maverick" personality. A maverick personality is one that is comfortable taking risks and receiving criticism and that perseveres through difficult situations.
   • Getting it right. Rarely is the product, service, or innovation right the first time. Failure is the norm; thus, one learns, evolves, and moves forward.

Many innovators had several failures before their ideas were accepted. Steven King had Carrie rejected thirty times before getting it published, Tom Monahan went through several bankruptcies before establishing Domino's, and Sir David Tyson went thorough 5,126 failed prototypes before amassing a net worth of $5 billion. Stamina is also essential to innovative people because of their ability to keep trying to achieve success. From the examples, it is obvious that successful innovation doesn't happen on the first try. It is important that innovators keep persevering to achieve the goal they set out to accomplish. Therefore, the ability to maintain the original vision and drive is essential for success.

The following are traits the good innovators possess and use to drive success:

1. *Innovators must be leaders.* **Leaders** *can motivate a team of employees to accomplish the mission, vision, and purpose of the task at hand. Leaders must have a passion that is contagious to their subordinates and excite them to want to carry out the goal at hand.* Leaders must also inspire people to work together to bring the creative innovative concept to life. In addition, good leaders use data to help drive decisions. A key point to note is data. Intuition is great and necessary but too often innovative projects are the result of someone's thought process, or "my idea without data to substantiate." The result is that projects move through the innovation process until the business case is analyzed, not just the financials but the data as well (industry, consumer, society, etc.) to determine that it support the financials. The result is that the data usually does not support innovation because of the singular perspective.

HOW DO YOU TAKE THIS FROM THEORY TO PRACTICE?

How did Created to Create (C2C) use data to understand the shortage of global drinking water? What kind of system could they develop to solve this problem? What parameters did they have to consider when designing a system to purify water?

In 2017, C2C focused on developing a water purification system that was lightweight (less than 10 lbs.), low cost (less than $500), and had a low power usage (less the 1 amp) that was efficient enough to produce over 1,400 gallons of drinkable water per day.

C2C used data to ask a simple question: Why was this so important? Their research found the following:

1. Bottled water is the fastest growing bottled beverage in the world.
2. On a planet of seven billion people, 2.5 billion people or 33 percent do not have adequate sanitation available to them;[1] 3.4 million people per year die of water-related diseases;[2] and solar is the most widespread power source due to its availability.[3]

The data intuition indicates that a system to purify water will play a key role in solving the world's global water crisis plus serve other markets. Therefore, by using data, C2C is working to solve the need for supplying drinkable water to people who previously had no safe source to obtain it.

2. *Another trait of leaders is the ability to manage a diverse team. Innovation teams should be comprised of a diverse group of employees to reduce groupthink, explore a greater variety of thoughts, and understand how new products affect others. Leadership is essential in innovation to motivate, excite, and guide the process to achieve maximum success.*
3. *Innovators understand the need for establishing and maintaining both internal and external networks. **Internal and external networks** are groups of stakeholders that are found inside and outside the organization that provide the opportunity to succeed.* Great innovators are continuous learners. They seek to understand things they do not always have knowledge of if they feel it is relevant. It's not that innovators think out of the box; they simply do not have a box. The world, all its people, and the universe are their box used for innovation.

---

1   Thilde Rheinländer et al., "Redefining Shared Sanitation," *Bulletin of the World Health Organization* 93 (2015): 509–510.

2   Jessica Berman, "WHO: Waterborne Disease is World's Leading Killer," VOA, October 29, 2009, https://www.voanews.com/a/a-13-2005-03-17-voa34-67381152/274768.html.

3   Andrew Blakers, "Solar Is Now the Most Popular Form of New Electricity Generation Worldwide," The Conversation, August 2, 2017, http://theconversation.com/solar-is-now-the-most-popular-form-of-new-electricity-generation-worldwide-81678.

4. *A key element of innovation is the support of top management. Managers are the internal network that knows how to innovate with speed due to having the authority and trust of their employees. Innovative people realize this and work with C-suite executives by keeping them abreast of the progress and accomplishments of their work. External networks are also important as the talents, expertise, and skills needed to succeed may not be available to innovation teams internally. Therefore, a collaborative approach may be needed to succeed, and top innovators realize this and form needed networks to gain success.*

5. *Innovators are risk takers. Innovators are not afraid to take chances to accomplish the goal of improving a current good or service, or to create a new-to-the-world one. The ability to take risks or have the courage to take chances is not typical, as most people don't want to jeopardize their careers. Taking chances also opens one to criticism on the part of management and coworkers. Risk takers are often chastised when their ideas don't work, but when their ideas work, they are praised for their success. Innovators can look beyond their peer's* assessment of their work and strive to achieve the goals they set forth to accomplish. *Therefore, the ability to take chances, endure criticism, and have the courage to try new things is what motivates innovators.*

While this list is not exhaustive, it gives the reader an idea that innovators are unique and embraced by their company. When people see their world in one way, innovators see it in another. This ability is unique and requires people to train their minds to see opportunities that are present to them, but not necessarily visible. The good/great news is that innovation and creativity are the most sought-after talents today. Nothing happens without people who are energized, aligned, and working together, thus everything ultimately revolves around people and talent.

It is important to make connections in the world we live in to see how different ways of doing what is normal can be achieved. To do this, people need to take time and reflect on what is currently done and find alternatives that can be utilized to do things more efficiently or better.

Talent and Community

The hiring practices of the twentieth century are as outdated as leisure suits and bell-bottom jeans. To recruit the best talent focused on innovation, companies must change the way they hired employees in the past. A major contributor to this is the emergence of Generation X and Y replacing the baby boomers in the workforce. While these three generations coexist in the workplace, each generation is distinct from the other. For example, baby boomers (1946–1964) seek monetary rewards, stability, and a flexible retirement plan. They aren't in need of constant feedback from managers and are very goal oriented. They also seek promotions, feel valued for their expertise, like large offices and reserved parking spots, and like having prestigious job titles to reaffirm their hard work. Gen X (1965–1980) seeks a good work-life balance as they have watched the baby boomer parents work so hard to make money and climb the corporate ladder. They prefer to work without a lot of supervision and a high percentage start their own businesses. They value opportunity, flexible work schedules, being recognized for their accomplishments, telecommuting, and opportunities to grow. Gen Y (after 1980) seeks ways to give back to the community and is attracted to corporate social responsibility, thrive off environmentally friendly work spaces, value a good culture, and like flexible work schedules. They also like the latest technology, time off, immediate feedback, and prefer structure and continued learning.

Employers must realize that gen X and Y will replace baby boomers by 2020, accounting for 60–75 percent of the global workforce. As gen X and Y take over as the dominate workforce, hiring practices must be adapted to what is most important to these generational workers.[4]

Besides generational differences, other changes in the modern workforce are the flattening of the organizational chart due to inefficiencies of multiple layers of management and the ineffectiveness it causes, hampering the ability to compete in a global workplace. Today's workforce is promoted much faster based on proven leadership, performance, and demonstrated skill sets. In addition, the hiring practices of the past relied on human resources to fill spots to bring about innovation with little help from top-level managers. As our competition is more global than regional or local, companies must adapt their hiring practices to a strategic approach involving C-suite executives.

A study conducted by Strategy and PWC looked at global workforce trends and found that top managers need to change the old hiring practices to attract the most innovative employees. The study identified demographic and generational shifts in the marketplace that require a change in the way attracting and hiring top innovators takes place. Of interest was that the global workforce is made up of only 17 percent white males. The greater piece of the labor force is composed of women and people of color. More specifically, the growing number of Chinese and Indian college graduates, more women graduating from college than men, and a massive generational switch into the global market have changed traditional hiring practices.[5]

Therefore, changing demographics, generational differences, and new ways to access promotions will require the human resource practices of the past to be revamped to attract the best people to innovate and support the mission and vision of companies.

To build an innovation workforce and recruit the best employees to support the innovation needs of companies, firms must first see what capabilities they need to grow, how to nurture leaders, how to get to market faster, and how to develop the right community of continual learning. A study conducted by PWC on global talent innovation identified four fundamental building blocks of talent innovation:

---

4   John Rampton, "Different Motivations for Different Generations of Workers: Boomers, Gen X, Millennials, and Gen Z," Inc., https://www.inc.com/john-rampton/different-motivations-for-different-generations-of-workers-boomers-gen-x-millennials-gen-z.html

5   DeAnne Aguirre, Sylvia Ann Hewlett, and Laird Post, "Global Talent Innovation: Strategies for Breakthrough Performance," Strategy &, May 15, 2009, https://www.strategyand.pwc.com/report/global-talent-innovation-strategies-breakthrough.

1. *Differentiated capabilities*: Does the company have the skills, knowledge, and abilities to capture a competitive advantage?
2. *Performance acceleration*: Does the ability to attract the right talent improve the workforce?
3. *Leadership development*: Is the right leadership in place and being developed?
4. *Talent culture*: Is the right culture in place to attract a diverse workforce?[6]

Differentiated Capabilities

Differentiated capabilities are the collective skills, abilities, and expertise that allows one company a superior advantage over its competitors. Differentiated capabilities rely on a cross-functional approach that allows companies to change the way business is conducted to gain a strategic advantage by utilizing the skills and knowledge of the people that comprise the team. The key is the ability of the team to recognize the talents of the members and to fill gaps or provide training to stay competitive.

The study also indicated that top managers must segment employees who are core employees (possessing the most skills, knowledge, and abilities), support employees (those who add value through other means) and noncore employees (those who no longer possess the skills needed). By segmenting employees, companies can assess more effectively the innovation team and how they can seek an advantage based on the members they have in place or the talent they need to recruit both internally and externally.

Performance Acceleration

Performance acceleration refers to the method in which companies manage performance in terms of how to measure, compensate, and promote employees. The ability to properly motivate employees requires an understanding of what they value to drive behavior. Some employees are extrinsically motivated, so awards, cash, and promotions would serve to increase their efforts. Others are intrinsically motivated; therefore, a thank you or the feeling of bettering the company, others, or society may be enough. Most employees are a mix of both, so the top managers who are understanding of their teams' needs for motivation and increasing performance is vital to stay competitive. In other words, leaders must show they care by rewarding both the company and the employees. Employees want to know if they are important or not, so the ability to cater to their needs is important. In addition, the high cost of replacing employees makes it advantageous for firms to retain the workforce they have if they perform at an acceptable level. High hiring costs, training, and mistakes due to lack of experience, are just a few things that add to the cost of bringing in new employees, so retention is a very viable option for firms.

Many businesses foster a sense of community among their members, and those members get out what they put in. Performance acceleration is much the same way. Members of the

---

6   Ibid.

cross-functional teams realize their performance will be evaluated by top managers; therefore, their performance will have an impact on the rewards they receive.Also, the keys to increasing performance are to establish goals that are measurable and obtainable, place the core employees in key positions, have the support of top management, and reward those who accomplish the goals established.

Leadership Development

Leadership development is identifying those individuals who possess the ability to take charge, have a vision for success, and have the mental capacity to handle rapidly changing market complexities. In addition, due to a changing global workforce, leaders must learn a variety of cultural differences, perspectives, and views that differ from traditional workers in the US.

It is important for companies to develop a leadership program supported by top management to cultivate future leaders. It is important to recognize individuals who demonstrate the ability to motivate, lead, and work with a variety of individuals. The old view of promoting someone from within who has tenure with a company or hiring outside of the company due to experience fading. Too many companies hire failed CEOs to manage a company, just to watch that company falter like the previous ones they managed. Today's leaders have a grasp of the whole company; they are proven innovators, have global experience, and are good change agents. Once an individual is found who represents these variables, it wise to develop them with the help of top management. This practice should be carried out for not only one person but as an ongoing practice for proven leaders to foster future leadership and direction.

Talent Culture

Talent culture is community's reputation that attracts and retains the best talent needed to innovate. As described earlier, a community is made up of beliefs, values, and behaviors needed to empower its members and give the sense of inclusion. The PWC study reveals that four factors drive engagement:

1. The level of respect, value, and recognition felt on the part of employees
2. The perception that an employee's job betters the company
3. The level of pride in the organization and its mission and vision
4. The level of trust and ability in top managers

The ability of companies to attract innovative employees is the key to future growth and success. The hiring practices and ways of promoting employees of the twentieth century have changed drastically. As generational change from baby boomers to more gen X and genY employees occurs, ways to stimulate these generations will need to be recognized to retain and attract core employees. In addition, companies need to develop ways to foster and grow leaders. One way to do this is through empowerment. Let young leaders take on projects and initiatives and give them the right to fail. Too often there is a fear-of-failure culture, but if young leaders learn from their mistakes, it will make them stronger leaders in the future.

Leaders exhibit the ability to motivate, think quickly and decisively, work with a variety of people and cultures, and promote innovation. Identifying these people and nurturing them will help to increase the pool of leaders to drive growth and success now and in the future.[7]

Where Should We Be?

To recruit and retain the best talent possible should be consistently one of the top five strategic and operational priorities for any company. *The Economist* published a study entitled "Talent Strategies for Innovation" where they indicated that C-Suite involvement in talent management has increased dramatically. The study also indicated that 75 percent of executives indicated that talent management is very important to their organization. In addition, the question of where to locate research and innovation centers was asked. The findings include areas where there was an abundance of talent and universities with accessibility to well-trained individuals. The ability to find talent and the innovative mind-set will force companies to collaborate with organizations they never thought of in the past and to seek talent in places never thought of.[8]

While the emphasis placed on seeking talent is a top priority for managers, the execution of the strategies usually falls on lower-ranking managers. This puts the burden on middle- to lower-level managers to find and hire these core employees and introduce them to the community. Therefore, there is a greater need on the part of top management to communicate to the middle- and lower-level managers the expectations and desires of hiring innovators who will help grow the company and provide a good fit for the community.

McKinsey & Company published a study entitled "Leadership and Innovation" and noted that top managers indicated that innovation is one of the top three drivers of growth for their companies. While innovation is recognized as an accelerator of growth, is was also noted that top managers were baffled by the process to innovate, thus, creating a dilemma. Ninety-four percent of the top managers surveyed admitted that mimicking other companies with successful innovation strategies and relying on the company's community involvement were the key drivers they used for innovation. Therefore, without a defined innovation strategy, how can a successful innovation plan be instituted? McKinsey & Company recommend three building blocks to create an innovative organization:

1. Use innovation as a strategic agenda created by top management to encourage growth within the organization.
2. Recognize existing innovators or innovation opportunities already in existence. Many times, the catalysts for innovation are present but without an assessment of the skills and knowledge present within the organization, top managers have no idea what assets they have at their disposal. As discussed earlier, human resources need to have

---

7   Ibid.

8   Economist Intelligence Unit, "Talent Strategies for Innovation," *The Economist* (2009): 1–16.

this information documented to internally fill the innovation needs of the company and to then seek external candidates to fill the gaps.

3. Foster a community of trust with employees. Top managers need to create a community based on trust between themselves and the employees to promote the ability to convey their ideas, promote innovation in a manner that is nonthreatening, and grow the company following the established mission and vision.[9]

What can top managers do? Innovation must be part of the strategic plans of the organization. It must be designed to support the mission and vision of the company. Therefore, top managers must create a mind-set that fosters innovation, is open to listening to ideas from employees, and encourages this type of behavior. Innovation has historically been encouraged in times of economic prosperity and discouraged in down times. Top managers must be consistent and encourage innovative suggestions and create strategies regardless of the economic state, as innovation gives companies the ability to prosper in both good and bad times.

What needs to happen to create this innovative mind-set? Top management must be held accountable by the CEO or board of directors to keep innovative strategies and behaviors in the forefront of the planning process. McKinsey & Company offer three suggestions to advance innovation:

1. Define the innovation that drives growth and meets strategic objectives. Top managers must lead the charge to drive the innovation efforts for the rest of the company. Without continuous encouragement from top managers, innovation efforts will fall short.

2. Make innovation part of the meeting agenda. Including an agenda item highlighting innovation sends a strong message that innovation is always a part of the plans the company wishes to pursue.

3. Establish measurable and obtainable targets and goals for innovation. Top managers should reward (extrinsic or intrinsic) innovators and encourage their behavior. An example of a measurable goal for financial strategies could be launching a product within a year (goal 1) and obtaining 10 percent market share in six months (goal 2). For behavior, an example could be including 20 percent of the innovative ideas that come from within the company through cross-functional teams in one year. Whatever the strategy employed, goals that are defined and obtainable both motivate and hold teams accountable. It also encourages healthy competition, which also is a motivator for success.

---

9   Joanna Barsh, Marla M. Capozzi, and Jonathan Davidson, "Leadership and Innovation," *McKinsey Quarterly*, 2008, https://www.mckinsey.com/business-functions/strategy-and-corporate-finance/our-insights/leadership-and-innovation.

Review Questions

1. What are characteristics of innovators?
2. What are traits needed to maintain a long-term vision?
3. List the differences between baby boomers, Generation X, and Generation Y in job needs.
4. How has hiring changed from the twentieth to the twenty-first century?
5. How can companies build an innovative workforce?
6. What is performance acceleration?
7. What are differentiated capabilities?
8. List some ways companies can develop leaders.
9. List the four factors that drive engagement.
10. What are the three building blocks to create an innovative organization?

Discussion Questions

1. What additional characteristics of innovators, not listed in the text, do you feel are important? Why?
2. What are some additional traits that can help innovators maintain a long-term vision? Why is a long-term vision important?
3. What are some of the needs you will have when you graduate and obtain that first job? Which is most important to you?
4. What are additional ways companies can build an innovative workforce? Of these ways, which do you feel are most important?
5. What are other ways to accelerate performance that are not listed in the textbook? Why do you feel this will be successful?
6. What are ways you would identify differentiated capabilities in employees? Once discovered, how would you get the most out of them?
7. What are other ways to drive engagement? Why do you feel they are important?
8. Of the three building blocks of innovation, which one is most important? Why?

Extension Activity

Discuss with a classmate the different ways you would use to discover the best talent. How does this talent make a positive impact on community? How does it impact the organization?

BIBLIOGRAPHY

Rheinländer, Thilde, et al., "Redefining Shared Sanitation," *Bulletin of the World Health Organization* 93 (2015): 509–510.

Berman, Jessica. "WHO: Waterborne Disease is World's Leading Killer," VOA, October 29, 2009, https://www.voanews.com/a/a-13-2005-03-17-voa34-67381152/274768.html.

Blakers, Andrew. "Solar Is Now the Most Popular Form of New Electricity Generation Worldwide," The Conversation, August 2, 2017, http://theconversation.com/solar-is-now-the-most-popular-form-of-new-electricity-generation-worldwide-81678.

Rampton, John. "Different Motivations for Different Generations of Workers: Boomers, Gen X, Millennials, and Gen Z," Inc., https://www.inc.com/john-rampton/differentmotivations-for-different-generations-of-workers-boomers-gen-x-millennials-gen-z.html

Aguirre, DeAnne, Hewlett, Sylvia Ann, and Post, Laird. "Global Talent Innovation: Strategies for Breakthrough Performance," Strategy &, May 15, 2009, https://www.strategyand.pwc.com/report/global-talent-innovation-strategies-breakthrough.

Economist Intelligence Unit, "Talent Strategies for Innovation," The Economist (2009): 1–16.

Barsh, Joanna, Capozzi, Marla M. and Davidson, Jonathan. "Leadership and Innovation," McKinsey Quarterly, 2008, https://www.mckinsey.com/business-functions/strategy-and-corporate-finance/our-insights/leadership-and-innovation.

CHAPTER SIX

The Art of Disruption and How We Select the Best Stakeholders

INTRODUCTION

Not all disruption is bad and in fact is a normal part of the innovation process. Companies continually disrupt products in the market or totally transform those we thought were obsolete. Cell phones were once a tool for business people to communicate faster to gain an advantage. Today, the smartphone is a computer and a camera, and it fulfills its original purpose as a communication device.

When reviewing what is important for a firm to be successful, it is hard to not acknowledge that stakeholders are a key part of any organization. So how do companies pick the people and suppliers needed to be successful and gain a competitive advantage? What are the desired characteristics and skill sets of highly innovative individuals and personality traits of top performers? The answer may lie with identifying mavericks who are high-performing individuals that companies seek to guide the innovation process. They are, however, unique from most people in terms of their personalities and their vision of the world around them. Companies must also look for certain personality traits necessary to obtain top job performance. While every person is not a maverick, certain traits can help with hiring the best people with the knowledge and skill sets to give firms a superior competitive advantage and to innovate at higher levels.

To launch products, firms must also possess five necessary skills. These skills will help companies be successful and help to foster positive working relationships with key suppliers. It is important that successful product launch be documented and that managers have experience, technical skills, an understanding of legal aspects, and a knowledge of fostering relationships within a channel and to be trained and nurtured to ensure costs are minimized while distribution is maximized.

Understanding how disruption and the role of key stakeholders in innovation can positively impact companies is a necessary means to success. Without these two attributes, companies will not gain the necessary competitive advantage needed to be a market leader.

Learning Objectives

In this chapter students will learn about the following:

- The stages disruption cause in the market and how products are affected
- The top personality traits that lead to higher job performance
- A maverick personality and its characteristics
- Ways in which top managers can work with mavericks to encourage them to enrich the innovation process
- The five skill sets needed to launch a product

Learning Outcomes

By the end of this chapter students will be able to do the following:

- Describe how disruption can positively impact products and provide examples
- Understand why maverick personalities are good for firms and suggest ways top managers can get the highest level of performance from them
- Understand what personality traits managers should look for to increase performance
- Suggest what skill sets are needed to successfully launch a product and why these are important

Key Terms

Disruption of incumbents: Established companies (incumbents) ignore a new challenger's ability to disrupt their current market position until they lose market share

Rapid linear evolution: A phenomenon that occurs when the challengers develop products that are better suited to satisfy customers' needs more so than the unsuspecting incumbent

Appealing convergence: Describes how challengers introduce products the incumbent ignores until they take market share and create disruption

Complete reimagination: The reimagining of a product or category is typically the result of technological improvements that build on a past idea but that vastly add value to consumers

Maverick personality: "One who is open, not afraid to take chances, perseveres, and is a risk taker." Mavericks are those who are bold, can think "outside the box," and are not afraid of taking chances

Experience: The understanding or knowledge gained by one who has observed, interacted, or witnessed a phenomenon

Theoretical knowledge: The understanding of why something happens based on theory. It helps to understand why an event will occur in various situations and why it doesn't in others

Practical knowledge: Applying the theoretical knowledge to put the theory in practice; requires experience to put in place the things you wish to accomplish

Interpersonal skills: The ability to interact and work with others in a positive manner

Communication: The ability to convey information between one or more individuals

Noise: Anything that can interfere with the communication exchange, including speaking different languages, no Internet, poor cellular service, and so on

Persuasion: The process that causes people to act or believe in something

Motivation: Provides a reason to act in a certain manner or to accomplish a common cause

Leadership: The art of leading organizations or individuals

INNOVATION IS DISRUPTION WHEN PROPERLY EXECUTED

Any innovation, from continuous to disruptive, changes the marketplace's landscape. Innovation gives companies the ability to compete and to increase their profitability regardless of the size of the competition; in other words, it levels the playing field for smaller firms. It is important to recognize that innovation should be a continuous practice that is undertaken by companies to remain a market leader or to compete in a competitive business environment. However, the goal of any company is to develop products that disrupt the market while minimizing the negative effect on their product portfolio (i.e., cannibalizing their own products). Examples of this disruption include digital photography versus film, online classes' popularity over being in a classroom, Blackberry being overtaken by the iPhone, and smartphones replacing cameras. The benefits for the disrupter are tremendous and possibly devastating for the disrupted.

Research conducted by Steven Sinofsky asked the obvious question, "If companies are so aware of disruption, why do their products get disrupted?"[1] Sinofsky also indicates that while the goal of companies is to fend off disruption, it is usually unlikely to do so. His work outlines four phases of the innovation pattern for technological products and how disruption affects them. These four phases include the following:

1. Disruption of incumbents
2. Rapid and linear evolution
3. Appealing convergence
4. Complete reimagination

Disruption of Incumbents

In any business environment, competitors are constantly introducing new products they feel can give their company a competitive advantage and increase market share and profits. **Disruption of incumbents** allows new firms to introduce products that disrupt the way established companies (incumbents) have typically operated. Incumbents typically ignore a new challenger's ability to disrupt their current market position until they realize they are

---

1   Steven Sinofsky, "The Four Stages of Disruption," Vox, January 6, 2014, https://www.vox.com/2014/1/6/11622000/the-four-stages-of-disruption-2.

losing market share and sales. When the incumbent tries to react to this threat it is typically too late, as the challenger has gained momentum and taken customers from the incumbent, thus disrupting the market. Some of the challengers' products represent new technology or an attribute change that can create an advantage to increase their market share and profits. Other times introductions are inferior to the incumbent's products and are created to be sold through different channels at lower prices.

Based on this, how do companies decide whether the challenger's products could disrupt the incumbent's current products? The secret lies in determining the adoption rate of a challenger's product by current customers and to determine the impact it has on key market variables. The adoption rate is an indicator of how many of the incumbent's customers are buying the challenger's products. This gives the challenger an indication of how successful the innovation is and if their new product is meeting the needs and wants of the target market. The key market variables include sales, customer blog posts, recalls, and market data giving clues to their success. All too often, incumbents fail to monitor challengers' offerings and their success is found out to late. An example is the downfall of the Blackberry to the iPhone. Incumbents need to identify potential threats, gain market intelligence, monitor the challenger's product development, develop contingency plans for the challenger's product, and then adjust as needed to counter the threat to not sacrifice lost sales and profits.

Rapid Linear Evolution

As the development of a product is nearing completion, challengers are in a favorable position versus the incumbents regarding speed to market. Incumbents have little idea what is about to happen in the market once the challenger introduces its offering, thus creating rapid linear evolution. *Rapid linear evolution* is a phenomenon that occurs when the challengers develop products that are better suited to satisfy customers' needs than the unsuspecting incumbents. An analogy of this may be two cars who are about to race. One takes off from a dead stop, while the other accelerates to 100 miles per hour, and the race starts from the same starting point. The car going 100 miles per hour gains the advantage immediately. The challenger has had the benefit of seeing what the incumbent has failed to improve on (i.e., not moving) and then creates disruption by offering a product that is better suited to satisfy customers' needs, while improving the attributes or needs of the customer over the incumbent. This is the starting point of how the challenger can get its products adopted in the market faster and to replace that of the incumbent, thus disrupting the market.

Appealing Convergence

A challenger's product offering is usually the result of finding a weakness in the current product offerings and then introducing a new product that exploits this weakness to satisfy the needs of the target audience. *Appealing convergence* describes how challengers introduce products the incumbent ignores until they take market share and create disruption. Incumbents, as indicated, typically are slow to realizing the disruption that is caused by early adopters and to accept this product as a threat. Incumbents who are slow to innovate their products to counter this threat typically rely on comparative advertisements stating how good their product is over the challengers, or through promotional campaigns focused on regaining market share. An incumbent's response in this manner gives the challenger a clear message that its offering has disrupted the incumbent and efforts should continue to exploit this. Ways to exploit this could include innovating new products that build off the first one's success, entering newer markets, finding new ways to use the product, and conducting focus groups to gain consumer insights.

Complete Reimagination

Products that were once the disruptors will one day be less relevant in the market. Think of smartphones, laptop computers, booking travel, and so on. Technology changes, new challengers find ways to capture the opportunities, and process improvements give competitors the ability to seize an advantage in the market. One way to disrupt the market is to completely reimagine a product or product category. *Complete reimagination* of a product or category is typically the result of technological improvements that build on a past idea but vastly add value to consumers. Examples of this include artificial intelligence, electric cars, the Cloud, block chain, and so on. Each of these product categories were reimagined from previous ideas and perfected to disrupt the market again.

Innovation provides needed disruption on the part of companies that execute correctly. This past section provided ways to gain advantages by spelling out strategies that use disruption to a company's advantage. It also spelled out how failing to monitor the market can hurt a company due to disruption that takes place that handicaps a firm's success. Companies need to stay in contact with their customers to determine what they seek in new products and to be aware of their competitors' activities. Satisfying consumer needs and using technology are just a couple of ways to create products that disrupt the current market and to create opportunity for innovative companies in the future.

HOW DO YOU TAKE THIS FROM THEORY TO PRACTICE?

How do consumers affect product selection? How does competition slowly affect normal business? What are the potential outcomes if the competition is ignored?

Professor Ferguson was a small business owner for over 25 years before entering higher education. One of the businesses he owned was a retail liquor store located in a small rural town. The store was focused on catering to both blue-collar workers who lived in town and a more affluent customer building on land located outside of town. The store offered brands of products that catered to these two groups of customers and the store did quite well. The store was the incumbent based on the section just discussed.

Professor Ferguson started working in higher education at the same time a challenger opened its doors. Professor Ferguson gave little thought to the challenger as he felt the location was poor and he had a loyal following. The challenger offered expensive brands of products and the décor was nicer than his retail location. After two years of decreased sales, Professor Ferguson started to question what was happening. When he realized the challenger had established a loyal customer base built on his customers it was too late to react, as the challenger had eroded the Professor Ferguson's business. So, what happened? One, Professor Ferguson gave little thought to the challenger, as described in the previous section. Two, Professor Ferguson figured his loyal following would reject the challenger, but Professor Ferguson was no longer active in operating the business, so loyalty shifted. Finally, the challenger did a better job of catering to the more affluent customers moving into the area. This example details what the previous section was describing. Professor Ferguson failed to monitor the challenger until it was too late, thus causing disruption and affecting his business's performance.

PICK THE RIGHT TEAM

The ability to pick the right team hinges on several leadership variables including: experience, possessing theoretical and/or practical knowledge, interpersonal skills, being a strategic thinker, and having a key relationship with suppliers and channel members. These five skill sets will greatly help the firm's ability to be successful based on the leadership behind the innovation.

Five Demonstrated Skill Sets Needed to Get the Product Launched

Launching a product is the culmination of our innovation process. To this point, the company or innovation group has conceived a product that will satisfy a substantial target market's needs, tested its ability to perform as designed while being safe, performed marketing research to determine if it will increase market share and profits, and now it's time to introduce it to the market. While this summary may make launching a product seem easy, it's not; in fact, there are skill sets that managers must have to be able to launch a product successfully.

THINK ABOUT THIS!

What skill sets do Yanfeng look for in their innovation teams? Do all members share the same experience? Why do their diverse teams add value?

Yanfeng is an automobile interior designer and manufacturer. They are a very progressive company that takes the approach their innovation team must be provided the resources to exist while developing products that will differentiate them from their competitors. The funds provided to the innovation team represent sunk costs, and the ability to recoup them is a gamble they take to stay competitive. Therefore, their innovative interiors result in providing funds to continue their work and in the support from top management. This approach helps to motivate the cross-functional team to continue to develop new and innovative automobile interiors and give Yanfeng a competitive advantage.

The cross-functional team adds value by having its group members from all areas of the company. This approach helps to understand how products can be manufactured and what the potential potholes may be that slow the innovation process down, thus losing speed to market. Professor Ferguson's brother-in-law, Michael (Mike) Phillips, is a senior engineer who works on this team. In conversation, Mike described how he felt inadequate on the team because he was not creative. Mike developed a new interior material made from recyclable components but had to test it to ensure safety and functionality. Mike conducted all the testing both on computer-aided design (CAD) and in the lab where he tested the interior by detonating the airbags to test the material on an actual dashboard under simulated scenarios. Mike reported to the group the findings and his supervisor told him how glad he was Mike was on the team. Mike was the only one who could test the product due to his expertise. He also told Mike that his strong engineering background was the reason they selected him. This made Mike happy to know that his lack of creativity was not a mistake and supplemented by his engineering knowledge of how the interior works and if it was safe for consumers. Mike has since been awarded the highest innovation award bestowed to an employee at Yanfeng, the Iexpress (innovation express) award or "Vigor Cup" for bringing the most recognized new technology or product to production.

So, what are these managerial skill sets and why are they important? How can the company's managers train or provide the guidance necessary to successfully launch products? Following is an overview of the top five managerial skill sets needed when launching a product.

1. Experience

2. Theoretical and practical knowledge
   - Ability to collect and analyze data
   - Training others
   - Understanding of legal issues
3. Interpersonal skills
   - Communication
   - Prioritizing
   - Persuasion and motivation
   - Leading and mentorship
   - Integrity
4. Being a strategic thinker
5. Having a relationship with key suppliers and channel members

Experience

It is almost impossible to do any job effectively without some type of experience. *Experience* is defined as understanding or knowledge gained by one who has observed, interacted, or witnessed a phenomenon. Can you imagine hiring a consultant to offer suggestions on ways to improve sales when he or she has no experience in selling or selling strategies? The same goes for companies who want the best people in place to launch products. The act of launching a product requires the experience of coordinating all functional areas, knowledge of how the process works before and after the launch, how to work with suppliers and vendors, and so on. With any organization or process there is a learning curve that is present, and launching products is no exception. Therefore, it is important to have in place experienced managers who understand all facets of the launch process to ensure the optimal level of success companies strive for when launching their latest products.

Theoretical and Practical Knowledge

Closely related to experience is practical and technical knowledge. While both require experience to some extent, there are differences with each. *Theoretical knowledge* is the understanding of why something happens based on theory. It helps to understand why an event will occur in various situations and why it doesn't in others. While it is important to understand the theory, it also helps to understand how to practically apply the theory. *Practical knowledge* is applying the theoretical knowledge to put the theory in practice. Practical knowledge requires experience to put in place the things you wish to accomplish. An example may include understanding how the innovation process works (theoretical) and being able to guide the process from start to finish with an actual product (practical). The ability to launch a product requires both types of knowledge, as well as the experience to put these into practice. Therefore, finding managers who possess these traits will lead to higher levels of innovation success.

Ability to Collect and Analyze Data

The ability to satisfy customer needs requires collecting information or data and then determining if a firm can satisfy them while making a profit. Without having data or being able to effectively analyze it, companies are severally handicapped. Launch managers must know what they need in terms of data and analysis to make important decisions regarding product launch. Without data and analysis, these important decisions will be in jeopardy.

While specific data is needed for specific product categories, some of the basic needs addressed by launch managers may include the size of the target market. We have stated throughout the text that target markets must be substantial to increase profits, achieve economies of scale, and gain a favorable market share. Demographic information is important to determine where this target market lives, what the gender percentages and median income are, if the company currently operates in these areas, and what the ethnicity of the residents is. These determinants will help to gain access to the areas that can provide the greatest potential for success. Conducting focus groups is another way that managers can gain insight, speaking with the target market regarding the firm's proposed innovation. Questions focusing on the price, product functionality, ease of use, and gathering additional suggestions would be pertinent questions to ask. While these few examples are not a comprehensive list, they offer an idea of information and insight managers may want to collect to answer questions leading to successful product launch.

Once the data is collected it is important to analyze it to make sense of the findings. As with data collection, the analysis is specific to each product category, but some areas of importance include what price range customers would pay for a product, product attributes (features, colors, feasibility of use, etc.), expected units sold, and profitability. Data analysis provides consumer insights and financial details that cannot be overlooked by managers. Therefore, collecting data and properly analyzing it are integral steps that must be addressed in the launch process.

Training Others

Launch managers must provide the experience necessary to launch products. Launch managers choosing to withhold information do so to retain the power they possess regarding the launch process over other less experienced people in the firm. This is not healthy for organizations as it can severely cripple the firm's ability to be successful in the event the manager retires or leaves the company. What is more practical is to assign one or more assistant managers to work with the launch manager to make the launch phase easier, but to also provide a learning platform for the assistant managers.

Launch managers should coordinate the step-by-step process in a way that educates others and is easy to understand. They should share both the potholes they see and the troubles that arise in the process to equip others with the education necessary to one day do the job effectively. Managers should also give their subordinates an increased level of responsibility, preparing them for the launch manager's position or to lead a product launch on another project within the same organization. Finally, a good practice is to create standard operating procedures that document each step in the launch process and reduce the risk of relying too heavily on one person to take on this duty.

HOW DO YOU TAKE THIS FROM THEORY TO PRACTICE?

Professors are constantly being asked to teach classes that maybe new to them. Professor Ferguson was asked to help a new assistant professor to teach a course that she had never taught before. The new professor was overwhelmed with the new class and had little idea on how to begin to teach this new but familiar subject (e.g., launching a product). Professor Ferguson had two choices regarding this matter. First, he could offer a few suggestions and withhold information that would protect him in the future to teach the class again if the assistant professor's evaluations were substandard. This approach would erode the quality of the class and students' ability to learn what they need to be successful. The second was to actively educate the assistant professor on what she needed to concentrate on and guide her in terms of materials necessary for the class. Professor Ferguson has taught several sections of this subject and deeply cares for the well-being of the students, so he selected the second alternative. He added the assistant to the educational software used to give her an idea of how he administered the course. He provided the textbook, contact information for the textbook representative, invited her to experience a lecture, spoke at detail how he uses case studies, and offered tests for the course. When the assistant professor launched her version of the course she was prepared to teach with authority and increased the level of success for her students.

This example provides the reader with insights on how a manager can educate his or her subordinates and provide the necessary training and materials to duplicate the launch process. While this example may not seem the same as launching a product, it is still the same as launching a service, which higher education is to the clients (students) who pay for it.

Understanding of Legal Issues

A launch manager is obviously not a lawyer, but he or she must know a little about laws that can affect the launch process. Launch managers will work with the company's legal team to ensure contracts are in place between vendors and suppliers regarding how their products will be distributed and by whom. Companies launching products want to be sure they are legally covered when selling their products. Any misrepresentation on the part of the parties involved in the launch can be held accountable in a court of law. The competitive landscape has changed in the global economy; therefore, the days of operating by the shaking of hands between the parties is long gone. Today, legal agreements help to bridge a lack of trust among parties doing business with each other. Legal agreements also spell out what is expected between the parties and give tangible goals each party is expected to abide by to maintain the relationship. Therefore, launch managers should have a good working knowledge on agreements that should be put in place and for working with the legal team to administer them before launch.

Interpersonal Skills

Interpersonal skills are the ability to interact and work with others in a positive manner. A positive working environment is a key ingredient to innovation. A manager who has excellent interpersonal skills can communicate and motivate others in a way that creates an environment full of cooperation. Cooperation helps to get a product to market faster because everyone works with each other in unison and strives to satisfy the goals of the company. Therefore, managers with superior interpersonal skills help to foster a team that works together to achieve a common goal. Next, we will look at some attributes that contribute to effective interpersonal skills.

Communication

Communication is the ability to convey information between one or more individuals. Communication takes many forms including: verbal, nonverbal, written, and electronic. The basic process of communication takes place when information is exchanged by a sender, who encodes a message, then sends it via one of the ways mentioned to a receiver. The receiver decodes the message and either understands the message or encodes a response, seeking clarification by the sender, thus encoding a message. This basic process of exchanging messages takes place until the conversation is complete. One facet of communication that can interfere with the exchange of information is noise. **Noise** is anything that can interfere with the communication exchange including speaking different languages, lack of the Internet, poor cellular service, and so on. Therefore, it is important to clearly communicate information in the innovation process to ensure everyone understands what is expected and to solve problems that come up during the process.

Nonverbal communication is also important in conveying information between parties. Although less effective in conveying information than verbal communication, forms of nonverbal communication can include such things as body language and facial expressions. Simple body language such as crossing one's arms while in a conversation can indicate a level of discomfort, while arms unfolded expresses a sense of agreeableness. Facial expressions such as frowning or rolling one's eyes can indicate unhappiness, while smiling can mean acceptance. Other forms of nonverbal communication include a person's lack of response to an email, protesting a company, defying company policies through symbolism (e.g., wearing jeans when prohibited), and taking longer breaks than allowed.

Written communication is a form of communication that is becoming less favorable due to electronic forms (e.g., email and text) that are more favored. Written communication is generally reserved for formal communications, such as offering one a job, reprimanding or promoting an employee, or some other official means of communication. There are more electronic means being used to replace written communication due to the speed they offer companies and the increased level of security afforded them. Therefore, future communications will focus less on written forms and more on electronic versions.

Electronic communication can take the form of email, text and instant message, cellular call, social media, and so on. The world of electronic communication is growing so fast that it is hard to predict what forms will be the most prevalent form in the next two to five years. The various generations also affect electronic communication. Baby boomers cling to more traditional communication types as their level of technology adoption is lower than gen. X, Y, and Z. Text messaging, Snapchat, Facebook messaging, and so on are all considered accepted means of communication today. Younger generations will refer to text messaging as "talking" to someone, which is not viewed the same by older generations.

The corporate world's preferred means of communication is through email, the Internet, and telephone. Information exchange has greatly sped up due to these instant ways of communicating, plus it greatly enhances the ability to send visual information (e.g., files, pictures, quotes, etc.). Smartphones have the ability to link work electronic communication to personal devices, which makes escaping work impossible. This has perpetuated an instantaneous expectation that working hours are 24/7 and vacations are no longer a way to get away from work and relax. While these downfalls exist, electronic communications have given a global economy the ability to effectively communicate with each other and increase the speed of innovation.

One important item to note about communication and all the forms discussed are that they vary by culture. Tone of voice, colors, body language and facial expressions, translation of words, and so on vary, so it is important that firms understand what is acceptable and not acceptable in the markets in which they conduct business. Many companies have fallen victim to not understanding the cultural differences that exist, so it is important to understand these to be successful.

Prioritizing

The innovation process is one filled with many steps, hurdles, regulations, and processes that must be followed to be successful. The ability of managers to prioritize these items is essential to ensure the innovation is continually moving forward and that anticipated potholes are addressed before they slow the process down.

One common pitfall of managers is to try to do too much at once, which creates a lack of focus. Imagine a storm causing damage to a house where the roof was torn off, the windows were broken, and the siding was ruined. What would you do to fix this? Would you fix the siding before the roof? The priority would be to get the roof fixed to make the house waterproof, then the windows, followed by the siding. Priorities are given to what is most important followed by the least important. Innovation follows the same steps. Would the inability to locate key raw materials needed to produce a product get less attention than deciding on the colors to use on the packaging? Managers must prioritize what is most important to less important. When priorities are set, the speed of innovation increases and products get to market faster.

Persuasion and Motivation

Managers must be able to persuade others within the organization to first pursue the innovation and then continue to see it through fruition. *Persuasion* is the process to cause people to act or believe in something. Opinions among functional and innovation team members may vary regarding the innovation being pursued. A manager with good interpersonal skills can persuade others that the innovation is worthwhile and adds value to the organization. This ability, however, can also pose a threat to the organization. Managers who are very persuasive can sometimes convince others that a new product is beneficial to the organization when in fact it isn't. Therefore, top managers must listen to the suggestions of managers leading innovation teams and then evaluate the real benefit the new product brings to the company in terms of supporting the mission and vision, increasing profits and market share, and adding value to the product portfolio.

Motivation is another trait that is necessary to get results. *Motivation* provides a reason to act in a certain manner or to accomplish a common cause. Once team members are persuaded to act, a good manager gives them the motivation to do so. Managers provide the reason and motivation to act in a way that will successfully see the innovation through from ideation to launch. Some of the ways to motivate others are to demonstrate that the innovation aligns with the aims, purpose, and values of the individual or organization. A key to be a good motivator is to know your subordinates and what inspires them. Motivation can also be triggered by one's intrinsic and extrinsic needs, or a combination of both. This has been discussed previously, but knowing what motivates subordinates is a way for managers to encourage actions that support the cause. Therefore, alignment of goals and understanding the triggers of motivation can help managers get their subordinates to act in a manner that supports a firm's innovation efforts.

Leadership

Leadership quality affects the performance of any organization. *Leadership* is the art of leading organizations or individuals. The word "art" was included in the definition because anyone can lead, but the effective leaders have made it an art form. There are many examples of effective and ineffective leaders, but certain traits are present that help shape a good leader. We have focused on five that we feel separate good leaders from poor leaders.

The first is confidence. Confident leaders are those who have a successful record of accomplishment and can motivate others to follow them because they are proven to be successful. Confident leaders can anticipate adversity and devise a plan to persevere and be successful. Experience, decisiveness, and an innate ability to persuade others to follow shapes confidence. Therefore, good leaders must be able to have the confidence that once a plan is put in place, they do the right things to accomplish their goals.

The second trait of a good leader is focus. Many times, leaders lose sight of the long-term plans and concentrate on the short-term obstacles that present problems. A good leader can stay the course of action developed in their strategic planning, while simultaneously dealing with situations that affect tactical planning. This is like adhering to the mission and vision of the organization discussed earlier. It is imperative that leaders maintain their long-term focus and not lose sight of the reason they pursued a course of action.

The third trait is integrity. Leadership integrity has come under scrutiny recently due to increased availability of information. It is hard to find political leaders who have not come under fire from the media and individuals because of their unethical or immoral behavior. While there are examples of leaders who lack integrity, there are many who display a high level of it. Leaders with high levels of integrity run organizations and treat their people with respect, display high ethical standards, and deliver on the promises they make. Leaders who display integrity in how they treat people and run companies are sought out by potential employees and shareholders and are respected by stakeholders. Therefore, integrity on the part of leaders is a valuable trait.

The fourth trait of a good leader is humility. Good leaders are humble and easy to approach. Humility allows subordinates to feel they can make suggestions to improve the firm, thus increasing their loyalty to the company and the leadership. An example of this when leaders leave a company and others follow them. Humility is free of arrogance. It is common to find that employees lack support for arrogant leaders. The major benefit of humility is the perception that the leader is just another one of employees trying to make the organization the best, which motivates others to strive for the same result.

The fifth trait of a good leader is the ability to be inspirational. Inspirational leaders get the very best from others. They create sayings that make others feel the message is directed at them personally, while being directed to everyone. Their actions motivate their subordinates to act because they are inspired. Inspiration requires longevity, trust, and integrity. It is a rare gift to inspire others, but the best leaders have this ability and can motivate others to be their best.

While there are several other traits of good leaders not discussed, these are a few that provide what it takes to successfully lead others and organizations. Good leaders are difficult to find, but the best ones are in high demand to run organizations. They accomplish what they set out to do and get the most out of their subordinates, which adds value to all stakeholders.

Being a Strategic Thinker

Being a strategic thinker is difficult for most of us and for managers. Their roles over time shift from performing all jobs in the company to overseeing and guiding the organization for extended periods of time. Strategic plans are those that last greater than one year, while tactical plans are short term and support the strategic plan. Indeed, being able to plan strategies that will be utilized for many years to come are difficult. It is very difficult to be strategic when the business climate changes so rapidly. This rapid change places a greater importance on seeing the future and deciding how the company can gain an advantage. Therefore, managers must be strategic to guide the organization for extended periods of time while devising short-term plans needed to address issues that arise and support the strategic plans.

Skill Sets Needed by Strategic Thinkers

What skills define good strategic thinkers and allow them to successfully guide their organization? The following are skills that will provide what is necessary to be a strategic thinker and to successfully guide the organization through dangerous waters.

The first skill is environmental scanning. Managers learn to scan the external business environment to determine where the threats will come from and what opportunities exist. Factors that comprise the external environment are possible to influence but impossible to change. These factors include socioeconomic, political-legal, technological, and competitive factors. Ways in which managers can scan the external environment include market intelligence from networks and sales people. Trends are another method to determine changes in the market presenting both opportunity and threats to the organization. A competitor developing a product that is an improvement to one a company currently sells presents the threat, while one that satisfies the needs associated with the trend is an opportunity. For example, autonomous vehicles pose a threat to current automobile manufacturers who fail to introduce it first. Pharmaceutical companies developing drugs to counter the rising trend of juvenile diabetes is an opportunity.

The second skill is evaluation of current practices. Good managers constantly strive to improve current practices to make the organization more efficient. Evaluating current practices also leads to discovering problems a company has but fails to correct. By discovering the cause of the issue, managers can critically devise ways to correct the problem and to improve the process to streamline effectively. One additional way to evaluate current practices is to audit the way decisions are made to determine if they are done without prejudice and if they are made in the best interest of the organization.

The third skill managers must possess is the ability to obtain different perspectives. Managers who fail to seek and understand the value derived from a variety of viewpoints pose a serious threat to the firm and stakeholders. The C-suite executives bring to the organization several years of experience (both good and bad) on what they have learned works in business. Seeking input from these talented executives will only benefit the organization and help it to thrive in the future. Therefore, open discussion should take place to determine the best courses of action to guide the organization.

The fourth skill of the strategic thinker is being decisive. When managers have analyzed all the data, formed a consensus between the executives, and determined what needs to be done, they should be decisive and make decisions that follow the determined course of action. All too often managers second guess their decisions or data presented. This leads to slowing down the organization and its ability to compete (i.e., paralysis by analysis). An example was when Toyota introduced the Prius. The data showed the anticipated sales, but Toyota didn't believe the numbers. They hesitated and produced less vehicles than forecasted.[2] The actual sales were closer to what the data suggested, thus causing Toyota to try to catch up and not

---

2   Del I. Hawkins, David L. Mothersbaugh, and Roger J. Best, *Consumer Behavior: Building Marketing Strategy* (New York: McGraw-Hill, 2013).

deliver the number of vehicles to meet demand. Therefore, managers must analyze the data to make decisive decisions that will give the company every advantage.

The fifth skill needed by strategic thinkers is to be able to be conductors. Strategic leaders must be able to bring all parties together and guide them on the same course of action. Once the organization adopts a strategy, a good manager gains alignment regarding how to achieve the goal. The ability to gain alignment means top managers must seek out others within the organization who oppose the strategy and discuss their reservation. They must let the opposition voice their concerns and then share why the innovation is in the organization's best interest. While this process is uncomfortable, it is necessary so that all members of the organization are striving for the same goal and to prevent the opposition from slowing the innovation process.

The final skill strategic leaders must possess is the ability to benchmark best practices. Benchmarking has been discussed previously, but it is an important skill needed to speed the innovation process by using past processes to drive future ones. Processes are usually transferable, so benchmarking what works best to implement strategy should be documented and repeated in the future. Benchmarking also helps to improve processes for the future that give firms strategic competitive advantage by increasing the speed of the innovation through the development channels, making the organization more efficient. Benchmarking also allows companies to change what was not efficient and improve the process of developing strategy. Benchmarking is a continuous process that should be utilized to help optimize the strategic process. Just as the business environment changes, so should the process of developing strategy and getting "buy-in" on the part of subordinates within the company. Therefore, benchmarking is a means to create an efficient system of developing and implementing strategies within companies.

The list of skills presented are a representation of what is necessary to be a strategic thinker.[3] What is important to remember is that strategy guides the organization in both the short and long term. It is important for leaders to devise a strategy to guide the organization and then adhere to the plans to ensure the company is successful and the process of innovation is not slowed down.

ESTABLISHING A RELATIONSHIP WITH KEY SUPPLIERS AND CHANNEL MEMBERS

There is a growing trend toward building relationships between suppliers and channel members. The Supply Chain Resource Consortium reported that suppliers and channel members can improve their relationship by building trust through sharing information. An example used to demonstrate this was the relationship between Dell and Microsoft, where information

---

3   Paul Schoemaker, "6 Habits of True Strategic Thinkers," Inc., https://www.inc.com/paul-schoemaker/6-habits-of-strategic-thinkers.html.

was shared to help each stay compatible with their products. Suppliers and channel members can be more effective and efficient by working together. The Consortium reported that relationships have a direct correlation with performance, meaning stronger relationships have a positive impact on performance, while poor relationships have a negative impact. Working together allows all parties to see what value the relationship brings and how each party brings mutual benefits and fosters ways to improve performance. In addition, there are a few ways to build relationships including increased use of technology, proper ways to manage inventory, and being more efficient with transportation systems. Finally, when each party is fair and honest with each other it fosters a sense of collaboration that helps to build positive relationships. Each party feels supported and works together to improve the relationship, thus increasing performance.[4]

In addition to the suggestions by the Supply Chain Resource Consortium, relationships can also be enhanced when each party receives benefits that are mutually acceptable. More specifically, suppliers and channel members must ask "Is this a good deal for me and can my partner deal what they say they can?" Relationships that provide mutual benefits and that can satisfy promises help both parties to accomplish their goals of increasing their sales and profits and of gaining market share. Therefore, forming solid relationships between parties provides many advantages and helps to satisfy the goals each has.

A final suggestion for establishing relationships between key suppliers and channel members is to avoid conflict and communicate together to resolve issues. Members can do things like pay their bills when due. Consumer-to-consumer markets are used to paying bills by a specified due date or else pay a late fee. Business-to-business markets typically do not pay in a timely manner. One way to build the relationship is to pay bills on time. This good faith strengthens conducting business together, as most companies will want to do business with ones that pay their bills. A second way to reduce conflict and resolve issues is to be ethical regarding returned merchandise. Claiming a credit for merchandise that is not outdated or damaged is unethical. Suppliers and channel members must communicate what the policies are regarding getting credit for these types of products. They must also figure out what is the easiest for both parties, so suppliers can give credit to channel members and not tie up available funds. A third way to reduce conflict and resolve issues is for suppliers to provide what the channel members specify for the products they will manufacture or sell. Companies have conducted research to determine what they will sell to their target markets, so suppliers must deliver those exact goods. If a suppler cannot do so, the channel members will lose sales, which will have a negative effect on the relationship. It is important to communicate what is specified for products to be sold and work toward delivering those. More specifically, quality, performance, attributes, and so on should be discussed and product samples should be provided to ensure the specifications are what the channel members deem acceptable for their customers. Finally, suppliers must be punctual on their delivery dates and times. Channel members

---

4 "Managing Relationships in the Supply Chain," Supply Chain Resource Cooperative, February 1, 2002, https://scm.ncsu.edu/scm-articles/article/managing-relationships-in-the-supply-chain.

that cannot get product will suffer stock-outs and lose sales. Suppliers must be sure to have enough inventory on hand to satisfy orders. In addition, suppliers must treat all channel members fairly. Favoring the largest accounts and ignoring the smallest ones will create tension. Therefore, ensuring the proper inventory is on hand, delivering when needed and on time, and providing high levels of service will reduce conflict and help good working relationships.

Review Questions

1. Describe the four phases of the innovation pattern for technological products and provide examples of each phase.
2. What are five managerial skills needed to launch a product?
3. Name the interpersonal skills that positively impact innovation.
4. What skills are needed to be a strategic thinker?
5. What are ways relationships can be strengthened between key suppliers and channel members?

Discussion Questions

1. Of the four phases of innovation patterns for technological products, indicate a product or product class that exemplifies its journey through the phases. Share with the class.
2. Do you feel mavericks are good, bad, or both for companies? Why?
3. Which three of the six ways top managers can support mavericks are most important to companies? Justify your response.
4. Which of the personality traits related to top job performance do you feel is most important? Do you think these traits vary by industry? Why?
5. What are the five skill sets needed to launch a product? What other skill sets do you feel would benefit a company and why?
6. List some additional interpersonal skills needed by employees. Explain why you feel these are important.
7. What are other skills not listed in text are important for strategic thinkers? How does you answer improve strategic thinking?
8. What are additional ways you feel are important to improve the relationship between key suppliers and channel members? Share some examples of each.

Extension Activity

Be prepared to discuss during class the following: XYZ, LLC is a manufacturer of kitchen appliances. They are thinking of adding a new line of toaster that can do three functions: toast bread without burning it by using a sensor, toast sandwiches like a local sandwich shop that uses an oven, and self-clean. What data would you want to collect as a launch manager and why? What type of questions would you want answered through analysis?

BIBLIOGRAPHY

Sinofsky, Steven. "The Four Stages of Disruption," Vox, January 6, 2014, https://www.vox.com/2014/1/6/11622000/the-four-stages-of-disruption-2.

Hawkins, Del I., Mothersbaugh, David L., and Best, Roger J. *Consumer Behavior: Building Marketing Strategy* (New York: McGraw-Hill, 2013).

Schoemaker, Paul. "6 Habits of True Strategic Thinkers," Inc., https://www.inc.com/paul-schoemaker/6-habits-of-strategic-thinkers.html.

"Managing Relationships in the Supply Chain," Supply Chain Resource Cooperative, February 1, 2002, https://scm.ncsu.edu/scm-articles/article/managing-relationships-in-the-supply-chain.

CHAPTER SEVEN

Why are the Consumer and the Market so Important?

INTRODUCTION

The consumer should be the focus of every business. Great business leaders never lose their customer focus, and innovators must strive to develop products that excite customers and create new markets. This chapter provides you with ways to identify new and tangible markets and to promote market expansion, identify the best entry-mode strategy, and determine if less obvious markets are available that provide opportunity. This chapter will also provide an overview of identifying a market's potential and ways to capitalize on both domestic and global opportunities.

Learning Objectives

In this chapter students will learn about the following:
- SWOT analysis and environmental scanning
- Factors that influence markets
- Various competitors
- Market expansion by geographical areas
- Best entry-mode strategy based on risk
- What additional market opportunities exist
- Ways to identify alternative markets

Learning Outcomes

By the end of this chapter students will be able to do the following:
- Perform a SWOT analysis and environmental scan
- Describe external environmental factors and how they can affect a firm
- List various methods of market expansion
- Discuss various entry-mode strategies and the level of risk associated with each

- Detail emerging markets and how population and demographic shifts present opportunities
- Discuss how social media, surveys, focus groups, and trends can be used to find new markets

Key Terms

Consumer: A person who purchases goods or services for personal use

SWOT analysis: A method of determining the strengths, weaknesses, opportunities, and threats of an entity

Environmental scanning: A process where external factors are analyzed to determine how they will affect the company's ability to compete

Population density: The number of inhabitants who live in a geographical location

Demographics: Factors that characterize the commonalities of a group of people based on such things as age, gender, education, occupation, income, marital status, and family size

Economic factors: Items that influence the profitability of a business including wages of employees, taxes, interest and exchange rates, unemployment rates, tariffs and governmental fees, recession/ boom, and management costs

Political-legal considerations: The effects politics and laws have on the operation of a company

Infrastructure: The components needed to support, maintain, and grow a society such as fresh water, sewer, roads, bridges, telecommunications, and electricity

Competition: A rivalry between two or more parties with the goal of seeking a superior advantage

Direct competition: Rivals competing in identical product categories

Indirect competition: Companies in similar product categories that compete against each other

Local markets: Those located approximately 10 miles or 10 minutes based on population density in proximity to the company offering goods and services

Regional market: An area that includes the same state as the local market or larger geographical area (e.g., Midwest, Southeast, South, West, Pacific-Northwest, etc.)

National market: One that sells products to an entire country

International markets: Those that include conducting business in more than one country, but not the entire world

Global markets: Those in which companies do business in at least three or more continents and have foreign direct investment in those continents

Entry mode: The method a company utilizes to gain access into a new market both domestically and globally, based on the level of risk it is willing to take

Emerging markets: Those that offer future potential and provide a good match for a firm's products

Population shifts: The movement of groups from one geographical area to another

Demographic shifts: The change in demographics through a period

Social media: An online community composed of various sites used by its members to share content, communicate, interact, and collaborate

Surveys: A collection of questions presented to customers directly or indirectly, seeking their opinions regarding questions by an interested party

Focus group: A collection of people who are asked questions by a facilitator to gain richer responses

WHAT ARE TANGIBLE MARKETS THAT WE CAN REACH?

Developing new products is at the heart of innovation, but if the market for our goods or services is not substantial for making a profit or capitalizing on economies of scale, our efforts are wasted. Companies have limited resources at their disposal so new products must not only add to the profitability of the company but should not take away material and process resources from other lucrative products the company produces. Therefore, innovators must ask the question, "What markets can we reach to maximize profits and effectively use the resources at hand while creating a better world?" Briefly, let's talk about a better world. "According to a 2014 Nielsen survey, more than half of online consumers around the world surveyed (55%) said they would pay more for products and services from companies that are socially and environmentally responsible."[1] In summary, reaching substantial markets, bettering society, and creating opportunities in markets is a perfect plan to place innovative products.

Another way to identify substantial and profitable markets teeming with opportunity is by performing a SWOT analysis. A *SWOT analysis* is a method of determining the strengths, weaknesses, opportunities, and threats of an entity. It can be used by companies, organizations, individuals, and so on to determine how strengths and opportunities can overcome weaknesses and threats. A SWOT analysis is usually the first thing marketing strategists do before they develop strategic and tactical plans for their companies.

A second analysis that should be performed is environmental scanning. *Environmental scanning* is a process where external factors are analyzed to determine how they will affect a company's ability to grow its business. These include scanning the following factors: economic, political, social, legal, competitive, and technical. While a SWOT analysis and environmental scanning are very similar in nature, there are differences between the two methods. The most noticeable is a SWOT analysis focuses primarily on the internal attributes of the company, while environmental scanning focuses on factors that are external to the company. One other consideration differentiating the two is a SWOT analysis allows companies to change or address these internal attributes to capitalize on strengths and opportunities, change the things that make the company weak, and devise strategies to address threats. Environmental scanning is external to the company; therefore, a company must learn to operate within these factors, but cannot change the environment in which it conducts business. One without the other will lead to bad decisions.

What Market Considerations Can Make Us Successful?

There are many factors that affect the markets companies wish to target. Considerations include population density, demographics (social), economic factors, political-legal environment, technical capabilities, infrastructure, competition, and the company's ability to

---

1   Anne-Taylor Adams, "Global consumers are willing to put their money where their heart is when it comes to goods and services from companies committed to social responsibility" Nielsen, June 17, 2014, https://www.nielsen.com/us/en/press-room/2014/global-consumers-are-willing-to-put-their-money-where-their-heart-is.html.

expand beyond local markets to regional, and if possible, national and global.[2] Key drivers of expansion are increased profits, achieving economies of scale, effective use of resources, and greater brand equity. Therefore, companies that can select the right markets will benefit both the company and their employees by sustaining growth, maximizing profits, and creating stable employment.

Population Density

Not every market has the same number of customers. *Population density* is the number of inhabitants who live in a geographical location. It is usually expressed in square miles and can be broken down by metropolitan areas (e.g., New York City) with high density, suburban areas (e.g., cities outside of a metropolis) with medium density, and rural locations (e.g., small towns that focus on farming as the main source of industry) with low density. Companies wishing to maximize their sales and profits typically focus on high- to medium-density areas. The population of these areas offers a substantial target market with typically elevated incomes, thus making sales and profits goals for the company realistic. While higher density is attractive for companies wishing to sell their latest innovative products, a few drawbacks also exist. The attractiveness of these areas also brings in large numbers of competitors. These competitors are usually well-established brands with considerable resources at their disposal. This could be a disadvantage to firms with fewer resources who will be forced to compete with these big names. Companies must analyze their strengths and weaknesses when thinking of entering these types of markets. Another drawback is the number of stores and traffic. Businesses operating in high-density areas need to add extra employees and fleet vehicles and be located nearby to effectively service their customers. This adds to the expense of the company, so a breakeven point must be determined to maximize profits and optimize service levels. Therefore, while high population density may seem attractive, companies need to assess their abilities to service this concentrated market effectively and determine what the impact on their profitability.

Low-density areas also provide advantages and disadvantage for companies. In contrast to high- to medium-density areas, low-density areas have lower levels of competition, making it easier to maximize profits by selling their goods and services at full price. Low-density areas are typically comprised on "mom and pop" or family-owned businesses, making them easier to place products quickly since the decision maker may be the person running the business. Some disadvantages include greater distances to service these businesses, adding to the firm's expense, plus sales volume will be lower than in higher-density areas, reducing the profit margins.

---

2   Rebecca O. Bagley, "The 10 Traits of Great Innovators," *Forbes*, January 15, 2014, https://www.forbes.com/sites/rebeccabagley/2014/01/15/the-10-traits-of-great-innovators/#2eaccc0e4bf4; Tomas Chamorro-Premuzic, "The Five Characteristics of Successful Innovators," *Harvard Business Review*, October 25, 2013, https://hbr.org/2013/10/the-five-characteristics-of-successful-innovators; "20 Qualities of an Innovator," The Heart of Innovation, August 13, 2010, http://www.ideachampions.com/weblogs/archives/2010/08/are_you_an_inno.shtml.

Many national brands have done a nice job of servicing all areas. Walmart offers their superstores in high-density areas, Walmart in suburban locations, and Walmart Express in rural locations. This format gives them ability to service all areas by altering the store size and number of items offered for sale. In addition, the internet accounts for 96 percent of all American's shopping behavior. The following will give the reader an idea of the population density of the US and where the opportunities may lie depending on the type of market sought.

Demographics

The types of products being offered to a company's target market are affected by the demographical make-up of the markets being served. *Demographics* are factors that characterize the commonalities of a group of people based on such things as age, gender, education, occupation, income, marital status, and family size. If you reflect on areas where you live it is common to find doctors, upper-level managers, and lawyers living in close proximity to each other, while blue-collar workers and laborers also live in a similar area. Products offered to these groups vary as well based on location. Luxury items are typically found near the towns with higher levels of disposable income, while lower-priced goods are offered in areas with lower income levels.

When innovators develop products, they must keep in mind who these products will be sold to and determine if they have the proper distribution channels available to place their products, what type of relationships are established to gain access to these locations, and if they can effectively service the customer base who is targeted to purchase the new products. While attribute-based innovation is easier to service than new-to-the world products, it is

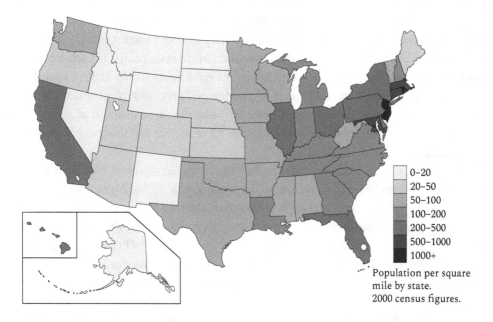

	0–20
	20–50
	50–100
	100–200
	200–500
	500–1000
	1000+

Population per square mile by state. 2000 census figures.

FIG 7.1 Population density in the US

important to prevent service failures by determining if current service levels can be maintained with new innovations, while offering established brands. The inability to service new products will increase customer churn (loss of business) and reduce profits. This is especially true today as the internet enables consumers to vent their disapproval to an infinite number of people via social media and company websites.

Economic Factors

Economic factors should not be confused with consumer income. *Economic factors* are items that influence the profitability of a business including wages of employees, taxes, interest and exchange rates, unemployment rates, tariffs and governmental fees, recession/boom, and management costs. It is important for businesses to evaluate the economic factors of the areas they wish to sell their products and manufacture them to maximize profits and minimize the cost of doing business.

While it is common to think that economic factors are similar throughout the US or the world, they vary greatly. The cost of living is higher in California and states along the Eastern part of the US, thus wages and manufacturing costs are also increased. Many manufacturing companies in the US have shifted their operations to the South, where the cost of living and doing business is less expensive and there is less unionization. On a global scale, many firms have shifted manufacturing to countries with lower labor rates to cut costs and increase profits. To show a comparison, Australia's average hourly wage is $21.50 compared to Vietnam and Southeast Asia at $0.39/hour. This simple example explains the rise in manufacturing of products in Vietnam, due to cheap labor costs.[3]

Lower labor costs as an economic factor that affects business is just one example. Consider exchange rates and how their fluctuation can give a company an advantage or disadvantage. Companies that operate in countries whose currency is worth more than US currency will provide additional profits due to the exchange rate. More specifically, if I sell a product for 1 euro in France and the exchange rate equates to a euro being worth $1.12, I have a 12 percent gain on the exchange. In addition, if companies sell products in countries with a lower exchange rate, they must increase their price to make the same amount of money. Therefore, it is important to understand how exchange rates impact the selection of markets and pricing strategies.

Another economic factor to consider is the state of the economy. A recession will have a negative effect on purchases of new innovative products due to the higher savings rates and lower spending by consumers. Recession is also characterized by higher interest rates, which affects the ability of businesses to borrow money to expand, innovate, and fund growth. While there are many negatives in a recession, there are glimpses of hope for companies. Due to layoffs and job eliminations during a recession, companies can find new and successful innovators to add to their staff, thus creating an opportunity! Finally, new innovations during

---

3   Robert Malone, "In Pictures: Where Is the World's Cheapest Labor?" *Forbes*, May 29, 2008, https://www.forbes.com/2008/05/25/change-security-internet-oped-cx_rm_outsourcing08_0529data_slide.html#34e69f631fa2.

a recession can be a means of seizing an opportunity while competitors are doing less, thus giving a potential strategic advantage.

Economic boom offers opportunities, as spending and available credit increase, making it an ideal time to innovate and introduce new products. Another benefit of boom is credit is cheaper, as interest rates tend to decline, thus giving the opportunity for expansion. While the benefits of economic boom outweigh those of a recession, labor is difficult to find, as most innovative people are employed. Also, the level of competition tends to increase, making it more difficult to attract new customers and maintain existing ones. Therefore, no matter what the state of the economy, both opportunity and obstacles are present. It is essential that companies maintain a long-term vision of what they are trying to accomplish through their innovation.

Political-Legal Considerations

The political-legal environment of any country has an enormous impact on innovation and company success. **Political-legal considerations** are the effects politics and laws have on the operation of a company. In the US, a change in political parties can change the laws, benefits, regulations, the way business is conducted, and so much more. When Donald Trump was elected president, he vowed to dissolve the Affordable Care Act, withdrew from the Paris Climate Agreement, and threatened to end relationships with Cuba. Both presidents George W. Bush and Barack Obama established these initiatives over the past 12 years, and within six months of being elected, President Trump was seeking to change them. While not identifying any political party affiliation, the dissolving of these initiatives can bring both opportunity and threat to companies and society. Insurance companies once excluded from the Affordable Care Act can gain a new opportunity to compete or lose it. Leaving the Paris Climate Agreement opens the door to mining coal once more at the sake of increasing CO_2 emissions, while benefitting coal manufactures. It also hurts the development of sustainable products, since the incentive to produce products that have less effect on the Earth's ecosystem is reduced or made unimportant.

These examples are just a few of the ways that innovators must anticipate the way politics can influence business in both a positive and negative manner. While these examples are from the US, political change affects companies on a global scale. Therefore, when considering establishing manufacturing facilities in other countries or opening new markets, the political system must be analyzed, and any changes should be evaluated to see what impact they could pose on the company seeking expansion.

Just as changing political climates can affect businesses, legal restrictions have similar ramifications. Laws vary by city, state, region, and country. In China, foreign companies cannot open a new business without collaborating with a Chinese-sponsored business. While this may seem a hindrance, many companies have done this with success. GM and SAIC collaborated to produce Buick, Chevrolet, and Cadillac in China. Businesses in India also must form a partnership to do business with a 51/49 ownership ratio (favoring the Indian firm) or a wholly owned subsidy if allowed by the Indian government. In contrast, companies originated outside the US are free to do business and build factories without the need for domestic sponsorship. Therefore, before companies decide to establish subsidiaries outside the US, they must be aware of the laws that could restrict their efforts.

Another way laws affect businesses is through zoning requirements. Certain local laws restrict the type of business and facility that can be used to conduct commerce. Some communities will not allow certain types of businesses to be established by schools and churches (liquor-related and adult novelty stores), there are restrictions where factories can be built in relation to housing developments, and hazardous types of businesses must be located anyway from residential areas (refineries, chemical plants, etc.). Therefore, companies must understand the local laws that affect the type of business they wish to locate in certain municipalities.

Technical Capabilities
Technical capabilities of both businesses and consumers have an impact on innovation. A good example of this is Silicon Valley and manufacturing in the Midwest. Lower levels of technological resources restrict the type of innovation that can be developed on the part of consumers and manufacturers. Innovation characterized by low levels of technology are typically attribute change or continuous innovation. High levels of technology allow for new-to-the-world products or disruptive innovation, if the level of technology a company possesses and incorporates into product matches what is available to consumers. For example, when Apple introduced the iPhone, it had to match the phone's capabilities with a network that could support the capabilities of the phone (e.g., provide the internet). Therefore, technology gives companies a strategic advantage based on the level of development and its use in the products consumers purchase.

Infrastructure
The availability of fresh water, ample and constant electricity, the internet, and stable roads, to name a few are keys to an infrastructure that is needed to support innovative companies. **Infrastructure** is the components needed to support, maintain, and grow a society such as fresh water, sewer, roads, bridges, telecommunications, and electricity. A strong infrastructure is what defines a developed country from an undeveloped country. With these attributes in place, businesses can effectively produce, manufacture, and ship final goods and service their customers.

The United States takes for granted the privilege of having fresh drinking water available. In fact, 90 percent of the US has safe drinking water[4] compared to the rest of the world where 663 million people have no access to drinkable water and 2.4 billion live in areas with no sanitation.[5] These impoverished areas suffer from higher disease rates and death when compared to areas with safe drinking water and sanitation. The unfortunate irony is companies locate

---

4   Joel Beauvais, "Moving Forward for America's Drinking Water," *EPA Blog*, April 26, 2016, https://blog.epa.gov/2016/04/26/moving-forward-for-americas-drinking-water/.

5   "The Water Crisis," https://water.org/our-impact/water-crisis/.

their operations in many of these areas due to cheap economic factors, but the conditions for employees is substandard. Therefore, to be successful, companies must provide the infrastructure needed to eliminate the problems these countries experience to increase their profits and employ workers with decent lives. Careful analysis must be undertaken to determine if the tradeoff of improving the infrastructure is worth the investment, but this also brings into account the need to be socially responsible to the people who work for the firm.

Competition

Every business faces competition in one form or another. Competition in business can be internal (e.g., departments competing for company resources) or more common, external (e.g., direct competition or internet competition) where companies must determine which markets they wish to address and target based on the level of financial gain. **Competition** is a rivalry between two or more parties with the goal of seeking a superior advantage. Competition surrounds our very existence, yet we are sometimes too immune to see it. Religions compete to convert members to their faith and rule societies, animals compete for mates and feeding ground, sport teams compete to determine who is the best, special interest groups compete to promote their ideologies, and the list continues. We have provided several examples of competition; however, businesses focus on rivals that can affect business including the following:

1. *Direct*: Rivals competing in identical product categories. Examples include GM trucks against Ford trucks, Android phones versus iPhones, and McDonald's pitted against Burger King and Wendy's. In each of these examples, the product class is similar for each competitor. Direct competition finds companies challenging each other on superior features, better quality, special pricing, better warranties, and superior performance, to mention a few. Companies also try to gain customer loyalty with their products to provide repeat purchases and spread positive word of mouth. Therefore, direct competition finds intense rivalry between customers to gain market share and maintain long-term customers.

2. *Indirect*: Companies in similar product categories that compete against each other. Examples include buying a car versus a motorcycle, flying instead of driving, and ordering from Taco Bell or getting a pizza. The product categories are all similar but not identical. Indirect competition focuses on value of one choice over the other, convenience, overall savings, and satisfaction of choice. In summary, while consumers may not see how air travel is a better choice than driving, companies should stress the advantages their service has over driving to gain acceptance on the part of consumers. Offering an airfare deal and then pointing out to consumers the benefits including not dealing with traffic and the convenience and time saved flying versus driving is an illustration.

3. *Budget or share of wallet*: Competitors vying for a share of the disposable income customers have available characterizes budget competition. More specifically, companies

compete against each other in unrelated product categories. Examples include McDonald's competing against a grocery store, a cruise line competing against a car manufacturer, and a college bookstore competing against a travel agent for a spring break trip. In all these examples, there is not the presence of direct competition, but a share of the available income consumers could spend to satisfy wants and needs.

There are many ways companies compete, and those are better suited for a management or a marketing strategy course. From an innovation perspective, companies (no matter how large or small) compete through innovation. Innovation gives the smallest of companies the ability to compete with larger firms in the market. An example of this is start-ups such as Tesla finding a niche in the once-exclusive auto manufacturing world, Airbnb reshaping the hotel industry, and Uber creating a new mode of transporting people and driverless cars. These companies are taking on old and established companies through innovation and are succeeding. Therefore, the need for innovation as a means of competing in a global market has never been so important. Innovative ideas stem from news paths or different perspectives of thought. The ability to bring them to market makes any company a formattable foe and gives it ways to compete with anyone.

How Does Market Expansion Help Us Gain an Advantage?

Thus far we have identified factors that help companies identify markets that could help their innovations become successful. This next section identifies specific markets and the characteristics useful for targeting them to offer products. More specifically, we identify local, regional, national, and global markets and indicators that help to identify the right time to expand. It is extremely difficult for companies to start out as global companies, so a more methodical plan needs to put into place to determine the best plan for expansion. This section will provide some guidelines needed for expansion.

Local

Local markets are typically located near the innovative company. **Local markets** are those located approximately 10 miles or 10 minutes based on population density in proximity to the company offering goods and services.[6] Local markets offer advantages to companies because people like to shop close to their homes and form mental maps of business and their locations. Other advantages of local markets include convenience, word of mouth, business reputation, fewer competitors, concentrated advertising, meaningful sponsorship, community involvement, lower operating costs, and so on. Local markets, therefore, give an advantage of gaining much-needed attention to their product offerings, which leads to easier trial rates and repurchases.

---

6   "Local Marketing," Marketing Schools, https://www.marketing-schools.org/types-of-marketing/local-marketing.html.

Disadvantages of local markets include limited growth, possibility of negative word of mouth from a few bad experiences, lower profits, less product and company recognition for regional growth, limited labor resources, limited availability of financial and material resources, and so on. In summary, while local markets offer a wide variety of positives, there are also negatives to be considered. Companies need to look at their strategic plans and vision to determine what is right for them. Also, local markets are where most start-ups begin due to the nature of just entering business markets and their lack of experience on a regional and global basis. Therefore, local markets should be evaluated with both short-term (tactical) and long-term (strategic) plans to guide future growth and innovation to accomplish these strategies.

Regional

Regional markets cover a slightly larger geographical area than local markets. While it is hard to quantify what a region is based on the literature, for the sake of this text, a *regional market* is an area that includes the same state as the local market or larger geographical area (e.g., Midwest, Southeast, South, West, Pacific-Northwest, etc.). Regional markets present many opportunities for companies including a larger geographical area, increased profits, expanded segments and target markets, a larger labor pool, similar psychographics, the ability to make supply chains more efficient, expansion of local brands, the ability to cater to similar cultures, comparative economic factors, and so on.

Some disadvantages include increased advertising and supply chain costs, new competitors, escalation of operating expenses, decentralization of organizational structure, slower growth, reduced profits, and more employees (e.g., payroll and HR issues). While the disadvantages must be weighed against the advantages, increasing the size of the market, profitability, and economies of scale present opportunities for companies to take advantage and increase sales and profits.

While there may be some drawbacks to regional expansion, it should be viewed from a long-term perspective if resources are available to promote this action. Namely, regional expansion should be a prelude to national expansion, which will be discussed next. Regional expansion gives companies the opportunity to perfect an organizational model that will allow for selling products to a larger audience within a defined area. If this model is successful, then a national expansion could mimic this model and be rolled out. It is important that a model built on covering a state be different than covering a region, like the Midwest, so companies should remember to be aware of regional differences and consumer preferences when going national. If planned correctly, the result can lead to more sales and profits and to covering a greater market.

National

A *national market* is one that sells products to an entire country. This type of activity is an extension of regional selling and allows for greater sales and profits on the part of companies. National markets, depending on their size, give companies the opportunity to experience markets with varied tastes to start to tailor their offerings to further accommodate their target audiences. It also provides increased economies of scale, efficient use of facilities and equipment, higher levels of brand awareness, access to less expensive raw materials, greater brand equity, a larger variety of suppliers, and increased availability of diverse employees needed for innovation.

Disadvantages of national expansion are loss of control from a central headquarters, increased pressure on supply chain functions, greater expense due to increased manufacturing sites and employees, increased organizational structure, and an increase in competitors.

National expansion allows companies to prepare for their next move, which is international. National expansion is also a good exercise to prepare all the functional areas of the organization to prepare for servicing a greater market. In sum, national expansion is a positive step for companies that achieve this level and should be viewed as a symbol of success not achieved by many. If the company is a publicly traded firm, national and pending international expansion should also increase stock prices, which gives the company more resources to operate. Whatever the outcome, if a firm remains national or plans to expand internationally, it will achieve more sales and profits and be allowed to carry out its mission and vision on a greater scale.

International

When companies expand internationally, they are taking a logical next step and a risk all at the same time. *International markets* are those that include conducting business in more than one country, but not the entire world. Examples of international markets include conducting business in the US the U.K., and France, where there are different countries involved but that don't address more markets. Companies usually select countries that are homogenous, as it helps when adapting for cultural differences. They also select countries that have a stable political system and have fewer barriers of entry. Advantages of international expansion are regional markets, which include increased market opportunities, possible tax benefits, greater sales and profits, economies of scale, a greater pool of employees, and more suppliers.

Disadvantages of international markets are higher expense of operation, the possible need to decentralize operations, possible loss of income due to exchange rates, understanding a new culture, vague knowledge of foreign laws, and language barriers.

International markets present both opportunities and challenges, so a good thing to consider is to hire managers native to the country you expand to. This will help the firm understand the language, culture, how business is conducted, the laws, how to obtain raw materials, and where to locate your operations. Overall, an international model allows companies the opportunity to spread their risk by conducting business in more markets, thus exposing the products to a greater number of consumers, which could help to increases sales, economies of scale, and profits.

Global

The definition of a global market varies between authors. This text will use the following definition as it incorporates aspects needed to be considered a global firm: **Global markets** are those in which companies do business in at least three or more continents and have foreign direct investment in those continents. An example of a global market is General Motors doing business in North America, Europe, and Asia with assemble facilities located in each continent. The difference between a global market and a domestic market is that products can be made in the host country (e.g., the United States) and then shipped to foreign markets (e.g., Europe). Global markets contain the manufacturing facilities and employ a local workforce, which are separate from their domestic operations.

There are many advantages of operating in global markets including greater target markets and segments to service, availability of raw materials, a diverse labor pool, reduced supply chain efforts since manufacturing is performed on home soil, increased profits, greater brand equity, and cheaper labor costs.

Disadvantages include inability to standardize products, resulting in increased costs; language and culture barriers; poor infrastructure; loss of control; time differences making meetings with the central office difficult; laws that vary by country; and fluctuating exchange rates. Therefore, companies must understand cultural differences, language gaps, local customs, laws regarding labor and doing business, and the stability of the government and must determine how much disposable income is available to purchase products and what the level of competition is before entering these global markets. However, with the growth of the internet, one can become a global company instantly. Mid-year 2017, Facebook announced that two billion people get on Facebook at least once per month. So, with this rise of connectivity, going global by staying local helps to reduce costs and increase opportunities for increasing sales and profits.[7]

What Entry Mode is Right for Your Company?

The ability to expand from one market to the next is shaped by the entry mode strategy the company seeking to expand institutes. **Entry mode** is the method a company utilizes to gain access into a new market both domestically and globally, based on the level of risk it is willing to take. Now that we have discussed the various ways to expand to different markets, it is time to discuss the various entry-mode strategies that are available to companies. While there are many opportunities to expand to various markets, companies take risks when doing so based on the stability of host government, laws, and the threat of losing proprietary information. Therefore, companies must evaluate the level of risk and what form of entry is best suited to do business in various markets domestically, regionally, internationally, and globally.

---

7   Kaya Yurieff, "Facebook Hits 2 Billion Monthly Users," Money, June 27, 2017, http://money.cnn.com/2017/06/27/technology/facebook-2-billion-users/index.html.

Internet, Exporting, and Licensing

The least-risky form of market expansion is selling via the internet, exporting, or licensing products to be produced in other markets. The internet has provided many opportunities to countries once off limits to the sale of US products. Selling via the internet also allows companies to reduce their costs since customers will never visit their facilities; therefore, location and warehouse space can be placed in lower-cost areas. The internet also allows for easier access to countries that were once difficult to conduct business in as a sole enterprise (e.g., China and India); however the laws are rapidly changing to accommodate this style of business, so companies should consult with customs and their attorneys to determine the best means of selling and shipping products.

Licensing is another low-risk way to enter new markets. The risk of conducting business is minimized by allowing companies located in a desired market to be licensed to produce a host company's product. Once produced, the producing company then uses its established distribution system to sell to consumers. While this is a desired way to do business in countries with restrictive entry requirements, there lies a problem. The proprietary information that may be contained in manufacturing a product is exposed to another entity and could be used by the host companies for future unlicensed products. Therefore, it is important to weigh your options when entering into a licensing agreement. Based on the level of risk and opportunity, doing business via the internet, exporting, and licensing offers companies many advantages to maintain a domestic operation while conducting business in expanded markets.

Franchising

Franchising offers companies the ability to sell the rights to use their proven products and business model in new markets. Franchising is very popular in the US, and some of the bigger companies have been successful in international and global applications. Some of the risks involved with franchises include inconsistent raw ingredients used to produce the products, different cultures requiring products to be adapted to local tastes and preferences, decentralized organizational structure, and doing business in unstable countries. While there is a level of risk, franchises allow for greater brand recognition, increased market area, the ability to dictate policy from a centralized headquarters, and achieving economies of scale. Therefore, companies offering franchises must identify markets that will complement the product selection and capitalize on market gains.

Acquisition and Joint Ventures

Another, more risky entry-mode strategy is acquiring a company in a different market or forming a joint venture. *Acquisition* allows for a turnkey operation for an entering company that is expanding. Firms must consider that there may be some restrictions on ownership and some of the products produced by the acquired company may not support the mission and vision of the company. Therefore, companies opting for this type of entry strategy should be aware of the laws that govern their acquisition and evaluate the benefits of buying this type of firm. However, the advantages of acquisition include buying an established customer base, having a supply chain network in place, having the ability to service an established retail network, and having the ability to project sales and profits.

Joint ventures are characterized by forming a business with another company in a different market maintaining an ownership position in the venture. While the ownership percentage may not be equal, it is important to note that the firms involved have a stake in the profits and loss of the joint venture. The risks of a joint venture include limited participation in operations based on percentage owned, changing ownership, and increased expenses. The positives include access to new markets, the ability to buy out the partner or increase the percentage of ownership if the joint venture is prosperous, cheaper labor rates, and greater access to raw materials for domestic operations if they provide a cost advantage.

Foreign Direct Investment
Foreign direct investment is the riskiest of the entry-mode strategies. It requires companies to own property in markets different from the host country's headquarters. The risk increases as companies expand to international and global markets, as political and legal considerations must be evaluated. Foreign direct investment gives firms the ability to reduce costs by producing products in the countries where they will be sold. Supply chain expenses are also reduced as a result when selling locally, thus increasing profits. Companies that use this strategy usually select countries that are homogenous with the country where they are headquartered. The risks include political upheaval, poor exchange rates, and weak infrastructure. In sum, most foreign direct investment is carried out by companies that seek stable markets and have access to enough raw materials to make this strategy successful.

This section on markets has presented various options businesses have when choosing expansion. Not every business has the resources or expertise to be an international or global firm. Companies must understand the various cultures of the nations they seek to do business with and determine if their products are a good fit. They must also seek countries with a stable government and ones that have laws that are easy to operate under. Firms seeking to expand their markets must perform careful planning and be honest with themselves about benefits and drawbacks of moving into a new territory. When done correctly, expansion increases the available customer base, provides economies of scale, raises brand awareness, provides a larger labor pool to hire from, and provides a more efficient use of facilities and equipment.

What Other Markets Should We Watch?
We have discussed factors that influence markets we can reach and the various types of markets available to companies. We listed the advantages and disadvantages of each and the rationale for expansion. Before moving to ways to identify opportunities, let's discuss what other markets we need to watch to maximize the potential of our company and innovations.

Emerging Markets
While some markets are ideal for our innovative products, others are developing, so while currently not ideal, they will eventually be a good choice to enter. **Emerging markets** are

those that offer future potential and provide a good match for a firm's products. Examples of emerging markets include East Germany when the Berlin Wall came down; the rising wages and population in China and India, which make these countries a good market to do business with; and as the infrastructure and investment in African countries continues, this will also be an emerging market to capitalize on.

While these examples are all countries that pose emerging markets, there are other emerging markets to identify. The rising life expectancy of Americans has created opportunities for assisted-living facilities and nursing homes; technological advances in products due to demand by gen X and gen Y; colleges and universities offering a greater number of online classes that are filled to capacity, and autonomous vehicles that provide many advantages to commuters, creating a race by companies to perfect this innovation. And as the number of millionaires increase among gen X and gen Y, financial planners understand these generations will be in hot demand. Therefore, emerging markets offer potential for companies to capitalize on both domestically and internationally. The ability to recognize emerging markets is based on trends in society, but innovators must do their research to identify trends and find ways to take advantage of them.

Population Shifts

There is once again a population shift in the US thanks to a better economy than that of 2008–2009, resulting in more people moving to the sunbelt and out of the snowbelt. ***Population shifts*** are movements of groups from one geographical area to another. The US is seeing more people moving to the West and South.[8] The shifts in population in the US are also contributed to nicer weather, cheaper housing costs, young professionals moving to city centers, availability of employment, lower taxes, and high-tech jobs. There are an estimated one thousand people a day moving to Florida due to these reasons.[9]

There will also be a shift in the world's population and growth. The population of Africa will increase as Asia, North America, and Europe will decrease. Latin America and Oceania will still be relatively stable.[10] Therefore, companies with new and innovative products would be wise to establish operations in these growing markets and capitalize on the rising growth and increasing disposable income levels.

---

8   Tim Henderson, "Americans are Moving South, West Again," Pew, January 8, 2016, http://www.pewtrusts.org/en/research-and-analysis/blogs/stateline/2016/01/08/americans-are-moving-south-west-again.

9   Katie Sanders and Amy Sherman, "Will Weatherford Says 1,000 People a Day Move to Florida Because of Freedom," Politifact, April 2, 2013, https://www.politifact.com/florida/statements/2013/apr/02/will-weatherford/will-weatherford-says-1000-people-day-move-florida/.

10   Shawn Langlois, "The Massive Shift Coming in World Population, Captured in One Animation," Market Watch, March 31, 2017, http://www.marketwatch.com/story/a-massive-shift-in-the-world-population-captured-in-one-animated-graphic-2017-03-29.

Demographic Shifts

Like population shifts globally, there is a shift in demographics in the US. **Demographic** **shifts** are the change in demographics through a period. Some major demographics in the US include a greater number of millennials versus baby boomers, decreasing marriage rates and increased cohabitation, and the growth rate of Asians and Hispanics greater than Caucasians.

On a global scale, demographics shifts include Muslim women giving birth to babies surpassing Christian women by 2035, immigrants filling the gap in hiring due to the retirement of baby boomers, and an increase of refugees in the US and Europe. Therefore, demographic shifts can provide opportunities for companies that can make available products that consumers are accustomed to in their previous locations and introduce them to new and innovated products to make their lives better.

What are Alternative Ways to Find These Elusive Markets?

Thus far, we have discussed what is needed to locate markets to target and identify other market considerations. Let's now look at alternative ways to find markets. While there are several ways to find the best markets to serve, we will concentrate on several ways to locate additional markets using various methods.

Social Media

Due to the increased use of social media, companies are constantly scanning sites to find out what customers are saying about current products and competitors and what consumers would like to see different in the current product offerings. **Social media** is an online community composed of various sites used by its members to share content, communicate, interact, and collaborate. Opportunities using social media have many advantages including cost (it is free), finding information with key words, contributors viewing content as credible, customers expressing their open feelings, sharing content using pictures, sharing consumer interaction experiences, and reading competitor product comments. Many larger companies have full-time employees who monitor social media sites to address any issues and to report on trending competitive information. Therefore, social media provides companies with a multitude of opportunities to assess the need for new products located in various markets.

Surveys

Another way to get information about current and future products and markets is through a survey. **Surveys** are a collection of questions presented to customers directly or indirectly seeking their opinions regarding questions by an interested party. Surveys can be issued online, in person, via the telephone or mail, and by mall-intercept. Common questions asked are to rate the performance of the product purchased or used, suggestions for improvement, likelihood of a repeat purchase, different applications of the same product, and likelihood to tell a friend to buy the product, among other questions (i.e., positive word of mouth). Surveys can use a variety of methods to collect data including true/false, Likert scales (e.g., ranking responses 1–7), emojis, sliders (e.g., ranking responses 1–100), and so on. Surveys can either be issued

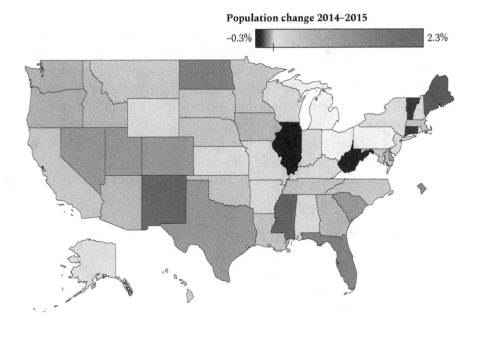

Population change 2014–2015

−0.3%   2.3%

FIG 7.2 **Population shift in the United States**

anonymously or customers can provide their information for follow-up if they choose. Surveys are a way to get direct responses from customers, which could hopefully help to provide needed insights for future innovation or improvement of the current product offerings. While this direct feedback is crucial for future success, there are drawbacks to surveys including low response rate, not being truthful (bias), high dropout rates, if not anonymous then not being truthful in responses, and the need to send reminder emails about a pending survey to boost response rates. Regardless, the ability to get responses to questions driving innovation is the key to providing what customers want, satisfying their needs, and determining the optimal place where they can buy a firm's products.

Customer Complaints

While not intuitive to common thinking, customer complaints, when handled correctly, can provide many opportunities to innovative companies. *Customers complaints* are usually a result of a customer feeling wronged in some fashion by a product or company. Companies have a unique opportunity to discover more about the products and ways to improve them by listening to complaints. While all complaints are not legitimate, most are, so companies must scrutinize the ones that are valid.

There are several reasons to address customer complaints. These include reducing customer churn (i.e., losing a customer). It costs five times as much to attract a new customer than to maintain a current one, so maintaining a customer base is vital and profitable. Long-term customers provide a stable revenue base, so it is advantageous to keep the customers we have. Also, complaints open the door to ask questions regarding the performance or the product and what can be done to improve it. This leads to future innovation by taking customer suggestions and noting them for product improvements. Negative word of mouth harms the reputation of a firm and creates a lack of trust on the part of consumers. Therefore, addressing the problem early can reduce this by satisfying consumers' complaints and making them happy. Finally, the company's ability to provide excellent customer service can help to develop loyal customers by taking care of their issues and solving the problem for them. In summary, while companies do not typically address customer complaints, it is an excellent way to drive innovation and retain customers who would normally be lost.

Focus Groups

Like surveys, focus groups provide insights directly from consumers concerning questions companies have regarding product performance or ways to improve them. A *focus group* is a collection of people who are asked questions by a facilitator to gain richer responses. The facilitator will typically elaborate on the responses given by the panel to gain further insights about their answers. An advantages focus groups have over surveys is the ability to probe deeper into the answers given by the group members to find additional insights. Another advantage is the ability to record or videotape the sessions for review later. Disadvantages include expense, response bias when you assemble many people, and lack of participation.

Many companies will sponsor a focus group at the beginning of a project to gain ideas from consumers on what they would like to see in a product. Focus groups can also be used for beta testing on a prototype a company has developed for input. Finally, a focus group can be conducted using the finished prototype to gauge the response of a new product and get consumer feedback. This feedback can be used in advertising and adjustments to the final prototype if deemed appropriate.

Trends, Their Importance, and the Ability to Predict the Future

There are really three types of trends:

1. *Global*: Trends that span the planet Earth. The growth of the internet is a great example
2. *Social*: Trends that relate to people, their mannerisms, and their habits
3. *Market/Industry*: Trends that relate to a market or industry

It is key that individuals, leaders, sales, marketing, and really all operational disciplines obtain a grasp of how trends affect the firm. Some ways to accomplish this include the following:

1. Understanding the importance of all three types of trends to ensure the organization focuses on the opportunities they present

2. Learning to follow emerging trends, determine which are substantial, and monitor data points within all three and how they can benefit the firm.

A perfect example of monitoring trends is the rising rate of obesity. In September of 2016, 20 percent of adults were classified as obese in all states, which was the highest rate ever reported in the US. Factors contributing to this include the mass consumption of soft drinks made with corn syrup, processed foods, genetics, community factors, and a lack of exercise due to internet use or playing video games.[11]

These trends regarding obesity present opportunities to gyms, diet plans, pharmaceutical companies, and health care providers to offer ways to improve our quality of life by becoming more active and reducing this type of epidemic. Trends are an important area for innovators to capitalize on and lend themselves to offering solutions to fix problems while providing opportunities for innovation.

Review Questions

1. Perform a SWOT analysis for one of your favorite restaurants. What are ways it can use its strengths and opportunities to counter its threats and weaknesses?
2. What are three opportunities you feel are present in your town using environmental scanning?
3. Why is population density evaluation important? Are there shifts in your state? What are they?
4. Select a business and describe the three levels of competition and provide examples.
5. What are the five levels of market expansion? Provide examples of each that are not covered in the text.
6. Why is it important to evaluate entry-mode strategies before entering markets?
7. Provide three examples of emerging markets. Why do you feel they are emerging?
8. Where in the US are we seeing population shifts? Describe them.
9. Are customer complaints bad? Based on your answer, how can companies use complaints to identify new markets?
10. Name two types of market trends. Give two examples of these.

Discussion Questions

1. How would infrastructure in developing countries affect the ability to conduct business versus infrastructure in developed countries?
2. Why is it difficult for a start-up company to go global immediately?
3. How are company resources, level of competition, and population density related?

---

11 "Adult Obesity Causes and Consequences," Centers for Disease Control and Prevention, https://www.cdc.gov/obesity/adult/causes.html.

4. What are some social external environmental factors you see are opportunities in the US?
5. Based on political-legal external environmental factors, risk, and entry-mode strategies, what do you feel is the best strategy for conducting business in China? Why?
6. What are some emerging markets you see in the US?
7. How do population and demographics shifts influence the types of products companies offer? Provide some examples.
8. Review a few company's social media sites. If there are complaints, how did the company handle these? What types of improvements do you see your company could utilize to capitalize on these?

Integrative Learning Exercise

1. Gather into small groups to discuss societal and market trends, then share your findings with the class.
2. What are three societal and market trends that you feel are available for improved innovation? What types of products would you offer to capitalize on these trends?

Extension Activity

1. Perform a SWOT analysis of yourself. Identify each of the four components and how you can use your strengths and opportunities to overcome your weaknesses and threats.
2. Based on the metropolitan area you are from, do you see demographical trends as determined by the cities, products offered, and housing types? Are there shifts you have observed?

BIBLIOGRAPHY

Adams, Anne-Taylor. "Global consumers are willing to put their money where their heart is when it comes to goods and services from companies committed to social responsibility"

"Adult Obesity Causes and Consequences," Centers for Disease Control and Prevention, https://www.cdc.gov/obesity/adult/causes.html.

Nielsen, June 17, 2014, https://www.nielsen.com/us/en/press-room/2014/global-consumers-are-willing-to-put-their-money-where-their-heart-is.html.

Bagley, Rebecca, O. "The 10 Traits of Great Innovators," *Forbes*, January 15, 2014, https://www.forbes.com/sites/rebeccabagley/2014/01/15/the-10-traits-of-great-innovators/#2eaccc0e4bf4.

Tomas Chamorro-Premuzic, "The Five Characteristics of Successful Innovators," *Harvard Business Review*, October 25, 2013, https://hbr.org/2013/10/the-five-characteristics-of-successful-innovators; "20 Qualities of an Innovator," The Heart of Innovation, August 13, 2010, http://www.ideachampions.com/weblogs/archives/2010/08/are_you_an_inno.shtml.

Malone, Robert. "In Pictures: Where Is the World's Cheapest Labor?" *Forbes*, May 29, 2008, https://www.forbes.com/2008/05/25/change-security-internet-oped-cx_rm_outsourcing08_0529data_slide.html#34e69f631fa2.

Beauvais, Joel. "Moving Forward for America's Drinking Water," *EPA Blog*, April 26, 2016, https://blog.epa.gov/2016/04/26/moving-forward-for-americas-drinking-water/

"The Water Crisis," https://water.org/our-impact/water-crisis/.

"Local Marketing," Marketing Schools, https://www.marketing-schools.org/types-of-marketing/local-marketing.html.

Yurieff, Kaya. "Facebook Hits 2 Billion Monthly Users," Money, June 27, 2017, http://money.cnn.com/2017/06/27/technology/facebook-2-billion-users/index.html.

Henderson, Tim. "Americans are Moving South, West Again," Pew, January 8, 2016, http://www.pewtrusts.org/en/research-and-analysis/blogs/stateline/2016/01/08/americans-are-moving-south-west-again.

Sanders, Katie and Sherman, Amy. "Will Weatherford Says 1,000 People a Day Move to Florida Because of Freedom," Politifact, April 2, 2013, https://www.politifact.com/florida/statements/2013/apr/02/will-weatherford/will-weatherford-says-1000-people-day-move-florida/.

Langlois, Shawn. "The Massive Shift Coming in World Population, Captured in One Animation," Market Watch, March 31, 2017, http://www.marketwatch.com/story/a-massive-shift-in-the-world-population-captured-in-one-animated-graphic-2017-03-29.

Figure Credits

Fig. 7.1: Source: https://commons.wikimedia.org/wiki/File:USA_states_population_density_map.PNG.

Fig. 7.2: Source: http://www.pewtrusts.org/en/research-and-analysis/blogs/stateline/2016/01/08/americans-are-moving-south-west-again.

CHAPTER EIGHT

How Does Innovation Add Value to Society?

INTRODUCTION

Innovation has contributed so much to society through existence. Simple things like fire, the wheel, weapons, healthcare, and technology, to name a few have increased our life expectancy and improved our way of life. We continue to innovate at a faster pace due to a global economy and to technology. In this chapter, we will identify innovation over time. We will also discuss how innovation adds value to society, the impact social media has on the company/customer relationship, and how companies add value to society outside of innovation in the form of philanthropy. We will also speak about the need for companies to provide leadership in markets and the importance of ethical behavior to benefit stakeholders. Finally, we will share strategies that help us connect with our customers and the importance of retaining them.

Learning Objectives

In this chapter students will learn about the following:
- How innovation has changed over time
- Ways companies add value to society
- The impact social media has on connecting consumers and companies
- Ways companies add value to society outside of innovation
- The importance of leadership in the market
- Strategies to connect companies with customers

Learning Outcomes

By the end of this chapter students will be able to do the following:
- Describe how companies satisfy needs, improve economic well-being, improve our quality of life, and advance technology
- List ways social media positively affects the company/customer relationship

- Identify why philanthropy and CSR have a positive influence for companies
- Describe ways in which leadership can create value in a market
- Develop strategies to connect with customers

Key Terms

Switching costs: The negative costs consumers incur when switching products or brands due to the increased time and effort to find and learn how to use a new product

Wealth creation: The accumulation of wealth by an entity for their betterment

Economic growth: Growth measured by gross domestic product (GDP)

Entrepreneurship: The act of creating a business that is either for profit or nonprofit with the intention of creating wealth or helping society

Intrinsic quality: The feelings you have toward a product

Extrinsic quality: The attributes that are external to the product

Reverse distribution channel or *reverse logistics*: The return of unwanted or used product to the manufacture for reuse, disposal, or recycling

Mass marketing: Sending a message or advertisement to the mass population in hopes the potential target market sees, reads, or hears the message

Applications (apps): Desktop, mobile, or web programs that allow direct access to the company via the internet

Geotracking: A way for companies to find customers by tracking their travels using their GPS from their smartphones

Cell phone optimization: Used to allow consumers to use their mobile device in the same way as they use a computer

Social media: Online communities that allow users to communicate directly with each other and companies that participate

Philanthropy: The donation of time or funds for humanitarian- or cause-related purposes

Corporate social responsibility (CSR): The initiatives that companies take to produce products that are not harmful to the environment and have minimal effect on society, while generating a profit to sustain this activity

Channel captain: The dominate member of a distribution channel that controls the flow of products due to their size

Learning curve: The knowledge that is gained through experience while working at a task

HOW HAS INNOVATION PROVIDED VALUE TO SOCIETY?

Before we identify how innovation adds or will add value to society, it is first important to see how innovation has added value to our lives. Many of the innovations of the past are forgotten because they have assimilated into everyday life, and we never think of how they have changed the course of history. The earliest innovations may seem simple in the present day, but at the time they transformed how people lived and added value to society, propelling it in a positive direction. Table 8.1 identifies a brief history of innovation and how it made an impact on bettering society.[1]

TABLE 8.1 *Innovation throughout History*

INNOVATION	ADDED VALUE TO SOCIETY
Fire (400,000 BCE)	Provided the ability to stay warm and cook food without the effects of contracting parasites.
Language (100,000 BCE)	Provided a means to communicate locally and with other societies.
Commercial trade (17,000 BCE)	Produced products from other societies available for trade, expanding civilization.
Farming (15,000 BCE)	Provided a means to feed multiple people and create wealth. Still a viable concern as the world's population increases and available land decreases.
Shipping (4,000 BCE)	Provided a means for trade and expansion of territory.
Wheel (3,400 BCE)	Allowed for efficient mobility and work.
Money (3,000 BCE)	Provided a way to trade without bartering for goods or services.
Iron (3,000 BCE)	Allowed for the development of weapons and durable farm equipment.
Written language (2,900 BCE)	Allowed for a means to transmit a message and a means to record historical events.
Legal system (1,780 BCE)	Gave society a set of rules to follow to guide behavior.
Steel (650 BCE)	A more durable metal than iron, which is the precursor to building modern day skyscrapers, cars, ships, and so on.
Water power (200 BCE)	Allowed for a means of energy to run engines, grist mills, and drive the first machines.
Paper (105)	Allowed for a vehicle to communicate written language and record history.
Movable type (1040)	Gave society the ability to print mass messages for distribution to others.
Electricity (1600)	The predecessor to how modern society was transformed. The ability to run a variety of mechanisms with an efficient power source.
Telescope (1608)	Provided a means to study the universe and to realize the Earth was not the only planet in the universe.
Steam engine (1712)	Allowed manufacturing to occur anywhere versus using water power, which required factories to be placed by streams. It also provided power for the first forms of mechanized farm equipment.
Light bulb (1800)	Edison perfected the light bulb in 1879, but it allowed society to work after sundown and provided more efficiency.

---

1   Ryan Allis. "The 40 greatest innovations of all time." *Startup Guide*. December 11, 2018. https://startupguide.com/the-40-greatest-innovations-of-all-time.

INNOVATION	ADDED VALUE TO SOCIETY
Telegraph (1809)	This was the first means of long-distance communication and gave society the ability to send messages instantaneously. A prelude to the modern-day telephone and later smartphone. It also helped to communicate the outcome of Civil War battles.
Petroleum (1859)	A highly combustible power source that would later aid our ability travel more efficiently than riding a horse.
Telephone (1860)	Allowed for an enriched ability to communicate not only in spoken language, but by hearing the voice of the caller. It also gave society the ability to reach others at long distances and was a direct descendant of the cell phone.
Vacuum tube (1883)	The vacuum tube improved our ability to communicate via the radio and later the television. It was the first step toward modern-day communications.
Semi-conductor (1896)	The semi-conductor resulted in our ability to develop computers and other devices that run from a microchip. In modern day, almost everything we use uses a chip, which is a product of the first semi-conductors. Your cellphone has more computing power than the first spaceship to the moon!
Penicillin (1896)	Penicillin gave the medical world the ability to stop infection. Infection and how to control it was virtually unknown until its discovery. This increased the life expectancy of humans and prevented the early demise of many who contracted an infection. It also gave hope to wounded soldiers in wars that occurred after its discovery.
Radio (1897)	The vacuum tube allowed the invention of the radio, a form of communication that could transmit mass messages to listeners. It also gave way to advertisements and public service announcements and was a form of entertainment before the television.
Airplane (1903)	The airplane was quickly adapted for many purposes. It would be used in war and enable travelers to be taken to destinations at great distances in a short amount of time. More recently, airplanes are used for delivering packages and are an alternative to traveling by car due to the cost.
Television (1926)	Another product of the vacuum tube was the television. The television brought another dimension to reaching audiences the radio lacked: a visual of the person sending a message. The television was also the precursor to the computer screen.
Transistor (1947)	The transistor replaced the vacuum tube and made electronics more efficient. Later the inventor of the transistor would go on to form Intel.
DNA (1953)	The discovery of DNA helped scientists understand how we inherent traits and uncover diseases.
Integrative circuit (1959)	The integrative circuit could fit more circuitry into a confined space, giving electronics more features. It was also the predecessor to the microprocessor.

INNOVATION	ADDED VALUE TO SOCIETY
The internet (1969)	The internet was invented to connect researchers doing work for the government in different locations. In 1992, researchers at the University of Illinois developed the Worldwide Web. The contributions the internet has made in the world are indescribable.
Microprocessor (1971)	Intel developed the microprocessor, which later revolutionized the world. The current chip allows for us to carry devices with more computing power than the first computers and spaceships that went in orbit.
Mobile phone (1973)	The mobile phone is an adaption of the first telephone and microprocessor. Technology gave the ability to call from virtually anywhere if there was service. It made business more efficient and instantly connected people without the use of desks or payphones.
Facebook (2004)	Enabled the world to visually communicate
Smartphone (2007)	The iPhone gave consumers the first device that combined a phone, MP3 player, computer, and camera in one unit. The smartphone revolutionized the cellular phone industry and gave way to doing the same things on your phone as on a computer, plus taking and posting pictures, using instant chat and text messages, and using apps to make life convenient.
Additional innovations for the future:	Value to society:
Driverless Automobiles	More efficient use of travel time.
Web 3.0 or the internet of things	The next version of internet that will allow you to obtain information from an interconnected web.
Genetic Modification	Help to stop birth defects and disease.
Geoengineering	Help to combat climate change

These past innovations and future innovations show how innovation builds on each other to add value to society. For example, language developed into written word. Written word, with the help of paper, gave society a means to transmit messages and store information. In addition, the telegraph, telephone, radio, and television transmitted messages and entertained. The vacuum tube allowed for the creation of radio and television, which gave way to the transistor. The transistor became the modern-day microprocessor. Microprocessors are found in most products and have made life easier for society. Therefore, without innovation, we would never have advanced our society to the point it is today. We take for granted the ability to post pictures to social media anywhere in the world, to stop cancer, to travel around the globe with ease, and to instantly communicate with anyone on the planet. It is due to innovation that these things are possible and why we have a superior quality of life.

We have identified the way companies added value to society in the past. This is not to say that innovation has not fulfilled adding value in the same eras. Such innovations as the automobile, the assembly line, television, commercial air travel, electric appliances, penicillin, curing of polio, pasteurization, and so on have made the lives of this world better and added a higher quality of life. For example, in 1800 the average life span of a US citizen was 30 years. In 2017 the average life span is 80 years, which represents a 266 percent increase. Innovation conducted properly ultimately creates a better world.

SPEED MATTERS

This section will focus on how innovation continues to add value to stakeholders on a global scale now and in the future. We will cover many topics, but the list is impossible to be all inclusive. It will feature many innovations and how they add value to our lives and the world in which we live. Keep in mind that at the time of writing this text, companies who fail to innovate quickly are seen to be a poor investment with ineffective leadership. This fact is why we stress the need to "move" and to not procrastinate when you are developing new products for the marketplace. The inability to "move" will slow down the process and put your company at a severe disadvantage in the market. As a perfect case in point, Spartan Motors Inc., over a thirty-year period (1985 to 2015) had a compound annual growth rate (CAGR) of 13.97 percent per year. These were astounding numbers for a non-tech company. Over that thirty-year period over 15 market redefining innovators were brought to life, or one every other year. Today the pace of change is exponential as the average life of a company is now just 15 years, thus proving that speed matters.

Needs Satisfaction

At the heart of innovation is the ability to satisfy the needs of our customers. This is not a new realization, but it should drive why we innovate. Most consumers are reluctant to switch products or try something new due to switching costs. *Switching costs* are the negative costs consumers incur when switching products or brands due to the increased time and effort to find and learn how to use a new product. Therefore, if we can determine what needs they have in a product category, switching will be easier if the time and effort to learn how to use the new product are minimal.

We will highlight a few areas of consideration before identifying specific categories and areas of determining ways innovation brings value to society. In order to determine the ways our innovations can satisfy customers' needs, we first must identify who the customer is. We must select our target market and determine demographical, geographical, and psychographic information about them. Only by determining these traits can we identify who the customer is and where they are located to satisfy their needs. Next, we will identify three areas of innovation that will add value to society through their continued improvements. These three characteristics are economic benefits, health, and the product.

Economic Benefits

Innovative companies add many economic benefits to society in a variety of ways. This section will focus on a few including wealth creation, economic growth, job creation, job stability, lower consumer prices due to competition and efficient manufacturing, and greater access to product variety due to global marketing. The *economic benefits* help to drive a better quality of life through greater earning power, stable employment, and higher buying power but also a better world as with wealth and people.

Wealth Creation

Wealth creation happens for both the company and the consumer because of innovation. We will touch on the consumer side when we discuss lower prices due to competitive pressure. We will discuss how wealth creation by companies are both a fringe benefit and a necessary part of innovation. *Wealth creation* is the accumulation of wealth by an entity for their betterment. Innovative companies create wealth through many sources including lowered costs, efficient processes (manufacturing, supply chain, marketing, etc.), brand reputation, quality, and loyalty ultimately benefiting its associates and the consumer.

Initially, companies will incur higher costs when innovating due to research and development and sunk costs. Once the product is in the market, companies begin to recoup their upfront costs by selling more products as the recent innovation is adopted by the market. Also, existing products may benefit from the innovation as customers discover a new brand. Companies can lower costs through innovation by achieving economies of scale (spreading fixed costs over more units produced). Also, by utilizing efficient manufacturing processes such as just-in-time manufacturing (producing products when ordered and not stored for future orders) and just-in-time inventory (products are manufactured and shipped the same day or soon), they can reduce raw materials costs, perfect efficient supply chain including warehousing (locating merchandise near target markets to reduce delivery times), and improve logistics (movement of products in the most efficient manner possible). In 1975 the minimum wage in the US was $2.10. In 2015 the minimum wage was $7.25, a 345 percent increase. One could argue this is not enough, but when you triple any "positive number" that is very good for society and improves the buying potential.

Marketing can also help to reduce costs and increase wealth by effectively targeting consumers and obtaining products more easily. Electronic marketing gives companies the ability to send and receive information from targeted customers. The target market can subscribe to emails from a company, then the firm uses these to send marketing messages and offers back to the inquiring customer. Most companies have an easy-to-maneuver website that allows customers to search, order, and pay for products, thus eliminating the need for large numbers of employees to service their customer base and increasing profits.

Brand reputation, quality, and loyalty are positive side effects of innovative companies. Studies show that there is a positive relationship between the innovativeness of companies and the level of loyalty, quality, and reputation.[2] Therefore, not only does innovation provide needed products for survival, but it also builds a stronger customer base. Loyal customers act

---

2   Ravi Pappu and Pascale G. Quester, "How Does Brand Innovativeness Affect Brand Loyalty?" *European Journal of Marketing* 50, no. 1/2 (2016): 2–28.

as marketers for innovative companies by spreading positive word of mouth, thus helping to market the products offered and increase sales and profits.

Economic Growth

Innovative products are a major contributor of economic growth. Advances in existing products or new-to-the-world products fuel the satisfaction of human needs and create opportunities for companies to expand the scope of business. Innovative products give companies the ability to expand their market, increase profits, and further innovate to maintain growth and existence. *Economic growth* is measured in gross domestic product (GDP). On average, the US GDP increases 2–3 percent per year and the US is ranked first in the world for the highest GDP behind China and Japan based on prices. When using purchasing power parity (PPP), the rankings are China, the US, and India.[3]

Let's briefly look at the job creation of several companies:

- Spartan Motors Inc., created in 1975, increased jobs from 0 to 1,700 by 2015
- Apple created two million jobs by 2010
- Google/Internet created 10.4 million jobs by 2016

Innovation and growth create jobs, which drives GDP in the right direction. As evidenced by the data, one product class that is a major contributor of economic growth is technology. The technology industry provides high-paying jobs and is related to fields that support tech companies. The technology field allows companies to be located anywhere due to the availability of the Internet. This gives them the advantage of lowering costs for facilities, labor, rent, and taxes over locating strictly in Silicon Valley. The effect of technology growth and its effect on job creation allows consumers to spend more money, thus driving economic growth while reducing costs.

Another area of economic growth is through entrepreneurship. *Entrepreneurship* is the act of creating a business that is either for profit or nonprofit with the intention of creating wealth or helping society. Being an entrepreneur has spurred the "gig economy," which is independent contractors or entrepreneurs with one goal: to set out on their own and not work for another party. It is estimated that by 2020, 40 percent of the US labor force could be "1099-ers" (independent contractors). Entrepreneurs create new products, use goods and services in their businesses (cleaning, office supplies, office equipment, automobiles, etc.), buy or rent space, and support communities. The innovative ideas entrepreneurs devise help grow the economy and fuel new and creative products that society uses. Entrepreneurship also helps to create new jobs and stabilize the workforce, lower the cost of goods through competition, and seek out ways to be more efficient (e.g., just-in-time manufacturing and just-in-time inventory).

---

3   "World GDP Ranking 2018," Knoema, https://knoema.com/nwnfkne/world-gdp-ranking-2018-gdp-by-country-data-and-charts.

New Jobs and Improved Quality of Life

Entrepreneurs create new products to satisfy unmet needs or address current needs and demands of their potential or current clients. A result of entrepreneurial activity is the creation of jobs and improvement of the quality of life for those who are employed. Entrepreneurs provide a means to uplift and support the communities they operate in by offering opportunities for their stakeholders through jobs.[4] A study conducted in 2002 found that 3.9 million jobs were created, of which entrepreneurs accounted for 2.8 million of these opportunities. Entrepreneurs also have a positive effect on the workforce.[5]

Creating Efficiency

Entrepreneurs, especially new start-ups, cannot afford to be inefficient. Inefficiency costs businesses up to 30 percent of their revenue each year. Entrepreneurs must use their resources to place a necessity on improving inefficient practices. The following are five ways entrepreneurs can change inefficient practices into efficient ones and become more profitable.

1. Entrepreneurs must identify what is causing inefficiencies and seek a way to reverse these practices. One way is to fully utilize the capabilities the firm has to operate at peak performance. For example, a restaurant owner has a lull between lunch and dinner. They could offer reduced menu prices during the lull, send employees out to pass out menus to businesses in the area, operate a split shift, and so on. The entrepreneur must step back and see the big picture and overcome what is causing the business to lose resources.

2. Entrepreneurs can democratize their business by giving their customers a greater say in when they want to purchase the goods offered. The traditional way of doing business is for firms to set hours for when customers will patronize the business. This practice is changing as firms are offering online ordering 24/7 and being open 24 hours a day and banks are offering ATM machines and scheduling appointments that fit consumer schedules. Giving customers more of a say frees time for the firm and increases sales, while satisfying customer needs.

3. Entrepreneurs can also integrate technology into their business to ease consumer utilization. Technology, such as apps, reduces the need to call a firm or miss a customer's call. Inefficient digital integration has cost firms up to a 25 percent loss in business. Other technology entrepreneurs can use are employee remote access to the firm, more automation to improve quality and reduce labor costs, and utilizing machines to do counting procedures and eliminate human error.

---

4 Ed Sappin, "7 Ways Entrepreneurs Drive Economic Development," Entrepreneury, October 20, 2016, https://www.entrepreneur.com/article/283616.

5 Ying Lowrey, "Estimating Entrepreneurial Jobs: Business Creation is Job Creation," 2011. American Economic Association Annual Meeting.

4. Entrepreneurs must also look at the big picture (the entire industry) and determine if their firm is fully integrated or just partially integrated. Full integration finds new opportunities by not focusing on how to satisfy a customer's needs for one segment of the business but by asking "What are the overall needs a customer has that we can satisfy?" For example, a rental car company can focus on providing a car to get their customers from point A to Point B, but what else does the customer need? Perhaps navigation, roadside assistance, lodging at his or her destination and places to eat, entertainment, a place to refuel the car, and so on. By fully integrating a firm's services, they can improve their efficiency and profits.

5. Identify ways the entrepreneur's products can be used for different uses or be sold in different markets. This is a form of disruption and helps to increase sales and profits by finding new ways to offer the products sold. This is found in products like Dawn dish soap, where it is used to clean dishes and remove oil from sea faring birds after the BP oil spill of 2010, but is also mixed with other ingredients to clean grout, kill insects, and so on.[6]

Health

The world's life expectancy continues to be extended through innovative drugs, procedures, and discoveries. In addition, medical research continues to find ways to reduce child mortality worldwide, cure cancer, treat a growing world population, and is even experimenting on how to stop aging. These advances will have a tremendous impact on economic growth by supporting an aging population, curing illnesses, and even altering genes to stop birth defects and disease passed through heredity.

The top innovations in medicine for 2017 include medicine that will reduce the risk of cardiovascular disease and death of diabetic patients, using cellular immunotherapy to treat leukemia and lymphomas, a 3D visualization system for surgeons to alleviate the problem of being hunched over a patient for hours, and absorbable stents to replace metal ones that are left in the patient and cause a potential for blood clots.[7]

Prolonging Life Expectancy

Innovations have also helped to prolong life. Swiss pharmaceutical company Novartis is working on a pill containing certain proteins that have been shown to reverse aging and reinvigorate brain and muscle function in older lab mice. Finally, flying drones are being used and tested to retrieve patients in remote areas suffering a heart attack. Tactical Robotics

---

6   Amy Osmond Cook, "6 Ways to Make Your Business More Efficient," Entrepreneur, October 31, 2017, https://www.entrepreneur.com/article/292833.

7   "Top 10 Medical Innovations for 2017 Revealed," Cleveland Clinic, https://consultqd.clevelandclinic.org/top-10-medical-innovations-2017-revealed/.

has successfully used this ambulance drone in Israel and is working with the FDA to make it available in the US by 2020.[8]

As the population of the Earth continues to live longer, innovative companies will continue to develop new products that will cure disease and illness, reverse the effects of aging, provide better joint replacements, perfect imaging equipment, and much more. These innovations will add to the quality of life for many and add value to global society. For example, the annual GDP (per capita) in the US in 1960 was $428 compared to just less than $11,400 in 2010. This represents a significant change demonstrating an improved quality of life for US residents.

Product Characteristics

Characteristics of products vary in the way they add value to society. Innovators seek to offer products that give their company advantages in terms of reputation, brand image, excellent customer service, customer satisfaction, convenience, and efficiency, to name a few. The ability to offer these types of products gives companies a strategic competitive advantage over their competitors and other products available in the marketplace. Therefore, companies strive to innovate to gain this advantage and to ensure they will survive in the future.

Quality

Quality products offer companies and society many advantages. When we identify quality, there are two factors that signify it. One is **intrinsic quality** or the feelings you have toward a product. For example, consumers buy hybrids because they are less environmentally harmful than gasoline vehicles. They feel they are doing what is right for the environment by purchasing these vehicles. The second is **extrinsic quality** or the attributes that are external to the product. For example, a consumer buys a Corvette because it is a symbol of power and wealth.

Higher prices are a surrogate for quality (e.g., is a Cadillac an inexpensive vehicle?), as are brand names and packaging. Consumers see high-quality products costing more, but this is offset in their minds by the performance and durability of the product. Quality also boosts the reputation and image of the company as it signifies that a firm offers high-quality products, so it is a superior company.

Quality also has different indicators for services including atmosphere of the location the service is provided, word of mouth on the part of previous service users, service provider reputation, consumers' experiences, and price. What is important to note is indicators of quality for both goods and services provide value to customers based on their level of expectations. This isn't to say that some consumers cheat and seek convenience of alternatives, such as fast food versus a well-prepared meal. Therefore, the value that products offer society is based from the perception and expectations on the part of consumers for the products they seek.

---

8   "Israeli 'Flying Ambulance Drone' Aims to Save Lives," EMS1, January 6, 2017, https://www.ems1.com/ambulances-emergency-vehicles/articles/158543048-Israeli-flying-ambulance-drone-aims-to-save-lives/.

Sustainability

Products that are sustainable in nature offer value to society by using fewer natural resources, causing minimal harm to the environment, and can be recyclable. As indicated later in this chapter, consumers prefer to purchase products that are made by socially responsible companies. Responsible companies indicate on their products what can be recycled or are using reverse distribution channels to promote product reuse. A *reverse distribution channel* or *reverse logistics* is the return of unwanted or used product to the manufacture for reuse, disposal, or recycling. An example is an automobile battery where the shell of the battery is reusable, but the inner core can be recycled and then replaced. The benefit of reverse distribution is the reduction in harvesting natural resources, creating unneeded waste, or responsible recycling on the part of the manufacturer.

Waste generation is expected to grow from 1.2 to 3.5 million tons per day in 2010 to 6 million tons per day in 2025. In addition, cost goes up from $205 billion in 2010 to $375 billion per year in 2025. As mentioned, sustainable products typically use fewer natural resources, which is better for the environment. Hybrid vehicles use less fuel, LED light bulbs burn less energy, high-efficient appliances use less electricity or gas, and so on. The result is a product that preserves the planet, provides responsible consumption, and can save consumers money. While climate change is a subject of debate, the need for sustainable products by most segments of the population have indicated that they support manufacturers of these types of products and would even pay a premium for their use.[9] (Therefore, sustainable products are valued by society and promote the image and reputation of the innovative companies that develop and manufacture them.

Technology

Technology adds value to society in many ways. When we speak of technology the first thing the research shows is how social media makes innovation effective. In the past, marketers have targeted customers through mass marketing, a generalized message targeted toward a minority of the population. *Mass marketing* is sending a message or advertisement to the mass population in hopes the targeted market sees, reads, or hears the message. This is effective for popular brands but doesn't benefit smaller companies. Another drawback of mass marketing is the expense. A more effective use of technology is to direct the advertisements toward the target market using social media. There are many ways to do this that add value to society including applications (apps), social media channels, cell phone optimization, and well-developed websites.

Applications (apps) are desktop, mobile, or web programs that allow direct access to the company via the internet. Apps are a means to access the customers who have downloaded it for companies to have direct communication with the target market. Companies use apps to build loyalty by offering deals and for ease of ordering. This technology adds value by being available anytime, anywhere the consumer needs it. Apps also help companies find their

---

9   Keith Ferguson. "An investigation of sustainable product purchase behavior: A social cognitive perspective of consumer action." (2014).

customers by using geotracking. *Geotracking* is a way for companies to find customers by tracking their travels using their GPS from their smartphones. Once these consumers are near a location tracking them, the company can offer a deal to lure them to shop at their location. A downfall of apps are companies that don't have their e-commerce (electronic commerce) sites optimized. *Cell phone optimization* allows consumers to use their mobile device the same way as they use a computer. All images and websites are the same as using a computer, so special offers can be presented, and interaction is identical to a computer. One of the biggest advantages today versus twenty years ago relative to innovation and growth is the internet. Today, in a matter of microseconds one has access to worldwide portals of information. The result is the opportunity for intuition and data, and innovation, happens much faster.

One of the biggest technology features that adds value to society, consumers, and the company is social media. *Social media* are online communities that allow users to communicate directly with each other and companies that participate. Social media sites are rapidly forming due to their effectiveness at reaching their members. Some social media sites include Instagram, Facebook, Pinterest, Twitter, and Snapchat. Companies rely heavily on monitoring social media sites because these are the online communication vehicles of many users, especially millennials, to share likes and dislikes of products or services and communicate with each other. Following are some data points regarding social media that add value to society.

1. *Co-create products*: Companies use their community to crowd source ideas to make their products better and to find new products to develop.
2. *Demand forecasting*: The aura created by a new product can help companies estimate demand for a product to ensure it's available to customers.
3. *Distributing business processes*: Making travel more efficient for companies to use social media to predict traffic patterns and flow to help their users.
4. *Market research*: Social media helps market researchers by monitoring the comments (i.e., good and bad) about products to reduce the time needed to develop new insights about the products and find ways to effectively target advertisement toward the right market.
5. *Marketing communications*: Social media allows companies the ability to communicate directly with customers to address their needs more effectively, make a sale, or answer any questions they may have, thus increasing the customer service experience.
6. *Lead generation*: Social media also allows companies to generate leads by monitoring the number of times a consumer clicks on their site, makes an inquiry, or asks others about a product. The lead generated is better than a random lead because companies can determine the amount of interest by a consumer's online activity.
7. *Social commerce*: Companies benefit by opinion leaders, friends, or family who like or recommend using word of mouth. As discussed previously, word of mouth is a recommendation by a reference group member and is effective because of the level of

trust we have for that person. Social media has a unique advantage of gaining word of mouth, which helps to sell products.

8. *Customer care*: Companies can avoid customer service disasters by monitoring problems reported on social media sites. They can also advertise offers to customers, thus providing a boost to their customer service efforts.

9. *Collaboration*: Social media sites provide a collaborative way for internal and external stakeholders to communicate with each other, thus making operations much more efficient.

10. *Matching talents to roles*: Social media sites that specialize in highlighting one's talents (LinkedIn, Indeed, Glassdoor, etc.) can be used by human resources to find the needed available talent for a company. It also allows individuals to demonstrate their

Ten ways social technologies can add value in organizational functions within and across enterprises

Organizational functions

| Product development | 4 | Derive customer insights[1] |
| | 1 | Co-create products |

| Operations and distribution | 2 | Leverage social to forecast and monitor |
| | 3 | Use social to distribute business processes |

Marketing and sales	4	Derive customer insights
	5	Use social technologies for marketing communication/interaction
	6	Generate and foster sales leads
	7	Social commerce

| Customer service | 8 | Provide customer care via social technologies |

| Business support[2] | | Improve collaboration and communication; match talent to tasks[3] |

Across entire enterprise

Enterprise-wide levers

(Social as organizational technology)

9 — Use social technology to improve intra- or inter-organizational collaboration and communication

10 — Use social technology to match talent to tasks

[1]Deriving customer insights for product development is included in customer insights (lever 4) under marketing and sales.
[2]Business support functions are corporate or administrative activities such as human resources or finance and accounting.
[3]Levers 9 and 10 apply to business support functions as they do across the other functional value areas.

Source: McKinsey Global Institute analysis.

FIG 8.1 **Ten ways social media adds value to society**

accomplishments and find employment with a company that is a good fit for their talents and desires.[10]

THINK ABOUT THIS!

How has social media changed your life? Does social media impact your product purchases? What does social media do for companies?

There are over 1.5 billion social network users worldwide
    80 percent of online users interact with social media daily
    70 percent of companies today use social media channels to target customers
What value does social media add to companies?
    Increases knowledge of a company and its products
    Increases brand recognition and consumer perceptions
    Adds to the credibility, trust, and loyalty of the company offering products
    Offers a more experiential way to sell products than just through looking at a picture by giving the customer the ability to use 3D modeling, various colors and styles, and videos[11]

WHAT ARE ADDITIONAL WAYS COMPANIES ADD VALUE TO SOCIETY OUTSIDE OF INNOVATION?

Today's companies are choosing to "give back" to the communities and stakeholders that have made them successful. This is done in several ways, including philanthropy, being socially responsible, teaming up with causes, volunteering, and involving employees and community. Through these types of value creation activities firms can better address society, increase profits, and increase their reputations and loyalty.

Philanthropy

Corporate philanthropy has changed over the past fifty years. Companies once donated large sums of money to charities or created foundations to share their wealth. This practice has been refined today to include employee contributions and matching, community participation, volunteering, donating on a global scale to better the world, and supporting a social agenda that addresses issues the world we live in faces. *Philanthropy* is the donation of time or funds for humanitarian- or cause-related purposes. Examples of philanthropy include donating

---

10   Jeff Bullas, "10 Ways Social Media Technologies Are Adding Value and Productivity," https://www.jeffbullas.com/10-ways-social-media-technologies-are-adding-value-and-productivity/

11   Ibid.

money to promote education, supporting the construction of a new hospital providing needed services to communities, or giving money for your business school's building to support the programs and university. Philanthropy is engaged by every level of business, as well as by individuals. It is typically viewed as giving back to society for its support in making a business or an individual successful. In other words, it is a way to share the wealth with those who helped create it.

The CEO of Force for Good identified philanthropy on the part of 272 multi-billion-dollar US companies with total revenues of $7.5 trillion and employing 14.3 million workers in 2016. The report indicated total contributions equaled $24.5 billion, 31 percent of the companies volunteered for social causes, seven out of ten companies gave to recipients on a global scale, nine out of ten companies matched employee donations; and of the causes supported, 29 percent were in education, 26 percent in social services, and 13 percent in economic development.[12]

The break down in figure 8.2 shows how philanthropy has changed. Companies are now encouraging their employees to volunteer their time and money to special causes. Employees are responding to this as well, which gives the company a reputation boost while reducing the amount of money it donates. In addition, the nature of corporate philanthropy is focusing on causes that better society versus donating to a charity that concentrates on one cause. Therefore, corporate philanthropy has reshaped the focus to be more inclusive and impact a wide variety of stakeholders.

Innovative companies must reach outside their core business to create a better world. In 2007 Spartan Motors joined forces with the National Volunteer Fire Fighters Council (NVFC) to create the Junior Leadership Program. The goal was to target tomorrow's leaders (our children) and to see them become involved in community service. The result was that in 2015, over three thousand individuals were registered and over two thousand fire departments were involved.

An additional means of corporate philanthropy is having customers buy products, round up their purchase, or donate a flat amount to a cause. Many retailers will encourage customers to buy items and then donate to a cause selected by the retailer. An example may be a discount store that is donating to a local school system and encouraging the purchase of school supplies to support this cause. Some retailers ask if you would like to round up your purchase to the next dollar amount and then donate that to a charity. Another form of this is to place a jar on a counter and allow customers to place their change in the jar. Finally, certain corporations will sell themed donation cards in which they can place their name to be displayed in a retail location showing their generosity. These forms of philanthropy both benefit the cause supported and the retailer who can increase sales or image in the mind of the consumer.

As Leila Janah observes, "You can teach a man to fish, but if he's living in a desert, there's no point." To irrigate that desert, she's founded two social enterprises. One is Samasource, which provides digital work for clients such as TripAdvisor and Microsoft to low-income

---

12   "Giving in Numbers," CECP, http://cecp.co/home/resources/giving-in-numbers.

people in Kenya, Uganda, and India. The other is LXMI (pronounced "LUX-me"), a line of fair-trade skincare products made from a rare type of shea butter derived from the nuts of Ugandan nilotica trees. LXMI works through nonprofit collectives to ensure that the women who harvest the nuts earn a living wage that is at least three times the local norm. Profits are reinvested into the companies so that they can expand.

Corporate Social Responsibility (CSR)

Corporate social responsibility is a broad term that describes a company's ability to take an interest in society and the environment and being economically sound for the betterment of its stakeholders. Other terms used to describe CSR include the triple bottom-line approach and people, planet, and profits. Whatever term used, CSR is rooted in responsibility and preservation of our planet. To be more specific, *corporate social responsibility* is the initiatives that companies take to produce products that are not harmful to the environment and have minimal effect on society, while generating a profit to sustain their activity. Cone Communications indicated that nine out of ten consumers would be more likely to purchase products from companies with a CSR focus, thus giving these companies both an incentive to practice CSR and to increase profits.[13]

Why the need for greater corporate social responsibility? There is a greater need than ever before to be more CSR based on the recommendations of the International Institute for Sustainable Development reports including six issues that drive the need for greater CSR:

1. *Governments' reduced role in legislation and regulation.* This reduced role puts greater responsibility on companies to be more ethical and self-regulate their actions.
2. *Higher levels of transparency.* Companies now have great transparency in their disclosures of actions they are undertaking, adding pressure to behave as good corporate citizens.
3. *Higher levels of customer interest.* As described, consumers are willing to reward or punish companies based on the level of CSR.
4. *Greater pressure by investors.* Companies that are CSR focused are less risky to invest in than those that are not and have higher levels of profit.
5. *Matching employee interests by being responsible.* Job seekers have expressed a need to match their interests with the company they want to work for. Therefore, candidates who feel strongly about the environment and society are more apt to apply at a company with higher levels of CSR.
6. *Aligning with suppliers that practice CSR.* For companies to be responsible, all stakeholders must follow suit. Therefore, suppliers and other stakeholders must provide products that will be included in the finished product that supports the triple bottom line.

---

13   "Global Consumers Willing to Make Personal Sacrifices to Address Social and Environmental Issues," CONE, http://www.conecomm.com/news-blog/2015-cone-ebiquity-csr-study-press-release

While not required to follow these practices, companies are rewarded through consumer insistence for their products, greater loyalty, higher profits, committed workforce, and overall confidence that they are bettering the world and its citizens through their business practices.

THINK ABOUT THIS!

What benefits does CSR give companies? How does CSR affect employment? Does CSR influence where customers shop?

Here are some data points regarding CSR found by Cone Communications:

1. 62 percent of consumers would work for a socially or environmentally responsible company, even if their salary was less than other companies.
2. 80 percent said they would tell others about the company's CSR efforts.
3. 90 percent would boycott a company who did not participate in CSR.
4. 93 percent of global customers have a more positive image of companies practicing CSR than those that don't.
5. 84 percent said companies that engage in CSR practices influence where they shop.[14]

HOW CAN WE PROVIDE LEADERSHIP IN THE MARKET?

Leadership in a market is a wonderful position to be in, but it also has responsibilities. Ethical companies treat market leadership with a sense of fairness, as they could exploit the market to benefit themselves. In a supply chain, the dominate company is called a channel captain. A *channel captain* is the dominate member of a distribution channel that controls the flow of products due to its size (e.g., Walmart). While one would think that channel captains should take every advantage of their power, it is ethical that the channel captains share the resources and compete fairly in the market.

Forbes listed the top ten responsibilities of industry leaders that should be followed to be both fair and ethical in the market:[15]

1. **Are you an honest company?** Customers trust what companies claim to be true regarding their products. Therefore, the trust and positive word of mouth companies earn should not be wasted on making false claims about their products.

---

14   Ibid.

15   John Hall, "Is Your Company an Industry Leader?" *Forbes*, August 6, 2013, https://www.forbes.com/sites/johnhall/2013/08/06/10-factors-to-crown-you-an-industry-leader/#424279896088.

2. **Are you a trusted source of information?**—Customers trust the information given by companies, so it is important to give truthful information as this helps to build credibility with your stakeholders.

3. **Are your executives thought leaders?** Does top management of the company participate in the direction the industry should follow and put words into practice? Top management has a responsibility to shape the industry and guide future growth. It is their responsibility to lead the way for future innovation, which in turn will be followed by other companies.

4. **Do you have a meaningful relationship with your target market?** Top management has a good grasp of what their target market seeks in their products. They strive for a relationship with their core customers and constantly survey or seek their opinions on what they need. Continuous interaction builds both loyalty and keeps companies aware of changing trends in products. Therefore, the ability to monitor consumer wants, needs, and changing trends gives companies an advantage in the market.

5. **Are your key employees known experts?** Innovative companies seek experts in the area in which they are developing products. Experience on the part of key employees helps to work through the learning curve. The *learning curve* is the knowledge that is gained through experience while working at a task. Hiring experts helps to speed through the learning curve and to produce innovative products at a faster rate, thus increasing sales and profits.

6. **Are you recognized consistently with awards and placements in top industry lists?** Top management needs to know the motivators of each of their key personnel. Some are intrinsically motivated (i.e., motivated by things that motivate them internally such as a thank you, the happiness felt because of one's efforts, etc.), and others are motivated extrinsically (i.e., things that are external in natural such as awards, plagues, or any other visible signs of success).

7. **Do you have a reputation for treating people well?** Established companies have earned a reputation for the way they treat their employees. Companies should be fair and treat their employees well as this is used as a drawing for attracting the best employees. Innovation requires the best minds to be able to think outside of the box and come up with the newest techniques and ideas.

8. **Do you show up in the search results your target market is looking for?** The ability to relate to your target market is the new goal of marketing. Historically, consumer-to-consumer (C2C) was characterized as a transactional relationship. Now, companies strive to be more relationship oriented, which improves customer retention and builds loyalty; therefore, the ability to relate your products and advertising toward your targeted customers improves profits and success.

9. **What do people find when they're researching your company?** How well is your website designed? Does it show your company has achievements? Companies can

highlight their accomplishments to their stakeholders, showing how society accepts these efforts.

10. **Do you have a presence at major industry events?** As an image booster, does your company have a presence to solidify your market dominance? Market leaders need to be present at major events to highlight their accomplishments and to guide the industry toward the next area of innovation. The product categories you are doing business in rely on the market leader to guide the way. Therefore, market leadership or close to leadership gives the opportunity to set the rules for others to follow.

HOW DO WE GET AND STAY IN TOUCH WITH REALITY (OUR CUSTOMERS)?

Fast Company suggests seven ways to stay in touch with your customers to ensure future sales and increase sales. Companies need to not fall into the habit of forgetting who made them successful or losing their customer service focus. All too often, companies are built on a customer service focus but lose their innovativeness as business starts to thrive. Examples of this include Sears, Eastman Kodak, Blockbuster, and Yahoo. Companies need to realize that continuous innovation is a successful strategy for survival and profitability.

Fast Company suggests the following strategies for success:[16]

1. *Make it a habit*: Successful companies make it part of their everyday plan to communicate with their customers. This strategy allows for continuous communication and is useful as reminder advertisements. The one drawback is too-frequent communication results in ignoring the message or unsubscribing to the emails.

2. *Social media is your friend*: Social media allows targeted messages to be sent to your target market, thus making advertising more effective and reducing the cost of advertising. Most consumers are continuously on their devices, which increases the probability that the message sent out will be received. Therefore, social media is an important way to stay in contact with your customer base and communicate with them.

3. *Get a life*: There is a big advantage to networking and developing a group of contacts that provide ways to increase business and reach new clients. Networking is a key to successful business as it provides a trusted way to expand your client base. Networking also is a key element in relationship marketing, which makes adding new clients and gaining leads easier than trying to establish new customers, which is more expensive.

---

16   Laura Vanderkam, "7 Non-Sketchy Ways to Stay in Touch with Your Contacts," Fast Company, August 9, 2014, https://www.fastcompany.com/3034456/7-non-sketchy-ways-to-stay-in-touch-with-your-contacts.

4. *Know everyone's birthday*: Wishing your clients a happy birthday is an inexpensive way to promote relationship marketing. The only drawback is when it is sent as a matter of business and not sincerely. All too often, salespeople send a birthday greeting to clients with no idea who they are. When that client sees the salesperson and thanks them, they have no idea who they are, thus ruining the sincerity of the message. Therefore, if you are to follow this strategy, know the person you are sending the message to.

5. *Sign up for alerts*: Another means to build relationships is to stay abreast of notices about your network. Google, LinkedIn, Facebook, and so on notify contacts of important events in the lives of the people with whom they are connected. Take a moment to acknowledge the achievements and birthday of your contacts. This helps to nurture the relationship and to remind them you are still connected and in touch.

6. *Be helpful*: As a leader, it is important to be a person who makes connections, is resourceful, and makes business happen. The one who has been granted so much is one who is expected to provide so much. Therefore, help to make connections and facilitate business as others will see the benefit you bring to them.

7. *Look at the big picture*: Most leaders are caught in the now and not in the future. Business planning consists of tactical (short-term) plans and strategic (long-term) plans. Business strategy dictates that tactical plans support strategic plans to ensure the success of the company. All too often, businesses get too involved in competitive actions that focus on tactical plans and lose sight of their strategic plans. Leaders need to step in and keep the company looking forward toward the goal they have established and to see the big picture. Leadership of any company is responsible for their long-term vision and seeing all the options available is the beginning to success.

DO OUR INNOVATIONS MOVE THE WORLD IN THE RIGHT DIRECTION?

Once we have come up with an innovation we must determine if the innovation follows the mission and vision of the company. We must also ask if it adds value to society. While simple questions such as "Does the innovation benefit our bottom line?" seem obvious, they also ask if your company is doing its part to be a good corporate citizen. Companies often ask for the profit picture before the mission and vison question. What is important is that the innovation developed by our companies adds value to society and satisfies the needs of the target market. As indicated earlier, consumers value innovative companies that make a positive contribution to society and that better their lives. Consumers also develop brand loyalty for a product that has been in the product life cycle for an extended period, so it is imperative for consumers to try and use the products developed that have a positive impact on society and the stakeholders. Ethical companies will guide their business practices in the right direction, which will preserve the legitimacy of their innovations and help to dictate strategies for the future to ensure survival.

Review Questions

1. What are some other innovations that contributed to bettering our modern society not shown in table 8.1?
2. What are switching costs? Provide an example of how switching costs affected you.
3. Why is wealth creation important? What is your plan to create wealth?
4. What are positive side effects of innovative companies not discussed in this chapter?
5. Why is entrepreneurship important for economic growth? Provide examples.
6. How has innovation helped life expectancy? Give three examples not discussed in this chapter.
7. What is the difference between intrinsic and extrinsic quality? Which one is more important to you and why?
8. What are reverse distribution channels and how do you feel they are effective?
9. Why is geotracking beneficial to companies? Do you feel it infringes on your privacy?
10. What is the difference between philanthropy and corporate social responsibility? Provide three examples of each.

Discussion Questions

1. Why is satisfying consumer needs so important? Share some examples of ways companies satisfy your needs.
2. What are other areas of value not used in this chapter that add value to society?
3. Do you feel living to 130 years old is important? Why or why not?
4. What are surrogates that you use when making a purchase selection? Share three examples.
5. What are your three favorite apps? Why?
6. What are your favorite social media sites? Why?
7. Give examples of philanthropy in an area with which you are familiar. Share with others if it impacts your purchase behavior.
8. Who are some of the best leaders you have experienced? Why?
9. What drives you today and in the future?
10. Why is a "better world" important?
11. Who are companies you admire and why?

Integrative Learning Exercise

Students will be given time to discuss how and where a company's leadership lost touch with reality and why. They can share this with the class.

Extension Activity

1. How have innovations in the past build on the future innovations? Provide some examples to share.
2. What are future innovations, not listed in table 8.1, that you feel are sure to be developed and adopted?

BIBLIOGRAPHY

Allis, Ryan. "The 40 greatest innovations of all time." *Startup Guide.* December 11, 2018. https://startupguide.com/the-40-greatest-innovations-of-all-time.

Pappu, Ravi and Quester, Pascale G. "How Does Brand Innovativeness Affect Brand Loyalty?" *European Journal of Marketing* 50, no. 1/2 (2016): 2–28.

"World GDP Ranking 2018," Knoema, https://knoema.com/nwnfkne/world-gdp-ranking-2018-gdp-by-country-data-and-charts.

Sappin, Ed, "7 Ways Entrepreneurs Drive Economic Development," Entrepreneury, October 20, 2016, https://www.entrepreneur.com/article/283616.

Lowrey, Ying. "Estimating Entrepreneurial Jobs: Business Creation is Job Creation," 2011. American Economic Association Annual Meeting.

Cook, Amy Osmond. "6 Ways to Make Your Business More Efficient," Entrepreneur, October 31, 2017, https://www.entrepreneur.com/article/292833.

"Top 10 Medical Innovations for 2017 Revealed," Cleveland Clinic, https://consultqd.clevelandclinic.org/top-10-medical-innovations-2017-revealed/.

"Israeli 'Flying Ambulance Drone' Aims to Save Lives," EMS1, January 6, 2017, https://www.ems1.com/ambulances-emergency-vehicles/articles/158543048-Israeli-flying-ambulance-drone-aims-to-save-lives/

Ferguson, Keith. "An investigation of sustainable product purchase behavior: A social cognitive perspective of consumer action." (2014).

Bullas, Jeff. "10 Ways Social Media Technologies Are Adding Value and Productivity," https://www.jeffbullas.com/10-ways-social-media-technologies-are-adding-value-and-productivity/

"Giving in Numbers," CECP, http://cecp.co/home/resources/giving-in-numbers.

"The New Competitive Advantage: Giving in Numbers Brief 2016," CECP, http://cecp.co/wp-content/uploads/2016/11/2016_GIN_8x11_High_Res_FINAL.pdf?redirect=no.

"Global Consumers Willing to Make Personal Sacrifices to Address Social and Environmental Issues," CONE, http://www.conecomm.com/news-blog/2015-cone-ebiquity-csr-study-press-release

Hall, John, "Is Your Company an Industry Leader?" *Forbes*, August 6, 2013,https://www.forbes.com/sites/johnhall/2013/08/06/10-factors-to-crown-you-an-industry-leader/#424279896088.

Vanderkam, Laura, "7 Non-Sketchy Ways to Stay in Touch with Your Contacts," Fast Company, August 9, 2014, https://www.fastcompany.com/3034456/7-non-sketchy-ways-to-stay-in-touch-with-your-contacts.

Figure Credits

Fig. 8.1: Source: https://www.mckinsey.com/~/media/McKinsey/Industries/High%20Tech/Our%20Insights/The%20social%20economy/MGI_The_social_economy_Full_report.ashx.

Thinking through the Details before Launch

CHAPTER NINE

What Do "Intuitive-Wise" and "Data-Informed" Mean?

INTRODUCTION

Innovation requires companies have leaders who can use their intuition (experience), available data, and input from cross-functional teams to make sound decisions. There are countless examples of leaders who have only used one of these three factors and that lead to failure. This chapter discusses why intuition is important but at times it is flawed. It also discusses how to collect data from several sources and why this data is important. In addition, the chapter speaks of ways to analyze data using statistical and non-statistical techniques. Finally, we conclude with what to do with both data and intuition when making decisions to give companies an advantage.

Learning Objectives

In this chapter students will learn about the following:

- The importance of intuition
- Why managers need to trust their intuition, but also their experience and knowledge to make sound business decisions
- The importance of why good managers must be data-informed and not just data-driven
- Why data is collected from both internal and external sources to help make decisions
- Methods we can use to analyze collected data to make sound decisions
- Why companies must use their intuition, data, and cross-functional teams together to reduce bias
- Ways to capitalize on our decisions using intuition, data, and input from cross-functional teams
- The pros and cons of gap analysis

Learning Outcomes

By the end of this chapter students will be able to do the following:

- Explain why using intuition alone is not good for managers to make decisions
- Understand why data is an important part of decision making, but it must be used to inform not drive the decision
- Know the purpose of cross-functional teams to provide the internal expertise needed for decision making based on the knowledge of all parts of the organization
- Understand how companies analyze their decisions based on several factors including increased profits, market share, customer satisfaction and loyalty, needed product portfolio additions, and benefits to stakeholders
- Explain the various biases that exist in decision making

Key Terms

Intuition: The ability to perceive things without the use of rationale thought that are or easy to understand without explicit instructions, or "knowing without knowing"

Data-driven: Uses available data to solely drive the decisions for new product development and neglects the human decision-making element

Data-informed: Uses available data to help make decisions but does not solely rely on its predictions to drive the final decision

Gap analysis: A method companies use to determine their status in the market based against their competition and then find where gaps are located to concentrate their innovative efforts in these gaps

Gap map or perceptual map: A visual way for companies to see where their company or products are placed in the market using two parameters

Management information system: A system used to make decisions by management utilizing a collection of technology, people, and processes that gather, store, and produce information

Data mining: Using big data to discover relationships, patterns, trends, and unexpected usage of products by companies

Census data: The collection of information regarding a population and the economy

Market intelligence or *market research*: Information gathered from the firm's external environment and used to make strategy decisions

Business intelligence: Information gathered from a firm based on internal functions

Social media scanning: The act of utilizing tools to listen to what customers are saying about a company, product, or service on social media

Trend: A tendency, style, or general direction followed by society

Multiple regression: Statistical technique that allows several independent variables to be compared to a single dependent variable

Partial least squares–structural equation model (PLS-SEM): Like multiple regression, but it allows the researcher to test multiple constructs of the dependent variable

Psychological bias: The act of making decisions in a manner that is illogical

Confirmation bias: Dictates that people seek information that supports their opinions and beliefs and ignore facts that refute these opinions and beliefs

Anchoring bias: Occurs when people hear a fact about a phenomenon believed to be the absolute truth

Overconfidence bias: Happens when people who have been successful feel overconfident in their abilities, thus causing them to take greater risks because they feel their decisions will be successful

Outcome bias: Results when only the outcome is quantified for success and not the process on how the decision was made

Adoption rate: The rate at which technology is accepted and adopted by consumers over time

Customer lifetime value: The amount of revenue that loyal customers will provide a business

WHAT IS INTUITIVE-WISE?

The ability to "trust your gut" or make decisions based on intuition either ends with the greatest achievement or sheer defeat. From a young age, we dream of being the hero. How many of you remember playing basketball and counting down the clock in your head to take the final shot? You would win the game or lose it in your mind. Many times, coaches devise a plan for these clutch situations focusing on getting the ball to the best shooter for the final attempt for glory. Sometimes it works and a hero is born, and other times it ends in a loss. This analogy may seem trivial, but it's one that most of us may have experienced and one that is experienced in innovation. Top managers must learn to use their intuition to develop new products that will satisfy customers' needs while using data to support their decision (we will touch on that next).

While it may seem obvious, you may be asking yourself, "What is intuition or being intuitive?" *Intuition* is the ability to perceive things without the use of rationale thought or that are easy to understand without explicit instructions. Intuition is simply knowing without knowing. So why is intuition so important in the world of business and innovation? Due to the global marketplace, the pace of business moves faster than ever before. One of the key points of this book is to stress the ability to get to market fast or make decisions quickly, as speed matters. This ability relies on one's intuition and the ability to be right when faced with limited time to make decisions. Without that ability, companies will be left behind wondering what happened to their ability to compete due to their inability to decide what is best for the firm.

THINK ABOUT THIS!

A study conducted by UCLA in 2014 found that we are exposed to enough data to fill 174 newspapers daily. This amount of information is five times the amount we received twenty years ago and the ability to use it to gain an advantage for our business is important for success.[1]

---

1   Simone Wright, "The 7 Attributes of Intutitive Business Leaders," *Huff Post*, November 17, 2014, https://www.huffpost.com/entry/business-intuition-what-d_b_5833396.

What are some of the key attributes possessed by intuitive leaders that can drive business and capitalize on trends and information available in the market using their experience to make good decisions? The following are seven attributes of intuitive business leaders:[2]

1. *Inter-vision guides their actions*: Leaders are not motivated by external goals but by satisfying the mission of the business in ways not realized by others.
2. *Intuitive leaders are trend setters, not followers*: They are not the type of leader to follow a routine or just rely on past practice. Intuitive leaders are innovative and transformative and create new processes and products they feel will satisfy the needs of their customers and better society.
3. *They don't dwell on past practices that are no longer feasible*: Just because a process or practice worked in the past doesn't stop intuitive leaders from abandoning outdated methods for new and improved ones.
4. *Intuitive leaders are team players and share the spotlight with their team*: Intuitive leaders know that they must create trust and connectiveness among the group to bring out the best innovation and to allow everyone to receive credit for their efforts.
5. *They can be described as mavericks, rogues, or rebels*: They thrive on being told "it can't be done" or "it's impossible" because their intuition allows them to think in ways not performed by others to solve the problems.
6. *They ask evolved questions*: Evolved questions are "how" questions that help evolve into solutions. Intuitive leaders know the questions to ask to get to the solution.
7. *Intuitive leaders do not think linearly, but in multiple directions*: Very rarely in business does planning take a linear direction. Intuitive leaders can think about situations and select courses of action that are in multiple directions to reach a viable solution.

Intuitive leaders are unique and have a gift to think on different planes, see situations in different lights, and help transform organizations. It is a trait usually found at the strategic management level in many successful organizations.

Next, we will discuss the need to back up intuition with data, but the starting point of innovation is having the intuition to recognize ways to successfully build your business's product portfolio and listen to your customers.

WHAT IS DATA-INFORMED VERSUS DATA-DRIVEN?

There is a misconception in the business world that data-informed and data-driven are the same concept. The difference is huge as **data-driven** uses available data to solely drive the decisions for new product development and neglects the human decision-making element. **Data-informed** uses available data to help make decisions but does not solely rely on its

---

2   Ibid.

predictions to drive the final decision. Data-informed recognizes the need for the human element to take into consideration all the factors that will ensure success of the contemplated decision. Data-informed uses experience, knowledge, and information to decide the best course of action. An example of this is auto-pilot on an airplane. Auto-pilot is helpful when flying, but with our current technology, taxiing a plane for takeoff and landing is better suited for a human to drive the decisions. There are many documented cases of an airplane's auto-pilot (data-driven) resulting in crashes, when ultimately humans should have driven the decisions, thereby making adjustments as new information presented itself. The same scenario should be followed in business. Companies use the data to drive the decisions and not rely strictly on data to make the final decision. Therefore, companies use data to be quick in the market, responsive to customer needs, continually improve their processes, and react to a rapidly changing business environment.

WHAT KIND OF INFORMATION CAN BE USED TO BE INFORMED?

Companies have a wide variety of information at their disposal that they can use to make decisions. We will concentrate on several types, but this list is not conclusive. Information companies' need varies by type of industry and niche. For example, retail stores would use consumer purchase information while a machine fabricator would use trade information. Whatever the industry, information and data are a vital part of decision making, and they drive innovation.

Before we focus on ways to collect information, we should first ask ourselves why are we collecting data. Innovators must first determine where the opportunities are in the market and how can they satisfy the needs of their customers now and in the future. These questions are easily answered if there is a need to innovate and a place for it in the market. One of the ways innovators can determine areas to focus their efforts on is to perform a gap analysis. A *gap analysis* is method companies use to determine their status in the market based on their competition and then find where the gaps are to concentrate their innovative efforts. A way to see where the gaps are located is to construct a gap map to determine where the opportunities lie. A *gap map or perceptual map* is a visual way for companies to see where their company or products are positioned in the market using two parameters, price and quality.

A visual map diagram is key as people remember 50 percent of what they see and hear.[3] Plus, visuals are processed 60,000 times faster than text.[4] Never forget, speed matters and you

3 "Do People Remember 10% of What They Read, 20% of What They See, 30% of What They Hear ... ?" Quora, https://www.quora.com/Do-people-remember-10-of-what-they-read-20-of-what-they-see-30-of-what-they-hear.

4 Rachel Gillet, "Why We're More Likely to Remember Content with Images and Video," Fast Company, September 18, 2014, https://www.fastcompany.com/3035856/why-were-more-likely-

are being paid to be right. As Paul Martin Lester, professor of communications at California State University Fullerton, stated, "We are becoming a visually mediated society. For many, understanding of the world is being accomplished not through words, but by reading images."[5]

HOW TO COLLECT INFORMATION

We will focus on several sources of information companies can use to make decisions. These include management information systems, big data, census data, market and business intelligence, vendor information, purchase data, trade data, and trends.

Management Information Systems (MIS)

MIS is not just one thing, but a collection of hardware, software, people, and systems used to produce information and data. More specifically, a **management information system** is a system used to make decisions by management utilizing a collection of technology, people, and processes that gather, store, and produce information. MIS adds efficiency to all levels of an organization by having a central point of accessing information needed to make decisions.

MIS is a generic term to describe how information is gathered, stored, packaged, and then dispersed throughout a company, the decision structure and the information systems used by various layers of management.[6] Based on the level of management, there are several systems used to gather information, as well as different structures used to interpret this information. The strategic level of management is unstructured as they try to devise strategies using raw data. The tactical level refines the work of the strategic level, and the operational level is very structured because the strategies are refined as the planning moves down through the organization.

The type of information system that a user uses depends on his or her level in an organization. The following diagram shows the three major levels of users in an organization and the type of information system that they use.

Decision Support Systems (DSS)

Top-level managers use decision support systems to make semi-structured decisions. The output from the management information system is used as input to the decision support system. DSS systems also get data input from external sources such as current market forces, competition, and so on.

---

to-remember-content-with-images-and-video-infogr.

5   "The Power of Visual Communication," https://policyviz.com/wp-content/uploads/2015/10/power-of-visual-communication.pdf.

6   "What Is MIS?" Guru 99, https://www.guru99.com/mis-definition.html.

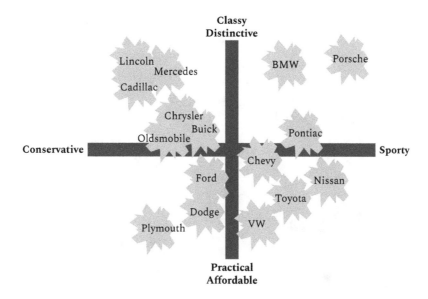

FIG 9.1 Perceptual map

Transaction Processing Systems (TPS)

Transaction processing systems function to monitor the daily business transactions of a firm. This information provides firms with valuable insights as to how they are doing and assists in making decisions that can help improve operations. Without daily monitoring of a firm's function, its performance will suffer as short- and long-term issues arise and must be addressed. Constant monitoring is key to maximize profits and to combat competitive threats.[7] This type of information system is used to record the day-to-day transactions of a business. An example of a transaction processing system is a point-of-sale (POS) system. A POS system is used to record the daily sales

Big Data

Companies gather data to try to determine trends, target and potential customers, popular items, demographical and geographical information, and so on. This information comes from purchases, social media, digital processes, and interaction. The only entity besides the federal government that stores more big data is Walmart. Walmart processes 2.5 petabytes of data per hour. So, what do they do with all this information? Forbes reported that Walmart uses this information to solve complex business problems, because what used to take weeks or days can now be resolved in minutes.[8]

---

7   Ibid.

8   Bernard Marr, "Really Big Data at Walmart: Real-Time Insights from their 40-Petabyte Data Cloud, *Forbes,* January 23, 2017, https://www.forbes.com/sites/bernardmarr/2017/01/23/really-big-data-at-walmart-real-time-insights-from-their-40-petabyte-data-cloud/#62bfb6a96c10.

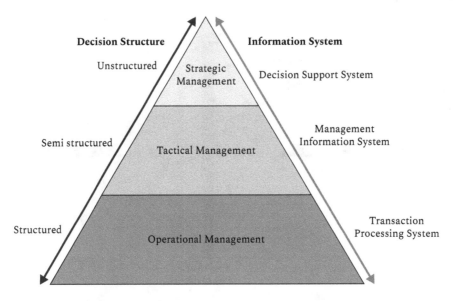

Decision Structure   **Information System**

Unstructured — Strategic Management — Decision Support System

Semi structured — Tactical Management — Management Information System

Structured — Operational Management — Transaction Processing System

FIG 9.2 **Decision structure and information system**

What does big data do for the companies that use it? There are many advantages of monitoring the data companies have available to them including gaining a competitive advantage by discovering which items sell the best, monitoring competitor's pricing, and knowing which items to feature in advertisements or put on sale in the store. Other advantages include tracking demographic shifts, gaining a better understanding of who the target customer is, and using historical data to predict future sales.

While the term *big data* is relatively new, the act of gathering and storing large amounts of information for eventual analysis is ages old. The concept gained momentum in the early 2000s when industry analyst Doug Laney articulated the now-mainstream definition of big data as the three V's (volume, velocity, and variety) and two additional dimensons.[9]

Volume

Organizations collect data from a variety of sources, including business transactions and social media, and they collect information from sensor or machine-to-machine data. In the past, storing it would've been a problem, but new technologies (such as Hadoop) have eased the burden.

Velocity

Data streams at an unprecedented speed and must be dealt with in a timely manner. RFID tags, sensors, and smart metering are driving the need to deal with torrents of data in near real time.

---

9   "Big Data," SAS, https://www.sas.com/en_us/insights/big-data/what-is-big-data.html.

Variety

Data comes in all types of formats, from structured, numeric data in traditional databases to unstructured text documents, email, video, audio, stock ticker data, and financial transactions.

SAS added two more to this collection, variability and complexity, as they felt they more realistically define the nature of big data today.

Variability

In addition to the increasing velocities and varieties of data, data flows can be highly inconsistent with periodic peaks. Is something trending on social media? Daily, seasonal, and event-triggered peak data loads can be challenging to manage, even more so with unstructured data.

Complexity

Today's data comes from multiple sources, which makes it difficult to link, match, cleanse, and transform data across systems. However, it's necessary to connect and correlate relationships, hierarchies, and multiple data linkages or your data can quickly spiral out of control.

Together, these dimensions of big data help transform the use of big data to gain a competitive advantage in the market by discovering trends before the competition. They also help to support the GT-MAP by providing a way to discover consumer needs and trends, thus getting to market with speed to capitalize on this information.

One area of big data usage that is very popular is data mining. **Data mining** is using big data to discover relationships, patterns, trends, and unexpected usage of products by both consumers and companies. Many companies have a plethora of data available but do little with this information. Data mining allows the company or outside firm the ability to use this information for the betterment of the firm. A result of data mining is innovation that is finding new ways to satisfy consumers' needs by using information. Data mining allows companies to find the unexpected in the data collected. Determining trends, usage, and relationships gives the firm an opportunity to develop new and innovative products that will add longevity and maximize profits.

Census Data

One data source that is sometimes overlooked is census data. **Census data** is the collection of information regarding a population and the economy. In the US it is collected every ten years and describes population characteristics, population shifts, demographic information, housing conditions, and social characteristics. Companies can use census data to determine where their target market lives or is moving to; population numbers and income levels are used for retail expansion; age can be used to determine the need for nursing homes or daycares; and, finally, population, education levels, and income can be used to locate factories or office spaces. No matter what the case for using census data, certain groups fall into categories that can be used to determine products, locations, and services to offer the population. One final note is that census data is free of charge and advantageous for smaller firms with limited resources needing to make decisions quickly.

Market Intelligence

Companies need intelligence to make business decisions that reflect the current events impacting their environment. When we speak of intelligence we are referring to two types: market and business. *Market intelligence* or *market research* is information gathered from the firm's external environment that is used to make strategy decisions. Forms of market intelligence include the following:

1. Surveys
2. Phone interviews
3. Focus groups
4. Observation or ethnographic research

Surveys

Once a problem is identified and clearly defined, companies can develop a survey to be administered to customers. Surveys are typically given online, but they may also be mailed to consumers to gather their opinions and attitudes. Survey questions can either be Likert type (e.g., 1–5), true/false, fill in the blank, slider bars (e.g., 0–100), rankings (e.g., 1–5), or faces that describe how the respondent is feeling. Surveys should be pretested to eliminate poor or confusing wording before the survey is administered and to cut down on expense and time lost. Sometimes to improve response rates, an incentive is offered to respondents such as a chance to win a prize, cash for taking the survey, or some other offer.

Advantages of surveys include saving time, reaching many respondents, and the ability to download information collected quickly. Disadvantages include cost, high drop-out rate, and the inability to ask respondents to elaborate on their answers. While surveys present both advantages and disadvantages, it is one of the most popular ways to gather information for analysis to make decisions.

Phone Interviews

While not as effective as surveys, phone interviews are another form of gathering data. Respondents are reached via the telephone and asked their opinions about the topic being studied using a rehearsed script. Phone interviews give the ability to ask respondents to elaborate on their answers, providing the researcher with richer answers to find the opportunities or solve problems. Phone interviews do have drawbacks, which include time and expense, decreased number of people with landlines, caller ID, and the inability to reach the targeted respondent.

Focus Groups

A focus group is a group of people invited to participate in a conversation with a facilitator by a company for compensation. These groups are usually videotaped and recorded for playback by the researchers. A facilitator asks the group their opinions, and like a phone interview, they can then probe deeper into the responses to gain valuable insights. This technique is excellent for discovering in-depth details about products, usage, competitors, and ways to improve the products a company offers.

Observation or Ethnographic Research

Although difficult, observing customers interacting with a product and then getting their opinions is a great way to find gaps that can be used for innovation. Observation typically is anonymous so that researchers can see how consumers act when they feel free of being observed. Products could be the company's own products, the competition's, or both. Observation provides new insights and uses for products that companies can use to improve or innovate from.

HOW DO YOU TAKE THIS FROM THEORY TO PRACTICE?

German company Miele observed families whose members were suffering from severe allergies. The observation was of them constantly cleaning their homes to reduce the effects of the allergic reactions.[10] This observation helped them develop a vacuum that has a light indicating when the area being vacuumed is dust free. This simple adaption would have only been discovered by observing German families and asking their motives for constantly cleaning.

Business Intelligence

Business intelligence is information gathered from a firm based on internal functions. Examples include gathering sales, fill rates for orders placed, percentage of orders shipped, receivables, and so on that allow the firm to determine how they are doing in business based on their internal actions. Business intelligence is used to accelerate business decisions, improve internal processes, increase efficiency, and identify trends and trouble areas on which to improve.[11]

Another form of intelligence often overlooked is information gathered from territory salespeople. Salespeople are the eyes and ears of developments in the marketplace. Friendships they

---

10   Kurt Soller, "It Seemed Insane to Spend $400 on a Vacuum, but Now I Like Cleaning," *The Strategist*, January 25, 2017, http://nymag.com/strategist/2017/01/best-vacuum-german-make-miele-complete-c2-review.html.

11   Margaret Rouse, "Business Intelligence," Search Business Analytics, https://searchbusinessanalytics.techtarget.com/definition/business-intelligence-BI

have with purchasing representatives or other key people often reveal important competitive activities that can help the company prepare for new products, programs, or other changes.

Why does this happen? The answer is simple: Sales people are not in the home office, thus they are working to connect, collaborate, and garner the right inputs.

Together, market and business intelligence provide a big picture view of the opportunities and troubles that face companies. The use of this information can provide strategies to help companies to innovate by seeing what is truly happening in the internal and external environments in which they do business.

Social Media Scanning

The advent of electronic marketing has opened the door for many companies to discover ways to produce innovated products based on consumers' use of social media. Consumers post their comments on social media regarding brands, likes and dislikes, product performance, and customer service satisfaction; they express their true feelings. Social media sites allow firms to follow them and utilize advertisement that is targeted directly toward these targeted consumers, thus reducing the expense of using mass advertising. *Social media scanning* is the act of utilizing tools to listen to what customers are saying about a company, product, or service.

How is social media scanning performed to monitor what is being said online? There is software available to monitor URLs, hashtags, keywords, and companies, organizations, and products. This software helps companies see what is being said about their products and their competitors. Social media scanning is so important that many firms have internal analysts who monitor the web to address customer issues and communicate with potential customers. Some of the software available to monitor the web include Keyhole, Addict-o-matic, Brandwatch, and Buzzsumo.[12]

Other Ways to Gather Information

In addition to social media scanning, there are other ways to gather information to help innovators make good choices and exploit opportunities. These include collecting vendor information, reviewing information from trade associations, and finding trends happening locally, regionally, or globally.

Vendor Information

Vendors will gather information about their industry to make decisions and develop strategies. This information can be very helpful to companies within the sales area serviced by the vendors, especially for smaller firms that don't have the resources to collect or use the data they collect. Vendors look for current trends, such as which products are selling the best; a ranking of the companies in that territory; and other key information that can be used to find ways to increase sales and profits and develop strategies to compete. Vendor information

---

12   "The Top 25 Social Media Marketing Tools," Keyhole, http://keyhole.co/blog/the-top-25-social-media-monitoring-tools/.

can be considered a partnership between vendors and the companies they work with. Vendors use this information to improve their business and their partners so all involved can be more successful.

Trade Association

A trade association is an association formed on behalf of businesses that operate in a specific type of industry to promote the industry, gather data, and represent the best interests of all the participants. Data collected by trade associations can be very helpful to the companies within that trade to guide their strategies and to find shortcomings in the industry to develop new products or solutions.

Trends

We have all been exposed to trends in our lives. Fashion, music, dances, and others influence society and our lives. A *trend* is a tendency, style, or general direction followed by society. The ability of businesses to recognize trends gives them a competitive advantage in the market by allowing them to develop innovative products to meet the needs of trends in society.

WHAT KINDS OF ANALYSES OR TECHNIQUES CAN BE PERFORMED TO DISCOVER ADVANTAGES?

We have revealed ways to determine opportunities (gaps), use your intuition, and collect information to help discover ways to improve innovation processes. The question now is, "What do we do with the information gathered to make sound decisions?" There are several statistical methods that can be used, plus other brainstorming techniques to find ways to identify opportunities and get to market faster than our competition. The following are some of those methods and techniques to help the reader make sound innovation decisions.

Multiple regression is a statistical technique that allows innovators to see the relationship between several independent variables and the influence they have in predicting a phenomenon using a single dependent variable. Multiple regression gets its data from surveys (i.e., interval or ratio scales) administered on a sample of the target market. This information is initially run using exploratory factor analysis to eliminate multiple cross-loadings and then analyzed to reveal relationships affecting the feasibility of innovating products. Based on the level of variance explained (R^2), companies can compare independent variables to see which ones have the highest variance and thus provide the greatest predictability. This information can be used in new product development to determine which attribute(s) consumers see to predict purchase behavior and innovation success.

Partial Least Squares-Structural Equation Modeling (PLS-SEM)

A more advanced method of analyzing data is using the partial least squares-structural equation model (PLS-SEM). *PLS-SEM* is like multiple regression, but it allows the researcher to test multiple constructs of the dependent variable. This is not possible with multiple regression. For example, if a company is trying to determine constructs that influence purchase behavior of ice cream (dependent variable), a researcher could indicate outside temperature, flavor, serving size, and price, for example. If multiple regression was used, the dependent variable would state likelihood to purchase ice cream and nothing else. Therefore, PLS-SEM is an advanced statistical method used to discover many factors that influence the dependent variable, which gives companies an advantage of incorporating these important variables in their innovation.

Analyzing Survey Data

Another method of determining what attributes are perceived as the most important to consumers is using the results from your survey (i.e., comparing means). Questions are evaluated by comparing the highest Likert scores to determine which factors shape consumer preferences. The Likert scores per question are tabulated and then the averages (means) are compared to see which questions scored the highest. For example, if chewing gum was rated using a five-point Likert scale on such things as flavor types, duration of flavor, cost, texture, and freshness of breath, the company could compare the means to see which factors influence purchasing the chewing gum. Other ways to evaluate survey data include the following.

Brainstorming

It is not statistically motivated, but brainstorming among a diverse group can take information and yield some great ideas for innovation. There is a specific reason the word *diverse* is used to describe brainstorming. Without a diverse group of individuals, groups would think in a similar manner and stifle innovation. Diversity brings out a variety of different ideas and thoughts used in making a product better and more responsive to the marketplace. Another area that needs to be addressed for brainstorming is a group comprised of all functional areas of the company to be more efficient and upfront with problems. A functional group will be better able to strategize and know what is required to provide the best course of action for innovation based on their individual area of expertise.

Data used to make these decisions can come from surveys, focus groups, phone interviews, and so on, the results can be presented to the group, and then a brainstorming session can take place to reveal new ideas to capitalize on. The following are some techniques to use for brainstorming to achieve the maximum level of innovation:[13] (https://www.wrike.com/blog/techniques-effective-brainstorming/).

1. *Brainwriting*: Team leader shares the topic with the group and the members write down their ideas individually without discussing their responses with their group members. These ideas are then shared with the group, or the team leader reads the responses either identifying who wrote them or anonymously. Identifying who wrote

---

13   Brianna Hansen. "7 Techniques for More Effective Brainstorming." May 16, 2018. https://www.wrike.com/blog/techniques-effective-brainstorming/

the idea works well for groups that have worked together for some time and can help stimulate further discussion. If the group is new, being anonymous may be beneficial as new members will be reserved in their responses.

2. *Online brainstorming*: Virtual teams use a central website to propose a question, and the teams share their ideas. This technique is fast and eliminates bias that can occur from shy group members not answering the way they feel due to group pressure. It also eliminates bias from cues such as body language and vocal tone. Most people are online, so this technique is instant, requires little time to participate, and can include a large group for more idea generation.

3. *Rapid ideation*: This technique limits the time a group or individual has to create ideas. The reason this technique is so effective is it eliminates overthinking or filtering of ideas based on other responses. The group is given a deadline and has a short amount of time to complete the exercise. Ideas are then filtered and discussed to see which are feasible for pursuing.

4. *Round robin brainstorming*: The group sits in a circle and a facilitator presents a topic or question. The group is given a few moments to think about the topic or question and then the facilitator goes around the circle individually to hear responses and ask further questions.

5. *Stepladder technique*: This technique focuses on eliminating groupthink, which occurs when individuals answer in a similar manner due to the worry of offending group members, lack of diversity, or laziness. The stepladder technique has a facilitator who shares the topic or question with the assembled group. The facilitator then excuses the group, except for two members. The two members and the facilitator discuss the topic or question in detail. Once this is over, another member is added to the room who shares his or her idea. The discussion is further explored by the group and then the process is repeated until the group is all assembled again and everyone's answers have been discussed.

Another simple yet effective method is the five golden rules for innovation teams:[14]

1. **Provide a proven framework** for the innovation team and allow them to work together: Avoid allowing the "maverick" or management to try to do everything themselves. As pointed out earlier, diverse teams strengthen the innovation process and provide new ideas for the firm to take advantage of for success.

2. **Have empathy from a customer's perspective**, not just focusing on technology: Firms need to think what the customer wants, feels, and thinks when it comes to innovation. Too many firms concentrate on technology-driven innovation, ignoring the one

---

14   Gavin Jones, "5 Golden Rules for Innovation Teams," *Medium*, January 31, 2018, https://medium.com/room-y/5-golden-rules-for-innovation-teams-3514ce3a54b4.

person who is most important, your customer, and discovering what their needs and wants are.

3. **Run the innovation process like an experiment**: Monitor, measure, and evolve. This will be discussed later in the text, but firms need to have an idea of what they are trying to create in their innovation. Do they have an idea of what to monitor and measure to determine if they are achieving their goals? Can the innovation continue to evolve into a feasible product, or should the firm cut their losses and move on?

4. **Don't throw good money after bad**. Innovation costs are typically sunk, meaning they are usually not recoverable, so if the innovation will not evolve, cut your losses and go to the next idea without wasting the firm's financial resources.

5. **Do something incredible**. Innovations teams need to maximize their time together and do something that makes a big difference. Innovation teams should not always seek to create a new-to-the-world product, but they should do something that contributes to the firm and society in a positive way.

The statistical and ideation ideas shared will be useful depending on your level of skill, understanding, and experience. These techniques give innovation teams and firms an idea that they must use the data and talent they have within their company to be successful. Innovating blindly is not a very successful method. Therefore, firms need to use everything they have in their grasp to strive to be successful.

HOW DO YOU TAKE THIS FROM THEORY TO PRACTICE?

How does Spartan Motors or C2C brainstorm? What are additional ways to generate ideas for innovation? Thoughts from John Sztykiel.

During my time at Spartan and at C2C, I reflected on the stakeholders as often as possible. I tried to involve customers, dealers, suppliers, media, and influencers on the major decisions and problems we had to solve. Probably the most successful method for me personally was to ask our consumers one to three questions.

1. With the product(s) you're using, what can be improved? This was sort of simple: Make the lousy jobs have a less lousy approach.
2. In any industry, what is the bottleneck that is the most difficult to overcome? Our task was to then find a solution. At Spartan Motors, managing inventory while delivering custom products was the issue. In the specialty vehicle business, inventory management is the biggest issue as 50 to 75 percent of every dollar was spent on bills of materials.

C2C and one of the companies they partner with is No Lines (custom active wear). The business model is focused on "no inventory," as inventory is the biggest issue in fashion retail due to holding costs.

In 2017, 26 major retailers in the US went through some form of bankruptcy/restructuring, amounting to $50 million of liabilities. As of February of 2018, three major retailers filed for Chapter 11, amounting to $3 billion of lost sales.[15]

Based on lesson learned from these failed retailers, the formula at C2C is simple:

Start small and focus on the most critical/difficult issue.

Disrupt in a positive way.

Leverage growth from the point of disruption and continue to innovate

Innovation is as easy as breathing air if you do the following:

Have an open mind.

Listen to your stakeholders.

Look at data to make intuitive decisions.

Make the lousy jobs less lousy, that is continuously improve.

Solve the most difficult logistic hurdle first to perfect your processes.

Stay centered on people; humans are the ones who buy your products.

HOW DO INTUITIVE-WISE AND DATA-INFORMED FIT TOGETHER?

Thus far we have identified how intuition is helpful by using our experiences to make decisions and how to use ideation using that information to be sure firms are making the right choices. Therefore, the need to gather information is important to challenge one's intuition. Finally, we discussed methods that can be used to make better sense of the information gathered. This next section discusses the importance of linking intuition and data to make decisions.

Intuition and data-informed should be thought of as complimenting each other. In other words, one should not use just intuition without data, and vice versa. The reason for this statement is that sometimes our intuition is based only on experience, but our data may not be credible. This creates a problem trying to make good business decisions. Too many organizations waste lots of money because one person had this one great idea (i.e., "one-person theory") that was conceived not using data or other information but simply thinking his or her thought would be great and the firm should develop it. The reverse is true when a new manager has little experience to make decisions (little intuition), so he or she must rely more on data to reach a decision, losing the human element. In any organization there are many psychological

---

15   Ben Unglesbee, "The Running List of 2018 Retail Bankruptcies," Retail Dive, November 21, 2018, https://www.retaildive.com/news/the-running-list-of-2018-retail-bankruptcies/516864/.

biases that interfere with logical decision making including confirmation, anchoring, over-confidence, and outcome biases.[16]

Biases

Humans have many biases that affect their ability to make sound business decisions. While it seems foolish that we as humans cannot make a logical decision, certain psychological biases exist that hamper this process. *Psychological bias* is the act of making decision in a manner that is illogical. These same biases also affect the ability to use our intuition effectively, thus relying on data to substantiate our decisions. While there are many biases that affect decision making, we will focus on ones that pertain to business decisions.

Confirmation Bias

Confirmation bias dictates that people seek information that supports their opinions and beliefs and ignore facts that refute these opinions and beliefs. An example of confirmation bias is while there are scientific facts that carbon build up in atmosphere and rising temperatures over the past one hundred years points to global warming, people ignore this as a cyclical occurrence. Business leaders need to be objective in the information they seek to make decisions and not ignore the true facts, even if they contradict their own personal beliefs.

Anchoring Bias

Anchoring bias occurs when people hear a fact about a phenomenon that they believe to be the absolute truth. An example of this is once an idea goes through the initial innovation process and an estimated sale per unit number is established, any reduction to this number is refuted and the original estimate is believed to be inaccurate.

THINK ABOUT THIS: PROFESSOR FERGUSON

One of the businesses I had in my career was a construction company. I would meet with potential clients to discuss a job and quite often they would ask me at the end of our conversation what I thought the project would cost. Early on, I would say I hate to quote prices since I have not gotten bids and have not been able to put together a final price. Customers, out of excitement and/or curiosity, would ask for a rough estimate, which they would not "hold me to." Thinking it was safe to quote off the top of my head since they would not "hold me to" that number, I would give them an idea of what I thought the job would cost. When I returned the final bid, and if it was higher than my guesstimate, they would say to me "I thought you said the job would cost X?" What the customer did was use my guesstimate as an anchor for the job and any price higher had a negative connotation. After doing this a couple of times, I refused to quote prices and would

16   Shana Lebowitz and Samantha Lee, "Cognitive Biases That Affect Decisions," *Business Insider*, August 26, 2015, http://www.businessinsider.com/cognitive-biases-that-affect-decisions-2015-8.

ask them to be patient as I got a final number for them. This helped to stop the anchoring bias and increase my sales.

Overconfidence Bias

Overconfidence bias happens when people who have been successful feel overconfident in their abilities, thus causing them to take greater risks because they feel their decisions will always be successful. An example of overconfidence bias is CEO Carly Fiorina's success at Lucent Technologies, which spelled disaster for Hewlett-Packard when she became CEO, taking the tech giant down to almost bankruptcy. While leaders tend to have a "cookbook" formula (relying past practices to predict future success), every company and situation is unique, so leaders must approach any innovation with a clear understanding of what is at stake and not rely on past experiences to predict future success.

Outcome Bias

Outcome bias results when only the outcome is quantified for success and not the process on how the decision was made. An example is a blackjack player winning the night before from a certain dealer and who seeks that same dealer, feeling the outcome will be the same on a new night. His or her success may ignore certain criteria such as where they sat at the table, the spot in the two decks dealt when they won, and pure luck.

While there are several other biases that affect decision making, it is important to realize that intuition is important, but the human element does not make it a foolproof system for making decisions. Business leaders need intuition and data to make valid decisions to rule out bias and produce innovative ideas that make the company successful and secure longevity.

On final comment when using intuition and data together is that the opinions of cross-functional teams within the company are vital. Decisions may be the result of the intuition of the executive leaders and the additional input of data, but feedback from the cross-functional team (team made up of all areas of the organization) to analyze the decisions and give their input on the idea's feasibility is crucial. Cross-functional teams understand the opportunities and limitations of their areas of expertise and can therefore assist in how feasible an idea will be to pursue. Leaders have a good knowledge of running a company but may not understand how accounting and finance are important in deciding the method to write off new equipment or know the most advantageous way to finance new machinery. Therefore, having input from cross-functional areas can help aid in the success of the company and should be sought out when carrying out plans to develop new products.

WHAT TO DO WITH ALL THIS INTUITION AND DATA?

When we have enough data and solid intuition based on experience, what does top management do to innovate and create a strategic advantage? The following are steps companies can take to capitalize on the advantage of superior intuition and data when making decisions:[17]

1. **Make better decisions with the data you have**. High-quality data is a precious commodity, so it is wise to use it to your advantage. Top management should use this data and their intuition to develop products that are needed by society and are a good extension of their mission and vision.

2. **Innovate products and processes**. Use data mining or customer needs to develop products that are desired by the consumer base and add value to the manufacturing process. Adding products that do not support the mission and vison or product portfolio are a waste of resources for companies. The ability to have machines run constantly reduces costs through achieving economies of scale and prevents employees from being out of work. It is essential that top management innovates to ensure survivability and maintain market share.

3. **Informationalize products and processes**. Consumers, due to their high levels of technological knowledge, seek products that can satisfy this need. Products that are too simplistic are viewed as lower quality and not adding value to the lives of high-tech consumers. Therefore, the ability to add technology to consumer products adds a certain level of perceived quality and desirability if wanted. The level of quality and desirability is, however, dependent on the adoption rate of the consumers purchasing the products. An *adoption rate* is the rate at which technology is accepted and adopted by consumers over time. The adoption rate includes innovators, early adopters, early majority, late majority, and laggards. Think of yourself and your desire to get the latest cellphone versus an elderly family member. Figure 9.3[18] shows the adoption rate over time.

4. **Improve quality, eliminate costs, and build trust**. These items may seem like impossible feats, but intuition and data can provide the necessary answers to accomplish them. Another element discussed earlier to support this is using a cross-functional team. All four elements can be used to achieve this goal. These four elements are essential in building customer loyalty and increasing customer lifetime value. *Customer lifetime value* is the amount of revenue that loyal customers will provide a business through their purchase behavior. It is cheaper to keep an existing customer than to

---

17   Thomas C. Redman, "Does Your Company Know What to Do with All Its Data?" *Harvard Business Review*, June 15, 2017, https://hbr.org/2017/06/does-your-company-know-what-to-do-with-all-its-data.

18   Gilbert D. Harrell, *Marketing: Connecting with Customers* (Chicago: Chicago Education Press, 2017).

attract a new customer (five times cheaper); therefore, building customer loyalty is essential to long-term profitability.

The Disruptive Innovative Model

The diagram reveals the theory of disruptive innovation where an incumbent firm launches new products aimed at the upper end of the market where profits are most prevalent. New entrants have an opportunity to compete by focusing on satisfying the needs of the lower end of the market where the incumbent typically would not focus their attention. As the new entrant gains resources, they improve their products to satisfy the needs of the mainstream markets and move into the high end markets as well. By the time the incumbent realizes the threat the entrant poses it is too late to stop their momentum and the advantage shifts to the entrant.

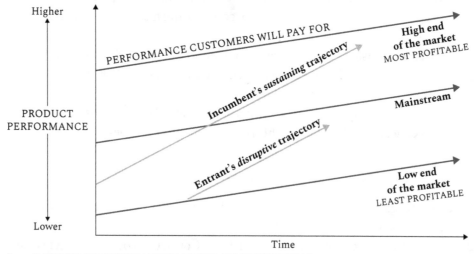

Source: CLAYTON M. CHRISTENSEN, MICHAEL RAYNOR, AND RORY MCDONALD
From "WHAT IS DISRUPTIVE INNOVATION?" DECEMBER 2015

FIG 9.3 Adoption rate of new products over time

5. **Exploit asymmetries**. All information or intuition is asymmetrical, meaning that not all information is present to weigh what should be adopted to innovate. Companies must use both the intuition of top management and data to get to a place of symmetry when deciding on the best innovation to pursue. Therefore, using all the tools at a company's disposal to make important decisions is crucial to avoid costly mistakes and reduced profits. The process is not easy but seeking input from cross-functional teams and customer input can help to make these decisions.

Companies have a great deal of information, experience, and expertise to draw from when making innovation decisions. While there exist the tools to be successful, top managers fall into biases that hamper their ability to make sound business decisions and thus put the longevity and ability to innovate at risk. Humble managers seek the input from their cross-functional team, customers and available data, and they use their intuition to make sound decisions. By combining all these factors, successful businesses thrive and those that don't eventually die.

Review Questions

1. What is intuition? Give an example of when you used your intuition to reach a decision. Was it successful? Why or why not?
2. What are four of the seven intuition attributes found in business leaders? Why are these important to innovation?
3. What is data-informed? Give three examples of a time you used data to drive a decision.
4. What is data-driven? How do companies use data to reach decisions?
5. How can a company use a gap map to determine ways to innovate?
6. Describe four ways companies can collect information. Which do you feel is most effective?
7. What are brainstorming techniques companies can use to be innovative?
8. Describe three psychological biases that affect business leaders and give an example of each that are not stated in the text.
9. Describe three ways top managers can use intuition, data, and cross-functional teams to make decisions. Do you feel this is an effective tool and why?

Discussion Questions

1. Share three reasons why you feel intuition is not a good choice to solely use to make decisions.
2. What is the purpose of doing a gap analysis? Construct a perceptual map of some of the colleges and universities in your area, basing the two axes on quality of education and starting salary and share the results with the class.
3. What is the difference between being data-informed versus data-driven? Share three examples of the differences.
4. Of the ways information can be gathered, what are the three most useful ways you can help companies? Why?
5. Which brainstorming technique do you feel is most beneficial? Share an experience you have had brainstorming ideas.
6. Give examples of psychological biases that have affected business decisions in the past. Share some ways you feel these can be overcome.
7. Why is using cross-functional teams a needed part of making decisions? Share a time you were on a diverse team and what your experience was.
8. What did we, the authors, miss?

Integrative Learning Exercise

You notice that your college or university has many franchised restaurants on campus. You feel you can capitalize on this by buying a franchise and securing a spot to open one. What are some of the intuitive reasons you feel this is good? What data would you collect to place your restaurant in the right building? Who would be on your cross-functional team and what would your agenda for a conversation look like?

Extension Activity

1. Do you feel using intuition, data, and cross-functional teams are all businesses need to use to make decisions? Share what else you feel can be used and why.
2. When you were choosing a college or university to attend, share some of the intuition, data, and cross-functional team experiences that shaped your choice. Was it beneficial?

BIBLIOGRAPHY

Wright, Simone. "The 7 Attributes of Intuitive Business Leaders," *Huff Post*, November 17, 2014, https://www.huffpost.com/entry/business-intuition-what-d_b_5833396.

"Do People Remember 10% of What They Read, 20% of What They See, 30% of What They Hear ?" Quora, https://www.quora.com/Do-people-remember-10-of-what-they-read-20-of-what-they-see-30-of-what-they-hear

Gillet, Rachel. "Why We're More Likely to Remember Content with Images and Video," Fast Company, September 18, 2014, https://www.fastcompany.com/3035856/why-were-more-likely-to-remember-content-with-images-and-video-infogr

"The Power of Visual Communication," https://policyviz.com/wp-content/uploads/2015/10/power-of-visual-communication.pdf.

"What Is MIS?" Guru 99, https://www.guru99.com/mis-definition.html.

Marr, Bernard. "Really Big Data at Walmart: Real-Time Insights from their 40-Petabyte Data Cloud, *Forbes,* January 23, 2017, https://www.forbes.com/sites/bernardmarr/2017/01/23/really-big-data-at-walmart-real-time-insights-from-their-40-petabyte-data-cloud/#62bfb6a96c10.

"Big Data," SAS, https://www.sas.com/en_us/insights/big-data/what-is-big-data.html.

Soller, Kurt. "It Seemed Insane to Spend $400 on a Vacuum, but Now I Like Cleaning," *The Strategist*, January 25, 2017, http://nymag.com/strategist/2017/01/best-vacuum-german-make-miele-complete-c2-review.html.

Rouse, Margaret. "Business Intelligence," Search Business Analytics, https://searchbusinessanalytics.techtarget.com/definition/business-intelligence-BI

"The Top 25 Social Media Marketing Tools," Keyhole, http://keyhole.co/blog/the-top-25-social-media-monitoring-tools/.

Hansen, Brianna. "7 Techniques for More Effective Brainstorming." May 16, 2018. https://www.wrike.com/blog/techniques-effective-brainstorming/

Jones, Gavin. "5 Golden Rules for Innovation Teams," Medium, January 31, 2018, https://medium.com/room-y/5-golden-rules-for-innovation-teams-3514ce3a54b4.

Unglesbee, Ben. "The Running List of 2018 Retail Bankruptcies," Retail Dive, November 21, 2018, https://www.retaildive.com/news/the-running-list-of-2018-retail-bankruptcies/516864/.

Lebowitz, Shana and Lee, Samantha. "Cognitive Biases That Affect Decisions," *Business Insider*, August 26, 2015, http://www.businessinsider.com/cognitive-biases-that-affect-decisions-2015-8.

Redman, Thomas, C. "Does Your Company Know What to Do with All Its Data?" *Harvard Business Review*, June 15, 2017, https://hbr.org/2017/06/does-your-company-know-what-to-do-with-all-its-data.

Harrell, Gilbert D. *Marketing: Connecting with Customers* (Chicago: Chicago Education Press, (2017).

Figure Credits

CHAPTER TEN

Data, Trends, and How We Innovate Using Insights

INTRODUCTION

Data, once thought to be the new oil, is a renewable resource that can be reused and refined over time, unlike oil. Firms use data collected from many sources to make business decisions and to gain insights that help achieve the goals of the organization. Firm success is obtained by following trends and then using data to understand in greater detail consumers' behavior and their changing needs. Trends are the general shifts we see in the world, while insights are the underlying reason people act. Together, they help to make firms successful by analyzing data to discover them. To gain success, firms us the 4 P's of marketing (promotion, price, place, and product) to devise strategies to compete using insights gained. By altering the 4 P's (the marketing mix), firms can respond to changing behaviors and create strategies to increase success.

Another aspect of data is the evolution of machine learning. Machine learning allows machines to learn versus being programed. In addition, artificial intelligence is a machine's ability to mimic human behavior. Together, machine learning and artificial intelligence are evolving, learning to speak to each other and humans. Other advances in technology include cryptocurrency, made possible due to blockchains and neural networks (computers that learn faster, are more accurate, and possess no bias). All these aspects combined have helped, and will continue to do so in the future, with ways companies can use data, trends, and insight to support the creation of goals and achieve the mission and vision of the organization.

Learning Objectives

In this chapter students will learn about the following:

- Why data is a renewable resource helping businesses to answer complex business questions
- How trends and insights differ and why they are important to making business decisions
- The relationship between big data, machine learning, and artificial intelligence
- The future of machine learning and artificial intelligence
- How firms conduct research and the steps they are recommended to follow

Learning Outcomes

By the end of this chapter students will be able to do the following:

- Identify a trend and explain ways to gain insight
- Explain where firms find data and why insights drive value
- Describe how data insights shape the 4 P's
- Discuss how machine learning, artificial intelligence, neural networks, and natural language processing are shaping the future, using big data to advance technology
- Make recommendations on how to harness data and insights

Key Terms

Trends: A general shift over time toward a prevailing tendency

Insights: Complete understanding of a phenomena or thing that dictates behavior

Data: Found everywhere in an organization. Every email, every purchase order, every machine operation, and every mouse click generates data that can be utilized by the organization to gain efficiencies

Machine learning (ML): Subset of artificial intelligence where computers use statistical techniques to learn with data versus being programmed

Artificial intelligence (AI): The ability of a machine to mimic intelligent human thinking

Big data: The seemingly unending structured and unstructured data that firms have at their disposal to mine and make business decisions

Internet of things (IoT): Devices that can receive and transmit data through the internet

Applied artificial intelligence: The ability to carry out tasks that mimic human behavior

Generalized artificial intelligence: Systems and devices that can handle any task put before them

Neural networks: Mimic the way the human brain classifies information received through its operating system while doing so faster, more accurately, and with no bias

Natural language processing (NLP): An application that tries to understand natural human communication, both written and spoken, and attempts to communicate back using a similar natural language

Ontology: The practice of defining the relationship of concepts or categories

Hypothesis: An assumption made and tested to determine if the assumption is true or false

Blockchain: A way to timestamp data using cryptography

IS DATA THE NEW OIL?

"Data is the new oil" has been a commonly used phrase. Clive Humby in 2006 coined this phrase, which means that unless refined, data will not be useful. However, more recent thought has suggested that data is different from oil; therefore, it is not the same. The comparisons of the two include the following:

1. Oil must be continually pumped from the Earth, while data can be replicated indefinitely.
2. The longer data is used, the more it is refined. Oil is refined once and then used to create a byproduct (e.g., gasoline, plastics, asphalt, kerosene, and lubricants).
3. The world's oil reserves are diminishing, but the data supply is increasing.
4. Oil has limited uses, while data has a plethora of uses.
5. Data is ecofriendly, while oil is not.
6. While data has many useful advantages over oil, it can also be harmful. It can invade personal privacy, be used to formulate the wrong assumptions, and give one group an advantage over another.
7. Data can be to reduce human issues, while oil can create them.
8. Data is not the new oil, but a renewable resource like the sun, wind, and tides.

These comparisons make a strong case for the difference between data and oil, but both are valuable, and without them the economy would not function. What is important is that data provides the information companies need to realize their goals and to find insights that will help them be successful and gain a competitive strategic advantage.

Those companies that understand how to utilize their data will quickly surpass those that do not. Today we are already seeing the use of data generating tremendous advantages for companies such as Facebook, Google, Netflix, and Amazon. Questions like where data can be found, how frequently it is created, and how it is visualized can make a tremendous difference in both the growth of a company and the value of it.[1]

Where is the Data?

Data is everywhere in the organization. Every email, every purchase order, every machine operation, and every mouse click generates data that can be utilized by the organization to gain efficiencies. There is data being generated everyday outside of the organization that must be considered as well. Examples of this include weather and traffic patterns, demographic and geographic patterns, which are can combined with a company's internal data to guide even better decisions such as new markets to enter, shifting target markets, and retail locations.

---

1   Bernard Marr, "Here's Why Data Is Not the New Oil," *Forbes,* March 5, 2018, https://www.forbes.com/sites/bernardmarr/2018/03/05/heres-why-data-is-not-the-new-oil/#33a634b83aa9.

The following vignette will try to demonstrate the need for data. For years you have wanted to buy this small convenience store by the beach. Every time you enter the store you see the owner, Joe, and it feels like he has been there forever. The store is always busy, especially on sunny summer days. Every time you go past the store, there are people coming in and out, carrying cases of beer and other beverages, snacks, ice, and so on. One day, the small convenience store comes up for sale, and you quickly buy the store, as Joe says he is retiring after working in the store for almost forty years. You start to run the store and quickly find out that Saturday and Sunday afternoons are extremely busy, and the main items you sell are beverages and snacks. On a sunny day, the business is booming. You quickly associate the stores purchases with the warm sunny weather. This might not feel like a big deal but as the owner, you need to make sure you have the correct number of employees and stock on hand. Because the store is small, you may have to schedule more deliveries from your key vendors. This also requires more employees to stock the shelves and manage the incoming inventory. The ice vendor, you determine, must make three deliveries per week determined by looking at sales data. After looking at your financial data, you determine that you are losing money on these sunny days due to increased labor costs. When you originally bought the store, you thought these would be your best days and now understand why you always saw Joe in the store. Faced with this dilemma, you are trying to determine what to do. Should you close the store? Can you physically work all the hours yourself? There's no way to decrease sales on a sunny day and even if there was, you wouldn't want to. This situation leaves you wondering what to do.

To find a solution you decide to use store-generated data to build a more profitable basket of goods for the consumer. When you look at the amount of people coming into the store and the data from the register receipts, you realize that just over one-sixth of the people have purchased some sort of sunscreen. You soon realize that sunscreen is more profitable than the beverages you sell. You quickly add additional space for sunscreen by eliminating a small greeting card rack that was there when you purchased the store. Suddenly you see in the data that sunscreen sales account for one third of your sales. By making this minor change in the product mix, you can utilize the labor that is needed on sunny days and become more profitable.

As another year goes by, you work to increase changes in the product mix by adding sunglasses, beach blankets, and a small assortment of sand toys. This increases profits even more as you come to realize that monitoring the shopping cart data you collect and understanding your consumers' wants and needs is highly correlated with increasing sales. You finally realize that continuing to improve your product mix and creating higher margins using transactional point-of-sale data is essential and the store you once thought as a financial disaster is now a money-making operation due to using data.

THINK ABOUT THIS!

How did the weather and traffic affect Professor Ferguson's retail liquor business? How did zoning impact his sales? How did demographic and geographic factors influence his product selection?

Professor Ferguson was in the retail liquor business for over 20 years. His stores were in Michigan, so this meant there were four seasons that impacted his business. Sales each year were tracked to gain a grasp on the what the expected volume for the week was historically. There were three locations, including one metropolitan and two rural. The demographics of each were different, so product selection varied by location. Also, two stores were in residential areas, while the third was in an industrial area. So, what effect did these factors have on business?

The weather was consistent, but the sales of items in a retail liquor store are greatly impacted by temperature. Cold drinks sell better in warmer weather, and the types of liquors sold varied as well. Brown liquors sold better in the winter and clearer products sold better in the warmer seasons. Also, demographics were different, so products sought varied, which meant learning consumer preferences were the key to survival.

Traffic also had an impact, as the industrial area had more traffic than the residential area, especially during the week when customers were working. In the industrial location, the intrastate the business was located on was under construction two summers in the ten years the location was in operation. Of course, road construction occurs in the warmest months, thus reducing the level of sales needed to sustain the slower sales in the winter months. The original road the store was located on went from two lanes to four with a center turning lane and an outside right turn lane added. Customers had to literally cross three lanes of traffic to enter the store's driveway. In the end, using the data collected, a decision was made to not renew the lease and shutdown the industrial location because of the increased traffic making it impossible to reach the store and negatively impacting sales. In addition, the two rural locations were located less than a quarter of a mile from each other, so the one location whose building was rented was shut down in favor of the one Professor Ferguson owned. The result of using the available data was profits rose, sales doubled, and payroll drastically decreased, managing only two employees versus 15.

What Value Do Trends Have on Success?

Trends are the window to the future. We have discussed trends in several chapters, so this is just a refresher as it adds meaning to this chapter's content. *Trends* are a general shift over time toward a prevailing tendency. An example of a trend is Spartan Motor's awareness that Americans are becoming overweight due to lack of exercise and eating processed foods. Trends don't happen from set periods but do change over time. Therefore, firms that can use information and data to discover these trends before they happen benefit from them.

WHAT ARE INSIGHTS?

Insights provide firms with more knowledge to make decisions. An ***insight*** is the complete understanding of a phenomena or thing that dictates behavior. Insights are important because they drive the strategies of the firm and help to satisfy its goals. An example of an insight is that Americans are becoming overweight and first responders are getting hurt lifting them into the ambulance. So, Spartan Motors installed hoists on their ambulances to lift patients in reducing the injuries to first responders. Insights provide a deeper understanding from which firms can use this information to be successful. We will discuss this in greater detail further in this chapter.

What is the Difference between Trends and Insights?

There are many trends for firms to observe. Trends do not develop at the same pace; some are slower to adopt, while others explode on the scene. Firms need to be aware of the external environment to detect these trends and to see if they can capitalize on them to be successful, like the example of Spartan Motors adding hoists to ensure first responder safety and increase sales.

So, while trends are numerous and need to be realized, insights are the way firms understand the trend and the behavior that guides them. Trends are a general understanding of a *way* an event is occurring; insights are the specific understanding of *why* it is occurring. It is the job of analysts to find out the specific reasons why people or things act the way they do, so top managers can use these insights to devise strategy and achieve the goals of the organization.[2]

It's Not the Data; It's the Insights That Drive Value

The past examples show that data is powerful and a person can literally build a business, turn around a company's performance, or grow a strong firm with the use of data and the insight it provides.

Insights are valuable to a business and data provides a means to them. With all the discussion of big data (which we will discuss later), there is less discussed, if any, about big insights. In fact, in my dealings with businesses big and small, the main discussion always revolves around data. Where does the data come from, how clean is the data, what tools are we going to use to make sure we can visualize the data correctly? These are all good questions. However, the insights that come from the data are the real value for the organization. They are the "so what" that the data provides. Let's say that you are looking at the nationwide sales of a $100 million company. By looking at the data, you see that 10 percent of sales, $10 million, and 8 percent of all the volume sales occur in California. This alone could be a good insight. Should the marketing budget next year include a 10 percent–line item for California? Should

---

2   Winifred Knight, "Trend or Insight? What's the Difference," Mortimer Harvey, April 1, 2016, http://www. mortimerharvey.com/blog/trend-or-insight-whats-the-difference/.

10 percent of the sales force be deployed to California? If we added one more piece of information, one extra piece of data, could a larger insight can be delivered? What percentage of the US population lives in California? The answer, 12 percent, leads to an insight that is key to the business efforts: There is a 2 percent dollar gap and 4 percent volume gap in the biggest state in the United States (i.e., California). This gap equates to $2 million, a $2-million insight by using internal and external data. This insight leads to action by adding more emphasis on sales and marketing efforts in California.

The insights to the data are delivered in many ways. They can be seen visually as outliers. For example, truck deliveries have been late the past six weeks to a specific location. By looking at traffic pattern data, and using a traffic app, we determine that road construction started six weeks ago. We must use that insight to give the strategy to fix the problem. The insight in this case may lead to a different route for the truck driver or customer notifications of delays.

Data Insights Shape the Four P's of Marketing

Marketers use the four P's of marketing (product, promotion, price, and place) to determine their strategies. Data insights can benefit the four P's by providing information firms can use to develop and implement these marketing strategies. Without insights, firms are blindly trying to implement strategies, which can lead to a waste of resources and can negatively impact sales. Next, we will look at the effect data insights have on the four P's.

Product

Insights can lead you to product innovations, especially if you have an ecommerce site and you are using analytics to quickly determine your customer's needs. Let's pretend that you are a $30 million manufacturing company. You currently make widgets that are used in the oil pipeline industry and have a variety of products sold through a distribution network of resellers. The resellers don't provide any data on their sales to you, but you have orders that are in your enterprise resource planning (ERP) system. You start to run some digital advertisements that target the resellers and you notice from your analytics that the ads with the most response come from your bestselling widget. This is usually the most expensive product and produces higher-than-normal profits for the company. The problem with this bestselling widget is that there is a longer lead time to produce it than other widgets the firm offers. When combining the insights of the bestselling widget's advertising with the data from the orders from your ERP system, a definite pattern emerges. The insight from the ERP system shows that orders have increased for the bestselling widget over the past several weeks. You begin to build a new type of widget that offers several attribute changes from the original and monitor the advertising and the ERP orders carefully. Soon, you have a line of widgets that represents 40 percent of your profits because you monitored the success of your product and satisfied the needs of your customers.

Promotion

The insights that can be gained from promotion are very impactful. Large retailers and consumer package goods companies have been using data insights for years to determine the exact promotion that works best to stimulate sales and address consumer needs. For example, an e-commerce company that sells active wear online through their own company store decides that they will discount their yoga pants to increase sales (the pants typically sell for $99). The company runs two ads to do some alpha (i.e., within the firm) and beta testing (i.e., outside the firm). The first ad is for 20 percent off and the second is for $79 dollars, while keeping everything else in the ad the same. After some testing, the company finds that the $79 ad performs better, so they continue to market the yoga pants using the price point versus the discount percentage.

The same company had been selling necklaces for $20 on their website but they had not been selling very well. One day someone in the office suggests that the necklaces should just be given away. Suddenly the company has a new promotion offering for full price yoga pants at $99 with a free necklace instead of the $79 price-point ad that was running quarterly. The lift is tremendous and now the company is selling more yoga pants than before with the $99 price point. There is also another benefit: The necklace carries a high gross profit margin (i.e., 50 percent); because of this, the promotion does not cost the company $20, but now it only costs the company $10. Therefore, the yoga pants net the company an additional $10 due to the higher gross profit percentage and reduces their inventory holding costs. This is a good example of how data and insights drive promotional activity.

Price

Data and insights can be used to generate pricing strategy as well. If you are a tennis player and you are headed to your local public tennis court to play tennis with one of your friends, you may stop at your local drug store to buy a new can of tennis balls. When you go to pick them up, you see they are priced at $3.98. You haven't played in quite some time, so you have no idea if this is a good or bad price. The court and the drug store are close to each other and that is all that matters, as you are seeking convenience.

However, a year ago the drug store did some data analysis and mined some insights of its own, finding it traditionally sold tennis balls for $2.98 at all stores. One day they decided to overlay the distance of the stores to nearby tennis courts using mapping software. The stores nearest public tennis courts would increase the price of tennis balls to $3.98 and stores not located near tennis courts would keep the price at $2.98. The insight they found was astounding: There was no decrease in sales due to this strategy, so the stores made an additional $1.00 per can just be using these data insights and potentially improved customer satisfaction. This may not seem like much until you realize that over 3,200 stores are near tennis courts, so selling two cans of tennis balls per week at each store increased company sales by 332,800 annually.

Place

Data insights are key when determining where the company sells its goods or services. It is critical to determine the best locations to place products or resources. For example, a home health care business has four hundred health care providers in two large Texas markets, Dallas and Houston. They have roughly three hundred people in Dallas and one hundred in Houston. They decided to mine traffic data to determine how much time the providers spend on the road versus in the homes of the people they service. After looking at the data, they see an insight. Houston providers spend only a few hours giving care, and most of their time they are stuck in Houston traffic. Because the health care providers are paid an hourly rate, it quickly becomes apparent that Houston is less profitable, and the service level does not meet the company's standards. After additional analysis, a decision is made to close the Houston branch and add more resources to the Dallas branch due to shorter drive times and being with more patients annually. Using these insights, companies big and small are driving their marketing decisions to increase revenue, decrease costs, develop more effective promotions, and have more efficient product development.

THE DATA OF MACHINE LEARNING AND ARTIFICIAL INTELLIGENCE

There is quite a bit of discussion in today's organizations about machine learning (ML) and artificial intelligence (AI). Although these terms are sometimes used interchangeably, they certainly should not be. *Machine learning (ML)* is a subset of artificial intelligence where computers use statistical techniques to learn with data versus being programmed. *Artificial intelligence* is the ability of a machine to mimic intelligent human thinking.

Artificial intelligence has a much wider scope than machine learning. Think of it this way: Machine learning is a key contributor to artificial intelligence but artificial intelligence is a bigger concept. Much of what is being worked on in artificial intelligence today is with machine learning, which explains why the two terms are used interchangeably.

What Exactly is Machine Learning and Why is it so Important?

First, we must disclose that machine learning is not new; in fact, machine learning (ML) is quite old. The term *machine learning* was used in 1959 by Arthur Samuel.[3] Machine learning is the concept that machines can build on inputs that they are given and continue to improve or learn. So, why has machine learning been such a buzzword in the past four years? The amount of data generated is becoming greater and greater, as much as 90 percent of all current data has been generated in the last two years! Because of the massive amount of data generated, machine learning programs have increasingly experienced more data inputs from which to learn. This massive amount of data is called big data. *Big data* is the seemingly unending

---

3   Arthur L. Samuel, "Some Studies in Machine Learning Using the Game of Checkers," *IBM Journal of Research and Development 3*, no. 3 (1959): 210–229.

structured and unstructured data that firms have at their disposal to from which mine and make business decisions. Big data allows firms to provide better results to build on, and as the amount of data continues to grow due to more devices being connected to the Internet, it will generate increasingly more data. This phenomenon is referred to as the internet of things (IoT). The *internet of things (IoT)* are devices that can receive and transmit data through the internet. It is estimated that there will be over 25 billion devices connected to the internet in the next two years, thus growing the amount of data available for the IoT.

Another relevant future fact about ML is that its ability to learn for itself versus being programmed has given some application to the ability to read text messages and email, then determine if the sender is criticizing or congratulating the receiver based on reading the message. The ability for ML to learn on their own has opened the door to such things as neural networks. *Neural networks* mimic the way the human brain classifies information received through its operating system faster, more accurately, and with no bias. It accomplishes this by using a system of probability that allows the machine to predict, give statements, and make decisions with a certain level of certainty. It uses a feedback loop to "learn" what was right or wrong, and then alters its decision making based off this learning in the future. The combination of ML and neural networks will allow machines to interact and communicate with other machines as easily as humans communicate with each other.

What is the Future of Artificial Intelligence?

Artificial intelligence (AI) is even older than machine learning. The ideas of artificial intelligence beings are as old as Frankenstein, but in today's business environment it is gaining increasing momentum as more data flows, more devices are connected, and machine learning becomes stronger. There are two types of AI, applied and generalized. *Applied artificial intelligence* is the ability to carry out tasks that mimic human behavior. This the most common form of AI and an example includes the ability to trade stocks or maneuver autonomous vehicles. *Generalized artificial intelligence* are systems and devices that can handle any task put before them. This form of AI is less common, but is the future of AI as technology advances, which helps to further develop this.

Today, more machine learning is being generated on natural language processing. *Natural language processing (NLP)* is an application that tries to understand natural human communication, both written and spoken, then attempts to communicate back using a similar natural language. This is the foundation of the devices that allow you to speak to them to perform tasks such as cell phones with voice recognition along with new devices such as Echo, Siri, and Alexa. This is possible by programmers classifying data into buckets defined as ontology. *Ontology* is the practice of defining the relationship of concepts or categories. For example, if you have an ice cream cone, an ice cream sundae, an ice cream sandwich, or bowl of ice cream, you are still eating ice cream. Using natural language, machine learning and creating ontologies are developing quicker because of better artificial intelligence, and this will only improve as the technology becomes more sophisticated (What is the difference between artificial intelligence and machine learning.[4]

Machine learning has paved the way for innovation through advances in artificial learning and this is evidenced by the dramatic increase of publishing companies and other educational-based firms selling simulations featuring AI. Artificial intelligence has allowed companies to give students real-world learning by mimicking their behaviors through the simulations, thus creating new learning opportunities. An example of this is McGraw-Hill's backpack simulation. The simulation pits students against each other and uses AI to learn how each student uses the four P's to sell their backpack. This student use of AI creates character and allows them to compete against each other.

WHAT ARE THE BEST WAYS TO HARNESS ALL THESE DATA AND INSIGHTS?

Having big data at your disposal is terrific, but what if you don't know how to convert it into information you can use to gain insights? Firms collect as much data as possible, only to find they are overwhelmed by it or they don't know what they are looking for. It is like the saying "trying to find a needle in a haystack." Firms must be able to harness the data they have and find insights that will answer the questions that will make their company successful.

When trying to gain insights using big data, firms must focus on factors that will help them to achieve this task. More specifically, firms must ask the following:

1. **What are the business's goals?** Firms must ask what the goal is for conducting analysis and the insights they are trying to reach. What is question or problem that needs to be answered? The business goals are the ones devised by management to help the firm be successful. They could include analyzing the US to determine the top markets for the firm regarding sales, profits, market share, and so on. The goal may also be to find areas of growth where the firm can provide resources to continue to cultivate success. Whatever the case, the goal of the firm will drive the research and provide a clear vision of what needs to be done, will devise the measurement strategy to be utilized, and will make recommendations to answer the research question, thus providing insights.

2. **What are the specific questions that must be asked to achieve the firm's goals?** A common mistake of using big data for analysis is that the research question(s) that will help obtain goals is too vague. There is a direct correlation between vague questions and results, thus trying to determine insights will be vague if the proper question is

---

4   Bernard Marr, "What Is the Difference between Artificial Intelligence and Machine Learning?" *Forbes*, December 6, 2016, https://www.forbes.com/sites/bernardmarr/2016/12/06/what-is-the-difference-between-artificial-intelligence-and-machine-learning/#740997ba2742.

not crafted. A great way to solve this dilemma is to ask questions a firm wants to find answers for. Build a timeline to find the answers to the questions so everyone working on the analysis knows what is expected. It is helpful to know the business, products, customers, level of engagement and satisfaction levels, and the mission and vision. These can act as a guiding force when formulating the research questions you wish to ask.

3. **What hypotheses must be tested to find the answers?** With the goals and research questions in place, the next step is to formulate hypotheses to test and provide the insights that can answer the research questions. A *hypothesis* is an assumption made and tested to determine if it is true or false. An example is the hypothesis that reducing the price of Brand X by 5 percent will result in a 10 percent sales increase. The hypotheses should be directly related to the research question and the goals you want to accomplish.

4. **How do we test the hypotheses to gain actionable insights?** To test hypotheses and gain action insights we must first us data that is valid and reliable. Researchers must measure the data that will provide the insights they need in a manner that shows it is significant and provides ways to be actionable. As mentioned, using data that is specific to the research question and that supports the goals will provide the specific answers needed to provide insights and help to tell the story of how a firm can achieve its objective. Therefore, actionable data, a good testing method, and well-written hypotheses will produce the answers needed to provide insights.

5. **What have we found through our testing and how do we tell the story?** In the results of testing, we will see the levels of significance that indicate if the hypotheses and relationships tested have meaning. Like having a blood test, the results are presented in a numerical form with ranges to demonstrate what is good, bad, or of concern for the patient to discern. To the doctor, they are indicators of the health of their patient. The bloodwork results fall within ranges to indicate if the individual functions measured in the blood (e.g., cholesterol, liver function, glucose, etc.) are within a normal range. If they are high that could indicate a potential problem, and the same holds true for measuring data. If the hypotheses tested are significant, the hypotheses formulated is true or significant. Take the example we used for lowering the price and increasing sales. If this hypothesis was significant, then we know that this could occur, so it would support the need to pursue this course of action. Sometimes the levels of significance indicate relationships that are a surprise. It is up to the researcher to determine why this has occurred and if it is of concern to the strategy or insights sought.

Once the data is analyzed and the results make sense, the researcher must provide managers with recommendations. What do the results say that will help achieve the goals and provide insights? Researchers must prepare an executive summary of the results that are written in non-technical terms to share with management as this will help to guide the strategies to achieve the goals by providing the insights necessary for success (49 analytics experts share their best strategy to turn data into actionable insights.[5]

Become a Data Detective

As data becomes cheaper to store and easier to visualize, a person must become a data detective. There is immense value in being a data programmer, data scientist, or a data analyst. However, the data detective should be able to investigate the clues the or she thinks will lead to the insights a firm seeks to gain a competitive advantage. The data detective will help the scientist save time, let the computer programmer write the code, and let the analyst look for important results. Together, the data detective brings many positives to the team to gain valuable insights.

Why Should You Become a Data Detective?

The employee of the future will have more data at his or her disposal than ever before and will be expected to use it to increase the value of the organization. The data in the company is a layer that exists over the entire organization, so every job is affected by it. This is also driving hiring decisions, as an ever-increasing number of jobs are offered to those who can manipulate data for insights or get data ready for those who can. Data is being tied back to profit and loss and balance sheets of companies. In many companies the chief technology officer has at least equal power to the chief financial officer to use data to benefit the firm. Therefore, data is of great importance to firms and helps provide many insights sought for success and innovation at a faster rate than others.

Should We Be Concerned about Becoming a Data-Driven Economy?

Older organizations are not yet using data to determine strategy. They are still relying on products and services that they have marketed in the same ways for years. Data driven companies are applying data rapidly through their organizations, allowing all contributors to see and act on the data to find insights.

Older businesses are being disrupted every day by data-driven companies, as these companies have not only embraced data strategy but are executing based on the insights that are coming from it. Should we be worried about data and the rise of artificial intelligence? The answer is maybe. It really depends on how data is collected and how it will be used in the future.

On the collection side, the rise of apps and gaming to collect data has proven harmful if a person interacts with games and/or gamification methods to collect data. When a person has moved into the "virtual world," a world designed to collect data, the lack of interaction and communication is yet to be seen. Other questions to ponder are, "Will this effect lead to less creativity in the future? Will there be a less and less musicians and artists in our

---

5   Paul Cox, "49 Experts Reveal How to Turn Data into Actionable Insights," Online Metrics, June 7, 2016, https://online-metrics.com/actionable-insights/.

future?" While the answers are not known, it is up to companies to adapt and change to benefit from them.

How data is used and the security of our personal data has become a huge concern, especially of late. We have already consented to have all our data collected, whether we know it or not, but the question is "How are companies using it and how secure is it from misuse?" This is not only important for our personal data, but for organization's data as well.

Enter Blockchain

Blockchain is the future of data security. *Blockchain* is a way to timestamp data. The data is organized in blocks, which are verified by previous blocks. It is this distributed ledger that makes the blockchain, by design, resistant to changing the data. This is what makes the blockchain so valuable for transactions that need to be traced. Although we may have heard more about bitcoin than blockchain, it is the blockchain that will provide some of the most valuable ways to use data in the future. These could be extremely useful in identity management as blockchain is being used in medical, transportation, and voting, along with its biggest use thus far, cryptocurrencies.

Data discussions can lead to many paths. From blockchain and artificial intelligence to machine learning and natural language data, the conversations are endless. Always remember that data provides you vision, and that vision creates insights. It is the insight that should drive the strategy and the strategy should be measured for effectiveness using data.

Review Questions

1. What does the phrase "data is the new oil" mean?
2. Why do critics say data is not the new oil? Provide three examples.
3. Give five examples of data not found in the text. If I were to seek trends regarding undergraduate cafeteria food consumptions, where would I find this data?
4. What is a trend? Provide an example of a trend you see today.
5. What is an insight? Using the trend provided for question 4, what is an insight you gained from this trend?
6. How do insights drive value?
7. How do insights shape the four P's of marketing?
8. What are the similarities between machine learning, artificial intelligence, neural networks, and natural language processing?
9. What factors help firms obtain insights using big data?
10. What does the term *data detective* mean?

Discussion Questions

1. Consider the phrase "data is the new oil." Do you feel it is or not? Why?

2. If your university sought ways to increase attendance at home football games, discuss five ways you would gather data.

3. I have hired you to find trends related to beverage consumption. What are three trends you would offer? Share some insights on how my firm could gain an advantage through your insights.

4. Discuss an additional way not listed in the text that you feel insights drive value. Why?

5. I have noticed a trend around campus that students are exercising more. I own a gym and want to take advantage of this trend. To gain insights, provide for me a manipulation of the four P's that could take advantage of this.

6. Share why you feel or don't feel artificial intelligence is beneficial to firms.

7. Discuss why big data is important for firms. Do you feel there are pitfalls to big data? Why or why not?

8. To harness big data to gain insights there were factors presented in the text. For the following business question provided, what are ways you would present information to finish the factors? Research question: Who is the target market for my new app that helps people find the shortest wait times at restaurants?

9. Share additional ways you feel blockchains can shape the future of business. Why did you state this answer?

BIBLIOGRAPHY

Knight, Winifred. "Trend or Insight? What's the Difference," Mortimer Harvey, April 1, 2016, http://www.mortimerharvey.com/blog/trend-or-insight-whats-the-difference/.

Marr, Bernard. "Here's Why Data Is Not the New Oil," *Forbes,* March 5, 2018, https://www.forbes.com/sites/bernardmarr/2018/03/05/heres-why-data-is-not-the-new-oil/#33a634b83aa9.

Marr, Bernard. "What Is the Difference between Artificial Intelligence and Machine Learning?" *Forbes*, December 6, 2016, https://www.forbes.com/sites/bernardmarr/2016/12/06/what-is-the-difference-between-artificial-intelligence-and-machine-learning/#740997ba2742.

Paul Cox, Paul. "49 Experts Reveal How to Turn Data into Actionable Insights," Online Metrics, June 7, 2016, https://online-metrics.com/actionable-insights/.

Samuel, Arthur L. "Some Studies in Machine Learning Using the Game of Checkers," *IBM Journal of Research and Development 3*, no. 3 (1959): 210–229.

CHAPTER ELEVEN

What Affects the Ability of Companies to be Decision Driven?

INTRODUCTION

When it comes to making innovative decisions, companies must consider many factors that affect this decision both positively and negatively. In this chapter, we will show how various types of innovation (continuous, incremental, and disruptive) offer companies both advantages and disadvantages, plus suggested uses for each. We will also identify the four rules of product development when considering a new idea that will guide the decision to move forward or go back to the ideation phase. We also ask, "Does the innovation match the company's mission and vision? Why this is important?" and suggest ways to get the corporate community to embrace the innovation. Finally, we identify how competition affects innovation and ways a company can press forward.

Learning Objectives

In this chapter students will learn about the following:
- The advantages of continuous innovation when making decisions
- The five reasons for adopting an incremental innovation approach
- How transformational innovation offers opportunities and risks for companies
- The four rules used to determine if an innovative idea is viable
- Techniques that can be used to get the corporate community to accept innovation
- How competition affects innovation and drives decisions

Learning Outcomes

By the end of this chapter students will be able to do the following:
- Determine which is the best form of innovation to adopt based on competition and satisfying the needs of the target market
- Analyze an innovative idea using the four rules to determine if it is feasible

- Understand how to determine if an innovation matches the mission and vison of the company
- Develop ways to address employees resisting innovation
- Understand how to adopt either a process or project innovation to stay competitive
- Decide when a horizontal or vertical product differentiation strategy is best

Key Terms

Continuous innovation: Type of innovation that requires no change in a consumer's behavior

Attribute: Something that adds value or is associated with an object, person, organization, etc.

Learning curve: How fast a new employee develops the assimilation of knowledge or skills

Pull demand: Customers asking retailers for a certain type of product, thus pulling the product through the distribution channels to be offered for sale

Organizational chart: Representation of the layers of management (authority) and how everyone with the organization is arranged based on how information flows and responsibility

Horizontal organizational chart: Indicates fewer levels of management and easier access to top executives

Vertical organizational chart: Indicates more levels of management so the company has more bureaucracy and communication flow in slowed

Incremental innovation: Type of innovation that requires a moderate change in consumer behavior while interacting with the new product

First-mover advantages: When companies introduce a product to market that is unique or the first of its kind

Cost-benefit analysis: An analysis that looks at the rate of return the monetary investment provides, dividing the costs by the expected revenue

Mass advertisement: Ad not targeting any specific consumer group but sent to the population via television, radio, or print

Targeted advertisement: Ad specifically targeted to a specific segment of the population via electronic messaging, email, mail, telephone, and social media

Transformational or disruptive innovation: The type that transforms or disrupts current products or markets and requires significant change in consumer behavior to use it

Jobs-to-be-done theory: Idea that an innovation must be able to accomplish the task a consumer seeks

Strategic business unit (SBU): Autonomous unit that has its own mission and vision yet reports to a central headquarters

Process innovation: Focuses on reducing a firm's costs through efficiencies

Product innovation: Characterized by the introduction of new and improved products to the market

Horizontal product differentiation: Similar to continuous innovation where the innovation is focused on attribute or feature changes and does not change consumer behavior

Vertical product differentiation: A strategy that categorizes products by their level of quality

WHAT TYPE OF INNOVATION DO WE CHOOSE?

We have previously identified three types of innovation (continuous, incremental, and transformational) and the differences between them based on behavior changes. In this chapter we will take a deeper look at these three types of innovation and discover why it is important for companies to select the correct type when they decide to develop new products. Innovation should be a never-ending process to ensure longevity and to remain in a dominate market position.

THINK ABOUT THIS!

Why did Kodak claim bankruptcy in 2012? What mistakes did they make? How did they correct what went wrong?

Kodak developed digital photography in 1975, but never pursued it to protect their highly-profitable film business.[1] This classic mistake allowed others to seize the opportunity, leaving Kodak with declining market share and profits. In 2012, Kodak, a once iconic household name, filed Chapter 11 (bankruptcy to help them reorganize).[2] This is a classic problem of companies that suffer from the biases and from not listening to their customers' needs and observing the world around them.

So, what did Kodak do to get out of bankruptcy and become profitable again? It is using their seven thousand patents and smaller corporate structure to innovate and develop touchscreen and other digital technologies. The results showed that in the first quarter in 2017, Kodak posted a $7-million profit and increased sales over the previous year.[3] While sales were down 5 percent, a smaller corporate structure helped to absorb this reduction.

Kodak, like so many other brands, are examples of why innovation is so critical. Customers didn't want to print pictures anymore, but instead wanted to post them. Without hearing the voice of the customer to drive innovation, companies like Kodak may all end up filing Chapter 11.

---

1   Nathan McAlone, "Inventor of Digital Camera Says Kodak Never Let It See the Light of Day," *Business Insider*, August 17, 2015, http://www.businessinsider.com/this-man-invented-the-digital-camera-in-1975-and-his-bosses-at-kodak-never-let-it-see-the-light-of-day-2015-8.

2   "In Chapter 11 Filing, Kodak Tries to Develop New Vision for Survival," *PBS News Hour*, January 19, 2012, https://www.pbs.org/newshour/show/in-chapter-11-filing-kodak-tries-to-develop-new-vision-for-survival

3   Mike Dickinson. "No Clear Path To Success For Kodak." *Rochester Business Journal. September 22, 2017.* https://rbj.net/2017/09/22/no-clear-path-to-success-for-kodak/.

Continuous Innovation

Continuous innovation is a type of innovation that requires no change in a consumer's behavior. This type of innovation usually involves an attribute change in the product or service. An ***attribute*** is something that adds value or is associated with an object, person, or organization. Examples include M&M's made with caramel, Coke Zero, iced coffee drinks, and so on. The differences from the examples to the original products are just changes in attributes and don't require consumers to change their behavior to consume the product.

There are several reasons why companies adopt a continuous innovation strategy. We will focus on the following:

1. Continuous innovation allows companies to respond to their customers' needs and changing attitudes by offering products that will satisfy them, all with speed.
2. It is a low-risk strategy.
3. Continuous innovation in large part is a marketing strategy.
4. Continuous innovation emphasizes the never-ending need to be innovative and makes this strategy part of the community or fabric of the company.

   - It changes the employee's mind-set toward how to innovate.
   - It improves collaboration among the community by sharing ideas openly.
   - It improves communication between all functional areas of the company.

5. It serves to perfect the innovation model used by a company when it seeks riskier innovations such as those that are incremental and transformational/disruptive.

Responding to Changing Customers' Needs

As discussed in *"Think about This" section* above, customers' needs change over time. Kodak, to protect its highly lucrative film business, ignored the fact their customers didn't want to print pictures but to post them online. While they had the technology to deliver, they ignored what their customers wanted for preservation of their own interests, which cost them market share in the digital camera arena and put them in bankruptcy.

Continuous innovation allows for quick responses to changing customer needs because the innovation selected is typically an attribute change (i.e., small change to an available product). Companies typically have all the processes and equipment present to adapt to this change, so the innovation can be adopted rather quickly and inexpensively. Another benefit of continuous innovation regarding satisfying customer needs is that the innovation typically doesn't need new distribution channels to sell the product. In addition, a company's current vendors or sales force can easily add the new product to their existing product offerings. For example, a potato chip manufacturer has customers asking to offer potato chips flavored like smoked ribs for summer barbecues. The company can develop the flavor and then add it to the plain potato chips they currently produce. The product is offered to stores as a new flavor and the consumer's needs have been met. In this simple example, the only change in the manufacturing process was the development of the smoked rib flavor. The manufacturing, distribution, and retailer network were all in place, so this innovation can happen rather quickly.

Low-Risk Strategy

Continuous innovation is a low-risk strategy for companies because it does not require large outlays of resources for research and development (R&D). As previously discussed, continuous innovation is typically an attribute change to an existing product. Therefore, a successful product with a slight change will typically bring positive results because of brand recognition, loyalty, and quality expectations. Therefore, companies will use an existing family brand or brand name to introduce products that are similar in nature. For example, the Ford F-150 pick-up uses a family name (Ford) and a brand name (F-150) for this vehicle. Consumers have images of what the Ford and F-150 brands represent, so these will influence, hopefully in a positive manner, consumer perceptions toward the type of truck they are purchasing.

Another reason continuous innovation is lower risk is if a new product is not successful in the market, demarketing (halting manufacturing) it results in a lower level of loss. As discussed, attribute innovation typically uses existing machinery, distribution channels, and retailers, therefore, discontinuing a product will result in loss but not on the same magnitude as using incremental or transformational/disruptive strategies. For example, Mountain Dew, a popular soft drink, especially among young Americans, frequently introduces new flavors to both satisfy customer's needs and to increase their market share. Mountain Dew has introduced forty flavors since its inception and while most have been discontinued (63)[4] the risk of introducing a new flavor is worth the reward if it becomes popular. Adding a new flavor poses very little risk to PepsiCo, their parent company, as all manufacturing, shipping, and retailers are currently in place. If the flavor is not accepted, PepsiCo discounts it, picks it up at the retailer, and exchanges it for something else, or sells it to a discount retailer.

A final thing to consider using a continuous innovation strategy is companies can use existing employees to develop the products. Since the process is similar, there is no need to bring in new people (i.e., a new innovation team). The *learning curve* of how fast a new employee develops the assimilation of knowledge or skills is very key. An example of the learning curve is the first five aircraft produced by Boeing, which will take longer to manufacture than the last five. Employees have learned all the processes and skills needed to improve speed and efficiency. Therefore, the learning curve lowers overall cost and risk and is realized by most companies to increase profitability through efficiencies.

A Marketing Strategy

Continuous innovation does not bring the highest return on investment as compared to incremental or disruptive innovation, but it does assist firms in continuing to provide a revenue stream needed to stay viable. The latter are new products that can seize top dollar in the market with no need to discount. When companies are customer focused and not concerned

---

4   "Mountain Dew," Wikipedia, https://en.wikipedia.org/wiki/Mountain_Dew.

with maximizing profits, using continuous innovation can work very well due to lower risk and taking advantage of existing processes. The classic example of this strategy is Apple. While most people will say Apple is a disruptive innovator, they are in fact using a continuous strategy. They capitalize on this strategy of continuous innovation by listening to their customers and then creating an aura around the new products they are launching to satisfy their needs.

The word *aura* has been introduced earlier in the text and is a key component of the GT-MAP as it is a way to gain consumer attention in an overstimulated world of mass advertisement. Companies create an aura around their product innovations to build excitement in the market and create pull demand. **Pull demand** results in customers asking retailers for a certain type of product, thus pulling the product through the distribution channels to be offered for sale. For example, Apple listens to their customers and then makes an attribute change to their existing products. The iPhone 6 had earbuds with a cord and the iPhone 7 is wireless, the camera was upgraded, there were a couple of design changes, and so on. The differences were subtle, but there is an aura surrounding the new iPhones, so the attribute changes marketed by Apple on the upgraded models creates value and aura; therefore, Apple uses this continuous innovation over and over as an effective marketing strategy. This strategy is also an example of an effective go-to market strategy as proposed in the GT-MAP.

Continuous Innovation Creates an Innovative Environment for the Community That Makes Up the Fabric of the Company

When companies are listening to customers, developing new products, brainstorming new ideas, and improving on what the current product portfolio offers, it strengthens a company whose members are in the mode of innovating. This mode has very important long-term implications for the company and its community. The biggest is being aware that listening to customers and then answering their requests through new products is a key to longevity. There are other benefits as well, which we will discuss next.

Creates a Mind-Set Focused on Innovation

Companies that practice continuous innovation have employees who are always thinking of new products and processes, which are designed to satisfy the needs of customers. Think of yourself. Since you enrolled in this class do you look for ways improve products or processes? The ability to create this mind-set is the responsibility of top managers. They should encourage this activity by offering suggestion boxes, open-door policies, and rewarding employees for making suggestions that lead to innovation. Another suggestion is they can give employees time to innovate as part of their daily work schedule and can celebrate failures. Celebrating failures reduces trying a new product for fear it fails and brings negative repercussions. Moreover, leaders can sponsor town hall meetings to have employees share their innovations and ideas of what the company is doing to innovate. Finally, top managers can also be transparent and let employees know they are part of the community in which innovation is everyone's responsibility (a form of social innovation to be discussed later in the text).

Improves Collaboration

Continuous innovation creates an atmosphere of collaboration. The community sharing their ideas is important, but when ideas that are similar or interesting to others are presented, this provides an opportunity for increased collaboration. We have discussed the need for cross-functional teams and diverse groups as a key ingredient for innovation. Improved collaboration provides a means to promote recruiting and attracting members to these teams and/or groups. A common problem for companies is the lack of collaboration outside of individual departments (i.e., working in silos). This is true for large organizations, but collaboration is a way to break down these silos and connect people within the community to share ideas and help develop new products.

Improves Communication within the Community

Along with increased collaboration comes better communication. Communication within the community stems from two sources. One is communication with top leaders. Innovative companies' organizational charts are more horizontal, giving easier access to top managers, thus making things more efficient and speeding the innovation process. Less innovative companies have a more vertical organizational chart and thus are slow to innovate due to barriers in accessing top managers. An **organizational chart** is a representation of the layers of management (authority) and how everyone in the organization is arranged based on responsibility and how information flows. A **horizontal organizational chart** indicates fewer levels of management and easier access to top executives. A **vertical organizational chart** means there are more levels of management, so the company has more bureaucracy and communication flow is slowed.

Continuous innovation has many positive effects on the community and is an integral part of a company. An innovative mind-set, customer focus, and better collaboration and communication are all part of what strengthens the top firms to develop new products. Top managers must encourage taking chances, listening to their employees, and being transparent to foster the trust and dedication needed to be top innovators.

Continuous Innovation Helps to Perfect Methods and Benchmark Best Practices when the Company Pursues Riskier Incremental and Disruptive Types of Innovation

We have discussed the lower risk that continuous innovation offers companies while monitoring the needs of our customers. It is through this never-ending goal of constant innovation that companies benchmark what was successful and strive for continual improvement of their processes and practices. The ability to perfect a system of innovation makes the process more efficient and speeds to market the new products being developed.

Proper benchmarking and continued improvement can also take away some of the risk with incremental and transformational/disruptive innovation. While these forms of innovation require a change in consumer behavior, the way a company utilizes processes learned from continuous innovation can help to streamline the process internally. Proven internal processes can help get the products to market quicker, which leaves more time to educate consumers and find a distributor network, the next hurdles facing the introduction of these types of new products. Therefore, learning from continuous innovation can pay dividends when attempting riskier forms of innovation.

Incremental Innovation

Incremental innovation is a type of innovation that requires a moderate change in consumer behavior to interact with the new product. The products developed using incremental innovation are like previous products but have features that require educating consumers on the proper way to use them. Examples of incremental innovations include hybrid vehicles, shopping online, and taking online classes. In addition, we previously discussed the adoption and diffusion rate of products, so incremental products will also be part of this process, depending on the consumer. To speed the adoption rate, firms use aura to gain attention and drive pull demand, as previously discussed.

Incremental innovation has advantages and disadvantages for the companies that seek this type of product. The level of risk associated with incremental innovation is greater than continuous, but not as great as disruptive innovation. This is due to product similarity but requires getting customers to learn how to interact with the new product and accept it. Therefore, while not a radical change in how to use the product, consumers need to learn new behavior. The problem is some consumers are risk adverse and do not like change. Therefore, firms need to emphasize the ease of use and the benefits of using the new product to increase the adoption rate.

We will address five areas that are synonymous with incremental innovation. These five areas include the following:

1. Gaining a short-term competitive advantage while increasing market share and profits
2. Improving an existing product as dictated by consumers
3. Increased cost to manufacture different products
4. The need to hire new employees
5. Increased advertising costs and customer education

Incremental growth is essential toward building brand loyalty and customer satisfaction. It provides many advantages to companies over continuous innovation. While more risky, incremental innovation builds on continuous innovation and sets the stage for transformational/ disruptive innovation. It is a necessary form of innovation needed to build brand equity and increase brand awareness while providing longevity. Most of the top companies innovate at every level and incremental innovation is a way to set a company apart from its competitors.

Short-Term Competitive Advantage

Incremental growth can provide the innovative company a temporary competitive advantage. The reason the competitive advantage is temporary is that while the innovation is unique, competitors easily copy it because of the ease of replication. When thinking of hybrid vehicles, Toyota captured the market with the Prius,[5] which gave them first-mover advantages. *First-mover advantages* are characterized when companies introduce a product to market that is unique or the first of its kind. Thus, it establishes quality, price points, and performance expectations from similar products that follow. Shortly after the introduction of the Prius, other car manufactures introduced hybrid vehicles, giving Toyota both a temporary competitive advantage and establishing what other hybrids should provide to consumers to be successful. From these new vehicles, we saw continuous innovative attributes added such as the Chevy Volt, whose car had a motor as a back-up charging the vehicle or propelling it when the battery was exhausted. Several other vehicles adopted continuous innovation including the Nissan Leaf and Tesla, which run strictly on battery power. These are all examples of vehicles that resulted from Toyota's Prius and the overwhelming acceptance by consumers.

Product Improvement Based on Consumer Needs

We have discussed ways to identify customer needs by revealing how companies must put them at the top of their innovation agenda to be successful and guarantee long-term success. Monitoring customer needs and ways to improve our current products are essential for incremental innovation. For example, if consumers expressed a need to clean their teeth while being less invasive on their gums, firms could seek to provide a product to accomplish this request. While researching this request, firms found a common problem expressed by consumers: trying to clean teeth without applying too much pressure while brushing. Philips introduced an electronic toothbrush named Sonicare, which was less invasive while providing cleaner teeth.[6] This innovation was incremental because consumers had to press lightly and brush their teeth in quadrants, versus providing the muscle action to scrub their teeth with a traditional toothbrush. It also provided different settings, which included a whitening setting. Therefore, consumers had to learn how to brush their teeth by changing their behavior, versus the traditional way, and Philips provided a way to brighten the consumer's teeth with one product.

Innovation should be focused on stakeholders and not a company's internal agenda. When the innovation does not match the mission and vision, add value to the product portfolio, or provide long-term growth and profits, it spells disaster for the company. As discussed previously, projects that are favored by top management or others within the organization based on intuition only need to be assessed based on the fit they provide the company and the available data. Customer needs should take precedent over "pet projects" and should always add to the value of the company and their stakeholders.

---

5   Michael Graham Richard, "Since 1997, Toyota Has Sold 6 Million Hybrids (1 Million of Those Just in the Last 9 Months," TreeHugger, January 20, 2014, https://www.treehugger.com/cars/1997-toyota-has-sold-6-million-hybrids-1-million-past-9-months.html.

6   "A New Level of Care," Philips, https://www.usa.philips.com/c-m-pe/electric-toothbrushes/sonic-technology.

Increased Cost of Doing Business

Companies must innovate, but there is a cost associated with it. While we discussed the relatively low cost of continuous innovation, incremental innovation has higher costs involved, which are attributed to greater research and development (R&D), the need for employees with a different skill set than the talent currently available, additional equipment, greater manufacturing space or warehousing, and other related (expenses vehicles, payroll, etc.).

While additional costs may be incurred to perform incremental innovation, companies must always perform a cost-benefit analysis to determine if the innovation is worth the investment. A *cost-benefit analysis* is an analysis that looks at the rate of return the monetary investment provides and divides the costs by the expected revenue. It should be cautioned that the cost-benefit analysis, as being data-driven, should not be the only analysis performed to determine profitability. Companies can determine if a product that just breaks even but completes a product line should be produced to add value. Therefore, the decision to continue with an incremental innovation must be discussed with the key financial officers, top managers, and the functional groups to determine if the costs are worth the rewards.

Hiring New People

We have also discussed in detail the need to have a human resource inventory to assess the talents and skills that are available to the company. When companies determine the need for additional talent, they can promote internally or hire externally to fill the space. It is important that the functional team provide the human resource department the skills needed and job duties that will be performed. This job can then be posted within the company so the current employees with the skills needed can be notified, or it can be posted externally through employment search engines.

It is important to remember that just as in innovation, companies must "move" and not delay finding the best employee to do the job. Delayed hiring of employees adds time, frustration, and possible product development delays, so a clear focus on what talents are needed is essential.

Increased Cost of Advertising and Customer Education

Incremental innovation involves changing consumer behavior, which means there is a need to inform current and future customers about the innovation, plus educate them on the way to use the product. Companies must determine what advertising strategies can be utilized when educating customers. Their choices include mass advertisements and targeted advertisements. *Mass advertisements* do not target any specific consumer group, but are sent to the population via television, radio, or print, digital, and so on. *Targeted advertisements* are specifically targeted to a specific segment of the population via electronic messaging, email, mail, telephone, and other digital means. Companies can target these customers by referencing their consumer lists, reviewing cookies from engaging on their website, responding to inquiries, and contacting past customers to inform them about the improved product.

Customer education is a key ingredient for successfully launching a new product. The ease of consumer's learning how to use the new product requires education. Existing customers must be taught how to use it in a different manner from which they are accustomed. Successful education assures existing customers will adopt the innovation, while the inability to show the benefits or changing behavior will mean they search for a different product with greater ease or will not adopt the new one. This form of education benefits consumers from targeted advisement because companies know who they are and want to retain them, so targeting the advertisements toward them adds great benefit.

Incremental innovation also gives companies the ability to attract new customers who are not satisfied with a product they are currently using or who see the benefits of the incremental innovation. To gain awareness, companies should follow a mass advertisement strategy to make as many people knowledgeable of the innovation as possible. Another strategy may be to offer demonstrations and post videos online or on the company website to let customers see the innovation in action. Moreover, demonstrations in stores for tangible products are also a good way to allow customers to interact with the new product. Salespeople provide the demonstration and then solicit a sale.

Incremental innovation provides many advantages to companies, a greater need to analyze the options, and an assessment of risks. Costs, type of advertisement, input from functional groups, support from top management, and educating customers are integrative factors that shape the success. While more risky than continuous innovation, incremental innovation gives companies a competitive advantage and leads the way to transformation or disruptive innovation.

Transformational or Disruptive Innovation

Transformational or disruptive innovation is the type that transforms or disrupts current products or markets and requires significant change in consumer behavior. Transformational or disruptive innovation is also called "new-to-the world innovation" as it introduces products into the market that are so radically new, consumers have never seen anything like them before, and they can change how cultures and the world operate. The most recent talked about transformational innovation is the autonomous vehicle. The race is on by firms outside the automotive sphere to introduce it. Companies like Apple, Google, and Yanfeng are developing a version that will totally transform the idea of what mobility has been. Imagine being able to have an autonomous vehicle pick you up for a meeting three hours away and you could work while it drives you to and from the meeting. While traditional automobile companies are trying to perfect this transformational innovation, it is interesting that firms outside are disrupting the auto space by developing this type of vehicle as well. This serves as an excellent example of the need to innovate constantly and to be aware of who the next players are in an industry once reserved for the select few.

Very early, disruptive innovation included the Ford Model T, commercial airlines, the electric circular saw, and the television. More recent disruptive innovations include the smartphone, electric vehicles, the internet, and biologic medicines.

Looking at these examples, think of how these disruptive innovations have changed society and required a significant behavioral change. The horse was the common mode of transportation until the automobile came along. The first automobiles were not disruptive due to the cost, but the Ford Model T became the first automobile that was mass produced, making it affordable to society and ushering in a new way to manufacture products reasonably. Builders had to rely on cutting wood with a hand saw when doing construction. The electric circular saw decreased the time it previously took to frame a house, increased production, and eliminated the need for jigs to cut rafter angles, thus reducing the cost of construction.

News was dispersed via horse-riding messengers until newspapers, telegraphs, radio, and then television were introduced. Television gave firms the ability to reach millions of people simultaneously. It also provided entertainment that was both visual and audible, something missing from traditional forms of media, like radio. Television allowed companies to advertise their products in a way that consumers could see and watch demonstrations of how they function. The smartphone changed the way people shop and communicate with each other and is central to how people in the twenty-first century live. These examples show how disruptive innovation changed society for the good and bad, and gives companies a lasting competitive advantage, until another company disrupts the industry again, ushering in newer products.

Origins of Disruptive Innovation

Dr. Clayton Christensen proposed the theory of disruptive innovation in 1995, but refined it in 1997.[7] Christensen proposed that smaller firms can compete or even up-end larger more established companies by focusing on the low end of the market that larger companies ignore due to tight margins and limited growth, allowing smaller firms the opportunities to take market share and grow profits. The rationale behind the theory was that of competitive response, which dictated that smaller companies innovating in the lower end of the market sought a way to gain entrance and monitor the reaction from larger firms.

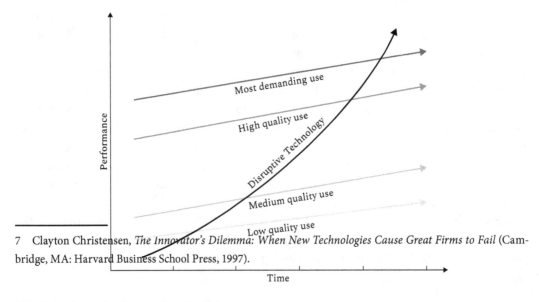

---

7   Clayton Christensen, *The Innovator's Dilemma: When New Technologies Cause Great Firms to Fail* (Cambridge, MA: Harvard Business School Press, 1997).

FIG 11.1 **Disruptive innovation model**

More recently, Christensen has refined the theory to add a complimentary theory referred to as the "jobs-to-be-done" theory.[8] *Jobs-to-be-done theory* states that an innovation must be able to accomplish the task a consumer seeks. This theory is rooted in the fact that besides a functional piece, innovations must also satisfy a social and emotional side. In other words, they must do what they are intended to do while satisfying the social and emotional aspects of users. For example, adults suffering from incontinence had to purchase adult diapers that were bulky and thus inhibited their ability to be in society for fear of embarrassment (emotional). Depends came out with a line that is effective and unnoticeable when worn; therefore, it gets the job done, reduces societal stigma, and allows for interaction with others (social).[9]

Additional Characteristics of Disruptive Innovation

Disruptive innovation gives smaller companies the ability to discover market segments that are typically not touched by larger firms and thus provides an opportunity to compete and gain market share and profits. Some other facets of disruptive innovation include the following:

1. Increased risk as compared to continuous and incremental risk
2. Targeting consumers who are interested in disruptive products
3. Opportunities for entrepreneurs and/or smaller firms

While there are other characteristics that define disruptive innovation, these three summarize and provide a good representation of what disruptive innovation means to a company. Next, we will examine them in greater detail to understand why they are important.

Increased Risk

We have been discussing the level of risk associated with innovation and how it is lowest for continuous and highest for transformational or disruptive innovation. One of the reasons for the highest level of risk involved in transformational or disruptive innovation is the high cost of research and development. Once a disruptive innovation is introduced it must recoup the investment associated with developing that type of product (i.e., sunk costs). As indicated, distributive innovations are typically associated with smaller start-up firms; therefore, financial resources are probably limited, and failure could have serious repercussions for the young company's long-term success. That is why many smaller firms seek to partner with larger firms with more resources to adopt their technology into a bigger product. This strategy allows the smaller firm to curve their level of risk and see their idea to fruition.

Another risk associated with transformational or disruptive innovation is the lack of awareness of future innovations. Companies think through and develop the first disruptive

---

8   Susan Adams, "Clayton Christensen on What He Got Wrong about Disruptive Innovation," *Forbes,* October 3, 2016, https://www.forbes.com/sites/forbestreptalks/2016/10/03/clayton-christensen-on-what-he-got-wrong-about-disruptive-innovation/#e43cdf6391bb.

9   Ibid.

innovation but have no awareness of future products. As discussed earlier, innovation in a global economy is a rapid process. If a firm is to be successful, it must seek ways to further innovate its products.

Ways to continue this success include monitoring disruptors (competitors working on products to rival our own), reviewing patents being filed, monitoring technology developments, and trying to not cannibalize your own products.[10] The innovation could be one of the three discussed in this chapter, but the lesson here is to always seek future innovation and not rest on the fact that since one was highly successful the company can sit back and reap the rewards. The GT-MAP is designed for continuous innovation to ensure viability and long-term success.

Targeting Customers Interested in Disruptive Products

Companies developing disruptive products must realize most of society will not adopt this type of innovation immediately, but over time. We have previously discussed the diffusion and adoption rates of products. Disruptive products typically start in smaller markets, so the adoption of the product will take some time. It is important to increase awareness of the new product and let ambassadors drive the growth, thus increasing the rate of adoption and recouping costs associated with the product. Increasing awareness is why the GT-MAP stresses creating aura. Aura helps break through over exposure of marketing messages and results in faster product adoption.

Another thing that should be considered is that disruptive products typically offer high performance or advanced technology. Not everyone is interested in all the high-performance features or knows how to use them. For example, some consumers (mostly older) see no need in using a smartphone and opt for using a flip phone. They seek a means to make a simple call and to be accessible, while seeing little value in apps, going on social media, posting pictures, and so on. Therefore, companies must understand how their disruptive innovation changes society and then use these points when selling the products based on consumer needs and wants.

Opportunities for Entrepreneurs and/or Smaller Firms

Disruptive innovation provides a way for start-ups to gain a foothold in the marketplace quickly. As stated previously, disruptive innovation targets the low end of the market (least profitable) because incumbents tend to focus on the more profitable segments, thus giving an opportunity to enter the market, build profits, and increase market share quickly. This gives entrepreneurs and smaller firms the ability to be successful and create future opportunities from their success.

---

10   "Cannibalization." The Economist. https://www.economist.com/news/2009/08/17/cannibalisation.

Assessing if the Innovation Satisfies the Four Rules of Product Development

Innovators are usually quick to come up with product ideas based on a need they see in the market. While this supports our contention that "speed to market" is essential, many of these innovators neglect to follow the four rules of product development:

1. Is it easy to duplicate?
2. Is it easy to understand?
3. Is it unique?
4. What is the emotional bond the innovation will create, and will it be a lasting one?

THINK ABOUT THIS!

What makes a great product idea a success? What are the long-term benefits a company can enjoy by pursuing this innovation? Will our innovation add value to customers and profits to our business?

We are constantly speaking with students about their innovation ideas. All too often, students will have a great idea to solve a consumer problem, but it does not satisfy the four rules. For example, a student group's final project in our class was an innovation that provided a peddle bike cab service for students that was powered by a driver peddling a bike that pulled a four-person cart. When asked after their presentation if this idea is easy to duplicate, the group replied "Yes!" This group was composed of students from Michigan State University, so when asked what they would do in the winter, they realized it was not a very practical idea. Therefore, the idea gave the group no advantage and created a commodity situation, where in the absence of no distinct advantage, price becomes the deciding factor. The alternative was to seek out a cab or Uber, which could operate year-round. The group quickly realized that their idea was less than ideal as it gave their company no competitive advantage. If they would have applied the four rules, they would have devised a different idea.

Is It Easy to Duplicate?

Innovation is based on answering the needs of customers, anticipating what they will need next, gaining a competitive advantage, and extending the life of the company, plus others. If it offers the same items as others or ones that are easy to duplicate, the company opens the door to failure. Products that are easily duplicated give no competitive advantage, create a purchase decision based on price, and do nothing for longevity. The world is full of "fast followers": companies in every market that do nothing but "follow" great products and figure out how to make it cheaper. Therefore, unique products should be sought to satisfy the needs of the consumer while giving the ability to charge a higher price point.

Is It Easy to Understand?

Products that are difficult to understand in both application and use are destined to failure. The American society is bombarded with so much information regarding things that are irrelevant they are disregarded or selectively not remembered. Today, when one fills up his or her car/vehicle, there is a commercial on the pump television screen, billboards display multiple messages, city buses advertise companies, messages are shown on social media, and so on. Products must make sense, as described previously. When consumers are presented with an innovation, they ask themselves, "How does this impact me and make my life better or more enjoyable?" Therefore, companies must be clear on how the new product impacts the consumer and the best way to comprehend how it benefits them.

Is It Unique?

Innovators must ask, "What makes my product unique? Why is my product so different from my competitors that people will buy it?" If the innovation is not unique, consumers base their purchase decision on price and availability. In addition, being unique makes the product standout against others, so it gives a company the ability to gain attention quickly. This helps reduce the funds spent on advertisement and assists in gaining market share and profits faster than "me too" products. Therefore, innovators will want to develop and broadcast the uniqueness of their products to benefit the company (i.e., create the aura).

What is the Emotional Bond the Innovation Will Create, and Will It Endure?

The emotional bond consumers have for products is another way of saying they're loyal. The emotional bond created between product, company, and consumer strengthens their purchase behavior and increases customer lifetime value. Being able to develop an emotional bond and maintain it is essential for companies. It is accomplished by offering loyalty programs, giving the ultimate in customer service, having fair pricing, and genuinely appreciating the consumer. Once consumers develop this bond, it is hard for competitors to gain their business. However, companies must continue to innovate and be customer centric to maintain and grow this bond.

Does the Innovation Complement Our Mission and Vision?

Earlier in the text we discussed why companies exist. The third component of this section identified the need to support the mission and vision of the company. All too often companies lose sight of their mission (purpose) and vision (the direction and what they seek to accomplish), which misaligns the overall strategy of the organization. This misalignment can occur through mergers, trying to stay competitive, and falling into the trap of short-term increases in market share and profits, to name a few.

When companies propose continuous innovation, it is simple to adhere to the mission and vision of the company because the new products are like what is currently offered. The challenge to follow the mission and vision comes with incremental and disruptive innovation. These types of innovation push the company to offer products that are different, or in the case of disruptive, very different to what was previously offered. It is important for companies to analyze how the innovation fits the mission and vision before the idea is pursued. Products that do not follow the mission and vision create confusion and blur the original intent of the company. It is important for companies to not make these mistakes and to always stay true to their original purpose and do what is necessary to seek what they intended when they started out.

You may be asking yourself, "How does a company diversify to meet multiple missions and visions?" That answer can be found in companies that have several strategic business units. A *strategic business unit (SBU)* is an autonomous unit that has its own mission and vision yet reports to a central headquarters. An example of this is Buick, GMC Trucks, Chevrolet, and Cadillac, which are SBUs of General Motors. Each has its own mission and vision yet reports to a central headquarters. Each SBU is independent in terms of the functional areas (human resources, manufacturing facilities, etc.), yet agile enough to respond to the needs of its target markets while maintaining separate mission and visions. This structure has proven very successful for companies that operate in several sectors of business (e.g., Proctor and Gamble, General Electric, Lever Brothers) and stay true to their original purpose.

WILL OUR CORPORATE COMMUNITY EMBRACE OUR INNOVATION?

Companies must not only consider if the innovation sought supports the mission and vision, but if the corporate community (i.e., stakeholders) will accept it. Earlier we defined community as a feeling of fellowship with others created by sharing interactions and forming relationships. We also described the differences between the two.

TABLE 11.1   *Community versus Culture*

COMMUNITY	CULTURE
Interaction based, not learned	No interaction required
Empowers its members	Learned behavior
Binds it members through relationships	Taught by family or through acclimation
Shares common interests	Common language, customs, or rules

Innovation provides companies many advantages, but also brings a level of uncertainty and change to firms adopting it. Resisting change is common practice for humans and while some people like change, most do not. People who like to know what to expect, are not willing to accept risk, and enjoy a routine. While innovation is essential for businesses to survive, top management must recognize that change and the feelings it brings to employees needs to be addressed. Evidence of this is human resource departments creating change agent positions within departments to address employee needs during change in a company. So, how can companies get employees to embrace innovation and the potential change that new systems or products may bring to their normal work routine?

Anita Campbell, CEO of Small Business Trends, suggests six ways to get employees to accept and embrace innovation:

1. *Accept what the employees are feeling*: Encourage employees to voice their concerns and share what is worrying them with management or change agents. Listening to employees ensures that their worries are heard and will be addressed.

2. *Address their concerns*: What is most important is feedback to employees on how their worries will be addressed. This is not the time for false promises or saying, "Don't worry; it will be fine," as this leads to lack of trust on the part of the employee and creates the possibility for rumors to be spread. Address the concern and provide a level of comfort for the distraught employee.

3. *Engage everyone*: Innovation most often involves small functional teams, yet it is highly beneficial to inform all employees why the innovation is important to the company, how it will benefit the company, and what the desired expectations are. Keep employees outside of the functional groups informed of the innovation and seek their feedback to encourage buy-in on the new product.

4. *Communicate clearly*: Let employees know everything about the innovation, what the expectations are once it is introduced, and how it will benefit the company and them. If some part of the innovation and the goals expected are not understood, then take the time to answer these questions, no matter how small. Probably the number one mistake made in innovation communication is not explaining in detail why innovating projects are stopped or killed. When people put countless hours into a project, then without notice are told to stop without adequate explanation, it is not acceptable. It is important that innovators do not go down this path and explain why they support the innovation while treating their people in an acceptable manner.

5. *Pump up morale*: Innovation projects require a lot of time, energy, and thought. The process can bring a great deal of stress and be mentally and physically draining for those involved. Therefore, it is important for top management to do things to take away some of the stress. Some examples include taking the innovation team to a baseball game, have a pizza party, going bowling, and so on, which will take the edge off the stress of the project and add an element of fun and comradery.

6. *Celebrate results*: When the innovation is complete, acknowledge the hard work of everyone. Discuss their role, how they went above what was expected to ensure success, and thank them for their hard work.

In addition, there is a need to monitor the innovations progress once it is launched. Launching a product is not the end of the innovation process but a start to see if it will be successful. Inform employees on the progress of the innovation and report how it is doing, as measured by the goals established before launch. In sum, employee acceptance of the innovation is crucial for success and the ability to keep them informed and listen to their concerns is an essential element of this success.[11]

HOW DOES COMPETITION AFFECT INNOVATION?

Ponder this question: How does competition affect the level of innovation taken on by companies? Does competition always have a positive effect on innovation? American business schools have always preached that competition is what drives the capitalist society we live in and thus drives innovation. While this is true to some extent, competition does affect the level of innovation and the type of innovation companies will partake in. More specifically, does a company focus on improving products or processes, or does it focus on attributes or quality? How do these strategies affect profits and the level of innovation?

How Does the Level of Competition Affect Innovation?

Psychologists will suggest people live by following the path of least resistance. This means that human nature will seek the easiest path to get something accomplished. Innovation is not any different. When competition is intense, the level of innovation tends to decrease due to pressure on cutting costs to stay competitive, which results in a minimal return of investment. When competition is too low, there is no incentive to innovate because there is no threat. So, when is innovation at its optimal point? The answer lies in the middle of these two scenarios. When there is a healthy level of competition and there is the opportunity for making a profit, companies will innovate to increase market share and profits. A steady level of competition allows companies to anticipate what to expect from their rivals, and this leads to committing funds for research and development to innovate. The only threat now is new entrants coming into the market, where very little is known about their capabilities and what products they bring to the competition.

Famed Harvard Researcher Michael Porter devised the model to provide businesses with a way to compare competitive strengths and know where a firm is in relation to competitors. Porter's model also helps to determine the profitability of new products based on these five forces:

1. Rivalry among existing competitors
2. Threat of new entrants
3. Threat of substitute products
4. Bargaining power of buyers
5. Bargaining power of suppliers

---

11   Anita Campbell, "6 Steps to Help Employees Embrace Innovation," American Express, May 25, 2012, https://www.americanexpress.com/us/small-business/openforum/articles/6-steps-to-help-employees-embrace-innovation/.

The five forces model helps to identify the opportunities firms may have and ways to gain advantages in the market. This model is especially helpful for innovation in determining a firm's relative strengths as a comparison to the competition that helps determine the level of innovation and to what extent a firm will carry it out (see figure 11.2 for the five forces model).

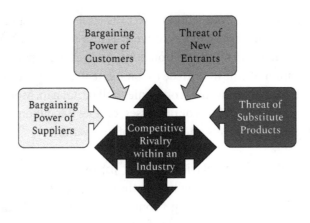

FIG 11.2 **Porter's five forces model**

How Does the Level of Competition Affect the Type of Innovation?

Innovation can be a couple of different types (process or product innovation) and the level of competition can impact both. *Process innovation* focuses on reducing a firm's costs through efficiencies. It focuses on existing processes and seeks ways to cut costs and give a firm the ability to maximize profits or cut costs and maintain a similar level of profitability. Process innovation is common in highly competitive environments where new innovations are threatened by lower margins, profits, and a reduction in the risk associated with research and development.

Product innovation is characterized by the introduction of new and improved products market. Unlike process innovation, product innovation involves both competitive and less competitive markets. Product innovation gives the firm an advantage in profitability by the introduction of new products and being able to demarket old products providing incentives to innovate forcing the competition to keep up with the product developments.

To capitalize on both types of innovations, firms can adopt a hybrid model. When the functional teams are developing products, manufacturing, shipping, and warehousing, the firm can develop new processes before the product is launched to improve the efficiencies. This two-pronged strategy will increase profitability by selling new and improved products while reducing costs through gain efficiencies.

What is Horizontal and Vertical Product Differentiation?

Horizontal product differentiation is like continuous innovation where the innovation is focused on attribute or feature changes and does not change consumer behavior. Companies offer products with various attributes to their target market. The target market decides which attribute it desires. This strategy is called horizontal because the products are similar and no one product is better than the other. It is the consumer who selects which product he or she desires. For example, picture your favorite brand of potato chip at the store. There are several choices you can choose from (regular, barbeque, sea salt, dill pickle, all-dressed, jalapeno, lightly salted, etc.), and you must make a choice. You may prefer regular, while a friend prefers sea salt. No one flavor is better than the other because of various tastes consumers have, plus the products are all priced in a similar way. It is this horizontal product differentiation that allows for companies to continuously add new flavors and drop unpopular ones based on a wide variety of consumer preferences.

Vertical product differentiation is a strategy that categorizes products by their level of quality. Companies use this strategy to price products at different levels, as price is a surrogate for quality. For example, Chevrolet, like most car companies, uses letters to differentiate products by quality, price, and attributes. LS has less features and is cheaper than the next step up, the LT. The same is true when consumers want to upgrade from the LT to the LTZ. A simplified version of this is when companies offer good, better, best. The attributes, features, and quality are all different and give consumers a choice when they are deciding to make a purchase.

Mixed product differentiation is found in certain product categories such as apparel. Certain styles of clothes (vertical) can come in a variety of colors and sizes (horizontal). Companies must decide which strategy works for their market segment and product category to be effective and capitalize on opportunities that are present.[12]

Review Questions

1. How does continuous innovation differ from incremental? Give two examples of each type of innovation that are not discussed in the text.
2. Of the five reasons for adopting an incremental innovation strategy, which do you feel is the most beneficial to a company and why?
3. Give an example of transformational innovation that started at the bottom of the market and worked its way up to compete.
4. List an innovative idea you have and compare it against the four rules. Explain how it satisfies or doesn't satisfy the rules.
5. How do mergers affect a company's ability to match their mission and vision with the new product lines they will acquire?
6. Of the ways to get the corporate community to embrace innovation, which suggestion do you feel is most beneficial and why?

---

12   Valentino Piana, "Product Differentiation," Economics Web Institute, 2003, http://www.economicswebinstitute.org/glossary/product.htm.

7. Give two examples of horizontal and vertical product differentiation that are not found in the text.
8. What are the Five Forces suggested by Porter? Give an example of how you could use these to stop competitors from eroding your business.

Discussion Questions

1. Why is continuous innovation more effective at satisfying customers' needs than disruptive innovation?
2. What are some ways continuous innovation can be used to benchmark best practices to move toward incremental and disruptive innovation?
3. Do you feel the increased costs of incremental innovation are worth the risk? Why?
4. How does transformational/disruptive innovation present opportunities for entrepreneurs?
5. List a product failure and success and compare it against the four rules of successful innovation.
6. The chapter lists ways to overcome resistance to innovation by employees. What else would you add to this list and why?
7. Of the two types of product differentiation (horizontal or vertical), which do you feel is the better strategy to implement? Why?

Integrative Learning Exercise

Presentation to the Board

Students will select an innovation idea that can be used for an existing company. They will then prepare a presentation to present to the board (instructor). Offer the CEO the type of innovation selected and why, how it satisfies the four rules, how it matches the mission and vision, how you will encourage the community to accept it, if it a process or product innovation, and if the product differentiated horizontally or vertically.

Extension Activities

1. What programs has your college or university added that are good representations of transformation innovation? Have they been successful? Why or why not?
2. What are some recent product introductions that failed the four rules of product development? What could the companies have done to change the outcome?

BIBLIOGRAPHY

McAlone, Nathan. "Inventor of Digital Camera Says Kodak Never Let It See the Light of Day," *Business Insider*, August 17, 2015, http://www.businessinsider.com/this-man-invented-the-digital-camera-in-1975-and-his-bosses-at-kodak-never-let-it-see-the-light-of-day-2015-8.

"In Chapter 11 Filing, Kodak Tries to Develop New Vision for Survival," *PBS News Hour*, January 19, 2012, https://www.pbs.org/newshour/show/in-chapter-11-filing-kodak-tries-to-develop-new-vision-for-survival

Dickinson, Mike. "No Clear Path To Success For Kodak." *Rochester Business Journal. September 22, 2017.* https://rbj.net/2017/09/22/no-clear-path-to-success-for-kodak/.

"Mountain Dew," Wikipedia, https://en.wikipedia.org/wiki/Mountain_Dew.

Michael Graham, Michael Richard. "Since 1997, Toyota Has Sold 6 Million Hybrids (1 Million of Those Just in the Last 9 Months," TreeHugger, January 20, 2014, https://www.treehugger.com/cars/1997-toyota-has-sold-6-million-hybrids-1-million-past-9-months.html.

"A New Level of Care," Philips, https://www.usa.philips.com/c-m-pe/electric-toothbrushes/sonic-technology.

Christensen, Clayton. *The Innovator's Dilemma: When New Technologies Cause Great Firms to Fail* (Cambridge, MA: Harvard Business School Press, 1997).

Adams, Susan. "Clayton Christensen on What He Got Wrong about Disruptive Innovation," *Forbes,* October 3, 2016, https://www.forbes.com/sites/forbestreptalks/2016/10/03/clayton-christensen-on-what-he-got-wrong-about-disruptive-innovation/#e43cdf6391bb.

"Cannibalization." The Economist. https://www.economist.com/news/2009/08/17/cannibalisation.

Campbell, Anita. "6 Steps to Help Employees Embrace Innovation," American Express, May 25, 2012, https://www.americanexpress.com/us/small-business/openforum/articles/6-steps-to-help-employees-embrace-innovation/.

Figure Credits

CHAPTER TWELEVE

Why is it Essential to Revise the Business Plan?

INTRODUCTION

To accurately allocate resources and predict profitability, a company must be able to project the number of units sold and their associated earnings. Common methods include identifying key market variables, conducting market research, analyzing data, and comparing it to a predetermined breakeven point. This data is also helpful in determining whether the innovation is worthwhile to pursue.

It is also critical to determine what kind of value the innovation will provide. A few ways to help determine this is to ask questions, such as "Will the new product reduce customer costs, increase efficiencies or productivity, reduce liabilities, and capitalize on consumer trends, and who might be a likely partner to manufacture or distribute the product?"

Firms must also identify the amount of their sunk costs, if there will be a competitive response, and how the company will respond. Answering these questions can help reduce a company's risk and provide direction for developing countermeasures. A successful company will have plans ready to enact should any number of factors change, and benchmarking is a common practice to measure the current state of a market and compare it to other time periods.

Learning Objectives

In this chapter students will learn about the following:
- How predicting units sold are calculated
- How to identify a breakeven point
- The value innovation brings to companies
- What resource allocation is
- Ways companies reveal their expected earnings
- What a risk analysis and countermeasures are

- How to use benchmarking to set an operating standard

Learning Outcomes

By the end of this chapter students will be able to do the following:
- Explain ways in which companies can estimate how many units will be sold
- Indicate the importance of market research and data to make sales predictions
- Explain why value helps companies and the manner in which it does
- Know how to identify trends
- Understand sunk cost
- Know the importance efficiency has on earnings
- Know ways to perform a risk analysis
- Indicate what a countermeasure is
- Know ways to documents successes and failures to guide future innovation

Key Terms

Surrogate: Something that is put in place of another

Breakeven point: The intersection between costs and profits where one more unit sold results in a profit and one less in a loss

Fixed costs: Costs that do not change with the level of product (e.g., computers, insurance, etc.)

Variable costs: Costs that fluctuate with changes in production (e.g., utilities, raw material, etc.)

Lean manufacturing: Concept using tooling and eliminating waste resulting in improved efficiency, effectiveness, and profitability

ISO: Non-governmental organization of 163 countries that voluntarily provides standards to minimize waste and errors for such industries as manufacturing, food safety, technology, agriculture, and healthcare

Project management software: All-encompassing software that manages a project from beginning to end

Social or open-source innovation: Focuses on ideas that are shared by others to perfect existing innovation for the betterment of society and are not concentrated on exclusivity

Resource allocation: The assignment of resources to help firms design, develop, produce, and sell a product to achieve its goals

Projected earnings: The amount of money a company expects to earn after expenses

Trends: Popular course or tendency that is temporary in nature and accepted by society in general

Sunk costs: Costs incurred that can't be recovered

Efficiency: The ability to accomplish a goal in an efficient manner utilizing reduced waste and effort

HOW DO COMPANIES PROJECT UNITS SOLD FOR THEIR INNOVATION?

Forecasting units sold requires a clear understanding of the targeted market to determine how many customers are likely to buy the product. A firm must include the worth of all invested assets to determine if the innovation is worth a true accounting of expenditures, thereby providing a clear picture of the profit or loss a company will likely incur by pursuing the development of the new product. A company can use the following to project the units sold:

- Develop a way to project sales by identifying market variables.
- Take advantage of marketing research.
- Utilize available data to support the projection.
- Use similar products to help with the projection.
- Identify sales in terms of a breakeven point.

What Market Variables Do We Need to Project to Identify Sales?

The way in which a market measures and sells units can vary in comparison to other markets. For example, some markets will measure and sell units individually, while others sell by weight, such as by the pound or ton, while others sell by volume, such as by the cubic yard. Therefore, it is important to identify the industry standard for the unit of sales you will be using to estimate total sales along with the period in which the units are sold. For example, will you measure units sold by day, month, quarter, or year? Establishing the measurable units of sale in a given time period provides a quantifiable way to determine if a company's goals are being met and if and how they compare to prior sales. For many analysts, this constitutes key metrics, which are used to determine if a company is a success or failure, or if a bank is willing to provide the needed capital to fund further growth.

How Do We Use Marketing Research to Gain an Advantage?

A key way to determine how many units will be sold to is to perform a market research. Market researchers devise questions to be researched, such as "Would you buy this product?" and "What do you feel is a price you would you pay"? The answers to these simple questions are used to give a company a general idea of how many units it can anticipate selling and the optimal price to charge. Based on the estimated size of the target market, researchers can project the number of anticipated units to be sold, which in turn provides a company with the profit potential of their innovation. If the responses to the researcher's questions are favorable, then a company should also determine the speed at which it should develop the new products. Therefore, marketing research can provide valuable insights into the company's ability to be successful and also develop an internal schedule for new product development.

How Do Companies Use Available Data to Project Success?

When companies innovate, many answers can be found in the past successes they have had. Firms collect data on customer purchase behavior, so it is likely that past successes will be dictated by the innovations that are similar in nature. Continuous innovation provides ways to estimate success by providing goods and services that satisfied consumers' needs or by answering their requests. In addition, firms can use past data to determine optimal times during which consumers shop, the results of various promotional strategies, and what forms of advertisement have been most successful. It is advantageous for companies to leverage their past successes to create a roadmap and to further build on their strengths and brand. Depending on how serious a company values market research, the cost to obtain information can be significant to nothing more than the time spent sorting through the free information that is available to companies or using social networks to poll users.

How Do Companies Use Surrogate Products to Predict Success?

In order to predict expected sales, companies can use similar or related products known as surrogates. The broad definition of a *surrogate* is something that is put in place of another. An example of a surrogate in a business context is a company that develops facial creams that contain aloe; you can research the sales of similar products. Another example may include using complimentary products to predict sales, such as increased sales in residential real estate could indicate an increased need for carpenters for a variety of remodeling projects over the next ten years. In both examples, a firm can use surrogates to better determine future sales. If the level of predicted sales is not what the company expects, its business plan should be modified to develop strategies to increase sales. Two solutions to address this fairly common situation is to conduct more market testing using actual prototypes of the innovation versus surrogates or reassess if there are other surrogates that might provide better data.

Why is it Important to Identify a Breakeven Point?

A *breakeven point* is the intersection between costs and profits where one more unit sold results in a profit and one less in a loss. The ability to know the breakeven point for an innovation is essential because a company will want to estimate total profitability of its new product. To do a breakeven analysis companies must identify both fixed and variable costs. *Fixed costs* do not change with the level of production (e.g., computers, insurance, etc.). *Variable costs* are costs that fluctuate with changes in production (e.g., utilities, raw material, etc.). Next, the company must identify the projected price of the unit to be sold. This can be done through marketing research efforts or by comparing the new product to similar products. To calculate the breakeven point, use the following formula:

Breakeven point = Fixed costs/(Unit selling price-variable costs)

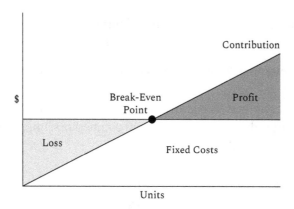

FIG 12.1 Breakeven point

By using the aforementioned methods of projecting sales, a company can determine if its business plan is valid or if it requires further revision. It also gives a company the ability to identify initial costs and search for ways to lower these costs to better compete in the market or to increase profitability. For instance, a company may determine that a significant portion of initial costs could be lowered by subcontracting the production of the product because another company is able to make it for less. This practice varies by market segments, such as manufacturing, where subcomponent parts are routinely placed out for bid, thereby leveraging existing market forces that reward subcontractors for reducing their own costs.

There are two primary benefits that occur when conducting market research, analyzing data, taking advantage of surrogates, and identifying a product's breakeven point. First and foremost, these methods can provide an accurate picture of the variable return on the resources invested. Depending on the market in which the company competes, such as technology, there may not be room for error, which means that a company will benefit from a business plan that is well organized and well informed and is flexible and dynamic, able to adjust to changes in market conditions. Lastly, practicing these methods will lead to greater fluency and result in improved execution.

WHAT VALUE DOES INNOVATION ADD TO THE COMPANY?

While this text primarily focuses on product (goods or services) innovation, another significant area that is regularly used to improve a business is process innovation. This type of innovation can result in improved business practices and create new efficiencies or any number of benefits; therefore, it is important for top managers to improve the quality of the products, increase profits, and add value to the company.

Firms that struggle with innovation should review their business plans to include innovative ways to address customers' needs, improve their operations, and help ensure their long-term success. This type of review should come from the top managers who guide the strategies of the company, and this approach will ultimately add value to the company. The following are ways innovation adds value to companies:[1]

- Improves processes that leads to increased efficiency and productivity, while decreasing costs
- Helps monitor customers' needs and provide products that satisfy them, therefore differentiating the products and services from competitors, improving brand awareness, and increasing market share
- Helps establish new partnerships and relationships
- Helps the company reduce employee turnover

How Does Innovation Lead to Increased Efficiency and Productivity While Decreasing Costs?

Innovation helps companies develop more efficient and productive processes, which results in decreasing costs. Increased efficiencies can be identified in several ways, and one of the most common is to develop a more efficient manufacturing process. This can be achieved through utilizing lean manufacturing. *Lean manufacturing* is a concept that leverages tried-and-true tools to increase quality while also eliminating waste, which translates into applying less effort to improved quality and efficiency, thus increasing profitability.

Lean manufacturing was fashioned from the Toyota Production System, which strived to drive out waste and create zero defects, thus increasing customer satisfaction. It did this in part by actively listening to the workers who produce the products, intentionally integrating their feedback regarding processes (with which they have firsthand experience) as being wasteful, and following up and creating new methods to improve the processes. Prior to the popularity of the Toyota Production System, all processes were developed by engineers and managers, but people in these roles have limited access or experience with processes that create the most waste for the company because they are not directly participating in the production process. It is the workers who have the most valuable input through their experience, both good and bad, and it is this feedback that is critical when a company seeks new ways to be more efficient and increase productivity.

Increased efficiencies can also be achieved by adopting industry-standard processes that improve how companies create products that are safe and reliable and that reduce waste, such as processes that are part of the International Organization for Standardization (ISO). *ISO* is a non-governmental organization with members spanning 163 countries who voluntarily provide standards in an effort to minimize waste and errors for industries such as manufacturing, food safety, technology, agriculture, and healthcare. Currently, there are 11 quality

---

1 "Use Innovation to Grow Your Business," Info Entrepreneurs, http://www.infoentrepreneurs.org/en/guides/use-innovation-to-grow-your-business.

standards in place to help companies increase their efficiencies, reduce defects, provide safe products, and reduce waste.[2]

Increased efficiencies can also be achieved by using project management software. **Project management software** is a tool many companies use that is intended to identify and track all aspects of a project from beginning to end, including tasks such as cost estimation, scheduling, cost control, resource allocation, communications, and more, depending the particular software title's desired attributes. For instance, a common feature of project management software is to send out a notification when collaborative groups must start their piece of the development, which provides a method of communication. By streamlining product development processes, companies can get to market quicker and more efficiently.

One final way (that will be discussed later in the text) to increase efficiency is by reflecting on the innovation process when it is completed. Like benchmarking, companies can review their successes and failures, how the results were derived, and then develop a system to improve their innovation process to make it more effective, efficient, and productive. Accurate notes should be kept throughout the development of any new product, and when a new best practice is identified, a formal policy should be established, allowing the company to get to market faster by using the latest successful processes.

How Can Innovation Increase Value to the Company by Monitoring Customer Needs?

We have discussed at length how satisfying customers' needs is one of the main goals of innovation. As a quick review, monitoring customers' needs is a key driver of innovation and allows companies to increase market share, sales, and profits; however, there are other benefits as well, such as differentiating the products and services of a company, thus increasing loyalty and sales.

In the market, there are many products that are copycat products associated with nationally recognized brands. These include private label brands, store brands, and competitive brands that seek to offer products that have the same coloring, shapes, and ingredients but that are typically offered at a lower price. This has proven to be a very successful way of competing with the main brands in any product segment, yet many consumers feel the original or popular brand offers a difference that distinguishes it from other "knockoffs." These differentiators are associated with quality, style, taste, safety, reliability, and durability, for which the consumer is willing to pay a higher price because these attributes, real or perceived, and they offer added value in satisfying consumer demand or expectations. The result of a company that offers products that satisfy particular consumer preferences is customer loyalty, as it increases brand equity. Brand equity adds value to a company by increasing the worth of brands it owns, which is driven by fairly predictable sales from a loyal customer base.

---

2   Mark Hammar, "List of ISO Quality Management Standards and Frameworks," 9001 Academy, https://advisera.com/9001academy/knowledgebase/list-of-quality-management-standards-and-frameworks/.

Innovation Adds Value through Partnerships and Relationships

Companies can benefit from various partnerships or strategic alliances that they leverage to promote their innovations. Partnerships can vary from short- or long-term durations, as well as by the amount of capital invested to cover expenses. Partnerships also allow companies to utilize another's assets or expertise in technology, processes, human capital, or other specific strengths that offset deficiencies or weaknesses. Therefore, a well-chosen partner can prove a strategic way to create a win-win opportunity for both organizations, compensating each other's weaknesses with the other's strengths. This is especially true for smaller companies with limited resources.

A relatively new area of innovation is social or open-source innovation. *Social or open-source innovation* focuses on ideas that are shared by others to perfect an existing innovation for the betterment of society and does not concentrate on exclusivity or profit. Social or open-source innovation seeks ways to improve existing products in a way that will lead to collaboration not by a group or individual within the confines of a company, but by society at large. There are four main drivers of social or open-source innovation:

- *A voluntary exchange of ideas*: Open-source innovation looks outward to groups or individuals, plus identifies trends that influence innovation.
- *A shift in the roles and responsibilities of who is an innovator*: Ideas are exchanged from voluntary participants and not limited to functional teams or an innovation team within a company.
- *Integrating private capital with public or philanthropic support to create a better world*: Many investors or companies are willing to invest in open-source innovation as part of their social agenda. Firms and philanthropists realize the importance of innovation to make a positive impact on society and this is reflected in their giving.
- *Sharing intellectual property for the betterment of society*: Similarly, in the past, intellectual property was considered a proprietary asset and as something sacred and not to be shared outside the company. Today information is shared with others to make a positive contribution to improving past innovations. For example, Ben Franklin knew his eyeglasses invention would better society, so he shared this to help others and to perfect it.[3] You may be asking yourself, "What are some examples of social or open-source innovation in the present age?" While there are many, we will highlight three that have made an impact on society.[4]

  - *Local Motors*: Local Motors was founded to solve urban mobility challenges in Berlin by 2030. Through social or open-source innovation, the "Ollie" was developed in 2016 and is a self-driving smart bus used to transport people.

---

3   Jeff DeGraff, "Open Source Innovation: What's In and What's Out," Inc., May 11, 2015, https://www.inc.com/jeff-degraff/open-source-innovation-what-s-in-and-what-s-out.html.

4   Merit Morikawa, "16 Examples of Open Innovation—What Can We Learn from Them?" Viima, November 20, 2016, https://www.viima.com/blog/16-examples-of-open-innovation-what-can-we-learn-from-them.

- *Lego*: Lego is not a new company but has opened a create-and-share site to allow for open-source innovation by providing ideas for new products. The result is a generation of over one thousand ideas annually, which keeps this iconic brand on the shelves and builds sales.
- *General Electric (GE)*: Connecting with Young Talent: GE has created an open-source model that encourages collegiate innovators to come up with new ideas and rewards the best products with scholarships, monetary awards, and a chance to work at GE.

Social or open-source innovation is in and of itself innovative because it breaks the traditional rules of business by sharing with other companies, and often times a company's competitors, ways to improve past innovations, and through an open network, improve on them, which also creates a much shorter and less expensive feedback loop. We have discussed the need to reduce groupthink in the text and to seek a diverse cross-functional group when innovating, and social or open-source innovation accomplishes this by allowing for a potentially limitless amount of input from which to innovate, which can also reduce the typical time it takes to get to market and offer an endless number of other new product ideas.

THINK ABOUT THIS!

Consider each major form public transportation in use today: automobiles via roads, trains via rail, boats via water, and airplanes via air. While none of these methods were ever owned by any one individual or company, what if another form of transportation was developed that proved to be remarkably faster, safer, and cheaper than any of our current forms of transportation? And what if this technology was owned by one person or one company?

In 2013, Elon Musk released plans to the public for what he referred to as the "fifth form of transportation" and called it Hyperloop. The open-source project was initially developed and documented by several hundred SpaceX and Tesla engineers, resulting in a 57-page paper with no strings attached or ownership claims to the technology. In the years since, thousands of engineers and engineering students from around the world have further developed and tested the idea of shooting levitating pods full of people through air-free tubes at speeds in excess of 600 mph. Additionally, dozens of companies have formed with the goal of capitalizing on this emerging and tantalizingly disruptive technology, including Sir Richard Branson with Virgin Hyperloop One.

What's more, several test tracks have been built, including one at SpaceX headquarters in Hawthorne, California, where every year since 2017 a competition is held to test the validity of different engineering approaches to the concept of the Hyperloop, and each year, all of the participants and attendees witness firsthand which designs outperform the others. Think about this! What are the benefits of encouraging teams of engineers from all over the world to wrestle with the engineering problems associated with Hyperloop? What would have happened to the idea of Hyperloop if Elon Musk had patented the technology and tried to develop and commercialize the idea himself? Is it better that these challenges are being addressed by open-source teams, or would it have been better to keep this technology closed and owned by a single entity?[5]

How Does Innovation Reduce Employee Turnover?

Talent is extremely important when developing innovations, and companies can use their innovations as a recruitment tool to attract the best talent who align with the company's mission and vision. Employee turnover is a significant problem for companies due the expense associated with recruitment, training, and the overall support of new employees; therefore, many companies offer incentives to retain and grow their workforce that benefit both the employee and the company. These incentives include flex time, telecommuting, gourmet cafeterias, on-campus pharmacies, free childcare, retirement matching plans, well-appointed breakrooms, and more.

So, how does innovation reduce employee turnover? One way is through a company's specific efforts to develop innovations that better society. Employees who feel their work is providing a meaningful difference to others is much more compelling than feeling their work does not. Millennials are particularly concerned about social justice and environmental issues, and it is especially important for this generation to understand how their work adds value to the world in a measurable way, so many companies that are considered innovative work to satisfy these needs and desires and thus retain their talent.

A second way innovation reduces employee turnover is by creating a stimulating work environment through the development of new products that are considered groundbreaking, revolutionary, or disruptive to the existing market. This excitement helps to drive employees' efforts, often much longer than a typical forty-hour work week, because they feel deeply invested in the outcome, and despite the additional effort, burnout is often much lower than expected.

A final way that innovation reduces employee turnover, among many others, is by satisfying both extrinsic and intrinsic needs of employees. Innovation satisfies both methods of needs satisfaction by providing a way to be rewarded both externally and internally. When external needs are met through mechanisms such as bonuses or other monetary rewards, promotions, or even symbolic gestures that recognize employees for their efforts, they feel appreciated. Additionally, when employees' intrinsic needs are met through recognition of their work and the values of the company align with their own internal values, it provides a deep level of satisfaction that is often conveyed as gratitude. Certainly, both are strong motivators for retaining employees, and many of the companies that are considered the most

---

5   Nick Easen, "Elon Musk's Hyperloop Debuts an Open Source Approach to Megaprojects," *Raconteur*, December 1, 2017, https://www.thetimes.co.uk/raconteur/technology/elon-musks-hyperloop-debuts-open-source-approach-megaprojects/; "Hyperloop," SpaceX, https://www.spacex.com/hyperloop; "Hyperloop," Wikipedia, https://en.wikipedia.org/wiki/Hyperloop; "Hyperloop One," Virgin, https://hyperloop-one.com/.

innovative employers provide ways for employees to be satisfied through a blend of both extrinsic and intrinsic means.

Just as it is important to consider all the methods described earlier in this chapter to develop innovation, the same is true of retaining talent, and as the values of the workforce change, a company should reevaluate the methods used to attract and retain talent, which should also entail a revision of its business plan. Top managers should constantly evaluate how the company adds value, and these methods of evaluation should be inclusive and transparent to their entire workforce to help identify waste and new areas of improvement. It is this holistic approach that transforms a typical company into a vibrant community and adds value to the overall organization.

How Do We Allocate Resources?

Resource allocation is at the heart of the planning that goes into innovation. *Resource allocation* is the assignment of resources to help a company design, develop, produce, and sell a product to achieve its goals. When a company reviews its success or failure with an innovation, the results can often be predicted, albeit through hindsight, in how the company allocated resources for the new product's development.

THINK ABOUT THIS!

What resources did you utilize to get into your school? Did you have a plan to select dorms and pay tuition? Do you have a plan in place to graduate on time with your selected major? What happens if your plans change? Do you have a secondary plan in place?

For most college students, showing up on move-in day was the result of a resource allocation plan set to achieve your goal of graduating with a degree in a field that will allow you to get a job that excites you. Perhaps your plan initially started by identifying schools that had majors that were in line with your career goals. Next, you probably started preparing for the SAT to achieve the score suggested by the school. After that, you visited the school to see if you had a good feeling about not only attending classes but living there for the next four to five years. You applied, assessed the costs, and probably discussed these issues with your parents or someone in your support network. If you received a loan, you needed to plan to apply so the money would be available when tuition was due, and so on. The bottom line is that a well thought out plan needs advanced planning to identify the resources that are available to you to help you realize your dream. The same holds true for innovators. Innovators must identify the resources they have at their disposal and formulate a plan that will allow them or their functional team to bring the product to fruition. Since resources are often limited, it is vital for innovators to develop a resource allocation plan to better utilize what is available to them for success.

How Do We Estimate Projected Earnings?

Calculating projected earnings is as important to a company as coming up with a key innovation. As we have stressed in this text, the importance of addressing customer's needs along with a company's ability to make a difference for society and itself by using profits to benefit its stakeholders and by earning a profit through successful projections is essential to short- and long-term survival, as it is indicative of why an innovation should exist in the market.

Projected earnings are the amount of money a company expects to earn after expenses. To estimate earnings, there are several methods that can be used to determine the projected income. One of the simplest methods is to forecast sales and expenses and then subtract the two. Another method is to identify the forecasted sales and multiple them by the projected net profit margin. Both of these methods will help the innovation team project the expense per unit, the projected number of units that can be sold to the target market, and the profit margin it will realize before the product is launched. More sophisticated methods include performing regression analysis using trends in the market to estimate earnings. An additional method includes using scenario analysis, which projects earnings at various ranges and allows a company to pit the worst-case scenario against the best-case scenario to decide the appropriate amount of money the company should allocate and expect to earn from the innovation. Typically, companies will analyze the business environment to determine what scenario is most likely to yield the best result. Factors that influence the scenario are the amount and level of competition, political-legal considerations, size of the distribution area, and complexity of the product, just to name a few.

Other Considerations for Estimating Projected Earnings

While estimating projected earnings involves the aforementioned methods, other factors that should be considered are as follows:

1. Trends
2. Sunk costs
3. Competitive response
4. Efficiency

Trends

Trends are a popular course or tendency that are accepted and supported by societal interests. When estimating how trends affect projected earnings, innovators must consider if the current trend affecting the need for innovation is a fad (product with short-term popularity) or if it will be supported as a long-term solution by the target market. Products that are a fad should be considered to provide short-term profitability and then possibly sold at the height of its popularity. Products that have the potential to be in the product lifecycle for the long term have projected earnings that are more easily calculated. Therefore, it is recommended that innovators determine, as best they can, if the innovation is likely to be a fad or a long-term trend when calculating their anticipated earnings.

While this may be easier said than done, there are signs that innovators should look for that help differentiate a fad from a trend. A fad has rapid growth and decline in the market. Fads tend to experience better-than-average initial sales, combined with the inability to replenish orders. However, repeat purchases tend to rapidly decline after the second or third reorder or version, depending on the market. Companies that experience this type of consumer behavior must recognize the need to sell the product at its popularity to other companies wishing to capitalize on this popular product, or quickly innovate an attribute to offer new value through the product to extend its lifecycle.

A trend is a product that grows at a consistent rate initially, but sales tend to strengthen as an increasing number of consumers adopt it. Examples of trends include online shopping and dating, increased student loan debt forcing graduates to return to their parent's home, and the use of debit and credit cards instead of cash. Trends are predictable if the marketplace is scanned to gain insights on consistent behaviors.

Sunk Costs

Sunk costs are costs that are incurred and cannot be recovered. Examples of sunk costs include employee training, consultants, advertising, and product research. While it can be argued that these costs are not recoverable, sunk costs do serve a purpose to better the company; therefore, it is important to incur some unrecoverable costs to improve or better the firm. Another way to avoid too many sunk costs is to put money into recoverable or billable areas for future expenditures after the sunk costs are incurred. For example, if a company bought a piece of equipment for $10,000 and then later discovered that it requires $5,000 in repairs, if another company offered to buy the equipment for $5,000 it would make sense to sell it versus investing another $5,000 into the equipment. As the old saying goes "Don't throw good money after bad," and in this scenario, it would make good sense to realize a loss and sell; therefore, when projecting future earnings, try to limit the sunk costs and utilize recoverable expenses.

Competitive Response

Competitive response is the reaction your competitors will have toward your products. Traditionally, to estimate projected earnings, an advertising budget is established to make people aware of your new product and counter any claims made by your competitors. Based on the competitive threat that exists, their response will impact your estimated earnings in the form of samples, advertising, sales expenses such as the sales force, vehicles, expense accounts, and so on, as well as discounts to gain market share. One proven method to counter a competitive threat is to enter a smaller market and then transition to a larger one. Another method is to expand your market through online channels, thus increasing your customer base at a global scale. Whatever the strategy used, a competitive response will impact your projected earnings and should be considered in your estimates.

Efficiency

Efficiency is the ability to accomplish a goal in an efficient manner utilizing reduced waste and effort. When a company is projecting earnings for their innovation, it is key that the new project target a substantial market, as this will increase the potential number of units sold. It is also important to be as efficient as possible to fully utilize the company's capabilities and leverage its particular strengths. Efficiency decreases expenses, which conversely increases earnings. What are ways companies can increase efficiency?

- *Technology*: Is the company utilizing the latest technology to make work more efficient? A few examples include software, automated phone systems, marketing, and machinery.
- *Production*: Does the company have machines that produce goods at a higher rate and with less waste? Rapid manufacturing equipment (machines that can do several steps versus just one) increase efficiencies by eliminating the space and time it takes to move from machine to machine and to manufacture the item. Companies also utilize six sigma principles to increase efficiencies to reduce waste incurred during their production processes.
- *Use of existing space*: Is the company using its available space as efficiently as possible? As previously discussed, just-in-time inventory (produce and ship) techniques help eliminate the need for warehouse space. Also, the use of rapid manufacturing equipment can be beneficial, as this type of equipment often frees up space that is typically used to house several machines. Companies are also implementing hoteling (sharing of desks between employees) to reduce the need for unused office space.
- *Suppliers*: Are a company's suppliers consistently providing quality products at the best price? Suppliers offer a wide variety of products used in the manufacturing of tangible products. Inconsistent quality means more waste and could damage the reputation of the company making these goods. Therefore, specifications must be given to suppliers to communicate the expectations of the companies buying their goods. Pricing should be reviewed periodically to ensure the firm is getting the best price with the best terms.
- *Sales force*: Is the company's salesforce being productive which is a key driver of profitability? Firms can increase sales efficiencies by encouraging the salesforce to upsell (offering higher price goods), cross-sell (sell complementary goods), and plan their sales routes so that time spent on the road is in front of customers rather than looking out a windshield.
- *Customer selection*: Is the company analyzing who their best customers are to maintain their loyalty and increase purchasing behavior? Customers with great potential need to be targeted, while the worst customers should be given less attention.

Projecting estimated earnings may seem simple, but it is imperative that a company understand these concepts and become proficient at projecting accurate estimates. While this section has presented some well-known factors that often impact projecting earnings, every sector faces different challenges at different times; therefore, it is important that estimating projected earnings be conducted by top management and all functional areas to determine if the innovation sought is worth the firm's time and resources. While the betterment of society and caring for the Earth are top priorities for companies when innovating, without profits the company will cease to exist. Therefore, a balance must be sought to improve the company and better the stakeholders that are part of the firm.

How Do We Perform a Risk Analysis and Devise Countermeasures?

Every step of the way, there are varying levels of risk associated with developing a new product. A company is wise to perform a risk analysis and devise countermeasures to either eliminate or minimize the adverse effects that risk could cause to the sales of the new product and to the company. This is a reinforcement from previous chapters.

Risk Analysis

When performing a risk analysis, there are five steps that must take place:

1. Identify the risks associated with the new product and the company.
2. Consider how the risks could adversely affect sales of the new product and the company.
3. Prioritize the risks and devise countermeasures.
4. Document the results and enact the best solutions.
5. Review the results and establish best practices.

Identify the Risks Associated with the New Product and the Company

When identifying risks, firms must identify the potential threats that jeopardize their success. Risks could include but are not limited to socioeconomic, political-legal, technological, competitive, environmental-physical, and global forces (i.e., the external environment). Risks are both generalized and specific to certain industries. Whatever the risk, companies must conduct a fair assessment of what the risks are and how to identify the ones that impact their innovation. A suggested method of assessing the risks is to conduct a SWOT analysis; however, it is essential to understand the environment in which a firm must compete, and a SWOT can help to analyze this.

Consider How the Risks Could Adversely Affect Sales of the New Product and the Company

Once the risks are revealed, it should be determined how they can affect the firm. Proactive strategies should be instituted to negate or minimize the risks, so their effect will not hurt the firm. Once discovered, these risks should be monitored, as they are recognizable obstacles the firm should avoid. The firm should enact strategies that will counteract these risks and formulate ways to neutralize them. It is better that firms be proactive than reactive, meaning that anticipating risks and ways to reduce their threat is easier to address when a firm has time to identify them and figure out ways to address them.

Prioritize the Risks and Devise Countermeasures

Risks should be prioritized by ranking them from most threating to least threatening. In addition, countermeasures must be instituted to neutralize their threat to the company. Countermeasures are specific to individual business sectors. For example, in the financial markets, a way to reduce the number of bad loans is to make the requirements for borrowing money more stringent. Therefore, once the risk is identified, a capable team of top managers should convene to devise counter measures to eliminate the risk.

Document the Results and Establish Best Practices

Countermeasures that are effective should be documented, and best practices should be implemented. Measurable means should to utilized to evaluate the countermeasures to determine their effectiveness. If a countermeasure is not effective, alternative measures should be enacted and evaluated. Due to the specificity of each industry, countermeasures that are effective should be benchmarked and utilized in times where threats to the firm occur. It is important that firms document what the risk was and the countermeasure utilized to counteract it with the results, so when risks of a similar nature are experienced again, a quick response can be utilized.

Review the Results and Benchmark Best Practices

Once the threat has been successfully countered, the results should be reviewed and documented. It is important that a firm determine if the company acted in a timely manner, if the countermeasure used appropriate, and the result of the damage. Due to the specificity of each industry, countermeasures that are effective should be benchmarked and utilized in times where threats to the firm occur. Benchmarking best practices is an effective way to deal with threats and should be reviewed for improvement (see future chapters for a full discovery of their benefits).

Review Questions

1. How can innovators project ways to determine units sold?
2. What are some market variable innovators we can use to project sales?
3. How does marketing research help innovators?
4. How can firms use available data to predict sales?
5. What are surrogates companies can use to estimate sales?
6. Why are partnerships important to innovators?
7. How does innovation reduce employee turnover?
8. How do firms allocate resources?
9. How do firms estimate projected earnings?
10. Why do firms calculate risk?

Discussion Questions

1. Why is projecting units sold so important for companies?
2. Share with the professor why market research is key for product success.
3. Do you feel open-source innovation is valuable for companies? Why?
4. When you graduate, what are ways firms can keep you to stay employed with them?
5. Share other means to project earnings not discussed in the text. Why do you feel these are important?
6. What are other factors to consider when conducting a risk analysis?
7. Share with the professor countermeasures that are not listed in the text.
8. What current industry do you feel presents the biggest growth and earning potential?

Extension Activity

1. Discuss how Monster energy drinks could innovate to make a new product. Would this new product add value to the company? Why?
2. Gather a group of students and perform a social innovation project based around a theme the professor selects. What did you learn working in a group? Do you feel you made progress? What group dynamics did you experience?

BIBLIOGRAPHY

"Use Innovation to Grow Your Business," Info Entrepreneurs, http://www.infoentrepreneurs.org/en/guides/use-innovation-to-grow-your-business.

Hammar, Mark. "List of ISO Quality Management Standards and Frameworks," 9001 Academy, https://advisera.com/9001academy/knowledgebase/list-of-quality-management-standards-and-frameworks/.

DeGraff, Jeff. "Open Source Innovation: What's In and What's Out," Inc., May 11, 2015, https://www.inc.com/jeff-degraff/open-source-innovation-what-s-in-and-what-s-out.html.

Morikawa, Merit. "16 Examples of Open Innovation—What Can We Learn from Them?" Viima, November 20, 2016, https://www.viima.com/blog/16-examples-of-open-innovation-what-can-we-learn-from-them.

Easen, Nick. "Elon Musk's Hyperloop Debuts an Open Source Approach to Megaprojects," *Raconteur*, December 1, 2017, https://www.thetimes.co.uk/raconteur/technology/elon-musks-hyperloop-debuts-open-source-approach-megaprojects/; "Hyperloop," SpaceX, https://www.spacex.com/hyperloop; "Hyperloop," Wikipedia, https://en.wikipedia.org/wiki/Hyperloop; "Hyperloop One," Virgin, https://hyperloop-one.com/.

Figure Credits

Fig. 12.1: Source: https://commons.wikimedia.org/wiki/File:CVP-FC-Contrib-PL-BEP.svg.

Disciplined Preparation: Communication, Presentation, and Validation

CHAPTER THIRTEEN

Storytelling and the Art of the Presentation

INTRODUCTION

People are drawn to compelling stories, and great stories are steeped in aura. So it is true of the markets' most compelling products: They all come with a story. What's more, when consumers learn of a compelling product, many will imagine using that product in a variety of scenarios or scenes, and in so doing, they begin creating their own association with the product through a story.

Take a moment to think of a time when you told someone about a great new product that you had just discovered. What did you say? How did you say it? Recall the tone of your voice and your body language. Think about how else you engaged the other person as you told him or her about this great new product. Pretty simple, right? You shared your personal experience using the same method as everyone else: You told a story. And this should be the foundation from which you deliver any presentation; however formal or informal, tell a story.

To observe this firsthand, watch any presentation with Steve Jobs, who is widely regarded as one of the best presenters to ever pitch a new product, and you will hear something more than how Apple approached a particular design challenge, or what the next generation's technical specifications were for their new device. As you listen and watch closely, ask yourself why so many of his audiences have described his charismatic presentations as something akin to being enveloped in a "reality distortion field." The answer is simple: He was a master at storytelling. And even though Steve Jobs will most likely be remembered as the CEO of Apple, let us also remember that prior to his return to Apple in 1997 he led one of the most profitable film studios, which was later purchased by Disney for $7.4 billion in Disney stock, and that company was Pixar.

Learning Objectives

In this chapter students will learn about the following:

- How PowerPoint presentations can be effective, as long as the presenter understands how to create slides that support a compelling presentation
- Ways to make a presentation heard and gain attention
- How to make a good first impression in three to five seconds
- How a great presentation boasts the aura of the presenter and company
- What risks and countermeasures are and why they are important
- Ways to use certain indicators to find global opportunities
- Why guided financial outcomes are better than financial pro forma
- Why getting your audience to ask questions is vital
- Why seeking what the audience expects from a presentation is key before you present
- Why one number or letter delivers an impression that is memorable

Learning Outcomes

By the end of this chapter students will be able to do the following:

- Put together a short, dynamic presentation
- Grab attention within the first three to five seconds
- Apply six techniques to get your presentation heard and remembered
- Prepare a dynamic presentation that can boost your aura
- Understand risks and develop countermeasures
- Use indicators to determine opportunities globally
- Understand why financial reporting for future results is guided versus absolute
- Incorporate questions into presentations at the appropriate time
- Know the importance of sending out an email before the presentation to deliver a message that will satisfy the needs of the audience
- Know why a number or letter is vital to remembering information shared during a presentation

Key Terms

Audience: An individual or group of people who are presented information in hopes of educating them and creating awareness

Five slides or less: An analogy for limiting the number of PowerPoint slides and including other methods of delivering information

Presentation: The act of presenting an object, material, or information to an audience in hopes they comprehend the information provided

Communication: The imparting or exchanging of information or news

Sender: A person who sends or transmits a message, letter, email, etc.

Receiver: A person who is given or accepts something that has been sent or given to them

Noise: Anything that interrupts the ability for a sender to send a message and the receiver to comprehend it

Three-to-five-second rule: An expression indicating one needs to make a good first impression within the first three to five seconds to gain attention and get the audience to like you

Guilty by association: A psychological fact that people are associated with other people, institutions, or groups and this forms the impression society forms of them versus the actual truth

Risk: The possibility of loss due to an event or occurrence

Countermeasure: An action used to stop a risk or threat from occurring

Gross domestic product (GDP): Total value of a finished goods and services produced in a specified period

Unemployment rate: An indicator of the number of people who are jobless

Rate of inflation: A percentage of the rising cost of goods

Consumer Confidence Index (CCI): An index that determines how Americans feel about the country's financial health, the economy's current financial health, and the state of the economy in the most recent six-month period

Producer Pricing Index (PPI): An index that measures price changes from a seller's perspective over time

Consumer Price Index (CPI): An index that measures the average of goods and services to determine inflation and deflation

Guidance: Advice or information aimed at resolving a problem or difficulty, especially given by someone of authority

Theory of constraints (TOC): A way to identify current constraints and discover ways to progress past bottlenecks

FIVE SLIDES OR LESS: WHY?

Even though you have listened to stories, read stories, and, in one form or another, watched stories unfold before your very eyes all of your life (if you are a gamer, you have likely interacted directly with other characters and players within a story for hours on end), it can be helpful to talk about some of the ingredients that make up a great story, especially in the context of delivering a presentation about a new product.

First and foremost, great stories engage our emotions. They cause us to feel differently than we normally do, and in the context of presenting a new product, the story you tell should do more than just excite the audience to either buy or invest in the product but also engage in the product's story, which includes a cast of characters, such as your company, your team of product developers and testers, existing customers, and, last but not least, the product's aura. Remember, most of the human brain is wired for emotions. To deliver a presentation that does not engage the audience's emotions is more than a missed opportunity; it's a waste of your time and your audience's, and it just so happens that the best way to do this is to tell a story. (After you have watched an Apple keynote by Steve Jobs, compare it to a Microsoft keynote by Bill Gates. Who told a compelling story, and who focused on facts, figures, and language that sounds like tired, bland marketing lingo?)

Second, when delivering a presentation, tell a story that builds a bridge to the audience's imagination in a way that stirs their emotions, convinces them to become active an listener in your story rather than passive and bored bystanders. Great presenters do this in a way that invites the audience to be included in the story rather than trying to convince them of what you are proposing or selling. Think about a recent time when you were listening to a speaker who compelled you to transform into an active listener. How did you feel? You likely felt as though the presenter was talking with you (not *to* you), and because of this, you likely felt *included* in the presentation and that your presence mattered, rather than then listening to some random person blather on about some meaningless information, where the speaker, his or her pitch, and your presence didn't matter at all.

Third, your story should include why the new product matters and how it will provide new and important value to anyone who uses it. If the new product is based on an existing product, your story should focus on the product's most compelling and valued features. Remember, your goal is not to drown your audience in the new product's details, but to tell a story where the product's new features are helpful agents that will make your audience rock stars when they either use or invest in your new product.

Last, your story should lead your audience to a conclusion that makes perfect sense; they should leave thinking to themselves, "Of course, they created this new product; it's a no-brainer that is practically guaranteed success, and of course *they* are the ones who created it; no one else in the market is capable of introducing a new product like this."

Yet, rather than engage an audience with a story, most presenters instead choose to create a series of PowerPoint slides. In 2018, Microsoft reported that there were 35 million PowerPoint presentations a day or four hundred per second used when presenting,[1] so it should come as no surprise that many audiences feel that they have experienced what is referred to as "death by PowerPoint." And while there is nothing wrong with using PowerPoint to supplement your presentation, presenters who rely too heavily on their slides usually never capture their audi-

| Emotional engagement with your audience | > | Energy expended reading, summarizing information, or conveying data on slides | = | Increased opportunity for a successful presentation |

FIG 13.1 **Presentation practice formula**

ence's attention. Consider the following formula as a simple test as you develop and practice your presentation.

1   "Best Presentation Software List: Complete 2019 Guide," Slide Bean, February 1, 2019, https://slidebean.com/blog/best-presentation-software-list-2018#best-powerpoint-alternatives.

An *audience* is an individual or group of people who are presented information in hopes of being educated and developing awareness. Think of a class when the lecturer lost your attention. What did you do? Many students resort to texting, checking social media, or completing homework for other classes. And how do lecturers respond when they notice they've lost their audience? Most often, they have become accustomed to being ignored and apathetic about presenting, or they double-down on trying to gain the audiences' attention, which is often driven by anger and comes off as aggressive, and this simply makes a poor presentation worse.

This section is entitled "Five Slides or Less" and refers to the fact that presentations should include more than just a PowerPoint to deliver the information. *Five slides or less* is a method that ensures the presenter limits the number of PowerPoint slides and includes other methods of delivering information. A *presentation* is the act of presenting an object, material, or information to an audience in hopes they comprehend the information provided, often with the hope of influencing the audience to do something, even if that is nothing more than increasing awareness or caring about a lesser known topic or issue. All communication occurs between what are called senders and receivers. *Communication* is the imparting or exchanging of information or news and the *sender* is a person who sends or transmits a message, letter, or email, while the *receiver* is a person who is the recipient of the communication. The interference of successfully sending a message and receiving it is called noise. *Noise* is anything that interrupts of ability for a sender to send a message and and the receiver to comprehend it (Refer to Chapter 6). What is important is that the message sent by the presenter be as informative and engaging as possible to capture and retain the audience's attention.

HOW DO YOU TAKE THIS FROM THEORY TO PRACTICE?

In Guy Kawasaki's book, *Art of the Start*, he recommends a simple and effective formula for presenting what has become famous among entrepreneurs and venture capitalists alike, which is known as the 10-20-30 rule. The rule works like this: Limit your presentation to no more than ten slides, plan to present for no more than twenty minutes, and use a font on each slide that is no smaller than thirty points. More specifically, your slides should be organized with no more than two slides for your introduction, seven slides for the body of your presentation, and one slide for your closing. If you choose to practice the 10-20-30 rule, it will ensure that your presentation is succinct, with only the most pertinent information, rather than usual onslaught of relentless PowerPoint slides that bludgeon audiences into a nearly unrecoverable state of boredom.

So, what are some other secrets to delivering a message that will gain attention and influence receivers? Forbes offers a list of the top six ways a presenter can deliver information without using a PowerPoint:[2]

---

2   Kristi Hedges, "Six Ways to Avoid Death by PowerPoint," *Forbes*, November 14, 2014, https://www.forbes.com/sites/work-in-progress/2014/11/14/six-ways-to-avoid-death-by-powerpoint/#5bd4084264d4.

1. Mix up the type of material in the presentation.
2. Provide the information before the presentation.
3. Break up the presentation by utilizing group discussions and exercises.
4. Provide a summary sheet.
5. Use attention getting software.
6. Include a show and tell.

Mix Up the Type of Material in the Presentation

Instead of relying solely on PowerPoint slides, the presenter should consider incorporating other types of material into the presentation, such as a photo, an item to pass around, social media, a meme, or other objects that will add meaning to the presentation and maintain the audience's attention. By introducing various types of material, the presenter is connecting with the audience at various sensory levels. Science has shown that increased attention and focus are positively correlated, gaining access to as many of the five senses as possible. Therefore, mixing up the material in a manner that will connect with all the senses will increase the attention and focus of the audience.[3]

Provide the Information before the Presentation

Providing the audience with the presentation material ahead of time is also a good way to inspire them to reflect on the information and increase the chances of the audience enriching the presentation with their comments and questions; however, it is not recommended that the audience receive a copy of the entire presentation because the audience may not show up for the presentation because they do not believe there is any other value to be gained by attending. Instead, the presenter should send a summary of the presentation that piques the audience's interest to learn more. Another approach to this method is to start a social media page and introduce some of the content to encourage conversation that will likely contribute to your presentation.

Giving the audience members a preview can also help explain challenging or difficult concepts so that the presenter can focus on engaging with the audience rather than getting bogged down by detailed explanations. This allows audience members the time to do their own research on the topics and increase their awareness and understanding, thereby increasing the audience's comprehension of the information.

---

3   Lena Groeger, "Making Sense of the World, Several Sense at a Time," *Scientific American,* February 28, 2012, https://www.scientificamerican.com/article/making-sense-world-sveral-senses-at-time/.

Break Up the Presentation by Utilizing Group Discussions and Exercises

The average human attention span in the digital world is only eight seconds. This is down from twelve seconds reported in 2000.[4] This means that gaining even one audience member's attention and holding it is virtually impossible, and the digital world is a temptation so great for many people that is often supersedes everything else.

One way to gain and maintain the audience's attention span is to encourage group discussions, exercises, and reflection. The presenter should consider his or her role more of a "facilitator" of active discussions by asking the audience thought-provoking questions to be discussed and answered by the groups. Plan on dedicating only two–four minutes on this activity because once the question is answered, the audience will likely begin conversing on other topics or become distracted in other ways. Once the groups have answered the question, the presenter asks for the group's responses.

Exercises are another way to maintain attention. Give the audience an activity to complete and then ask them to report their results. While the presenter should consider whether it is advantageous to ask the audience to perform the activity as individuals or as groups, the end goal is to have the audience report back on their results. Ideally, the presenter should be prepared to capture these results to honor the work of the audience and leverage their efforts to further develop and promote the idea(s) related to the presentation.

Finally, setting aside a few minutes for personal reflection can also be an effective way to engage an audience. Reflection is usually a time for audience members to quietly think about their thoughts and is particularly useful when the presenter wants the audience members to recall a personal experience of some kind or to imagine a different future if either the current set of circumstances were to change or remain the same. Again, the presenter should be prepared to capture their audience's reflections, and these often provide some of the most powerful and potent results because they usually are deeply rooted in the audience's emotions.

Provide a Handout of the Presentation

A handout provides the audience with a way to take notes and follow along with the presentation. The presenter should be cautioned to not cram the handout with too much information as it will likely confuse or overwhelm the audience. The most effective handouts contain a summary of the topics that the presenter will cover, yet the audience is still required to listen or participate in order to realize the value of the presentation. Another welcome aspect of a handout is that it gives the audience a ready-made opportunity to take notes alongside the material, which helps increase comprehension. Handouts also increase the opportunity for the audience to engage with others after the presentation by sharing or discussing the information that was provided.

---

4   Simon Maybin, "Busting the Attention Span Myth," *BBC News,* March 10, 2017, https://www.bbc.com/news/health-38896790.

Use Attention-Capturing Software

Compelling visuals are a very effective means of gaining attention. The brain processes visual cues sixty thousand times faster than text, so integrating visuals can dramatically increase the success of a presentation.[5] Software titles such as Prezi, Slidebean, and Apple Keynote can provide the visual attraction needed to inform an audience while retaining their attention, which is the greatest challenge for any presenter.

Presenters who take the time to learn how to use these technologies demonstrate to an audience that they care about their audience's experience, and it also conveys that they are keeping up with the latest trends, which is always positive. However, if the presenter is not well versed in a using a software title, it often results in disaster. Give yourself plenty of time to ensure that you understand how the software works and how to navigate through your presentation if an audience member asks you to return to a prior point. Lastly, ensure that the software is not what will distract from your presentation, but rather support it. Some presenters can distract their audience by overusing the "special effects" that are available with the software, so use these features sparingly and review your presentation to ensure the information remains in focus.

Have a Show and Tell

Using props or artifacts during your presentation can help deliver a message that informs the audience. For example, if the presenter is sharing information about a new phone app, it would be wise to have the app available so the audience can see how it works. Using props can help an audience visualize what the presenter is speaking about, or in the case of a physical prop, it can engage the audience's tactile senses versus trying to describe something with which the audience has no previous experience, thus delivering a more effective way to convey the message that is likely to be much more memorable.

THE THREE-TO-FIVE-SECOND RULE

In the first three to five seconds, the presenter should direct his or her efforts toward building an emotional connection with the audience. The *three-to-five-second rule* is an expression indicating one needs to make a good first impression within the first three to five seconds to gain attention and get the audience to like you. People chose to do business with people they like. If you can connect with your audience in a positive manner, they are more likely to be receptive to you and you can accomplish more.[6] The length of time in which we make first

---

5   Amanda Sibley, "19 Reasons You Should Include Visual Content in Your Marketing [Data]," Hub Spot, August 6, 2012, https://blog.hubspot.com/blog/tabid/6307/bid/33423/19-Reasons-You-Should-Include-Visual-Content-in-Your-Marketing-Data.aspx.

6   Amy Rees Anderson, "People Do Business with People They Like," *Forbes*, June 28, 2013, https://www.forbes.com/sites/amyanderson/2013/06/28/people-do-business-with-people-they-like/#e7bf35b309f7.

impressions varies by report. A study by Willis and Todorov found that first impressions are made in milliseconds,[7] while *Business Insider* claims it can take as long as seven seconds.[8] Whichever report you believe is true, it is imperative to introduce yourself to your audience in a way they will find appealing, which in turn will cause them to be more receptive to the information you are presenting and help form a lasting relationship.

There are several ways to accomplish the three-to-five-second rule, which include the following:

1. **Show a warm smile.** When meeting your audience for the first time, give them a warm and sincere smile. Facial expressions are a great way to make a good first expression. Try to smile naturally and not force a smile that is likely to be perceived as fake. It is always best to convey a feeling of sincerity and warmth while at the same time being authentic.

2. **Shake hands in an appropriate manner.** A good rule is to extend your hand, look down, place your hand in theirs, and then look up. This helps to prevent the "dead fish" handshake and ensures that your hand will successfully meet theirs, rather than causing a near miss or a half-handed handshake. Take care not to apply too much pressure. Slight pressure is acceptable, but don't overdo it, regardless of the person's gender.

3. **Introduce yourself to your audience.** An introduction is a good way to break the ice with a new group. If you are meeting an individual for the first time, consider repeating his or her name a few times early in your conversation, or consider rhyming his or her name with another word in your head, so that you are more likely to remember it. If you are meeting a new group of people, consider providing them with name tags so that you can call on any of them using their name during your presentation, further establishing an emotional connection between you and them. People are more attentive when you can call them by name, plus it shows you care. Whichever the scenario, a warm introduction sets the stage for a good relationship.

4. **Speak in a clear tone and at an acceptable volume.** Try not to speak too fast or loud, mumble, or use slang. Adjust your speech to the audience you are addressing. For instance, you likely talk differently to your grandparents than with your friends. A way to judge what is acceptable is to listen to the speaker first to gain a sense of what he or she considers acceptable speech and then adjust your style as best you can. Someone who adjusts his or her speech for better communication and who is articulate is someone who will most likely create a positive first impression.

---

7 Janine Willis and Alexander Todorov, "First Impressions: Making Up Your Mind after a 100-ms Exposure to a Face," *Psychological Science* 17, no. 7 (2006): 592–598.

8 Anna Pitts, "You Only Have 7 Seconds to Make a Strong First Impression," *Business Insider,* April 8, 2013, http://www.businessinsider.com/only-7-seconds-to-make-first-impression-2013-4.

5. **Maintain eye contact and avoid looking away**. People who avoid eye contact often create a poor impression. When speaking with someone new, maintain eye contact without staring. It is polite to look away briefly, but maintain a warm contact with your audience as much as possible.

6. **Be aware of how you look**. Ask yourself if you are dressed appropriately. If you have piercings or tattoos, would it be best if they were covered up? One way to determine this is to ask ahead of time about what is expected or acceptable. It is better to err on the side of caution than to make an incorrect assumption. Once you have established a rapport, you can often relax your appearance.

Some additional points for the three-to-five-second rule are as follows:

7. **Be aware of how you correspond**. Writing, texting, and emailing all provide a means for people to form judgments based on grammatical errors, misspelled words, or incomplete thoughts, all of which will leave an impression of you with your audience. Ensure that your written communication is free of misspellings or grammatical errors, avoid communicating at a time when you feel upset or stressed, and it is always a good idea to ask someone to proofread your communication before sending, especially when it is regarding a sensitive matter.

8. **Practice your presentation**. Rehearse your presentation until you are confident that neither slides nor notes are needed. Also, try to anticipate questions that may arise during your presentation. Consider telling a story that ties in well with your presentation. Your level of enthusiasm will be contagious, so it is best to convey excitement.

HOW WILL THE PRESENTATION ENHANCE OUR "AURA" (OUR BRAND) AND THE COMPANY'S IMAGE?

If a presenter follows the guidelines laid out in the previous sections, consider what impact the presentation may have on the company, its brand, or its image. Your goal should be to present in a way that helps the firm standout from its competition, make new connections with prospective clients, and impress industry leaders.[9]

A good presentation leaves a positive and lasting impression that will serve to elevate the company's image. New customers who may have never heard of the firm prior to the presentation can develop an affinity to the company through their positive experience. Finally, industry leaders who are in attendance may seek to form an alliance with an impressive firm

---

9   Katherine Paljug, "Presentation Skills Every Business Owner Should Have," *Business News Daily*, November 13, 2017, https://www.businessnewsdaily.com/6188-business-presentation-tips.html.

based on the quality of the presentation. Everyone loves to be associated with a winner as it stimulates the brain and helps make us feel good.[10]

In addition to the aforementioned qualities that help to improve a company's image, a good presentation helps an audience form an opinion of the company's culture and community. The audience will also form an opinion of what they think the firm is trying to accomplish and whether the company is likely to be successful. If their values align with the goals of the organization, this will help strengthen their bond to the company while simultaneously improving its image as well.

No matter how one analyzes the effectiveness of a good presentation, there are more benefits to improve the firm's image than to ruin it. Like most things, a presenter is guilty by association. *Being guilty by association* is a psychological fact that people are associated with other people, institutions, or groups and this forms the impression society forms of them versus the actual truth.[11] Guilt by association includes both positive and negative associations; therefore, while rehearsing a presentation, it is beneficial to consider what negative guilty by association factors may adversely influence the audience while maximizing many positive and meaningful examples.

TOP FIVE RISKS AND COUNTERMEASURES

In today's world there are five risks that ultimately affect the results of your innovation's success. *Risk* is the possibility of loss due to an event or occurrence; however, a great firm will use risk to increase its success by identifying ways to control it. Therefore, a firm can try to influence risks, but they can never change them, except for risks that are associated with the company's internal operations.

Risks

1. **Performance of the product/service.** The firm must determine the performance levels of the innovation based on the price and competition. As previously discussed, price is a surrogate for performance. The company must match the performance levels with the prices being charged and then synchronize these with the expectations of the target market to be successful. Failure to do so creates an increased risk that will be pitted against the company's success.

---

10   Eugene Sheeley, "The Winner Effect: How Success Affects Brain Chemistry," Gamification, February 21, 2014, http://www.gamification.co/2014/02/21/the-winner-effect.

11   Wendy L. Patrick, "Choose Your Friends Carefully: Avoid Guilt by Association," Psychology Today, May 12, 2014, https://www.psychologytoday.com/us/blog/why-bad-looks-good/201405/choose-your-friends-carefully-avoid-guilt-association.

2. **Timing, society, and the consumer.** Companies often run the risk of introducing a product at the wrong time, and possibly to a community or target market that will not welcome it. As previously noted, incremental innovation is the most common form of innovation because firms simply alter a limited number of the product's attributes and often reintroduce it to the same target market. While this is the less risky form of innovation, it is not foolproof. Many times, especially with food items, a new flavor may not be attractive to consumers and then the product will fail. What is key to determining the timing, how society will react, and if the consumer response will be positive is to conduct market research to help predict how the innovation will be received. Market research can reduce risk and provide a greater probability of success because it often provides answers to many of the most important questions when introducing or reintroducing a new product into the market.

3. **Competition.** When new products are introduced the firm must anticipate the competitive response. The product life cycle's first stage is introduction. During the introduction stage, a product is most expensive because despite spending countless dollars on the development of the innovation, the firm must now spend additional money to promote the product. It is at this point that the competition will often attack the product to prohibit it from getting a foothold in the market. Before launch, a firm must determine which markets are best to introduce the innovation and which target market will be the most susceptible to purchasing it.

4. **Government regulations.** While companies do not control governmental regulations, they can try to influence them. This is the reason companies hire lobbyists, to influence key governmental personnel to approve the release of their products. When innovating, it is best if a firm can anticipate the likelihood of their product being scrutinized by the government and its regulatory bodies.

   This is common in consumer products, especially pharmaceuticals, where the result of using a medication can substantially impact the health of a patient. Pharma companies must test their medications for years before selling it to the public and all their results must be disclosed to the Federal Drug Administration (FDA). This type of innovation violates one of our rules of innovation, which is that speed matters. This explains why pharmaceutical companies file for patents and why the price of their medication is so expensive, because they are trying to recoup a massive amount of research and development dollars. Outside of big pharma, other companies try to introduce products they can quickly introduce to the market to recoup their investment.

5. **Macro world events.** As the business climate shifts to more of a global economy, firms must also be aware of potential changes in the market that could benefit or adversely affect the business, such as shifting world populations, tariff, changing preferences for products, and policies regarding immigration to name few. Companies must be

informed about changing events to reduce their risk and be well positioned to capitalize on new opportunities.

Of all the risks presented, timing is the most significant and most difficult to predict. People can have a great idea for a new product or innovation, but if society or the consumer is not ready to adopt it, it will fail. A perfect example is electric vehicles. Electric cars have been available to consumers for over one hundred years, yet only in the recent past has the world started to embrace them.[12] Other examples of innovations whose timing were not synchronized with society include the Newton by Apple and the first smartphone because they were just too far ahead of their time. Timing is by far the number-one risk that must be discussed.

THINK ABOUT THIS!

How did Isuzu use risks and countermeasures to be successful? What did Spartan Motors learn? How are risks and countermeasures related?

In 2011, Spartan Motors was selected by Isuzu Truck to assemble the Isuzu N-Series cab and chassis. This required Spartan Motors to convert an empty plant into a production facility in order to assemble 15 vehicles per day with less than sixty people in an assembly space less than 35,000 square feet and do so in less than 12 months. This was no small feat as there was very little automation equipment or space available to do the work.

Throughout the process, Isuzu consistently focused on identifying the risks and the countermeasures. In retrospect it was illogical not to use risk and countermeasure techniques when considering how rare it is that anything goes as planned. Therefore, firms must identify and accept risk and plan for it with countermeasures. This method forces a company to assess all of the variables to determine the greatest risks along with the probability of the risks occurring. Then the appropriate countermeasures need to be devised to thwart the risk. Isuzu's approach to manufacturing and production completely transformed how Spartan Motors operated, and ever since it has assessed risks and countermeasures for every product developed and offered.

Countermeasures

Countermeasure is a term first used in 1923 to describe ways to counter a risk or threat.[13] A **countermeasure** is an action used to stop a risk or threat from occurring. The term is used

---

12   "The History of the Electric Car," Department of Energy, September 15, 2014, https://www.energy.gov/articles/history-electric-car.

13   "Countermeasure," *Merriam-Webster*, https://www.merriam-webster.com/dictionary/countermeasure.

extensively by the military to counter a threat from the enemy. Countermeasures can be passive or aggressive depending on the threat.

While countermeasures are utilized as part of the way the military operates, they can also be used by companies while developing new products. Business leaders must identify the right countermeasures when a risk occurs to address it properly and minimize the threat. The following are some examples of how leaders can use countermeasures in innovation to overcome the risks that face nearly all businesses.

1. **Performance of the product or service**. If the product has quality or performance issues, those must be addressed as quickly as possible. A great example of this is the Samsung Galaxy Note 7, which was introduced in August of 2016 and discontinued just two months later due to safety issues regarding the battery. When Samsung became aware of the problem, it halted production and announced a recall for the phone. This countermeasure to the risk posed by the Galaxy Note 7 did not occur without financial implications. Before the recall, Samsung was the smartphone market share leader at 21–28 percent market share. After the recall, Samsung's stock lost $14.3 billion. The countermeasure Samsung has used to recover from this is to introduce the Galaxy 8, which has extensive battery testing and features to rival the latest iPhone.[14]

2. **Timing, society, and the customer**. Using each of these as a countermeasure can be strategic, because if the timing is off, the market will likely not adopt the product. A classic example is Ford's introduction of the Edsel. Ford Motor Company wanted to produce a car that was equally attractive to both men and women. It also wanted to produce a car that had a comparable amount of chrome to match many of the other cars on the market. The result was the Edsel, but early polls showed that the American consumers weren't interested in the car. (Note: This is also a clear violation of striving to be intuitive-wise and data-driven).

   When the Edsel was released in 1957, it was a flop. It was too expensive, used too much gas, and was not popular with the press. What was worse, Ford introduced a complete redesign that fixed the issues in 1960, but by that time it was too late. Ford had invested $250 million into the Edsel and lost $350 million, making it one of the worst new car launches in history.[15]

3. **Competition will always react to an innovation launch**. You have a plan, but your competition has a plan as well, and they will react. Too often this risk is overlooked. As discussed, companies must anticipate risk associated with competition that may

---

14 Peter Paschal, "Samsung Rises Again," Mashable, https://mashable.com/2017/03/29/samsung-galaxy-s8-forget-note-7/#ELClKUGqSmqG.

15 Richard Feloni, "4 Lessons from the Failure of the Ford Edsel, one of Bill Gates' Favorite Case Studies," *Business Insider*, September 5, 2015, http://www.businessinsider.com/lessons-from-the-failure-of-the-ford-edsel-2015-9.

interfere with the innovation. An example of a countermeasure firms can use to stop a competitive threat is to drop the price below the initial retail price of a product before it is available (i.e., jamming). Another, in a business-to-business context, is to lock a client into a contract or underbid the competition before they can establish themselves in the market. Firms must anticipate the risk and use countermeasures to minimize it.[16]

4. **Government regulations will always alter markets**. Companies must consider how government regulations can dramatically change how we live, and companies must be proactive and well informed of changing policies. One countermeasure used to alter government regulations has been the National Rifle Association's (NRA) lobby to avoid stricter gun control. It did this by asking members for financial contributions to support lobbyists in Washington and by encouraging voters to tell their officials they would not vote for them if they passed stricter laws or banned certain weapons. The NRA's success is a result of incredible financial resources and a grass roots effort by US gun owners.[17]

5. **Macro world conditions and events** pose many risks; however, innovators can also utilize countermeasures to limit these and to gain an advantage. Historically, a popular countermeasure has been to shift production to countries that have a lower labor cost to save money. Many foreign companies have found great success by selling their products in the US because of high consumption and a higher standard of living.

Common Indexes and Economic Measurements

The following are ways to measure global opportunities and then assess both risks and countermeasures to discover opportunities:

- *Gross domestic product (GDP)* is the total value of a finished good or service produced in a specified period. The US typically measures GDP on an annual basis. It is a good indicator because it represents an overarching view of the strength of the nation's economy.
- *Unemployment rate* is an indicator of the number of people who are jobless. There is a positive correlation between the unemployment rate and the current state of the economy, meaning a recession usually occurs after a sustained period of high unemployment.
- *Rate of inflation* is a percentage of the rising cost of goods. High inflation means the cost of goods are more expensive, thus purchasing power among consumers is reduced.

---

16 Hans Östermann, "Sales Strategies: Dealing with Competition," Sales Pop, January 6, 2014, https://salespop. net/salespreneurs/sales-strategies-dealing-with-competition/.

17 Ryan Sit, "Here's Why the NRA is so Powerful and Why Gun Control Advocates Have Reason for Hope," *Newsweek*, February 22, 2018, http://www.newsweek.com/nra-gun-control-parkland-florida-school-shooting-campaign-donations-813940.

- *Consumer Confidence Index (CCI)* is an index that determines how Americans feel about the current financial health of the economy, as well as the state of the economy over the prior six months. It is administered by the Conference Board and surveys five thousand households every month to determine the index results.
- *Producer Pricing Index (PPI)* is an index that measures price changes from a seller's perspective over time. It identifies changing prices in three areas: industry-based, commodity-based, and commodity-based final demand of domestic goods and services.
- *Consumer Price Index (CPI)* is an index that measures the average of goods and services to determine inflation and deflation. CPI is also an indicator of the cost of living, which is used by both consumers and businesses to determine the expense of living or operating in one geographical area over another. While PPI is measured from a seller's perspective, CPI is measured from the consumer's perspective.

There are many more indexes and data points to consider, but this list provides a good way to evaluate the state of the economy and the current mind-set of the consumer.

Use Guided Financial Outcomes Rather Than Financial Pro Formas

Most presentations provide a one-sided view that is nothing but positive, and hopefully realistic. If there is one thing that is guaranteed in any presentation that includes a "financial pro forma" is that it will be either too high or too low. Identifying the current and future risks and countermeasures will help ensure that the financial pro forma will be understated, allowing the company a greater chance to overdeliver.

When including this type of information in a presentation, keep it simple and focus on one key data point, if possible. Do your best to cover all the potential scenarios, such as worst case, expected case, and best case. Note how public companies provide financial "guidance," which is the preferred way for a company to convey that whatever numbers are provided, they reflect a range rather than an absolute value. Therefore, *guidance* is advice or information aimed at resolving a problem or difficulty, especially given by someone in authority. Publicly traded companies provide guidance for investors by providing full disclosure of their financial records based on generally accepted accounting practices (GAAP). The numbers reveal the financial performance of the company along with data that may provide some indication of what could happen in the future, helping investors make an educated decision on whether to invest.

Question the Process and the Timing

Questions are an integral part of the presentation. This is an opportunity to involve the audience and develop physical and emotional buy in. It also helps discern what the concerns are and identify ways for the company to overcome them. To increase the opportunity for people to ask questions, consider the following methods:

1. **Allocate 50 percent of your presentation time to questions**. First, this will force you to avoid subjecting your audience to death by PowerPoint. This compression will also

ensure your messages are direct, clear, stimulating, and organized. There is a lot to be said for the theory of constraints and how it relates to the public. The *theory of constraints (TOC)* is a way to discover what is restricting a process and finding a way to either eliminate or reduce the effects of the constraint. TOC is a term commonly used in manufacturing, but it is equally applicable to delivering a presentation. Identifying constraints in your presentation will help develop a more streamlined presentation with improved clarity.

Next, it is improbable that the presenter will be able to influence anyone if he or she does not know how to speak well, much less be able to adequately address any concerns or objections and what will be done to overcome them. Consider the question-and-answer period of your presentation as an opportunity to demonstrate leadership. Your confidence, knowledge, and preparation will inspire your audience's trust. If you asked a question to which you do not know the answer, simply state that you do not know the answer and provide a timeframe as to when you will get back to them with the answer. No one expects you to know everything.

2. **The best time for questions is at the end**. Tell the audience up front that once the agenda topics are covered, there will be time for questions; otherwise, you may not be able to deliver your entire presentation. Many presentations never conclude at the end because the speaker was willing to field questions throughout the presentation rather than reserving time for the end. Let people know that you value their opinions and that they will have ample time for input.

Before the Presentation Draft Even Starts

It is recommended that a presenter email all attendees in advance with the following question: "What are the top three items/areas/questions you would like to see answers to when we discuss on such and such data?" The following are reasons why you should consider doing this:

1. It shows you care and value their input.
2. It gives you clarity as to the audience's expectations or concerns.
3. It gives you clarity as to whether you have enough time allocated.
4. You will be prepared and it shows you are taking this seriously.
5. Presentations are about approval, alignment, and the proverbial business phrase "buy in."

By sending this simple email out ahead of time you are immediately differentiating yourself. Too often people, especially leadership, believe everyone thinks like them; this is wrong. Never ever underestimate the importance of showing people you care and value them and their opinion. Remember the quote from the three-to-five-second section: How you make people feel can make all the difference.

Speed Matters

It seems the world today spins a little faster every day, as we have become accustomed to immediate feedback from text messages, social media, and email, and multitasking has become a way of life. Think in your own life about how many tasks have you taken on at once. It has become part of our being to do several things at once.

Speed is crucial to innovation as it is advantageous to release a new product to market as quickly as possible to recoup the financial commitment made by the company and to gain an advantage.

Speed matters for one simple reason: time. Time is the only resource that we can never recover, replenish, or acquire more of. When that second, minute, hour, day, week, month, or year is gone, it is gone forever, and that makes time the most precious sought-after commodity on the planet. Time is also important to any consumer; therefore, your innovation should take advantage of time as a resource to create more opportunities to get your products in the market.

Prepare your presentation so that you take the breath of your audience away. As mentioned in the beginning, we live in a world where data and information overload is a daily occurrence. Simplicity will help you deliver a message that is memorable and easy to understand. Don't try to complicate things, as your audience will block out the information you are sharing with them.

Review Questions

1. What are common problems when conveying information to an audience?
2. What are six ways to avoid death by PowerPoint?
3. What is the three-to-five-second rule? List three ways to make a good first impression.
4. What are three ways to mix up the information in a presentation to maintain attention?
5. What are the five risks firms face? Provide examples of three risks and related countermeasures that are not used in the text.
6. What financial data points can innovators use to discover global opportunities?
7. Why do firms provide guidance for financial outcomes versus a financial pro forma?
8. What are two ways to encourage asking questions during a presentation?
9. What are four things a presenter can ask of his or her audience before the presentation?

Discussion Questions

1. Discuss with a classmate a product whose timing was too late or early. What could the company do differently?
2. The list found in the section "Speed Matters" contains a list of things that move faster today than ten years ago. Discuss what else has accelerated and why.

3. It has been said people first want to know how much you care before you share how much you know. Discuss a time when you felt compelled to show compassion over knowledge toward someone or something.

4. Is it possible to create and move time, not literally but figuratively? Explain your response to a classmate.

5. What is a huge benefit of driving toward one number or letter? Have you ever experienced this? Share with your professor or a classmate.

6. Discuss with a classmate ways to make a good first impression. Do you think the three-to-five-second rule is a valid concept? Why?

7. Share with a classmate a letter or number that has meaning to you. What is the meaning and why?

8. Provide suggestions to a classmate on other indicators innovators can use to determine global opportunities.

9. Discuss some of the best lectures you have had and the worst. What was the difference? Did the best lectures follow ways to mix up the presentation discussed in the chapter?

10. Discuss how the presentation can enhance the aura of the firm and the presenter.

Extension Activity

Select a product you feel would be good to sell in another country. Using the five risks and countermeasures, identify all five for the product and list them for your professor to review.

BIBLIOGRAPHY

"Best Presentation Software List: Complete 2019 Guide," Slide Bean, February 1, 2019, https://slidebean. com/blog/best-presentation-software-list-2018#best-powerpoint-alternatives.

Hedges, Kristi. "Six Ways to Avoid Death by PowerPoint," *Forbes*, November 14, 2014, https://www.forbes.com/sites/work-in-progress/2014/11/14/six-ways-to-avoid-death-by-powerpoint/#5bd4084264d4.

Groeger, Lena. "Making Sense of the World, Several Sense at a Time," *Scientific American*, February 28, 2012, https://www.scientificamerican.com/article/making-sense-world-sveral-senses-at-time/.

Maybin, Simon. "Busting the Attention Span Myth," *BBC News*, March 10, 2017, https://www.bbc. com/news/health-38896790.

Sibley, Amanda. "19 Reasons You Should Include Visual Content in Your Marketing [Data]," Hub Spot, August 6, 2012, https://blog.hubspot.com/blog/tabid/6307/bid/33423/19-Reasons-You-Should-Include-Visual-Content-in-Your-Marketing-Data.aspx.

Anderson, Amy Rees. "People Do Business with People They Like," *Forbes,* June 28, 2013, https://www.forbes.com/sites/amyanderson/2013/06/28/people-do-business-with-people-they-like/#e7bf35b309f7.

Willis, Janine and Todorov, Alexander. "First Impressions: Making Up Your Mind after a 100-ms Exposure to a Face," *Psychological Science* 17, no. 7 (2006): 592–598.

Pitts, Anna. "You Only Have 7 Seconds to Make a Strong First Impression," *Business Insider,* April 8, 2013, http://www.businessinsider.com/only-7-seconds-to-make-first-impression-2013-4.

Paljug, Katherine. "Presentation Skills Every Business Owner Should Have," *Business News Daily*, November 13, 2017, https://www.businessnewsdaily.com/6188-business-presentation-tips.html.

Sheeley, Eugene. "The Winner Effect: How Success Affects Brain Chemistry," Gamification, February 21, 2014, http://www.gamification.co/2014/02/21/the-winner-effect.

Patrick, Wendy L. "Choose Your Friends Carefully: Avoid Guilt by Association," Psychology Today, May 12, 2014, https://www.psychologytoday.com/us/blog/why-bad-looks-good/201405/choose-your-friends-carefully-avoid-guilt-association.

"The History of the Electric Car," Department of Energy, September 15, 2014, https://www.energy.gov/articles/history-electric-car.

"Countermeasure," *Merriam-Webster*, https://www.merriam-webster.com/dictionary/countermeasure.

Paschal, Peter."Samsung Rises Again," Mashable, https://mashable.com/2017/03/29/samsung-galaxy-s8-forget-note-7/#ELClKUGqSmqG.

Feloni, Richard. "4 Lessons from the Failure of the Ford Edsel, one of Bill Gates' Favorite Case Studies," *Business Insider*, September 5, 2015, http://www.businessinsider.com/lessons-from-the-failure-of-the-ford-edsel-2015-9.

Östermann, Hans. "Sales Strategies: Dealing with Competition," Sales Pop, January 6, 2014, https://salespop.net/salespreneurs/sales-strategies-dealing-with-competition/.

Sit, Ryan. "Here's Why the NRA is so Powerful and Why Gun Control Advocates Have Reason for Hope," *Newsweek,* February 22, 2018, http://www.newsweek.com/nra-gun-control-parkland-florida-school-shooting-campaign-donations-813940.

CHAPTER FOURTEEN

What is the Product Validation Process and How Does it Affect Innovation?

INTRODUCTION

Firms must analyze several key factors when validating an innovation. Price is a key consideration as is how the target market will perceive the level of quality, status of use, and value the product gives them. Quality is another key component that adds validity to the innovation process. Manufacturers today build on quality through adopting various standards such as TQM, ISO, and Six Sigma. The perceived level of quality consumers feel a firm's product offers has a direct impact on the price they are willing to pay and helps validate the innovation process.

Another consideration firms must think of is using the best distribution channels to make the products available where and when consumers are ready to buy. Firms can also use the relationship among their suppliers to gain useful information that can be used in the innovation process. Firms can use the information they have and then do a SWOT analysis to identify the best way to address opportunities. One other tool that is effective is perceptual mapping, where a firm can survey its customers to see where their product is located on a map comparing two factors (e.g., price and quality) as compared to their competition.

Learning Objectives

In this chapter students will learn about the following:
- How price perceptions of consumers influence their purchase decision-making process
- How quality is the key to innovation in the twenty-first century
- The importance of distribution channels and supplier relations
- How firms analyze opportunities in the market
- How firms find ways to satisfy customer needs
- Ways to identify markets that present the best opportunities to firms
- How your product is perceived relative to the competition in the mind of the consumer

Learning Outcomes

By the end of this chapter students will be able to do the following:

- Identify the eight price perceptions that influence the consumer purchase process
- Recognize various quality standards and why firms use them
- Know the factors that benefit proper selection of distribution channels
- Know how to perform a SWOT analysis
- Know how to segment a market using segmentation variables
- Calculate price using various methods
- Know how to use a perceptual map

Key Terms

Price: The amount of money charged for a firm's offerings to consumers

Value proposition: The perceived value received for a product by a consumer versus the price charged as compared to competitive products

Second or third mover advantage: Strategy that allows dominate companies to establish parameters for a product category and then rival firms introduce a cheaper version of the product to gain market share

Price tolerance: A consumer's purchase response to an increase or decrease in the cost of goods or services

Quality: The way in which individuals' needs are satisfied through continuous improvement

TQM: Quality standard that seeks to reduce errors, streamline supply chain management, improve customer satisfaction, and ensure employees are properly trained

ISO 9000: Universal standards that seek to help firms to meet the needs of their stakeholders while meeting statutory requirements related to producing a product

Lean manufacturing: Focuses on the minimization of waste in manufacturing without sacrifice to production

Six Sigma: Techniques and tools that seek process improvements

Direct sales channels: Channels where manufacturers sell directly to the final consumer

Retailing: Involves buying goods through a wholesaler and then-selling them to the final consumer for a profit

Holding costs: The expense a firm incurs when buying products and then holding them until they sell

Wholesale distribution: Distribution channel where wholesalers buy products and then either warehouse products or sell them to either retailers or distributors

Online channels: Those that sell directly from the manufacturer to the final consumer via the internet

Supplier evaluation: The evaluation of a supplier to measure its ability to reduce costs and to determine if its level of service is acceptable to maintain a consistent level of production

Bill of material: Determines raw materials, sub and intermediate assemblies, and quantities of goods to complete final manufacturing

SG&A costs: Collection of direct and indirect costs related to selling a product

SWOT analysis: Analytical tool that identifies an organization's strengths, weaknesses, opportunities, and threats. It reveals factors influencing the company both internally and externally

Strengths: The things an organization does best and how it is able to realize an advantage over its competitors

Weaknesses: Areas where an organization lacks an advantage or needs improvement

Opportunities: Favorable factors that could give a company a competitive advantage

Threats: Factors that have the potential to harm an organization. Examples of threats include labor strikes, lack of trained skilled workers, new competitors moving in the area, shortages of raw material, etc.

Cost-plus pricing: Utilizes the premise that firms price products by estimating all costs, plus the desired level of profitability in dollars

Demand pricing: Factors volume and profits when determining a sales price

Competitive pricing: Used in established markets to price products at the same level as their competitors

Markup pricing: Factors in all costs and is then marked up based on a percentage of profit

S-T-P: Strategy used to identify markets to be segmented, what consumers will be targeted, and how to position the firm's product in the mind of the consumer, which guides promotions

Market segmentation: Strategy that divides the entire consumer market into subgroups (segments) based on similar characteristics

Demographic segmentation: Strategy that defines customers based on their age, income, family structure, education, marital status, sexual preference, gender, ethnicity, religion, etc.

Geographic segmentation: Identifies consumers with similar needs and wants by geographic location ranging from cities to countries

Geodemographics: Combines demographics and geographies to provide firms a richer means to segment consumers

Psychographics (lifestyles): Segments consumers based on their hobbies, interests, lifestyles, and opinions

Behavioral segmentation: Segments groups consumers based distinct behaviors

Positioning: Offering the target market a firm's products in a way that meets their needs

WHAT PRICE POINTS DO CUSTOMERS EXPECT?

Price is a surrogate for many products to customers including value, quality, and prestige. *Price* is the amount of money charged for a firm's offerings to consumers. Consumers make a clear value judgement when buying a product between the price charged versus the value received. This judgement is called the value proposition. A *value proposition* is the perceived value received for a product by a consumer versus the price charged as compared to competitive products. The ability of firms to deliver superior product value versus the prices charged can give them an advantage in the market. So, how do firms determine what are optimal prices to charge for products relative to offering value to their customers? The answer lies in gathering consumer insights to what they feel is a good value versus the price being charged. Marketing research plays a key role in determining these insights. A common theme of the text is the value of satisfying consumer needs through innovation. Gathering consumer insights is essential so firms can conduct surveys, focus groups, or ethnographic research to determine consumer preferences for products. A common problem firms experience is not understanding what consumers perceive as valuable and charging a premium for products that cannot be compared. More specifically, if a firm sees its offering as valuable and charges a premium but consumers have no point of reference, their value perception may be misaligned.

So, what are factors affecting the price perceptions consumers factor when making a purchase decision? Factors include the following:

1. Using past experiences to base current comparisons
2. How easy it is to compare products
3. Features desired by consumers
4. The competitive response to the new product
5. How effective a firm's advertisement is in the mind of the consumer
6. The ease of obtaining the product
7. The current economic situation
8. Their peer group/social network

Using Past Experiences to Base Current Comparisons

Humans learn from past experiences, which influences future behavior. This holds true for purchasing products, especially for services. It is hard to compare services without prior experience because each service provider is different. Just as you will have a different experience with professors teaching the same classes, a firm's ability to duplicate a service is difficult as well. Therefore, it is essential that firms provide a consistent experience every time a customer interacts with their products.

How Easy it is to Compare Products

Products that have no real differences are compared by price. It is essential that companies offer customers features that address their needs and to set their product apart from the competition to charge higher prices. In addition to the "differentiation," products must be hard to replicate; otherwise, they will be copied quickly by the competition. Customers will pay higher prices for products that satisfy their needs, but there must be an obvious difference separating the differences to charge higher prices. Therefore, firms must make their products be perceived as different, satisfying their customers' needs, and be superior to charge a higher price point. While this is easily said, some firms are comfortable with taking a second or third mover advantage and offering products that are copycats. *A second or third mover advantage* is a strategy that allows dominate companies to establish parameters for a product category and then rival firms introduce a cheaper version of the product to gain market share. An example of this is a soda that competes with Mountain Dew called Citrus Drop, and another called Citrus Pop. Both knockoff brands are like Mountain Dew but carry a much lower price tag, thus giving the firms that produce them a price advantage.

Features Desired by Consumers

As detailed earlier, marketing research and focus groups give companies a pulse of what consumers feel perceptions of a product means to them. It is through these discoveries that firms can capitalize on differences that allow them to charge higher prices based on perceived differences as compared to their competition. Features must be perceived as meaningful to add to the value perception of a product. Without this perception, added features will not be found to add value, and thus be viewed as too expensive. Therefore, adding features or attributes to a product must be determined through research and then tested to see if charging a higher price is warranted.

The Competitive Response to the New Product

The position a firm has in a market will play a role in the prices it can charge. Dominant companies can charge a greater price point due to their branding and recognition by consumers. Firms that are new to a product category must establish themselves as dominant players that threaten the dominance established by competitive firms to be afforded the opportunity to increase their prices due to a perceived difference in the products they offer. Once a firm has established itself as the dominate company, it can set the standards for what a product costs in a market based on the value and features ordered and provide the level of service that accompanies the product. Until this dominant position is met, firms must fight their way to the top by offering products that are seen by consumers as a better value to their target market and offer them at the right place.

How Effective a Firm's Advertisement is in the Mind of the Consumer

Advertisement effectiveness is typically measured in the level of increased sales or market share. Advertisement gives firms the opportunity to show the target market advantages that their product has over their competitors. The more advantages shown generally means the price will be higher. In addition, the more features a product has in comparison to its competition also indicates that the product will be more expensive. This is seen quite often in car commercials where luxury equates to a higher price vehicle.

Another indicator of higher price is branding. Do consumers value a BMW the same as a Kia? Branding gives consumers a clue to the level of price point the product will carry. Branding also gives consumers the ability to demonstrate their wealth, social status, and preference in products. It is common to see residents of similar areas driving the same make of car. Brands give firms the ability to charge more for their offerings based on consumers' perceptions and the value received by using the brand.

Ease of Obtaining the Product

Product distribution typically influences the price charged. Mass distribution, such as a bottle of soda, will carry a reduced price due to level of competition for the product. A product that has a limited distribution will carry a higher price. While firms want their products to be readily available, it is important to analyze the company's current distribution network. Many firms seek an exclusive opportunity for a product to create traffic and give themselves a price advantage. The product's retailer also informs the price. Do Nordstrom's products sell for a similar price as products from Dollar General? A store's location, the company's retail strategy, and its distribution network all play a role in the price charged for a product.[1]

The Current Economic Situation

The state of the economy has an impact on price perceptions consumers have when evaluating a purchase decision. In times of recession or economic downturn, consumers are more conservative and tend to let price influence their decision, as money is not as readily available. This is evident in the savings rates, which tend to increase in economic hard times and the number of businesses that go out of business. In favorable economic times, cash is more readily available, job growth is good, and consumers tend to let price not be such a dominant factor when deciding on a product. Consider how purchases of real estate, automobiles, and vacations are affected by a favorable economy. Therefore, firms evaluate the current economic environment when determining price.

Peer Group and Social Networks

Peer groups and one's social network also influence purchase decisions. Consumers want to avoid being chastised by their peers for buying a product that contradicts the group's values. For example, if one's peer group is environmentalists, purchasing a SUV may draw criticism due to higher consumption of fuel. In addition, the product purchased is evaluated based on exposure in use. If you are going to use a product in private, peer group influence will have a minimal effect. If use is in public, then peer group influence will have more of an impact in purchase evaluation.

In addition to price points that affect consumer behavior, there are three additional factors that contribute to pricing and innovation:

1. The effect price has on satisfaction
2. The influence price has on service quality
3. How customer satisfaction affects price tolerance

The Effect Price Has on Satisfaction

Price has a correlated effect on the prices charged for a product's satisfaction, meaning that the higher the price, the greater the expectation of the product's satisfaction. Would you expect the same satisfaction of food from McDonald's versus a gourmet steak house? Companies need to match their level of satisfaction with the prices charged. Consumers' expectations will have

---

1 "Expectation Pricing," Changing Minds, http://changingminds.org/disciplines/marketing/pricing/expectation_pricing.htm.

an adverse effect on high prices and poor service. Therefore, the higher the price charged for a product, the greater the expected level of satisfaction anticipated.

The Influence Price Has on Service Quality

Like satisfaction, price has a positively correlated effect on perceived quality, meaning that the higher the price, the higher the perceived level of service. This is seen in many facets of business. Examples include the level of service received at a Volvo dealership for service versus a Nissan dealership. Based on my personal experience, the Volvo dealership usually provides gourmet coffee, fresh cookies, and a nice waiting area, where the Nissan waiting area has no coffee and no fresh baked goods. Consumers are conditioned to receive higher levels of service based on the level of price. Retailers such as Nordstrom provide a higher level of service than the less expensive Walmart. Therefore, providers of expensive or inexpensive products usually cater their offerings based on price to their target market to broadcast the expected level of service.

How Customer Satisfaction Affects Price Tolerance

Price tolerance is a consumer's purchase response to an increase or decrease in the cost of goods or services. Price tolerance is another term for price elasticity. Price elasticity can be either be elastic or inelastic. Examples of these include a rise in price resulting in decreased purchased behavior, which results in price elasticity, while no response means inelasticity. Firms must strive to promote their product's benefits to reduce price elasticity. They must also provide reasons the product has no substitute, thus creating an inelastic demand scenario. Some product categories have been very successful in this endeavor, including cosmetics, cell phones, and college education. While it is safe to say most people would not do without these products, it is also safe to suggest a cheaper alternative may be sought. Exceeding the customer's expectations typically enables firms to charge a higher price. This loyalty also creates a relationship with the brand. Twenty years ago, clubs and loyalty programs hardly existed. Today they are everywhere, as consumers have shown they will be very loyal if their experience with the product or service warrants it. Therefore, it is the job of firms to stress the benefits and quality of their products to maintain a loyal customer following.[2]

Quality Expectations

Quality is a key factor that differentiates companies from each other. *Quality* is the way in which an individual's needs are satisfied through continuous improvement. A major influence on quality expectations is innovation. It is through the process of innovation that improving

---

2   Andreas Herrmann, Lan Xia, Kent B. Monroe, and Frank Huber, "The Influence of Price Fairness on Customer Satisfaction: An Empirical Test in the Context of Automobile Purchases," *Journal of Product & Brand Management* 16, no. 1 (2007): 49–58.

quality and standing apart from the competition that companies gain a competitive advantage. Without innovation, quality, efficiency, and product improvement would not be relevant.[3]

Components of quality may include reliability, performance, durability, and conformance to specifications.[4] Quality is important in the twenty-first century because consumers are more demanding and informed, have many choices, and technology dominates their life.[5] With more choices available in a global economy, the level of competition is at an all-time high. Firms use quality to differentiate themselves to avoid having to compete solely on price. Therefore, products that are reliable, perform well, and are durable will be perceived as commanding a higher price than ones that do not contain these attributes.

Probably the most popular area of quality comes from total quality management (TQM). *TQM* is a quality standard that seeks to reduce errors, streamline supply chain management, improve customer satisfaction, and ensure employees are properly trained. TQM was the work of William Deming in his efforts to help the Japanese rebuild after World War II. From the work of Deming came other improvements to quality standards including ISO 9000, lean manufacturing, and Six Sigma.

- **ISO 9000** are universal standards that seek to help firms meet the needs of their stakeholders while meeting statutory requirements related to producing a product.
- **Lean manufacturing** focuses on the minimization of waste in manufacturing without sacrifice to production. It is derived from the Toyota Production System (TPS), which focuses on reducing waste to improve customer satisfaction.
- **Six Sigma** are techniques and tools that seek process improvements. Their goals are to eliminate defects that affect the quality of a product to the point it has a 99.99996 percent success rate.

These quality standards, while slightly different, are focused on the improvement of ways to provide customers products and services that are superior and reduce waste. Improved manufacturing techniques and reduction of waste, while improving the success rate of products are a clear sign of a high-quality product. Quality exceeding expectations is first a mental commitment, which in turn affects behavior. Many times, the little extra steps cost nothing, yet firms miss this every day. A perfect example is four or five-star hotels typically fold the toilet paper in the bathroom, so it looks great and is easier to grab. This small step takes an extra two three seconds, but it is very important. Why is this not done by lower-cost hotels? Poor leadership and ignoring attention to detail act as a point of separation between the five-star hotels and the cheaper alternatives.

---

3   Juhani Anttila. "Quality and Innovation." http://www.qualityintegration.biz/HailInnovation.html.

4   David A. Garvin, "What Does 'Product Quality' Really Mean?" *Sloane Management Review* 26, no. 1(1984): 25–42.

5   Paulo Sampaio and Pedro Saraiva, Eds. *Quality in the 21st Century: Perspectives from ASQ Feigenbaum Medal Winners (Switzerland: Springer, 2016).*

Distribution Channels

Selecting a distribution channel or channels is a very important step once the innovation is ready for distribution. There are several types of distribution channels that firms can consider based on their level of service, price, and product image. The following are distribution channels available to innovators to offer their products to customers.

Direct Sales Channels

Direct sales channels are channels where manufacturers sell directly to the final consumer. There are many advantages to this type of distribution channel including controlling the customer relationship and eliminating the costs associated with using a distributor. However, there are limitations as well including limited growth opportunities and the need for more personnel to manage the manufacturing and sales of products. The internet has totally changed the world by allowing anyone the opportunity sell directly to consumers. Unfortunately, the biggest losers are firms that relied on "brick-and-mortar" outlets to be the primary source of sales. More of this is discussed in "Online Channels."

Selling through Retailers

Retailing involves buying goods through a wholesaler and then selling them to the final consumer for a profit. The advantage of this relationship is that retailers can eliminate the need to carry large amounts of inventory, thus reduce holding costs. **Holding costs** are the expense a firm incurs when buying products and then holding them until they sell. The longer they take to sell, the higher the holding costs. Retailers seek to limit their holding costs to free up cash to operate their business. When a firm's inventory gets low, they simply order from the wholesaler and receive the merchandise to sell to their customers. The negatives to this relationship are ensuring retailers are equally promoting all products and are at the mercy of the efficiency of their wholesaler to deliver the products.

Product Distribution through Wholesalers

Wholesale distribution is a distribution channel where wholesalers buy products and then either warehouse them or sell them to either retailers or distributors. As described, the advantage to retailers is wholesalers warehouse the products meant for distributors or the final consumer (i.e., reduce holding costs). A disadvantage to this channel is the increase in costs of products to sell. Anytime a channel member handles a product, it must charge a fee to do so, thus increasing the cost to the final customer. Therefore, it is important to determine how many channels are necessary to utilize to sell a product to the target market.

Online Channels

Online channels are those that sell directly from the manufacturer to the final consumer via the internet. The advantage of an online channel is the ability to reach all members of the target market if they are accessible to the internet. It also helps to reduce the costs of direct sales and gives firms the ability to bid on large institutional accounts. In addition, online channels give firms global reach to sell their products at a lower price. Finally, online channels allow firms to customize their offerings to customers by saving their cookies. The disadvantages include exposing your offerings to the competition in an accessible manner and allowing them to see your reviews, which can be good or bad. Bad reviews give competitors the opportunity to go after a firm's customers due to dissatisfaction by providing them with a product that is superior.

Innovative firms must scrutinize the distribution channels they wish to utilize to distribute their products. Key considerations of choosing a distribution channel include lowering the costs of the products sold to gain an advantage in the market, efficiently replenishing inventory, shipping costs, and maintaining a favorable image in the market. Market research will determine the optimal price consumers will pay for a product; therefore, the distribution channel and the number of members that will handle the product are a vital determination of which channel to use. Firms must always seek the most efficient means to distribute and sell a product to be competitive; therefore, the proper distribution channel will help to accomplish this.

Supplier Evaluation

Supplier evaluation is the evaluation of a supplier to measure its ability to reduce costs and to determine if its level of service is acceptable to maintain a consistent level of production. If suppliers are inconsistent, a firm's ability to maintain a consistent availability of products is severely hampered. Therefore, choosing the right suppliers should not be a trivial matter as it affects the profitability of the firm.

Suppliers must be measured with quantifiable means including percentage of fill rates, percentage of returned items, and the efficiency of billing. Effective and efficient suppliers give firms a competitive advantage in the market and allows them the ability to control costs. The net effect is increased profits, improved supply chain, and minimized costs.

Bill of Material, Labor, and Determining Selling, General, and Administrative (SGA) Targets

Expenses play a key role in the profitability of companies. Some of the major factors that influence profitability include material costs, labor, selling, and general and administrative costs. It is the task of firms to maintain a strong grasp of these expenses to be as efficient and be as profitable as they can. Profitability of a firm helps to attract investors, place an advantage for future investment, and to survive economic difficulties.

Bill of Material

A **bill of material** determines raw materials, sub and intermediate assemblies, and quantities of goods to complete their final manufacturing. A bill of material is also important to communicate the needs of manufacturers and suppliers as they must satisfy customers. A bill of material is also tied to production orders, which helps to reserve components that are either in stock or not, to ensure they are involved in the production of a product. The bill of sale is essential to ensure that a good is set for manufacturing and that it has the needed materials to produce it. In many firms, bill of material costs are the largest expenditures. Too often firms focus on just the cost and not the innovation side. Never forget the innovation side.

Labor

One of the most expensive costs for a company is **labor.** Labor costs have historically been tied to the economic state of the country in which it operates, meaning the better the economy, the higher the wages paid. In addition, companies tend to seek employees who possess certain skill sets needed to be innovative. Therefore, labor costs are a function of skills needed and the market price for individuals with certain skill sets.

Selling, General, and Administrative Costs (SG&A)

SG&A costs are a collection of direct and indirect costs related to selling a product. Factors that influence SG&A costs include shipping, delivery, commissions, advertising, and marketing, plus, travel-related expenses such as phone, travel, and salaries for sales personnel. In addition, rent, utilities, and salaries for non-sales personal are also included.

While there is a direct correlation between SG&A expenses and profitability, most firms focus on cutting expenses, improving product quality, and increasing the quality of management. While this strategy works for the short term, it is important that firms concentrate on developing a core group of employees who comprise a functional group able to develop and bring to fruition an innovation that will give the firm a competitive advantage. In addition, developing a firm's labor pool should be most important as this will ensure consistent innovation and a building of the talents available to the company.

HOW DO FIRMS ANALYZE OPPORTUNITIES IN THE MARKET?

There are two useful tools available to firms that help them analyze opportunities in the market. One is a SWOT analysis, which stands for strengths, weaknesses, opportunities, and threats (reference Chapter 7). The second is the five forces model devised by Porter. Both techniques help firms identify their abilities to compete in a certain market and to reveal ways to gain a competitive advantage by identifying their advantages over competitors.

What is a SWOT Analysis and How Does It Help a Firm?

A **SWOT analysis** is an analytical tool identifies and organization's strengths, weaknesses, opportunities, and threats. It reveals factors influencing the company both internally and externally.

Figure 14.1 shows the four quadrants that comprise a SWOT analysis. When performing a SWOT analysis companies must be specific to avoid ambiguity. Companies must also be honest with their assessment of the four quadrants for it to be used effectively. It is all too common that companies focus on their strengths but deny their weaknesses as they are not a favorable topic to discuss; therefore, an honest assessment is important. The SWOT analysis is a very useful and simple tool.

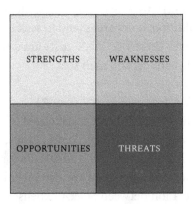

FIG 14.1 **SWOT analysis**

There are two more areas to consider around the typical SWOT analysis:

1. In the strengths and opportunities quadrants, list the items that are unique to you, the product, or your firm.
2. Perform the same analysis for one and two years out. It is amazing what changes and the healthy discussions that take place.

The following is a closer look at the components of the SWOT to better understand how each quadrant should be approached.

1. *Strengths* are the things an organization does best and how it is able to realize an advantage over its competitors. Examples of strengths include brands, loyalty programs, patents, abundance of financial resources, proprietary technology, and so on.
2. *Weaknesses* are areas where the organization lacks an advantage or needs improvement. Weaknesses include high debt, low receivables, decreased sales and market share, poor supply chain, and so on.
3. *Opportunities* are favorable factors that could give a company a competitive advantage. Opportunities include expanding to a new market, increasing sales, filing a new patent, and launching a new product.
4. *Threats* are factors that have the potential to harm an organization. Examples of threats include labor strike, lack of trained skilled workers, a new competitor moving in the area, and a shortage of raw materials.

A SWOT analysis is a valuable tool for determining where a company currently stands and where it needs to go. The SWOT analysis is useful to drive strategic plans that companies can use to develop long-term strategies. It is also useful to give all members of an organization the visual ability to see how they are doing compared to their competitors and what needs to be done to be a leader.

HOW DO COMPANIES FIND WAYS TO SATISFY CUSTOMER NEEDS?

Once the SWOT analysis is complete, firms need to use the recommendations to identify ways to gain an advantage by developing or refocusing products to satisfy consumer needs. Needs satisfaction is a common theme of this text, as consumers will not buy products that provide little benefit to them. Identifying consumer's needs, therefore, is at the heart of innovation and is a key factor as to why firms innovate.

A common mistake firms make is to assume they know what the needs of their clients are and how to satisfy them. They often have no formal processes in place to identify these needs and innovate blindly. This practice sets up a tremendous opportunity to fail. So, how can firms discover the needs of their customers and then respond to satisfy these needs?

Companies must seek out the "voice of the customer" to get a realistic idea what their needs are and then assess if they can satisfy those needs. All too often, companies ignore the customer because they tend to suggest needs that are too individual in nature. Ways to overcome this is to ask open-ended questions on what they see is needed to make products better and avoid asking what they would like to see improved. Another way of gaining customer opinions is to take suggestions and propose the solutions for needs satisfaction to a different group of people from similar areas. This is a form of test marketing that can be used to gain consensus.

Another way to identify consumer needs is to not make assumptions regarding their level of satisfaction. Many times, firms assume they know the needs of consumers only to find out they were wrong. Examples include Firestone assuming automakers would always buy bias tires only to have Michelin take the market with their radial tires, McDonald's failing to see that customers wanted healthier choices, and Kodak assuming customers preferred film over digital photography. Companies must never assume they know the needs of their customers and must always seek their input. The following are seven ways to accomplish identifying the needs of customers.

1. *Speak with customers.* The only way to identify the needs customers have is to speak with them. This can be accomplished in several ways including open-ended questions, surveys, focus groups, and phone interviews. The goal is to gain an understanding of the positives and negatives associated with a firm's existing product, or ways to improve current products. When seeking information, it is advised to speak with

individuals or smaller groups to prevent participants preserving their thoughts due to a large group or answering in a manner that is not like other responses.

2. ***Seek out employee input.*** Employees are the frontline contacts between the company and customer. They typically have relationships developed with their clients and hear their opinions on the products they purchase. Therefore, employees have access to the thoughts and opinions of the customers regarding the positives and negatives of products that are sold. Companies must also establish a way to obtain customer input from employees in a manner that is not threatening. Some corporate cultures are not very inviting of negative comments; therefore, a way to provide a safe haven for this information is needed. The ideal scenario is for employees to immediately share this information with their supervisors. This information, both good and bad, is necessary as it represents the true voice of the customer. Companies need to address customer comments and learn how to use this information to enhance innovation.

3. ***Speak with the supplier.*** It is amazing the amount of insight gained in speaking to this group. They are involved in the market place as deeply as you are. Leverage their wisdom. Another added benefit is their loyalty to you will grow and they now know you respect and value them.

4. ***Speak with dealers and distributers.*** This must be done in a measured, disciplined manner as dealers' distributions are trained to sell every day. However, since they interact with the consumer, their insight and wisdom are key.

   Note: At Spartan Motors an effective method was to get dealers and suppliers together as one group. They would discuss different states, but really focused on the future state. The interaction and discussions were tremendous as they provided valuable insight that could be used to improve business together.

5. ***Determine what is most important.*** Top managers should use the information from their customers to add attributes or create new-to-the-world products. Take the information gained from customers and determine what areas are most important and how the firm can gain a competitive advantage. The most important information should be shared with the cross-functional innovation team to determine what type of innovation will best serve the customer and the firm. The innovation team can then start their work of capitalizing on the best ways to innovate.

6. ***The job is never over.*** Once the needs of the customer are met, companies sometimes become complacent and stop the innovation process. The opposite of this is more of the reality in a highly competitive business environment in which firms compete. Companies must continue to monitor how their innovation is beneficial to their customers and then seek additional ways to innovate. In other words, innovation is a continuous process versus a one-time endeavor.

   As discussed in previous chapters, successful continuous innovation requires firms to benchmark best practices and build on their successes. Benchmarking helps firms develop policies and procedures that are transferable to future innovation. It allows companies to get products to the market faster and reduces failure and wasting resources. Therefore, benchmarking best practices will improve a firm's efficiency and increase its level of innovation.

7. ***Find ways to continue working with your customers.*** The ability to continuously work with your customers is essential. By working closely with customers, firms can monitor their needs, increase the level of service provided, and create a positive post-purchase experience. Ways firms can continuously work with their clients include follow-up calls or emails, sending surveys, and asking them to demo new products and seek their advice. The goal is to increase consumers' loyalty to your firm and to discover ways to satisfy their needs.[6]

WHY IS PRICING SO IMPORTANT?

Pricing has a correlated impact on success, meaning the more accurate the price charged, the more units a firm will sell. There are ground rules to establishing a price for products:

1. The price charged should meet the breakeven point and profitability goals of the company.
2. If you lower the price, you should lower the costs to maintain a sufficient level of profits.
3. A price audit should be conducted frequently to ensure profit margins are met and prices are competitive.

To determine a price firms must have a solid grasp on their costs associated with producing a product. All costs (fixed and variable) must be estimated for accurate pricing to take place. If all costs are not accounted for, a company could be operating in a negative cash flow position, so it is important to realize all costs. After the costs are determined, an acceptable profit must be established. This profit can be a percentage dollar amount, or others means established by the firm. It is important to keep in mind that costs affect profitability, so reductions such as markdowns, damaged goods, shrinkage, salaries/wages/commissions, employee discounts, and other incidental costs hurt profitability.

Ultimately, the price charged, especially in the US, is based on how competitive a firm wishes to be in the market versus its level of profitability. Companies must be able to compete against rivals, so charging the price that will give them a competitive advantage and profits is important. At the heart of determining the correct price is marketing research. Before a product is pursued in the innovation process, the marketing department needs to conduct an

---

6   "Five Strategies Companies Must Follow to Satisfy Consumers' Needs," TTI Success Insights, http://blog. ttisuccessinsights.com/5-strategies-companies-must-follow-satisfy-customers-needs.

analysis of the prices charged for similar products in the market and to interview potential customers to determine what the ideal price is for a product. If the innovation involves an attribute change, price will be a determining factor for success. If the product is a new-to-the-world product, price will not be the deciding factor, but charging the right price up front based on consumer expectations needs to be determined. That is where marketing research plays a vital role. Marketing researchers will interview customers to determine what they would pay for a product and then determine if their desired level of profitability can be achieved. Therefore, pricing is more than just developing a product and selling it. It involves analyzing costs and market prices for similar products, meeting a desired level of profitability, and providing a return on investment for the firm and its stakeholders.

There are several ways to determine what prices to charge consumers. Determining price for new products and existing ones can utilize any of the four types listed based on the product's position in the market, quality, company philosophy, level of service, and competitive comparison. While any of the proceeding methods work to establish a price point for goods to be sold, ultimately the major influence on price is competition and anticipated level of profits. The four ways to determine price are as follows:

1. **Cost-plus pricing** utilizes the premise that firms price products by estimating all costs, plus the desired level of profitability. This method requires an accurate assessment of cost, plus the ability to meet the desired level of profits as dictated by market pricing and corporate objectives.

2. **Demand Pricing** factors volume and profits when determining a sales price. In other words, the more volume sold, the lower the price of the product. This form of pricing is common for large wholesalers that can buy in volume, thus lowering their cost and then realizing higher profits when selling their products to retailers. Demand pricing has many advantages; however, one key disadvantage is if the buyer cannot purchase in large volume the unit costs go up, thus increasing the sale price of the goods due to higher cost of goods sold. This can obviously have a negative impact on sales and profit. It is important that firms using this method consistently purchase in high volume to reduce their costs.

3. **Competitive Pricing** is used in established markets to price products at the same level as their competitors. Competitive pricing is common for commodity products such as a bottle of soda, candy bar, and a bag of chips. As the price lowers below the competitive price it is perceived as a bargain by consumers. However, when price is higher, it is seen as price gouging and results in lower sales. Therefore, firms must have continuous knowledge of what their competition is charging to be competitive. One way to increase the sales price in a competitive market is to focus on attributes other than price. Companies can increase the level of service, offer nicer atmospherics than competitors, layaway, gift wrapping, and special terms for purchasing. These attributes make price less important and offers benefits to the consumer for buying that product.

4. **Markup Pricing** factors in all costs and is then marked up based on a percentage of profit. It is like cost-plus pricing but takes costs (fixed, variable and overhead) and uses a percentage versus a dollar amount. Following is an example of markup pricing:

> Sale price costs/sale price = margin percentage
> Costs/1 – desired markup = sales price
> Selling price = $100
> Cost = $50
> Desired markup = 50%
> $100 – $50/$100 = 50% margin
> 100/1 – 50% = $200 marked up price for the good

Profits for the sales of goods must be determined while considering the effect of competitive pressure and determining what pricing for typical products consumers will pay. In addition, firms must realize their needed level of profitability to meet their goals, provide a return on investment, and save funds for the future. Therefore, pricing is a vital part of any firm and should be given consideration when pricing new products.[7]

What Markets Provide the Best Product Opportunities?

Identifying the best markets to sell your product requires an understanding of who the firm's target market is and where they are located. Innovators, and especially the marketing members of the cross-functional team, must provide the team with a clear indication of who the market segments are, how to target them, and the method to position the product in the mind of the consumer. Therefore, effective marketing segmentation will help firms capitalize on the best markets and identify the target of the innovation.

Segmentation, Targeting, and Positioning

The ability to segment, target customers, and position products is referred in marketing a S-T-P. *S-T-P* is the strategy used to identify markets to be segmented, what consumers will be targeted, and how to position the firm's product in the mind of the consumer, which guides promotions. The three components of this framework allow companies to satisfy the needs of their customers by identifying them from the larger mass market. S-T-P makes marketing strategies more effective because it focuses on who the ideal customer for the firm and its products is. Therefore, it is a much-practiced strategy aimed at being more efficient to determine the needs of customers and finding them to sell a company's products.

Market segmentation is a strategy that divides the entire consumer market into subgroups (segments) based on similar characteristics. The characteristics of these segments include identifying consumers by demographics, geographics, geo-demographics, psychographics, and behavioral traits. In addition, marketers can use more specific segmentation variables such as

---

7   "Pricing a Product," Entrepreneur, https://www.entrepreneur.com/encyclopedia/pricing-a-product.

generational, online, and cultural. The text will concentrate on the first set of segmentation variables as it is most recognized and studied.

How to Define a Target Market

The process of segmentation begins with identifying the target market that is best suited to buy your products and to satisfy their needs or wants. There are guidelines firms should follow when they identify how their new product can satisfy the needs of their target market:

1. *Substantial*: The target market is large enough to earn a profit by offering the product to them.
2. *Identifiable*: The segments are easy to identify and address.
3. *Accessible*: Firms can contact the target market with offers and retail locations to sell their products.
4. *Responsive*: The target market will positively act to the marketing efforts of the company.
5. *Actionable*: Consumer behavior gives firms a clear indication of how their marketing efforts are perceived by the target market.

Firms that follow these guidelines will have more success because the market they are targeting provides the consumer base and profit potential they are seeking. As indicated in this text previously, while not all efforts are for realizing a profit, firms need to be profitable to maintain their existence. A key to doing this is properly identifying the correct target market that will buy the firm's products to satisfy their needs and wants.[8]

FORMS OF SEGMENTATION

This text will identify five forms of segmentation strategies, but there are other more specific methods used. The forms of segmentation most commonly used by firms are as follows:

1. Demographic
2. Geographic
3. Geo-demographic
4. Psychographic
5. Behavioral

---

8   Gretchen Gavett, "What You Need to Know about Segmentation," *Harvard Business Review* 70 (2014): 5019–5028.

Demographic

Demographic segmentation is a strategy that defines customers based on their age, income, family structure, education, marital status, sexual preference, gender, ethnicity, religion, and so on. Demographic variables have been proven effective methods of segmentation because similar groups exhibit similar purchase behavior, motivations, interests, and brand preferences. It should be cautioned that while demographic variables are a proven method of segmenting, there are outliers that should not be categorized. For example, a union plumber may earn $150,000 a year but live in a blue-collar area. The plumber's wages would be like a physician practicing family medicine, but the two may exhibit different purchase behavior. Therefore, firms should review census data to get a grasp on the make-up of the population targeted.

Geographic Segmentation

Geographic segmentation identifies consumers with similar needs and wants by geographic location ranging from cities to countries. Location impacts the buying behavior of consumers. Consumers in larger metropolitan cities (e.g., Chicago, New York, and Los Angeles) have different needs than consumers in small rural communities. For example, a consumer in Chicago may not have a car, may live in a high-rise apartment, and may utilize mass transit. This consumer seeks retail locations that are close to where he or she lives and purchases items more frequently because he or she must transport the items to his or her apartment by bag or cart. He or she may also utilize delivery services to bring items frequently purchased to his or her apartment. A consumer in a rural community most likely lives in a home, uses a car to shop and go to work, and purchases items in larger quantities. Therefore, firms must identify ways to address these various markets to satisfy consumers' needs and earn a profit. In the example just provided, Amazon has made great strides addressing consumers in metropolitan areas with their Prime Pantry program. They deliver to consumers food and assorted household goods, thus alleviating the need to shop at a physical store.

Geodemographics

Geodemographics combine demographics and geographics to provide firms a richer means to segment consumers. Similar demographics tend to congregate by each other, so this gives firms the ability to specifically target like groups who exhibit similar purchase behavior. As an example, think of the geographic area in which you grew up. Did the professionals (doctors, lawyers, business people) tend to live in the same part of town? Did the blue-collar workers do the same? Where was the Cadillac dealership located versus the Chevrolet dealership in your hometown? Where did they sell Rolex watches versus a Timex? The answers to these questions typically show that white-collar neighborhoods are in different places of the city than the blue-collar ones. The Cadillac and Rolex retailers are usually located in the same vicinity as the white-collar neighborhoods, while the blue-collar workers are located near the Chevrolet and Timex stores. While one may have not given a thought to why certain stores are in the areas they are, companies position their locations based on proximity to their target markets. Therefore, by understanding where and who lives in what areas, companies can capitalize on offering their target market the products they seek.

Psychographics

Psychographics (lifestyles) are segmenting consumers based on their hobbies, interests, lifestyles, and opinions. This form of segmentation identifies how people spend their time and the interests they have. Examples of psychographics include people who are active in fitness, biking, sailing, and yoga. It may also include those who participate in social causes, liberals or conservatives, and those who binge-watch shows. Firms need to do research to determine what psychographic profiles best describe a potential target market. This research cannot be found through census data or other external means. Firms must observe trends and speak with consumers to gain awareness of psychographic variables and determine if they can create products that will be profitable and address the needs of these groups.

Behavioral

Behavioral segmentation groups consumers based on distinct behaviors. These behaviors could include product usage, benefits sought, use status, purchase readiness, and so on. Firms that can identify similar behaviors stand to benefit by specifically knowing which type of offer to make the segments. For example, if a consumer is a first-time user of a product, marketers can make an offer for a second purchase by extending a coupon. Firms also want to identify heavy users of products to retain their business. Casinos in Las Vegas give customers players cards and then track their gambling activities. The heavy gamblers are given comps (compensation) by the casinos to gain their loyalty and keep them playing. The heaviest users are often extended free rooms and meals to keep them in a specific casino to win their money back.

In addition to the types of behavioral characteristics, occasions play a big part in behavioral segmentation. Events in one's life may trigger purchase behavior, so firms try to identify such occasions to take advantage of these events. An example is Pro Flowers (an online florist), which sends notifications to buy flowers for an anniversary, birthday, Mother's Day, and so on via email. Big Box home improvement stores will run special events for Father's Day, Memorial and Labor Day, and other holidays. Retailers also try to capture business on Black Friday and major holidays. Behavioral segmentation is an effective means of segmenting consumers and gives companies the ability to specifically target their customers.

PRODUCT POSITIONING

Once firms have determined the target markets and the type of segmentation to utilize, they must devise strategies and objectives to position the product in the mind of their target market. *Positioning* is offering the target market a firm's products in a way that meets their needs. Some consideration includes the quality, prices, the retailer, branding, and so on as to give the target market a sense of what the product stands for and how it can improve their lives by using it. One way to determine how the product fits in the mind of customers compared to other products is to have them use a perceptual map. Remember, a perceptual map plots two characteristics on a map and firms ask customers to place their products and the competitors on the map based on where they feel the competition fits into the two parameters. For example, a car company may want to determine two parameters such as mileage and safety. The four points of the map would include excellent mileage, poor mileage, extremely safe, and not safe. The consumers would then assign each type of vehicle based on their perception of these characteristics on the map. Companies can then use this information to see how safe and what mileage consumers perceive their car provides. The perceptual map will then help in their promotions, pricing, and future offerings (see figure 14.2).

In summary, perceptual maps help firms see the consumer's perspective as to where a firm's products and their competitors fit into two defined parameters. This knowledge can help firms improve and innovate based on these perceptions and gain an advantage in the market.

Review Questions

1. Name five of the eight influences on price perception and give a summary of each.
2. What are the three additional influencers on price and innovation listed in the chapter? Provide examples.
3. Why is quality a key factor in the twenty-first century?
4. Identify the various distribution channels listed and provide an example for each.
5. Why is a SWOT analysis so important to firms?
6. What are seven ways to identify customer needs?
7. What items should firms consider when identifying a target market?
8. Identify the various methods to segment a market. Provide examples for each.
9. Use price and quality and then construct a perceptual map of fast food restaurants.

Discussion Questions

1. Select three of the factors that influence price perception and share with the professor examples you have encountered for each.
2. Share why you feel quality is important or not important in the twenty-first century.
3. What is your preferred distribution channel? Why do you prefer this channel?
4. Why is identifying customer needs is important? Of the seven ways listed, why did you select that method?
5. What are other variables firms should consider when selecting a target market? Share why you feel they are important.
6. Discuss what method of segmentation you feel is most effective. Provide three examples for this method.
7. Share ways in which a perceptual map can identify opportunities for firms.

Extension Activity

Select a product you frequently use. Perform a segmentation analysis to determine who other groups would be a good candidate for the company producing it to target.

BIBLIOGRAPHY

"Expectation Pricing," Changing Minds, http://changingminds.org/disciplines/marketing/pricing/expectation_pricing.htm.

Herrmann, Andreas, Xia, Lan, Monroe, Kent B., and Huber, Frank. "The Influence of Price Fairness on Customer Satisfaction: An Empirical Test in the Context of Automobile Purchases," *Journal of Product & Brand Management* 16, no. 1 (2007): 49–58.

Anttila, Juhani. "Quality and Innovation." http://www.qualityintegration.biz/HailInnovation.html.

Garvin, David A. "What Does 'Product Quality' Really Mean?" *Sloane Management Review* 26, no. 1(1984): 25–42.

Sampaio, Paulo and Saraiva, Pedro. Eds. *Quality in the 21st Century: Perspectives from ASQ Feigenbaum Medal Winners (Switzerland: Springer, 2016).*

"Five Strategies Companies Must Follow to Satisfy Consumers' Needs," TTI Success Insights, http://blog.ttisuccessinsights.com/5-strategies-companies-must-follow-satisfy-customers-needs.

"Pricing a Product," Entrepreneur, https://www.entrepreneur.com/encyclopedia/pricing-a-product.

Gavett, Gretchen. "What You Need to Know about Segmentation," *Harvard Business Review* 70 (2014): 5019–5028.

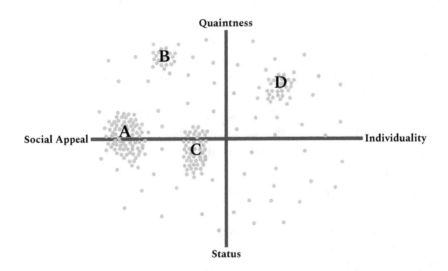

FIG 14.2 **Perceptual map**

Figure Credits

CHAPTER FIFTEEN

What is a New Product Development and Timeline Approach?

INTRODUCTION

Firms must find an approach to use to develop and test products. The ability to accurately predict what consumers will purchase is the goal of innovation. This chapter will identify some methods to develop products including a new product approach, which is designed to satisfy consumers' needs, reduce production costs, increase speed to market, and create a design that is easy to reproduce. Firms can also adopt a timeline approach, which spells out the process on how to innovate and who is responsible for what parts and when.

Firms must also test their products to ensure the intended target market is satisfied. Some ways they can do this are alpha, beta, and gamma testing and using test markets (standard, controlled, and simulated). Another way to test a product is through prototype testing, which provides firms with real customer feedback who interact with it to make changes. Testing helps to reduce the chance of product failure in the market, thus stopping the waste of valuable resources.

Finally, we will discuss the need to develop a timeline used to launch a product and determine which functional areas will be involved and when. In addition, firms must assess their available resources one more time before the launch to ensure success.

Learning Objectives

In this chapter students will learn about the following:
- What a new product development approach is and how it helps firms innovate
- How a timeline approach acts as a blueprint for innovation
- Advantages and disadvantages of various testing methods
- How test markets can help firms predict product success in the market
- How to use prototypes to gain valuable consumer insights before launching a product
- Why a timeline is important to launch a product

Learning Outcomes

By the end of this chapter students will be able to do the following:

- Understand and develop a new product development approach
- Explain why a timeline approach is beneficial to firms to get products to market faster
- Conduct alpha, beta, and gamma testing
- Explain why prototype testing is beneficial to gain consumer insights
- Know the difference in test markets and suggest which is more beneficial to firms
- Grasp the concept of developing a timeline to launch a product once the testing is complete

Key Terms

New product development approach: Conceptualizing, designing, developing, and introducing a new good or service to market that satisfies customers' needs

First mover advantages: When a firm introduces a product that is unique to the market, thus giving it an advantage until a competitor copies or improves the design

Timeline approach: One that presents the steps necessary to innovate a product from start to finish. It speeds time to market and helps communicate to the innovation team when and where each step in the process should fall

Alpha testing: Testing that is performed within a company to gain initial feedback on the product being developed

Beta testing: Testing that is performed outside the organization on individuals who mimic the intended target customer

Gamma testing: Testing done as a last step, primarily performed for safety concerns

Test markets: Consumer testing determining what factors influence their purchase behavior in an actual or simulated environment

Standard test market: Testing method that selects cities that are thought to represent the greater market where the product is placed in stores to sell and monitor the results

Controlled test market: One which customers are guided to controlled stores to analyze their purchase behavior

Simulated test market: Testing method where the purchase environment is totally controlled by the firm testing the products

Prototypes: Initial version of what the final product will look like or do after refinement

NEW PRODUCT DEVELOPMENT APPROACH (NPD)

The **new product development approach** is conceptualizing, designing, developing, and introducing a new good or service to market to satisfy customers' needs. The benefits of adopting a new product development approach include reducing waste, and introducing products that satisfy the needs of customers, which allows firms to compete on a local, regional, or global level, and if done correctly, will provide a strategic competitive advantage. It is imperative that all functional areas of the firm work together to develop new products. As stressed throughout the text, an innovation team must include all functional areas of the company to be successful. Their timing on developing new products will be more important at certain times, but what is needed is utilizing the expertise of these functional groups to ensure the success of a new product.

When designing new products, it is important that firms establish objectives to achieve the new product processes:

1. **Designing products that satisfy consumer needs and provide the expected level of quality.** Customers will not buy products they don't want or need. Firms must conduct marketing research to determine this by utilizing focus groups, interviews, monitoring blogs, and speaking to the target market to determine what they need. The brand will determine the level of quality as brands satisfy the expectation of consumers. Would it be unthinkable if Mercedes Benz had a car that was cheap and of poor quality? Brands are surrogates for price, quality, and customer expectations; therefore, these must be consistent for a product carrying a brand name.

2. **To formulate a design process that reduces costs and gives firms an advantage to profit more or offer their products at a lower price, while not sacrificing profits. This can be done through increased efficiencies and realizing economies of scale.** This is another topic that will be covered throughout the text, but successful firms reduce costs through efficiencies. Efficiencies are gained through utilizing machines that can perform multiple tasks, thus reducing the space needed, while taking advantage of the speed of today's manufacturing equipment. Another form of efficiency is practicing just-in-time manufacturing where products are produced and shipped without storing them. This helps to produce the same number of products in less space, reduce holding costs, and so on, thus saving money.

   The ability to produce more gives firms economies of scale. As a review, economies of scale are the ability to spread a firm's fixed cost among more parts, thus reducing their costs. It is important to achieve this as it helps the firm compete and increase profits.

3. **To increase the speed to market of new products to gain first mover advantages or competitive advantage.** Getting innovative products to market quickly is another popular theme of this text and a main part of the GT-MAP. Getting a product to market and being the first one to introduce it gives firms first mover advantages. *First mover advantages* are when a firm introduces a product that is unique to the market, thus giving them advantage until a competitor copies or improves the design. The firm is able to establish many things being first, including quality, performance expectations, price, style, and functionality. The originating firm can file for a patent or trademark to gain protection from competitors by legally protecting the innovation from being copied. First mover advantages also help increase the firm's value and its brand equity because a truly unique product adds value to the firm and there is a valued placed on brands.

THINK ABOUT THIS!

Hostess Brands filed Chapter 11 in 2012, so how much is a bankrupt company worth? Do iconic brands such as Twinkies, Ding Dongs, Wonder Bread, and Dolly Madison have value? What would you have paid for the right to own these brands?

In 2012, Hostess Brands filed Chapter 11 protection to reorganize the company and fight off bankruptcy. Hostess Brands was struggling due to Americans trying to cut their carbohydrate intake and lose weight. So, if a company is on the verge of bankruptcy, does its brands carry any value? The answer is it does. Gores Group eventually bought the company for $725 million. The Wonder Bread brand was also sold to Flower Foods for $360 million. The brand equity of legendary products are worth lots of money and although the companies were struggling financially, their brands are quite valuable.[1]

4. **Perfecting simplistic designs that allow for reductions in changes and are easy to reproduce.** Simplistic design allows for easy manufacturing and increases the speed of manufacturing products. It also allows for firms to invest less in machinery because the need for complex manufacturing processes are eliminated. Simplistic design also helps in horizontal line extensions (covered in another chapter). When the design is simple, making slight changes to extend the product lines are faster, less expensive, and very effective in satisfying the customers' needs and increasing the firm's profits.

To achieve these objectives, firms must formulate an integrated approach that identifies ways to satisfy its business strategy. As discussed before, accomplishing the mission and vision of the firm should guide the new product development process. New products should also contribute to the firm's portfolio in a way that increases the value and utilizes resources in an efficient manner.[2]

The following are ways to achieve the integrated approach to new product design:

1. Align the new product development with the firm's business strategy.
2. Use innovation teams to help streamline the design process.
3. Establish an efficient development process. As discussed throughout the text, benchmarking best practices can help achieve this.

---

1 Michael J. de la Merced. "Hostess Brands, Makers of Twinkies, Gets a New Owner." *New York Times,* July 5, 2016. https://www.nytimes.com/2016/07/06/business/dealbook/twinkies-gores-hostess-brands.html.

2 "A Strategic Approach to Product and Process Development," NPD Solutions, http://www.npd-solutions.com/pdstrategy.html.

4. Utilize digital tools to ensure quality, get to production quicker, and design the new products fast.
5. Use product design to increase the efficiencies of a firm to achieve more profits and efficiency.

As indicated, the new product design process must be linked to the firm's business strategy and ultimately its mission and vision. Research conducted by Hayes and Wheelwright found that there are five dimensions firms need to compete. These five dimensions include cost, quality/performance, flexibility, dependability, and innovativeness.[3]

1. *Cost*: Cost reductions can be achieved by limiting the breadth of products and concentrating on being efficient during manufacturing.
2. *Quality/reliability/dependability*: Firms must understand what their customers need and how their new products can satisfy these. Products should be tested to ensure they offer the consumer the highest quality and use computer-aided testing in the manufacturing process.
3. *Time to market*: Companies need to continuously scan the internal and external environments and understand their customers' needs to produce a well-designed development process. Strategies must be clearly spelled out and a chain of command is important to establish who is doing what functions to speed the development of the new products.
4. *Innovativeness/technology*: Firms must have a technology plan in place to effectively utilize it for the manufacturing or development of new products. Firms should invest in state-of-the-art technology that will speed production, simplify design, and produce products sooner and faster than in the past.

New product development is a vital undertaking for any firm. It helps them compete, enhances their product portfolio, and creates efficiencies in manufacturing. Firms that benchmark best practices have an advantage over ones that do not, and keeping a simple process in place both speeds the products to market and helps them be more profitable.

Timeline Approach

A *timeline approach* is one that presents the steps necessary to innovate a product from start to finish. It speeds time to market and helps communicate to the innovation team know when and where each step in the process should fall. When preparing to innovate, especially in the latter phases closer to launch, it is important to establish a timeline to help keep the launch on track. Launching a product is a very expensive endeavor for a firm, so the clearer

---

3 Robert H. Hayes and Steven C. Wheelwright, *Restoring Our Competitive Edge: Competing through Manufacturing*, Vol. 8 (New York: Wiley, 1984).

the timeline is laid out for the innovation team and company employees, the more successful the launch will be.

Since each timeline is unique to the type of innovation and company, we will provide some suggestions to establish a timeline. These suggestions can then be used to fill in the blanks to bring a product to launch.

1. *Test the product before developing it further and launching it*: The next section of this text identifies various methods to test new products. It is important that firms test these products with targeted customers to determine if they find the product acceptable. Customers can interact with a prototype or service to determine if it is acceptable in terms of use, functionality, and complexity. The biggest reason to test is to determine if the new product satisfies their needs, both realized and unrealized, while not endangering the consumer.

2. *Maintain excitement with the innovation team*: The excitement, first felt by a product innovation team, may wean as time goes on. This slow down in momentum and excitement can slow the launch of the product as well. Top managers can be sure to provide the team the time and resources to familiarize themselves with the new product and establish customer support protocol.

3. *Prepare for an increase in sales*: It may seem easy to increase sales, but much planning must go into this decision. Firms must prepare for an increase in the purchase of raw materials, ensuring there are enough and the right type of people on board; possess sufficient inventory to fill orders; and train employees to support the customer servic e efforts. In addition, wholesalers and retailers must be educated on the products and ample shelf space must be secured to bring the product to market. Therefore, the ability to bring a new product to market must be coordinated from manufacturer to retailer to ensure it will be successful.

4. *Don't forget about your core business*: While all the planning is going on to prepare to launch a new product, firms must not forget about the ones that generate revenue daily. It is exciting to create a new product and see it from ideation to launch, but firms must still focus on the products that are in the market. It is important that service levels and the ability to restock sold merchandise be maintained to make the new products more successful. It is very probable that firms will sell their new products to the same retailers they sell their current ones, so maintaining quality service will help when launching the new product.

5. *Establish measurable parameters for success*: Firms should establish measurable goals leading up to launch and then after. Pre-launch goals could include having X number of units of back stock in the warehouse and your wholesalers having X amount before launch. It could also include when the products will be shipped to retailers or service providers and the fill rate (i.e., the percentage of the product ordered versus what was shipped). Launch objectives include achieving a certain dollar amount of sales within

a certain time. Other things that can be measured are profitability, increase in market share, percentage of shelf space, and customer satisfaction rates. The ability to establish measurable goals gives the firm the ability to quantify its success.

6. *Get customer feedback after launch*: As discussed previously, post-purchase evaluation is very important to determine if a customer will repurchase the item and tell his or her friends (i.e., word of mouth) about the product. Firms sometimes shy away from customer opinions out of fear of them having a negative experience. The opposite should happen. Firms should contact consumers and get their feedback. If someone had a bad experience, the firm should do whatever is necessary to correct it. Gaining customer feedback also gives firms the ability to adjust, evolve, and lead. Corrections can be made to the innovation to correct any problems, while introducing it into the market quickly. Speed to market is vital, so obtaining post-purchase feedback and then adjusting any small problems will get the product into the market faster and not have a competitor steal the idea.

Another benefit of establishing a timeline is that it shares information with the team and employees. Employees can build excitement for the product as well by seeing a document that lays out the steps to be taken to introduce the new product into the market. Open communication is a key component to product development, and establishing a timeline is another method of practicing this.

Alpha/Beta/Gamma Testing of New Goods and Services

Before products reach the later phases of development, firms must test them to determine if there are shortcomings in the design or application. Due to the expensive nature of product development, not knowing if a product will function as designed and satisfy consumer needs is negligent on the part of companies. So, what can companies do to ensure they are on track with the development of a new product and satisfying the needs of their target market? The answer is testing! There are various kinds of testing that can be performed to accomplish this goal. We will focus on three types: alpha, beta, and gamma testing.

Alpha Testing

Alpha testing is testing that is performed within a company to gain initial feedback on the product being developed. It is thought that employees of the company will give uncensored feedback to the functionality and ease of use of the product and if it is perceived to satisfy the needs on the customer. It is also a quick method of testing as the people testing the product are housed on site, so companies don't have to arrange a focus group to test the product. While not a conclusive means of finalizing the testing of a product, alpha testing can give innovators a clear indication if there are initial problems that need to be addressed or weaknesses in the design of the product.

The following are pros and cons of alpha testing.

TABLE 15.1   *Pros and Cons of Alpha Testing*

PROS	CONS
It is used primarily for use testing by internal candidates, so it speeds the development process along by seeking early feedback by "experts."	Data gathered may be biased since it was tested internally. Employees may not be honest if the design is poor for fear of discipline.
It allows firms to address problems that were discovered and allows for a quick fix to the issue, and then for a retry.	Usability focus, reliability and security may not be addressed as firms seek initial feedback on functionality.
It allows firms to refine the objectives of the design to better suit customers' needs.	Internal candidates may not represent the final consumer using the product and bias the results and feedback.

While both pros and cons exist in alpha testing, it is a vital method to understand early strengths and weaknesses of a product. Firms should therefore utilize these types of testing methods, realizing that certain biases may occur, which may prompt them to do additional testing or to alter design.

Beta Testing

Beta testing is testing that is performed outside the organization on individuals who mimic the intended target customer. Beta testing is done in real time to discover if there are issues that need to be addressed before the final work is performed on the new product. It is one additional step that innovators can use to reduce product failure and maximize the needs' satisfaction of the product. The following are pros and cons of beta testing.

TABLE 15.2   *Pros and Cons of Beta Testing*

PROS	CONS
Beta testing helps to realize the gaps between the actual performance of the new product and anticipated performance.	Duplicating the anticipated target market may be hard, especially if marketing doesn't target the right group.
Customer validation of the new product helps to reduce failure and the loss of financial resources.	Testing the product in real time doesn't allow firms to control for certain variables; therefore, close attention to the testing must be maintained.
Post-service requirements may be detected in beta testing by interviewing customers.	

Beta testing is the first opportunity to test the product on a sample of the anticipated target market and thus gives a clear indication of the benefits and problems the product may encounter in the market once released. Therefore, it is essential that firms accurately target the correct consumer and then test the product on a representative sample to increase success and gain insights on the product's potential.

Gamma Testing

Gamma testing is testing done as a last step, primarily performed for safety concerns. It is used to validate the performance and functionality of the product to be launched. While this is a worthwhile step, it is slowly being phased out due to competitive pressure, trying to get a product to market quicker, and satisfactory beta testing results. The following are pros and cons to gamma testing.

TABLE 15.3   *Pros and Cons of Gamma Testing*

PROS	CONS
It helps ensure the product to be launched is reliable, safe, and functional.	Not focusing on changing the product by just testing the reliability and functionality doesn't help with any last-minute design changes.
It saves time as it doesn't continue to test modification of the design.	As indicated early, this step is often deleted due to trying to launch a product to market quickly.
It provides greater satisfaction of consumers' needs.	

The purpose of gamma testing makes it a worthwhile means to determine if a product will perform as expected once it is launched. Due to firms trying to get to market quickly with their innovations, it is slowly being phased out. If firms have time to perform a function and reliability test, this would be a worthwhile endeavor, as poor product performance can hamper the adoption of a new product or hurt initial sales with problems associated with a new product.[4]

Test Markets: Another Way to Test Products?

Alpha, beta, and gamma testing are not the only ways firms test products. The duration of testing products is based on the nature of the product. More specifically, products such as pharmaceuticals and medical devices are tested for extended periods of time, while some consumer goods are hardly tested at all. Therefore, firms must do their best to provide a product that is safe to consumers and will not harm them in any way. So, what are other means of testing products?

Test markets are another form of market testing that gives marketers an indication of what will trigger customer purchase behavior. **Test markets** are consumer testing determining what factors influence purchase behavior in an actual or simulated environment. Firms can test the effect various scenarios will have on purchase behavior by three test market methods: standard, controlled, and simulated. The use of each gives companies the ability to test their products to determine their potential success before a major roll out, thus reducing the financial burden a product failure could cause a firm.

---

4   "What Are Alpha, Beta, and Gamma Testing," Testbytes, http://www.testbytes.net/blog/alpha-beta-gamma-testing/.

Standard Test Market

A **standard test market** is a testing method that selects cities that are thought to represent a similar market where the product will be placed in stores to sell and monitor the results. This is a long-proven method of determining product success as products undergo normal purchase evaluation by similar consumers as the target market. If the product does well in these test markets, it can be rolled out to a greater area or go national with the offering. While test marketing doesn't ensure success, it is a method that can help predict if a product is worthy of greater distribution.

Controlled Test Market

A **controlled test market** is one in which customers are guided to controlled stores to analyze their purchase behavior. Unlike the standard test market, only certain stores are included, and consumers are directed to those stores to test new products. It has been found to be a cheaper and faster way to evaluate consumer behavior. However, it is difficult to judge consumer reactions to the products and it also gives the competition an exact store location to see or possibly purchase the new product.

Simulated Test Market

A **simulated test market** is a testing method where the purchase environment is totally controlled by the firm testing the products. A simulated test market gives firms the ability to test different advertising schemes, display arrangements, and how altering the marketing mix i.e, the (four P's) affects the purchase of the new product. It is a very effective method of testing because instead of allowing purchase behavior to happen naturally as in the first two methods, this form gives marketers the ability to try various scenarios on customers to fine tune the offerings, which will hopefully lead to increased sales.[5]

Test marketing a product before launch does slow down getting to market quickly. Decisions to test the market may include the type of innovation being tested, if product failure will have a devastating effect on the firm, the cost of the product, and so on. The biggest threat to test marketing is the exposure of the new product to the eyes of the competition. There lies a fine balance between speed to market and product testing. As we have discussed previously, benchmarking best practices can help to get to market quicker by utilizing proven techniques by the firm. Therefore, companies must benchmark and make the decision in their timeline approach as to what type of testing will be used before launching a product.

Evaluating the Changes That the Prototype Needs Based on Consumer Reaction

Prototypes are essential for product development as they give end users an idea of how they can satisfy their needs. **Prototypes** are an initial version of what the final product will look like

---

5   "Test Markets," Causal Marketing Research, http://media.acc.qcc.cuny.edu/faculty/volchok/causalMR/CausalMR8.html.

or perform after refinement. Their purpose is to determine if the design or function is acceptable to the final consumer and thus will undergo extensive changes leading to the final design. Prototypes give firms many advantages including reduced time and cost of development. The goal is to have a representative sample of the target market to interact with the prototype to determine if further changes are needed, if the design satisfies their needs, and to finalize it to start production. Another benefit is increased user involvement. The only way companies can determine if the prototype is successful is to get it in the hands of the end user. The faster the firm can determine if the design is successful, the quicker it can get to market. Therefore, prototyping is a necessary step in the product development process.

Prototyping also has many disadvantages, including insufficient analysis. Developers may focus too closely on the prototype and fail to see obvious changes that need to be made to satisfy the customer. Developers need to ask the customer if there needs to be any other changes made or how the prototype can be changed to make it better and not focus on the minimum to get by. User confusion is another disadvantage of prototyping. Users interacting with the prototype must be aware that the unit is not the final product. The prototype is a representation of the final product and thus consumer insights are being sought. Users' opinions should be cautioned for clarification as the firm is seeking input regarding the functionality and usefulness of the prototype to perfect the final design. Another disadvantage is the misunderstanding of the users' objectives. Companies and users must be on the same page regarding the objectives to test the prototype. If not, it can lead to failure and miscommunication. Finally, prototypes need to act as a guide, but firms must not spend too much time in development. Excessive development time can lead to delays in launch and give the competition an advantage in countering the new product. Firms must test the prototype, make changes, and then launch the product as quickly as possible. The inability to do so, or excessive testing, can lead to delays, which can be costly in terms of time to market and loss of competitive advantage.[6]

Establishing a Timeline to Further Development and Launch

There is a fine line that occurs when a company plans to introduce a product and the time it takes to test it. Often, companies utilize test markets to try out the product before rolling it out into bigger markets. The benefit is that firms can be sure the product will be successful; however, it may also give the competition the opportunity to capitalize on the product and steal the momentum. Therefore, launching a product requires a rapid launch and follow-up to ensure it is successful.

This topic will be discussed in more detail later in the text, but as a prelude to this conversation here are some things to consider when establishing a timeline and preparing to launch. A timeline is essential to give the cross-functional team a realistic expectation of what they need to do. Without a timeline, the innovation process would drag out and the opportunities

---

6 "The Pros and Cons of Prototyping," Rapid Reproductions, https://rapidsrepro.com/advantages-disadvantages-prototyping/.

sought would be wasted. Cross-functional teams can use the timeline to motivate their efforts and use it as a template for what they need to accomplish and when. What is important is that the innovation under development needs to be launched as quickly as possible to gain an advantage in the market place. The product must be tested to ensure it will not harm the user, it functions as expected, the quality and price match the target markets expectations, the product will lead to repeat purchases, and it supports the mission and vision of the firm while adding value to the product portfolio.

The innovation should be tested using alpha, beta, and gamma testing, but testing the product internally and externally can give firms the ability to ensure the innovation is ready to launch. We have shared stories of firms that have tested far too long only to find out that a competitor has stolen the idea and introduced the product first. This limits the effectiveness of gaining a first mover advantage and puts the firm in a position of not market dominance but trying to compete with the same product they developed. Therefore, a timeline can help give everyone a realistic idea of what they need to accomplish to be successful.

Launch is an essential part of innovation. We stress in great detail and emphasize launching a product with speed is essential for success. The timeline discussed will help establish when the launch will occur, but the product must be introduced as soon as possible. If the testing results are favorable, the product must be introduced and monitored. Feedback can come from customer surveys, focus groups, monitoring social media, blogs, sales data, reorders, and any other method customers use to communicate their pleasure or displeasure for the firm's innovation. We will discuss this in more detail, but firms must introduce a product and then adjust the product as needed, evolve the product so it is found to be worthy of purchase, and then lead in the market.

Products that are too similar can only compete on price. This puts firms at a disadvantage as price has a direct correlation on profits. If price is the only factor consumers will consider because a product is seen as a commodity product, they will have to discount it to compete. Innovations that are unique can give the firm the ability to set a higher price and recoup R&D dollars more quickly, plus increase sales and profits. Therefore, getting to market quickly is not a catch phrase; it is reality in the world of innovation.

Establishing What Functional Areas Will Be Delegated to Launch the Product

Firms must determine which functional areas are needed to launch a product. The question as to which areas should be involved is simple; all areas must be involved. Just as all areas should be involved in the development of the innovation, the same holds true when launching the product. It is rare that any one person has the expert knowledge to orchestrate the development and launching of a product; therefore, it is important to use all functional areas to do so. Product launch requires the expertise of all functional areas to ensure it will be successful. As discussed previously, the ability to adjust elements of the launch quickly is vital to a product's success. Product launch must be done quickly to not give the competitors the ability to copy the innovation, but also it must be introduced to recuperate sunk costs involved in the development of the product. Therefore, the ability to launch a product involving all functional areas is vital to its success.

What are some requirements needed for successful cross-functional teams? The following are suggested requirements needed for firms wishing to create a representative cross-functional team:

1. **The cross-functional team should be open-minded and motivated**. We have discussed the need to prevent groupthink, and a well-comprised functional group can prevent this from happening.

2. **Cross-functional groups should come from all functional areas of the organization**. It is vital to represent all areas participating in the innovation to make it successful. Therefore, a cross-functional group made up of all areas of the organization will make it successful.

3. **The team leader must have the authority to act and possess good communication skills**. Each cross-functional group must have a leader who has the authority to act on behalf of the group. Each innovation team needs an advocate to promote their project. Top executives at times are biased toward groups, so a person leading the group with similar authority can be helpful to see the project gets equal consideration. Another reason having someone of authority on the team is to be sure the mission and vision of the firm drives the innovation. All innovation must support the reason the firm is in existence and add value to the product portfolio.

4. **Innovation is not possible without adequate financial resources**. Research and development require funding on the part of companies wishing to launch products. Without the needed funds, innovation is not possible. Imagine trying to attend school with no money to pay for tuition. It is vital that a realistic picture of what the development and launch of a product will cost be properly accounted for to ensure its success. This ties back to having all functional units involved in the process, so a firm can properly determine what the sunk costs will be. Without proper funding, innovation may never be realized, so a budget must be established at the beginning to ensure it will have the means to be created and launched.

5. **Teams must have adequate communication between its members**. Open communication skills are a vital part of success. It requires team members to communicate perceived problems as well as successes while the innovation process is occurring. Open communication should not be limited by the fear of discussing problems with the executive in charge of the innovation team. Any member must be given access team members concerns' and information they feel is worthy of sharing. Without this, the efforts of the team are useless, so open communication is vital to the success of the product.[7]

---

7   "Cross-Functional Teams," Inc., https://www.inc.com/encyclopedia/cross-functional-teams.html.

Review Questions

1. What are the objectives of the new product development process?
2. Describe the ways to achieve the integrated approach to new product design.
3. List and elaborate on Hayes and Wheelwright's five dimensions needed to compete.
4. What are suggestions to develop a timeline approach? Describe each one.
5. What are the pros and cons of alpha testing?
6. What are the pros and cons of beta testing?
7. What are the pros and cons of gamma testing?
8. List and describe the three different types of test markets.
9. What is prototype testing and why is it important for firms?
10. Describe the requirements needed for firms wishing to create a representative cross-functional team.

Discussion Questions

1. Considering all the objectives in the new product development process, which do you feel is the most important? Why do you feel this way?
2. Select three ways to achieve the integrated approach to new product design and describe why they are important to firms.
3. What else would you suggest to enhance Hayes and Wheelwright's five dimensions needed to compete? Why do feel this is important?
4. Which suggestion in the development of a timeline approach do you feel is most important? Describe to you professor why you feel this way.
5. Discuss the importance of alpha/beta/gamma testing. Do you feel we need to do all three? Why?
6. What are your thoughts on test markets? Are they important or do they slow down the launch of the product? Why do you feel this way?
7. Describe your thoughts on product testing. Should firms launch the product and make changes while it is in the market or test it and then launch? What is your rationale?
8. How important do you feel prototype testing is at gaining consumer insights? Why?
9. Share your thought with your professor on the importance of cross-functional teams. Do you see real value to them? Why?

Extension Activity

1. Simulating a timeline approach, have students devise a timeline for preparing for their next exam. Include the chapters they must cover, time for prep, assignments, and so on and then draw it out so it is visible.
2. Form groups and have students conduct an alpha test on a product of your choice. What did they learn about obtaining information?

BIBLIOGRAPHY

Merced, Michael J. de la. "Hostess Brands, Makers of Twinkies, Gets a New Owner." *New York Times,* July 5, 2016. https://www.nytimes.com/2016/07/06/business/dealbook/twinkies-gores-hostess-brands.html.

"A Strategic Approach to Product and Process Development," NPD Solutions, http://www.npd-solutions.com/pdstrategy.html.

Hayes, Robert H. and Wheelwright, Steven C. *Restoring Our Competitive Edge: Competing through Manufacturing,* Vol. 8 (New York: Wiley, 1984).

"What Are Alpha, Beta, and Gamma Testing," Testbytes, http://www.testbytes.net/blog/alpha-beta-gamma-testing/.

"Test Markets," Causal Marketing Research, http://media.acc.qcc.cuny.edu/faculty/volchok/causalMR/CausalMR8.html.

"The Pros and Cons of Prototyping," Rapid Reproductions, https://rapidsrepro.com/advantages-disadvantages-prototyping/.

"Cross-Functional Teams," Inc., https://www.inc.com/encyclopedia/cross-functional-teams.html.

CHAPTER SIXTEEN

The Art of Exciting the Customer

INTRODUCTION

Consumers are exposed to approximately four to ten thousand marketing messages a day, so it is important for firms to seek new and more effective ways to gain consumers' attention.[1] Many successful firms accomplish this by creating aura around their brand and their products, which drives consumers to desire their offerings, which in turn helps create additional buzz for the innovation both locally, regionally, and globally. By identifying previously undiscovered consumer preferences and satisfying their unmet needs, firms can establish themselves as leaders creating new value for customers in ways that are completely unique from any other company, thereby presenting a strong differentiation in the market.

This chapter also looks at ways to launch a product quickly. One suggested method is to use consumer feedback to obtain key insights needed to decide to go to market. In addition, working cross-functionally helps for rapid launch by consulting with manufacturing, supply chains, sales, and marketing to determine if the firm is ready to launch and can maintain a steady flow of products in the market.

Learning Objectives

In this chapter students will learn about the following:
- How consumer perception influences product awareness and gains attention
- How advertisement retention is influenced by the level of consumer involvement
- What aura is and why it is important in innovation
- How to geographically create aura ("buzz") by identifying factors occurring in various markets
- Four trends that will drive growth among the world's leading companies

---

1   Ron Marshall. "How many Ads Do You See A Day?" September 10, 2015. https://www.redcrowmarketing.com/2015/09/10/many-ads-see-one-day/

- How feedback helps to launch products more quickly
- Areas of a firm that need to be addressed for rapid launch
- How marketers need to create market strategies using the four P's
- Why post-purchase product evaluation is important to success

Learning Outcomes

By the end of this chapter students will be able to do the following:

- Create ways to gain greater consumer perception
- Devise ways to get consumers to be more involved in information search and purchase decision making
- Describe ways to create aura around an innovation
- Analyze geographic differences that affect products and ways to find trends and compete by understanding differences that exist
- How to use feedback to launch products quickly
- Analyze a firm's capabilities and make suggestions to rapidly launch products
- Know how the four P's can be utilized to create marketing strategies
- Understand the need for positive post-purchase product evaluation and ways to handle dissatisfaction

Key Terms

Perception: The act of perceiving stimulus through one's senses, cognition, and level of understanding

Involvement: The act of being involved with something or the level of participation

Low involvement: Involves frequent purchase behavior and low price

High involvement: Involves little to no experience with a product and high price

Aura: The distinctive atmosphere surrounding a given source

Pull demand or marketing: Creates consumer interest resulting in their asking for the product to a retailer, thus causing the retailer to offer the product for sale

Differentiation: The ability to be heterogenous to solve customer needs quickly with solutions that are fast to market

Fixed manufacturing: A process where equipment is fixed to produce one part of the product, which then goes into a final good

Programmable manufacturing: A type of manufacturing that produces batches of products versus mass production

Flexible manufacturing: Like a program, where a variety of products can be manufactured using one machine, adding to the benefits of providing the ability to produce parts needed to assemble a final product

Supply chain: The movement upstream and downstream of components needed to produce a product and offer it to the final customer

Warehousing: The short- or long-term storage of a tangible good once manufactured

Inventory control: The ability to have a sufficient amount of inventory available to prevent out-of-stocks for retailers

Holding costs: The cost manufacturers incur when they produce and then store products without selling them

Sales channels: The way a product is offered to consumers, either directly or indirectly

Direct channels: When companies sell their products directly to consumers and then provide a means to deliver the product to them

Marketing strategy: A way firms turn their target customers into customers who buy their products

Marketing plan: A documented strategy dictating how the strategy will occur

Promotional tools: Ways companies connect with their target market from print, radio, television, and the internet

Integrated marketing communication (IMC): An integrated marketing method to broadcast a unified message to a target market using various, but common, types of media

Products: Objects (tangible, and intangible) a firm sells to a final consumer

Post-purchase evaluation: The evaluation of a product's functionality or performance, creating satisfaction or dissatisfaction

Buyer's remorse: A feeling of regret as a result of making a purchase decision

HOW DOES CONSUMER PERCEPTION AND LEVEL OF INVOLVEMENT AFFECT PURCHASE BEHAVIOR?

Consumers are exposed to thousands of marketing messages every day. This excessive exposure to marketing messages has reduced their attention to few messages and retention of the information broadcasted. Firms continue to effectively target their message to consumers based on the media sources (e.g., television, radio, print, and social media) with which they participate. Two factors that influence purchase behavior are perception and involvement.

Perception is the act of perceiving stimulus through one's senses, cognitions, and level of understanding. Perception influences how effective an advertisement is and the level of attention given by consumers. Consumers with no interest in a message will have low interest in the advertisement, and thus minimal retention, whereas an advertisement that gains one's attention will more likely be retained. The ability to gain a consumer's attention will create the desire to obtain more information concerning the features and benefits of the product. The information sought will increase the comprehension of the message and hopefully lead to a purchase response. Finally, if a consumer has no need to purchase a retained product immediately, he or she may store the information until he or she is ready. In this scenario the consumer remembers the information or brand and then pursues more information before purchasing the product. Therefore, the level of perception on the part of consumers is vital to gain their attention with a marketing message.

Another factor that influences advertisement retention and affects consumer purchase behavior is the level of involvement. *Involvement* is the act of being involved with something or one's level of participation. Involvement is directly related to the frequency of purchase activity and price. Involvement is characterized as low and high. *Low involvement* involves frequent purchase behavior and low price. Products that are purchased on a regular basis, such as morning coffee, are given little involvement by consumers. Habitual purchase behavior is routine, so involvement in the purchase behavior is not a necessity as the performance and satisfaction of the product is consistent. In addition, the price of low involvement products is routinely low, so there is no need for consumers to spend a lot of involvement in the purchase decision as their level of risk of not being satisfied is low. *High involvement* involves little to no experience with a product and a high price. Products purchased occasionally or possibly never, such as cars or a house, require high levels of involvement due to inexperience or no experience by consumers. Also, products that carry a higher price point will typically receive higher levels of involvement to reduce post-purchase dissatisfaction. Based on the level of involvement, firms must strive to be the brand that consumers have adopted for their low involvement behavior or provide sufficient information for the high involvement purchases.

The New Way to Attract Interest in Innovation: Aura and People

This text separates itself from other textbooks by introducing the concept of aura. Aura is a concept that cuts through the overexposure of marketing messages, as discussed earlier, to gain attention and create consumer demand. The word *aura* is defined in the dictionary as "a distinctive atmosphere surrounding a given source."[2] This definition, as it relates to innovation, is rather limited. So, why is aura so important? How does it separate one firm from another? The answer lies in the effective and efficient way it captures the attention of consumers.

As described earlier, capturing the attention of consumers is becoming more difficult. Aura gives firms the ability to engage consumers regarding a new product, especially in the age of social media. Consumers are given "teasers" regarding a product, which peaks their interest and gets them to follow the progress of the product innovation. It is the heightened level of engagement that is one of the keys to reaching potential customers at a higher level. It also creates what marketers call pull demand or pull marketing. *Pull demand or marketing* creates consumer interest, resulting in their asking for the product from a retailer, thus causing the retailer to seek out the product and offer it for sale. Pull demand is an effective way to get products into stores because retailers are being asked to carry certain items by their customers, which reduces the retailer's risk of carrying merchandise that may not sell.

THINK ABOUT THIS!

How do pharmaceutical companies use pull demand to sell their products? How does pull demand motivate consumers? Is this strategy effective?

---

2   "Aura." *Merriam-Webster.* https://www.merriam-webster.com/dictionary/aura

Many pharmaceutical companies utilize pull demand in the advertisement strategies. They do this by showing actors, who are representative of the target market, in scenes where their lives are positively impacted by using the drug they are selling. For example, drugs such as Humira, Enbrel, and Taltz show how psoriasis can cause embarrassment on the part of people trying to live a normal life. In their advertisement they show how their condition improves over time and then toward the end of the message how they are living a normal life. Why do these companies use this type of advertisement? The answer lies in the real target market seeing the advertisement. They will exhibit high purchase involvement because this condition has affected them personally. They will seek out a physician who can prescribe this miracle medication and make their life better. The demand for a certain drug comes from a consumer, thus reducing the chance the physician will prescribe only one brand of drug for psoriasis.

Pull demand is a very effective way to encourage purchases because it is motivated by consumers demanding a certain type or brand of product. It also helps companies estimate the need for the products they sell because sales tend to more consistent. It also helps to place products in markets that typically may be dominated by one or two firms; therefore, it creates many benefits for companies utilizing this type of demand.

Aura creates a mystic surrounding around a product that draws consumers in and keeps them engaged. Aura can send out messages and signals as a means of communicating on a personal level that deepens our involvement with the new product. A fascinating article entitled *"Why Apple Is Losing Its Aura."*[3] identified that Apple was losing its aura and why. The article speaks of ways Apple created aura through designs that delighted their customers and their products and provided great experiences. Apple users became a community by providing products that are compatible through their iOS, and Apple products were elegant and beautiful with a charismatic spokesperson in Steve Jobs that provided rituals for the community (i.e., the annual meetings).

This article speaks of four factors that create aura for any firm, including customer participation, firm participation, engagement, and creating an identity within a community. Aura provides the power of engagement by drawing community into its beauty and holding on to it. Aura doesn't satisfy a need or provide empathy; it creates lust and love, and it can become an obsession. We saw this with Apple during the Steve Jobs era(s), but as the aura is waning, the author points out the community turns to anger and demands the aura be reinstated or they will leave. Firms must try to create this aura and draw the customers in to create loyal and lifelong patrons.

---

3   Bruss Nussbaum, "Why Apple Is Losing Its Aura," Fast Company, January 28, 2013, https://www.ama.org/partners/content/Pages/why-customers-attention-scarcest-resources-2017.aspx.

Research conducted by Björkman[4] describes aura as the way firms create tangible feelings in the consumer's mind. He goes on to define aura as a "cover that is related to the feeling-experiences of beauty, exclusiveness, unique and authenticity that a product, service or a brand creates, gives marketing a new tool that can be explored much deeper than this introduction article shows."[5] The article also points out and supports Ferguson, Sztykiel, and Ingram's[6] contentions that aura's importance to companies comes from the constant bombardment of marketing messages we are exposed to everyday, thus decreasing the effectiveness of the marketing message. Björkman also describes that aura helps set firms apart in a world of products that are similar and markets that are overloaded with options.

Björkman (2002), suggests that factors that affect the building process of aura include the following:

1. Level of pricing
2. Customer validation
3. Type of organization
4. The marketing strategy employed

A consumer who possesses strong aura around a brand or product has a personal relationship with it which helps strengthen the consumer's commitment toward the product, company, or brand. We find this true with brands like BMW, Corvette, perhaps your university, Channel, and Coca-Cola. Firms must try to build the aura and draw the customer in to strengthen the loyalty and commitment that is shared between them.

4   Ivar Björkman, "Aura: Aesthetic Business Creativity," *Consumption, Markets and Culture 5,* 1 (2002): 69–78.

5   Ibid., 77.

6   Keith E. Ferguson, John Sztykiel, and Moss Ingram. *Contemporary Product Development: A Focus On Innovation.* California, Cognella Academic Publishing, 2019.

HOW DO YOU TAKE THIS FROM THEORY TO PRACTICE?

Harley-Davidson (Harley) is one brand that defines how companies can use aura to gain attention, deepen the emotional bond with the product, and provide connections when using or seeing the brand. Harley accomplishes the aura around their products in several ways. When a customer buys a Harley, he or she is part of a community of riders. Harley riders come from all spheres of society and the community is built around the product he or she rides not his or her job, income level, where he or she live, and so on. Harley has also done a nice job strengthening the community by forming the Harley Owner's Group or HOG. HOG. is a group composed of only Harley riders that links over a million people in over 25 countries together to share the love of the product. Harley also sponsors the annual Sturgis motorcycle rally held every year in Sturgis, South Dakota. Harley riders from all over the world gather to share stories, see each other, and take part in this fun event focused on Harley owners. Other things Harley-Davidson does to create aura is to honor the military and utilize product placement. Product placement is is placing a company's product in a movie to advertise it or create awareness. Harley-Davidson did this in the film *Easy Rider* using the popular Captain America bike ridden by Peter Fonda.

Harley-Davidson's are not technological wonders. Their design has not changed much in the past 25 years, but this is what attracts people to it. It is seen as the "All-American motorcycle" and the aura it has built around the product has formed a devoted community of riders.[7]

How Do We Create a Buzz for our Innovation Geographically?

In the section on aura, we discussed how in a world of oversaturated marketing messages, we need to find a way to gain consumer attention. Firms can do the same geographically by offering products to consumers that satisfy their preferences, identifying future growth markets, differentiation, and improving areas with limited distribution. Geographies are not limited to states, regions in the US, or just the US; it can also include specific continents or the entire planet. Therefore, offering new products that focus on satisfying consumer needs gives firms an opportunity to create excitement and increase profits.

Consumer Preferences

Consumer preferences vary widely in the United States as a preference is a generic term that can describe any number of product attributes, such as the brand, taste, color, price, or features. Consumers in the North may prefer automobiles that are all-wheel or four-wheel drive, have heated seats, and be rust proofed due to extensive salt use in the winter. In the South, consumers may want spicy foods, higher efficient air conditioning, and sweet tea. In the East,

---

7   Hydar Saharudin, "How Harley-Davidson Rode to Iconic Brand Status through Word-of-Mouth," Referral Candy, June 29, 2016, https://www.referralcandy.com/blog/harley-davidson-marketing-strategy/.

consumers will have a greater preference for seafood, and depending on the city one lives in, may prefer mass transit over owning an automobile. In the Western states consumers may prefer mountain bikes, camping equipment, and ski-related products. While these examples are very limited, it shows that in the US, consumers preferences for consumer goods varies.

Another area of interest is population shifts in the US as they indicate emerging markets and areas for opportunity. The 2010 US census showed how population growth continues to shift from the North to the West and South.[8] This shift gives companies the ability to adopt products to emerging markets and sell products once consumed in the North in these new markets. It also gives companies the ability to learn how consumer preferences change, thus creating opportunity. For example, Chick-fil-A, a fast-food restaurant chain that has dominated the South has enjoyed tremendous growth in the North as travelers demand their food.

Shifts in population also give companies the ability to innovate based on changing consumer preferences. As more people move to the South and West, the ability to provide fresh drinking water will become an issue. Global warming has affected snowfall in the West, which has had an impact on providing drinking water along the Colorado River states. In the South, the need for fresh water has created the need to develop inexpensive desalination plants. Firms must identify the changes and innovate to stay competitive and create new opportunities for themselves, stakeholders, and society.

We have identified changes in consumer preferences in the US based on population shifts. The world is not just limited to the United States, so where are the shifts and subsequent opportunities on a global scale? The Smithsonian reported shifts in the world's population and the impact it will have by the year 2050. The world will see decreases in population in China by 10 percent, 25 percent in Europe, 30 percent in South Korea, and 40 percent in Japan. Due to immigration in the US, people in the 15–64 age group will increase by 42 percent. Europe and East Asia will have a third of their population over 65 years old, while the US will have over 350 million people under 65. This equates to an additional 100 million Americans. While this number predicts opportunities for global companies, it also triggers environmental concern on how to support this many people.

There will be a need to ensure we provide new energy forms, cleaner air, ways to yield more food per acre, and ways to provide care to an aging population. Finally, firms must continue to monitor the needs and wants of a changing society as ethnicity changes. The basic form of innovation will always be to support the customer and the vision of the firm, but it may require more effort to determine who the customer is.[9]

---

8   "By the Grid: Population Shift to the West and South," US Census, October 18, 2012, https://www.census.gov/dataviz/visualizations/024/.

9   Joel Kotkin, "The Changing Demographics of America," *Smithsonian*, August 2012, https://www.smithsonianmag.com/travel/the-changing-demographics-of-america-538284/.

Differentiation

The ability to stand out amongst your competitors is a key to long-term sales and growth. **Differentiation** is the ability to be heterogenous solving customer needs quickly with solutions that are fast to market. It gives companies the ability to focus on consumer needs and wants and then offer solutions that are unique compared to their competitors. Thus, differentiation provides a way to gain a competitive advantage and consumer attention.

Deloitte Insights on the United States Economic Forecast for 2018 predicted the economy will continue to grow due to low unemployment, higher wages, low inflation, and job growth. There were four trends the study found that will drive growth among the world's leading companies:

1. Globalization
2. Innovation
3. Mergers and acquisition activity
4. Digitalization

Globalization

The global economy has given firms the ability to seek opportunities in emerging markets. The ability to offer products in emerging markets helps to strengthen a company's sales and profits. It also helps to identify ways in which innovation can satisfy the needs of new customers. Another benefit of globalization is the opportunity to collaborate with firms that are native to the emerging market. This gives firms access to doing business in countries where the firm may not understand the customs, language, ways business is conducted, and how to distribute products in the most efficient manner. Finally, globalization gives firms the opportunity to lower labor costs and to acquire raw materials at cheaper prices over current suppliers.

Innovation

This text has discussed many factors suggested by the Deloitte study, including new ways to innovate to increase the speed to market. It also suggests approaches to ideate new innovations based on consumer needs and discovering trends. Another factor mentioned in the study was the need to not market test for prolonged periods and introduce products to market quicker. This line of thought is what we have referred to as speed to market and adjusting on the fly once a product is introduced. The underlying message to the Deloitte study and this text is faster product introduction, the ability to monitor consumer responses, and the ability to adjust accordingly, which will provide firms practicing these to have an advantage over their competitors.

Mergers and Acquisition (M&A) Activity

The study also indicated seeking new opportunities through M&A activity. A strong US economy will provide the financial resources needed to support M&A activity. The benefits are like the ones indicated in the globalization factors, plus it allows firms the ability to buy technology they may lack. The result is the ability to innovate in new areas possibly never thought of before. One drawback found in M&A activity, previously discussed, is adding product lines that do not support the product portfolio and mission and vision of the firm. Companies must carefully determine which products will be kept in the merger or acquisition and then sell off or discontinue the ones that add minimal continuous value.

Digitalization

Deloitte suggests that firms align their technology in ways that optimize customer engagement and positively impact their purchase behavior. Firms must be creative and efficient in how it can achieve this. Customer digital engagement faces the same challenges as oversaturation of marketing messages. If customers have difficulty engaging with a firm digitally, they will go elsewhere. One improvement seen recently is cellphone optimization, which gives consumers the same feel as using a computer, but through their phones. Artificial intelligence will also continue to impact customer engagement through ease of ordering and information search. Therefore, firms must strive to seek what technologies consumers want and how to provide them.[10]

How Does Tight Feedback Help to Launch an Innovation?

This text has discussed on numerous occasions the need for speed to market. Getting to market quickly allows firms to potentially gain a competitive advantage, depending on the type of innovation, or to seek additional sales. Another advantage is not allowing a competitor to steal an idea and introduce it first in the market. One of the key factors to rapid launch is to seek customer feedback about the innovation and then to use this information to get the product out into the market.

Seeking feedback from consumers also opens the door to receiving negative feedback or feedback that is not representative of society in general and is specific to the individual giving it. If negative feedback is received, it should be viewed not as bad, but as a means to improve the innovation to increase the chances for success when it is launched. Companies must ask for constructive feedback to use the suggestions given to decide when the time is right to launch the innovation being developed.

Firms should seek feedback early on to guide the development process of the product they are enhancing or creating. We have discussed the need to involve all functional areas early to help launch a product quickly versus each group working separately. Passing the project from functional area to functional area creates a rather slow development process, which equates to slow product launch. All functional areas need to work simultaneously on the innovation to decrease development time, thus getting to market with speed.

---

10   "2019 Consumer Products Industry Outlook," Deloitte, https://www2.deloitte.com/us/en/pages/consumer-business/articles/consumer-products-industry-outlook.html.

What are Other Areas That Need to be Considered to Rapidly Launch an Innovation?

We have discussed many areas that need to be addressed to rapidly launch products. These include creating aura to gain attention, following trends to predict consumer demand, and obtaining customer feedback. These areas of interest are typically external to the organization, as they are meant to monitor and influence customers. So, what are ways we can rapidly launch products internally? The following sections focus on ways firms can address their internal capabilities to rapidly launch products. As discussed, innovation can be addressed in two ways. It can be a process that is step by step, meaning one functional group works on one aspect of the product and then hands it off to another functional group. Also, the innovation can be developed where all functional areas work on it simultaneously. For the sake of rapid launch, simultaneous development works best because all functional groups are working to perfect the product, thus reducing the learning curve needed to devise the final product.

Manufacturing

Rapid launch depends on being able to supply markets with products both initially and then after the product is introduced. When firms consider launching an innovation, they must assess their manufacturing capacity to determine if they can meet market demand for all products they offer. If companies cannot meet demand, they must increase their capacity by adding more manufacturing equipment or seeking an outsourcing agreement. It is essential that firms work simultaneously to determine these factors so that they can better prepare for dealing with the capacity they need when developing an innovation.

Manufacturing must also determine a more efficient process to manufacture new products. Questions to asked include what raw materials are needed, if a component approach works better (one where companies purchase components from other companies to be used in final assembly), or if they construct or develop the entire product in house. Manufacturing can be classified in three different ways.

1. Fixed
2. Programmable
3. Flexible

Fixed manufacturing is a process where equipment is fixed to produce one part of the product, which then goes into a final good. It involves a very capital-intensive use of tooling, and changeover of tooling is expensive and labor intensive. The changeover required creates a loss of revenue because the manufacturing process is halted. Fixed manufacturing is typically not conducive to rapid innovation as it takes time to set up the manufacturing process. It can have an advantage, once it is set up, to produce mass quantities of products. While mass production is beneficial to achieve economies of scale and keep up with consumer demand, rapid innovation typically requires adjusting, evolving, and leading to "tweak" new products based on consumer feedback, so it is not a preferred method of initial launch. This type of manufacturing is characteristic of the automotive industry.

Programmable manufacturing is a type of manufacturing that produces batches of products versus mass production. This form of manufacturing gives firms the ability to produce a variety of products in a shorter period, which helps to supply parts to produce a final product. The downside is the need to halt production to reprogram the machinery between batch production, adding to loss of revenue and time. This is characteristic of robotic manufacturing.

Flexible manufacturing is like a program, where a variety of products can be manufactured using one machine, adding to the benefits of providing the ability to produce parts needed to assemble a final product. The true benefit of flexible manufacturing lies in the fact that programming the machine can be done offline and then transferred to the equipment, thus eliminating changeover and reprogramming one piece of equipment. For the sake of rapid launch, flexible manufacturing is the most ideal method of manufacturing due to the variety of parts it can make and the speed at which it affords companies.[11]

Manufacturing capabilities play an integral part in the ability to rapidly launch products. As shown, flexible manufacturing gives companies the ability to manufacture products quickly and to adapt to changes in product design based on consumer feedback. It also allows for minimal changeover, thus giving companies the ability to meet initial and ongoing inventory needs. Firms must identify the manufacturing capabilities that best match their ability to produce products quickly and enable them to change designs minimizing the lost amount of money and time.

Supply Chain, Warehousing, and Inventory Control

As with manufacturing, the ability to have products available to initially fill and then resupply retailers is the goal of effective supply chain, warehousing, and inventory control. *Supply chain* is the movement upstream and downstream of components needed to produce a product and offer it to the final customer. *Warehousing* is the short- or long-term storage of a tangible good once manufactured. Services are perishable, as discussed previously, so they cannot be stored. *Inventory control* is the ability to have a sufficient amount of inventory available to prevent out-of-stocks for retailers. Supply chain, warehousing, and inventory control work together to provide the products necessary to launch and resupply tangible goods for consumers to purchase. Without coordination of these three areas, inefficiencies will result, affecting product launch and the ability to resupply.

Supply chain management also has a great responsibility to ensure raw materials are at the manufacturing site when needed, product is moved as necessary between production facilities, the finished product is moved to the firm's warehouse or a retailer, and then finally the product is made available. This view is a very simplistic one of supply chain. Supply chain encompasses logistics, which is the movement of products and allocation that sends the products to the

---

11   "Manufacturing Applications of Automation and Robots," Britannica, https://www.britannica.com/technology/automation/Manufacturing-applications-of-automation-and-robotics.

right market and optimal retail locations frequented by customers. What is important to note is that supply chains give rapid launch an advantage through providing materials needed to manufacture the product quickly and then supplying retailers as needed.

Warehousing products also plays a key in the rapid launch of innovations by initially stocking products to be sent to retailers and finally serving as an access point to restock products sold. Companies must determine the optimal amount of inventory to be warehoused initially due to the absence of purchase history. Manufacturers run the risk of incurring high holding costs if they stock too much versus not stocking enough and then create an out-of-stock scenario for retailers and customers. As previously discussed, but for sake of a review, *holding costs* are the cost manufacturers incur when they produce and then store products without selling them. Many manufacturers try to produce the products and then ship them directly to the retailer's warehouses as this eliminates the dilemma of incurring holding costs.

Inventory control is effectively managing inventory whereby retailers have stocked shelves, necessary backstock, and orders placed to prevent stockouts. The initial stocking of products supporting rapid launch must be closely monitored to ensure there is product available for customers seeking the innovation. A dilemma occurs when firms are unable to estimate the level of sales that will occur for the new products. Until a pattern of purchase behavior can be established, inventory control must be closely monitored. Just as holding costs affect wholesalers, holding costs also affect retailers. Money spent on inventory not moving takes away funds that can be used for ordering other products. Therefore, proper inventory control can increase profits and build a customer base by having available the products that customers seek.

Based on the information provided, it is obvious that supply chain, warehousing, and inventory control rely on each other to be effective and help launch products quickly. One cannot function without the other; therefore firms must find a balance to be effective and efficient in the market when it comes to launching a product quickly. Proper delivery of raw materials and final products, storing enough inventory to meet demand, and displaying and reordering at the key times helps innovators have an advantage.

Sales Channels

How the innovation will be sold also affects rapid launch and creates excitement among consumers. *Sales channels* are the way a product is offered to consumers, either directly or indirectly. Firms must determine what is the most efficient and effective way to get the product to the customer while maximizing their profits. There are many considerations that affect the decision to offer products directly to consumers (direct) or use traditional means (indirect). Such considerations include size of the organization, strength of the distribution network, presence of a sales force, having an established distributor network, and so on. Many firms use companies that specialize in logistics to get the products to their customer, including United Parcel Service (UPS), the United States Postal Service (USPS), Federal Express, and so on. While these logistics companies are very efficient and provide a means of delivery, they are more expensive than a company delivering their goods to a company's warehouse or to the retailer in bulk. Therefore, firms must determine how to get the product to their customers when they order in a way that is cost effective and provides high levels of service.

Direct or Indirect Sales Channels

Companies can choose between two different sales channels to promote their innovative products and excite consumers. The two ways to promote products include direct and indirect sales channels. *Direct channels* are those that companies sell directly to consumers and then provide a means to deliver the product. *Indirect channels* utilize wholesalers and retailers to accept goods and then provide them to consumers. This channel is efficient but will include a mark-up on the part of wholesalers to recover the costs they incur and to take possession of the product and then provide distribution.

Benefits of direct channels include knowing how your customer feels about your product and the effectiveness of your service to satisfy their needs. Some disadvantages include loss of distribution efficiencies and potential higher costs of shipping. Since a company is shipping its product to individuals, it may be more cost effective to ship directly or hire a secure third-party vendor to take on this part of the business. Benefits of indirect channels include utilizing efficient supply chain network and greater access to wholesalers and retailers. Disadvantage include the loss of customer contact and higher retail prices due to mark-ups by channel partners.

Marketing Functions

Companies take part in marketing strategies that revolve around the four P's (price, place, promotion, and product) to effectively offer their products in the market and to specifically target their customers. *A marketing strategy* is a way firms turn their target customers into customers who buy their products. Marketing strategy targets specific customers (target customers) and entices them to buy their products by altering the four P's in a manner that creates superior value to them. A *marketing plan* is a documented strategy dictating how the strategy will occur. The marketing plan is established to create a unified message to attract the target market to buy the product by creating the most attractive arrangement of the four P's. The marketing plan should be a long-term plan that utilizes ways to establish customer lifetime value.

Outlets That Cater to the Target Market (Place)

Having the innovative products available for customers is not the end of the story. Marketing must determine which outlets their target market will seek to find the new products, be it online, in a store, through kiosks, and so on. This task is accomplished by surveying the target market in the beginning of the process to determine what their needs are, how the innovation can satisfy their needs, and what channels they utilize to purchase products.

Many times, the target market may want to use more than one channel to purchase products. There is a growing trend of consumers to shop online and then go to a brick-and-mortar location to purchase a product. This type of shopping is characteristic of clothing, electronics, and other items that require trying the product on or interacting with it. If the product is one that is routinely purchased, then more online purchasing will occur, such as using Amazon's pantry program. Therefore, having a multi-channel strategy is beneficial to ensuring that consumers find and trial the product before they purchase it, or to encourage repeat buying behavior.

Pricing Considerations

Price is an important determinant in products as it affects the value, quality, and prestige a product represents. In consumer behavior, value is the subjective decisions consumers make when they feel price and the benefits derived from a product reflect the quality (e.g., a Mercedes-Benz is expensive and is perceived to be high quality). Another aspect of price is reference pricing. *Reference pricing* is the price consumers expect to pay for a product. For example, ask yourself what each of these items cost: a 2-liter of Coke, a candy bar, and a hamburger from a fast-food restaurant. Consumers, therefore, categorize pricing associated with product categories when making choices and have an idea of what the product costs should be based on past purchase experiences.

Promotional Tools

Company's use various promotional tools to attract existing and potential customers. *Promotional tools* are ways companies connect with their target market or potential customers through print, radio, television, and the internet. It is essential that company's use integrated marketing tools to send a unified message to their audience. *Integrated marketing communication (IMC)* is an integrated marketing method to broadcast a unified message to their target market using various, but common, types of media. IMC helps to create hype by sending a common message to all consumers who relate to the new product.

Product

Another element of the four P's is product. Examples of products include cellphone apps (i.e., service) and tangible products (i.e., goods). There has been a recent increase in services due to technology improvements. Therefore, consumers must be interviewed to determine which types of products they seek to satisfy their needs. Needs satisfaction is based on several criteria including prestige, demonstration of wealth, and the satisfaction of hedonic needs on the part of consumers. *Products* help to satisfy these needs and to develop both loyalty and repeat purchases. Products and the companies that sell them also can utilize aura to create excitement around them and encourage purchasing. Therefore, products give firms the ability to increase their market share, profits, and prestige in the market.

Post-Purchase Evaluation

One of the last steps in the consumer decision-making process is the evaluation of the good or service they select after the sale. *Post-purchase evaluation* is the evaluation of a product's functionality or performance, creating satisfaction or dissatisfaction. Satisfaction with a product purchase usually creates positive word of mouth on the part of consumers. Positive word of mouth creates excitement or enhances the aura with the product and encourages repeat purchases. This is the goal of innovators, to create a positive experience and enjoy the benefit of repeat purchases on the part of their customer base. The benefits to the company include a longer time the good or service is in the product life cycle, greater customer lifetime value, reduced need to advertise, faster recovery of R&D dollars, and greater profits and market share.

Dissatisfaction with a product leads to cognitive dissonance or "buyer's remorse." *Buyer's remorse* is a feeling of regret as a result of making a purchase decision. It can be triggered by several factors including poor performance, low quality, finding the product cheaper, or not knowing of a competitor's product then later discovering it. Buyer's remorse does the opposite for creating consumer excitement, and adds dissatisfaction to the post-purchase experience. It encourages negative word of mouth, does not stimulate repeat purchases, and may cost a firm profits and market share; therefore, consumer testing, helplines, and acting quickly when a problem occurs can help to overcome this phenomenon.

Firms must capitalize on the benefits of a positive post-purchase evaluation through consumer testimonials, increased availability, social media presence, and proper production planning to alleviate out-of-stocks. If a product is found to cause a negative post-purchase evaluation, firms must address this immediately. The text covers the concept of "adjust, evolve, and lead," which means to correct any problems that result with the launching of a product. Others strategies that innovators must do are to handle customer complaints fast, make them happy, seek why the product has caused dissatisfaction, and address social media complaints. Dissatisfaction gives firms the ability to create a positive experience if the complaint is handled fast and to the customer's satisfaction. As discussed previously, it costs firms five times as much to attract a new customer than to retain an existing one. Therefore, the goal is to make your customers happy and take advantage of their excitement to promote your business.

Innovators seeking to create excitement with their product must use aura to gain attention, stimulate satisfaction with the purchase, and make it convenient to purchase their products. The benefits associated with creating excitement help firms to continue to innovate due to the ability to generate profits to fund future innovation. Firms must also prepare for a fast launch through efficient manufacturing and to have the proper sales and distribution channels available to them. Finally, creating a positive customer experience is vital to retaining and attracting new customers. Therefore, consumer perceptions and involvement in a product, coupled with aura, are used by the best companies to dominate market segments.

Review Questions

1. How can perception increase a consumer's ability to receive a marketing message?
2. Give an example where a consumer would demonstrate high and low involvement. What types of purchases are categorized by each?

3. How does aura positively impact the innovation process?
4. What are customer preferences? Why are they important to determine?
5. What are four trends identified in the Deloitte Insights United States Economic Forecast for 2018? Give examples of each.
6. Why is customer feedback so important to launch products quickly?
7. What are areas a firm needs to evaluate to accomplish rapid launch besides customer feedback?
8. Give examples of the four P's in marketing. How do they contribute toward developing marketing strategy?
9. Why is post-purchase product evaluation so important to companies?
10. Why is it important for innovators to address negative post-purchase evaluation?

Discussion Questions

1. Why is perception so important in innovation?
2. How can consumer involvement help or hurt the purchase of a new innovation?
3. Share with your professor the relationship between aura and pull demand. Do you feel pull demand is a good marketing strategy for innovators?
4. What are some examples of changing preferences you have noticed in the US?
5. What are ways companies can monitor customer feedback? Which do you feel is most effective and why?
6. What are other factors that can be used to rapidly launch products not list in the chapter? Why did you select those?
7. If I were to successfully develop the first autonomous vehicle in the US, discuss how you would use the four P's to create marketing strategy to sell it?
8. Share a time you had a positive and negative post-purchase evaluation of a product. Did you share this with a friend or let the company know?
9. Do you feel post-purchase decisions are an important consideration for innovators? Why?

Extension Activity

1. Form groups and select a product that you feel has an aura built around it. Discuss and share with other groups the traits that create the aura and what else the company could do to build a community of engagement.
2. When thinking of levels of involvement in purchasing a product, think about a high- and low-level involvement situation you participated in. Share with a classmate what you experienced.

BIBLIOGRAPHY

Marshall, Ron. "How many Ads Do You See A Day?" September 10, 2015. https://www.redcrowmarketing.com/2015/09/10/many-ads-see-one-day/

"Aura." *Merriam-Webster.* https://www.merriam-webster.com/dictionary/aura

Nussbaum, Bruss. "Why Apple Is Losing Its Aura," Fast Company, January 28, 2013, https://www.ama.org/partners/content/Pages/why-customers-attention-scarcest-resources-2017.aspx.

Björkman, Ivar, "Aura: Aesthetic Business Creativity," *Consumption, Markets and Culture 5,* 1 (2002): 69–78.

Ferguson, Keith E., Sztykiel, J, and Ingram, M. *Contemporary Product Development: A Focus On Innovation.* California, Cognella Academic Publishing, 2019.

Saharudin, Hydar, "How Harley-Davidson Rode to Iconic Brand Status through Word-of-Mouth," Referral Candy, June 29, 2016, https://www.referralcandy.com/blog/harley-davidson-marketing-strategy/.

"By the Grid: Population Shift to the West and South," US Census, October 18, 2012, https://www.census.gov/dataviz/visualizations/024/.

Kotkin, Joel. "The Changing Demographics of America," *Smithsonian,* August 2012, https://www.smithsonianmag.com/travel/the-changing-demographics-of-america-538284/.

"2019 Consumer Products Industry Outlook," Deloitte, https://www2.deloitte.com/us/en/pages/consumer-business/articles/consumer-products-industry-outlook.html.

"Manufacturing Applications of Automation and Robots," Britannica, https://www.britannica.com/technology/automation/Manufacturing-applications-of-automation-and-robotics.

Launch

CHAPTER SEVENTEEN

Time to Go Live!

INTRODUCTION

This chapter focuses on how and why a disciplined approach should be used to prepare a new product for the market, and while many firms agree with this premise, many do not follow a formalized practice. There are four areas of particular interest to help ensure a product's successful introduction to the market: planning, pre-launch, launch, and operations. We will also review specialized areas inside and outside of the organization and how control varies widely from one company to another. This chapter also details how firms can accelerate innovation to gain an advantage and quickly recoup costs. Finally, we discuss traits that comprise a great team and why communication is key for reflection and review, adjusting, evolving, leading, and obtaining marketplace feedback.

Learning Objectives

In this chapter students will learn about the following:
- Disciplined preparation and its importance
- Why disciplined preparation is essential for planning, pre-launch and launch activities, and operations
- Specialized areas located within and outside the firm and their importance
- Acceleration and why it is important
- How preparation and teams win, not talent
- The importance of review and reflect and adapt and evolve to lead using marketplace feedback

Learning Outcomes

By the end of this chapter students will be able to do the following:

- Devise a disciplined approach for innovation
- Explain what the within and outside the firm means and the differences between them
- Prepare guidelines for acceleration of the innovation process
- Understand traits that make up great teams and formulate a plan to assemble a great team
- Know how to use market feedback to guide a review and reflection discussion

Key Terms

Disciplined preparation: A controlled form of behavior that helps prepare a firm to innovate and do what is necessary to be successful

Stealthstorm: The hidden politics innovators use to ensure top management supports the innovation being developed so it will be accepted

Lost in translation: Some of the original ideas are lost when innovators are developing a product

Next practice organizations: Those that improve their best practices to develop new business models that improve the firm

Kaizen: Business philosophy or system based on making continuous positive changes on a regular basis to improve productivity

Acceleration: The act increasing the speed or velocity of a product to gain a competitive advantage, prevent competitors from copying, and recoup research and development dollars faster

Focus: The speed needed for getting to market quicker

Agility: Accelerator because it allows a firm to change the direction it is traveling if it runs into issues and allows for open communication between team members to solve problems quickly and keep going

Motivation: The energy needed to accelerate in innovation

Efficiency: Accelerates innovation by having processes in place that have been proven

DISCIPLINED PREPARATION

Disciplined preparation is a controlled form of working to ensure everyone involved in the product is ready to assist in a successful launch and has ongoing support afterward. A disciplined approach helps firms perform better and achieve their goals by anticipating risks and having a good understanding of who the target market is, what the competitive response will be, and how to find the best channels to sell their products.[1]

An Accenture study surveying five hundred executives found that 93 percent believe innovation is crucial for their firm's long-term success; however, only 34 percent had an effective

---

1   "Manage Innovation Risk with a Disciplined Approach," Innovategov, http://innovategov.org/2013/11/27/manage-innovation-risk-with-a-disciplined-approach/.

innovation framework in place.[2] Therefore, the need for a disciplined approach to innovate should be part of every firm's innovation strategy for success.

As a disciplined approach is critical to success, consider the following six steps to prepare to launch your innovation:[3]

1. **Focus.** Innovation usually begins with a brainstorming session that includes many unfocused ideas. This is also called a charrette, which is a rapid ideation session where concepts are discussed by multiple groups to determine if an innovation has potential. When the session is over, the innovation funnel brings the ideas to fruition by accomplishing three things:

    - Clarifying the objectives of your innovation. Define what you are trying to accomplish and let that guide the process.
    - Defining your limitations and what is acceptable. Determine the level of risk the firm is willing to take, which will then define the type of innovation it can pursue.
    - Identifying new markets. What markets and innovations will best satisfy the needs of your customers to ensure success?

2. **Connect.** How can firms get people together to share ideas and collaborate more to innovate? We have discussed the need for innovation teams to be diverse to share ideas and offer a varied view to avoid groupthink. How can firms accomplish this connectiveness that needs to happen? Steve Jobs placed the restrooms in the center of the new Pixar building to encourage employees to meet more to increase connecting with coworkers.

3. **Tweak.** Too many times innovators want their "masterpiece" to be polished and complete before they show the executives and others what they have been working on. This is understandable, as who would want to draw criticism, have their efforts halted, or be seen as a failure? Unfortunately, many times the innovation being perfected falls short of what is expected by the firm's standards or by customers. A good practice to avoid this is to share the work or ideas frequently with the team or executives. This will help to tweak the ideas or innovation along the development stages and ensure the innovation satisfies the needs of the customer, can be produced economically, obtains buy-in, and supports the firm's mission and vision.

4. **Select.** If the firm is still in the ideation phase, tweaking ideas, as discussed in the last section, is a good practice. Gathering various comments from a diverse group within

---

2   Tamara Zimmerman, Stephen Gardiner, and Jodie Wallis. "A Guide to Self-Disruption: Driving Growth Through Enterprise Innovation Strategies in the Digital Age." Reviewed June 6, 2019. https://www.accenture.com/_acnmedia/Accenture/Conversion-Assets/Microsites/Documents21/Accenture-Self-Disruption-Enterprise-Innovation-Strategies-Digital-Age.pdf.

3   "Successful Innovation—A Disciplined Approach," Dentons, October 22, 2013, https://www.dentons.com/en/insights/articles/2013/october/22/successful-innovation---a-disciplined-approach.

the organization is a good practice for innovation. Once the tweaks are over, the best idea is selected, or the best innovation design is agreed on. This phase is important as speed to market is key, so there is little time to hesitate on the best idea or design to pursue.

5. **Stealthstorm**. A *stealthstorm* is the hidden politics innovators use to ensure top management supports the innovation being developed so it will be accepted. Any innovation is a risk to firms because money is allocated to a product that has no assurance of success. Top managers can be skeptical of innovation (remember the Accenture study mentioned) due to this risk. Innovators need to share the innovation and its progress with executives to get their buy in, which helps accelerate the process because they don't have to fight every step of the way. The result of stealthstorming is a smoother innovation process and speed to market.

6. **Persist**. Firms must not let setbacks or potholes experienced along the way stop or thwart their innovation efforts. Every innovation will experience difficulties that seem to make the innovation becoming a reality impossible. This scenario is a perfect time for firms to encourage tweaking. Get comments and ideas from others on ways to correct the problems being faced by tapping into coworkers who may have experienced similar problems and worked through them. Therefore, when a problem arises, it is important to not quit but to seek advice from others, so the product can be finished and launched.

Inside and Outside the Organization

Innovative organizations must learn to balance areas within the organization they have control over for success. This section builds upon the concepts first covered in Chapter Seven. Cross-functional teams should always be part of the innovation process and their specific understanding of how their department operates and develops an innovation is crucial for success. While the firm has control internally of departments and planning, outside the organization they do not. In Chapter Seven we referred to this as *environmental scanning* and indicated how firms can influence but cannot control these external aspects. This next section will review these concepts and further detail how important they are for innovation development.

Inside the Firm

Within the organization there are several areas that impact the innovation process. These key areas must work in unison to ensure the product innovation will be a success. This text has stressed in several chapters the need for cooperative cross-functional teams working to help produce a product that addresses the needs of the customer, gives the firm a competitive advantage, gains sales and profits, and satisfies the mission and vision of the firm. This can only be accomplished by specialized areas working together to ensure the innovation process is successful. When we speak of specialized areas within the firm we are referring to the following:

1. *Supply chain*: The internal department that oversees the logistics and allocation of the company's products. The **supply chain** is responsible for the delivery of raw materials, movement of these materials for production, transportation of finished goods to wholesalers or warehouses, or semi-finished products to manufacturing. Allocation is the practice of supplying the finished products to retailers or the final consumer. It includes estimating when to ship products to prevent out-of-stocks, what geographical areas will sell the most products, and the coordination with manufacturing to produce the needed quantities to ship.

2. *Manufacturing*: **Manufacturing** is the process of transforming raw or semi-finished goods into a final product. The responsibility manufacturing has is tremendous. If they fail to produce products, this can severely handicap the company. Manufacturing must be efficient to reduce costs (labor, waste, stock-outs, etc.) and to increase the speed of producing products to be sold.

3. *Human Resources (HR)*: The **Human Resources** department is responsible for recruiting and retaining individuals who provide the skill sets needed to innovate. As discussed in previous chapters, HR must have a file for each employee and his or her associated skill sets to provide the talent to innovate. HR also handles such areas as benefits, employee complaints, hiring and termination, and college recruitment to find the best talent.

4. *Quality control (QC) or the cost of poor quality (COPQ)*: QC is an important element for firms, as consistency of products is key to repeat purchases. Firms must maintain internal quality control levels, or if they outsource products, they must test to see if their suppliers are maintaining the level of quality established. **QC** follows strict standards and methods including six sigma and ISO 9000. Consistent quality gives the consumer an idea of time a product will be inexistence and dictates the price people will pay. If you recall, price is a surrogate for quality, so consistent levels help to justify the price being charged.

   Cost of poor quality (COPQ) includes all the costs that reflect poor innovation, design, validation, and manufacturing processes. Examples of COPQs include the following:

   - Overtime
   - Expedited shipments
   - Returns/defects
   - Warranty cost
   - Legal costs related to product performance
   - Delays in shipments

Once a firm starts to focus on COPQ and makes it inherent in the design process, all key objectives will naturally gravitate in the desired direction. It is critical this is understood, as every one of the aforementioned costs will negatively impact the innovation product development process.

5. *Customer service*: The **Customer Service** department caters to the needs of the customers. They provide information to help make decisions, handle complaints, perform exchanges and returns, and perform any other function that helps to maintain a healthy relationship with a firm's customers. Customer service is also found to differentiate firms from each other due the similarities of products. Customer service is key for the service industry where there is direct interaction typically between service provider and customer.

6. *Sales*: **Sales** is the internal area of the firm that drives revenue. Sales is comprised of both internal and external sales people. Internal salespeople make sales while being stationed inside the company's office or from home. They typically take phone calls or make phone calls to sell a firm's products. With the increased use of technology, may internal salespeople now conduct business via the internet or combine phone and the web to do business.

   Firms must ask if sales personnel are properly equipped to sell, promote, and create the demand in the marketplace. The two areas to focus on in this area include:

   - How does the innovation differ from the competition's current offerings?
   - What will the concerns be over the product or service, and what's the right strategy to overcome the concerns? Effective firms do this today in a subliminal way through the website and digital media, so if there is a perceived concern, the firm can address it as part of its social media strategy to overcome or address the issue before it is ever brought up.

   Training people is key to an effective launch and too often the organization expects the sales force and distribution to know all that they do. One problem is that they have not been putting enough development into it. Firms must provide training on what their expectations are for the launch and share the risk and countermeasures analysis with the salesforce to make this process operate smoothly.

7. *Marketing and the Go-To Market Aura Plan (GT-MAP)*: Marketing is responsible for orchestrating the GT-MAP. Marketing should magnify the high-performance aspects of the product to create an aura of authenticity around the innovation to gain interest. Marketing must also help conduct research to determine the sales potential for the innovation and what price they can charge. They must decide who the target market will be and which venues will provide the most sales for the products.

   Remember, the GT-MAP process must begin at the earliest stage of product development, rather than during the final stages when the product is almost done, and successful firms bring the creative agencies and people who will start the GT-MAP in the ideation and innovation process as early as possible. Their job is to first listen and understand the spirit and story behind the innovation and to understand the little things that make the product or service so special. "Lost in translation" is a phrase that many people have heard. *Lost in translation* means that some of the original ideas or meaning are lost when innovators are developing a product. Too often, the marketing/creatives do not get/understand the full story behind the innovation of the new product/service, and then they wonder why there is a lack of excitement. Tell the full story behind the innovation to build the aura and excitement.

8. *Information technology (IT)*: The **IT** department is responsible for both the internal customer and the way the firm interacts with the customer electronically. Internal clients include employees and utilize technology to do their jobs and for supporting the processes that take place in the operation of the firm. The IT department also helps develop innovative ways customers can interact. The interactions include providing information on the products sold, current pricing, ways to order, how to retain customers once they are on the company's website, and how to get them back if they click off. Therefore, in a world where people are well connected electronically, IT is vital to the image and sales a firm experiences.

   In Chapter Ten we discussed why the the biggest fault from an IT perspective during the product launch in a GT-MAP is that people perceive it is all social media. An epiphany for many leaders is if someone could manage his or her own Facebook page, he or she would be great in digital marketing. This is not always the case. Today, data analytics can drive the market to you or you to the right market. Data will either reinforce or challenge your innovation and business plan. Data also helps a firm grow and be great, and it makes a difference, so learn to love and embrace data, not all data, just the right data. The key is to be data-informed, intuitively-wise, and decision driven, all with speed.

9. *Finance and accounting*: The **Finance and Accounting** department helps firms make decisions that have an impact on the firm's ability to invest needed resources while maintaining proper documentation of its actions. When a firm seeks to innovate it must determine how to provide the funds needed to accomplish this goal. There is a certain amount of sunk costs that are involved in innovation; therefore, firms must determine the best way to provide funds and to record their use for both tax and profit reporting. These two departments are essential in providing resources and ensuring they are being used in the most efficient manner.

   Nothing happens without the right dollars allocated to the right areas to ensure the plan has the best opportunity possible to succeed. In most organizations, resource dollars are shorted in the GT-MAP area as people believe sales will fly the moment that the introduction/go-live event takes place. It is essential to have a reserve set aside for a slow start and not to handicap the new product by leaving it underfunded.

10. *Legal*: The **legal** team handles all contracts, lawsuits, licensing and patents, and a variety of other matters to keep a firm free from trouble with the law and consumers. Legal also helps establish internal policies that protect workers and minimizes the threat of lawsuits that can arise from such things as sexual harassment, unfair labor practices, policies written that affect employee job functions, and so on. Depending on the size of the firm, the legal department may be housed internally (i.e., a larger firm) or by retaining the services of a legal practice on an as-needed basis (i.e., a smaller firm).

Outside the Firm

What makes these key disciplines even more precarious is none are under the firm's direct control. With every launch, the GT-MAP is dependent both on variables you can control (inside the firm) and variables you can't control (outside the firm). We have discussed the ones you can control. So now it is time to focus on the ones you do cannot control. A common mistake made by innovators is that people trust and assume that outside firms have a tremendous, disciplined plan, when in fact, most do not. The key to solving this issue is to follow the same disciplined process used internally as well as externally. Firms must be very focused on the risks and devise countermeasures to minimize or eliminate the threats.

Firms also utilize the talents of others that are outside the company. Typically, firms that are smaller in nature will outsource duties it needs to save on cost and to be more efficient. In the last section we spoke of having a legal team as part of the firm's departments or retaining the services of a legal practice. A firm of ten people have no need to hire an attorney to be on staff as the firm doesn't have a large need for legal advice. A firm consisting of ten thousand employees may be a different story, as there are many legal issues that arise. Therefore, going outside the company for help is a common and acceptable business practice. The following areas are examples of departments that are typically outsourced (outside the firm):

1. *Advertising/creative agencies (ad agencies)*: These agencies work to create ways to communicate information to stakeholders of the firm. They are experts at developing ways to reach overstimulated consumers to tell them about the product, support the mission of the organization, or to provide information. There are many ways ad agencies deliver the message, including with humor and fear, for example. However, when ad agencies develop the messaging or advertising campaign, they must understand the goal of the company to ensure that consumers remember the ad in addition to identifying the best channels to reach the target market (e.g., print, radio, television, internet, social media, etc.). This takes many years of experience and the ability to conduct research to find ways to reach the consumer.

   Firms that are in place to promote and convince people to buy a product or service will be more successful than those that have no understanding. Execution is the biggest concern here as too often there is the chance that the message can be lost in translation. This is how the process typically works:

- R&D talks to Engineering.
- Engineering talks to sales.
- Sales talks to Marketing.
- Marketing talks to the advertising or creative agency.

Each of these four steps are an opportunity to miss something, either in part or entirely. The proper method is to have all five groups meet at the beginning stages and then on a consistent basis. The opportunity for miscommunication is huge and presenting the information to the group will stimulate conversation, prevent getting lost in translation, and save time relaying the message.

2. *Suppliers*: Many times, firms cannot produce subcomponents as efficiently and as cheap as firms that have great capabilities. In this case, it would do the firm well to outsource the products it needs to both reduce cost and maximize profits. Outsourcing through various suppliers is a common and proven method used in business. Seeking suppliers outside the firm helps companies find stable supplies of raw materials, obtain parts needed to produce their products, and allows the supplier to take the burden of the holding costs of the materials until it needs them.

3. *Distribution*: Firms are faced with a choice when they offer their products for sale. They can distribute them or retain a firm to do so. When a firm is large enough and has a reliable distribution network, it makes more sense for the firm to handle the distribution of the products internally. However, if it doesn't have established distribution networks in place, it is better to retain a firm outside the company to handle getting the products in the hands of the customers. Most firms rely on outside firms to distribute and warehouse products for them. This creates a more efficient way to sell their products and helps increase cash flow.

   The way in which something is shared or sold over a specific area varies. Here are several focal points firms must consider:

   - Do they understand the innovations as they align with the vision?
   - What makes it special and hard to replicate?
   - Do they understand the GT-MAP and embrace it?
   - Are they motivated, excited, and incentivized properly?
   - Do they have the data and information to overcome objections and concerns?
   - Do they have the right people in the right areas and are they supported properly?
   - Are demonstration pieces placed properly in the marketplace?

   Too often this is how new product/innovation rollouts work after the go-live event. Poorly thought-out strategies are only moderately effective. With a focus on these points, the firm's opportunity for success grows dramatically.

4. *Transportation*: Not every firm can transport its own product. In today's market, products are being sent locally, regionally, nationally, and globally. It is better in most

cases to utilize an outside vendor to transport the products to customers once they are produced. Modern transportation firms offer the advantage of tracking shipments, eliminating the need for expensive trucks and trailers, and saving on the need to hire drivers. In addition, using outside vendors to transport products reduces costs such as insurance, fluctuating fuel costs, and maintenance.

When you look at the number of departments discussed, 14 in total, ten are within the organization, while four are outside the organization. This can vary slightly depending on the industry, but this is the most common structure. Within the ten departments of the organization, each one has variables outside of its control. Table 17.1 identifies these variables to give the reader an idea of the things a firm must deal with.

TABLE 17.1   *Variables Outside of a Firm's Control*

WITHIN THE ORGANIZATION	AREAS OUTSIDE OF THE ORGANIZATION'S CONTROL WITHIN EACH DEPARTMENT
Supply chain	Supplier effectiveness
Manufacturing	Equipment
Human Resources	The right labor force
Quality control	Quality systems and supply base
Customer Service	Component troubleshooting/supply base
Sales	People trained
Marketing	Ad/creative agencies
IT	Hardware/software
Finance	Financial resources
Legal	Agreements

Imagine each operation having a disciplined preparation plan for each department with risks and countermeasures associated with it. That is a ton of work; however, it is essential the plan is in place to ensure success. Remember the GT-MAP is a framework firms can use to help plan and guide the innovation process.

As Angela Duckworth writes in her book *Grit,* the reason naturally talented people frequently fail to reach their potential, while other less gifted individuals go on to do amazing things, is passion. Duckworth's research found that when we are passionate about accomplishing something, we will go to great lengths to realize our goals. It is a term she uses to describe this as passion and persistence, where an individual who has true drive to accomplish a goal will persevere in the face of defeat because he or she is passionate about obtaining his or her goal.[4]

Next, we examine variables outside the organization where one's control of influence is even less:

---

4   Angel Duckworth, *Grit: The Power of Passion and Perseverance.* New York: Scribner, 2016.

TABLE 17.2   *Variables Even Further Outside of a Firm's Control*

OUTSIDE THE ORGANIZATION	VARIABLES OUTSIDE THE ORGANIZATION
Advertising/creative agencies	Execution
Suppliers	Raw materials
Distribution	Execution
Transportation	Labor
Currency exchange	Fluctuations

As you consider these, what other variables are there with each operating discipline? For many global organizations the currency exchange rate is a critical part of their financial/business model, yet they have no control over it. A great example of disciplined preparation is President Abe Lincoln. Following is a list of Abe Lincoln's issues and failures that he had to overcome before becoming one of the greatest presidents in US history:[5]

TABLE 17.3   *What President Abraham Lincoln Overcame*

YEAR	EVENT
1816	Family forced out of their home
1818	Mother died
1831	Failed in business
1832	Ran for state legislature—lost
1832	Lost his job and could not get into law school
1833	Borrowed money to start his own business went bankrupt
1835	Engaged to be married, but sweetheart died
1836	Total nervous breakdown; in bed for six months
1838	Sought to become speaker of state legislature; lost
1840	Sought to become elector; lost
1843	Ran for Congress; lost
1846	Ran for Congress; won!
1848	Ran for reelection; lost
1849	Sought the job of land officer in his home state; rejected
1854	Ran for US Senate; lost
1856	Sought the vice president nomination at the party's convention; got less than one hundred votes
1858	Ran for US Senate; lost
1860	Elected president of the United States

President Abe Lincoln had 44 years of disciplined preparation and never quit. He failed to be defeated despite his setbacks, which helped him get through one of the most turbulent times in US history, the American Civil War. While Lincoln's plan to win the Civil War was

5   "Lincoln Never Quits," http://www.rogerknapp.com/inspire/lincoln.htm.

often flawed by inferior generals, he persevered and eventually found a leader who could accomplish his goal by placing Ulysses S. Grant in charge.

DISCIPLINED PREPARATION AND THE PLAN

The plan/outline will vary for each operating discipline, but there are six keys, or indicators that firms should have to ensure they have the right plan:

1. A reasonable person looks at the plan to determine if it is well thought out.
2. There is a "purple cow," (something that is different, stands out), something that is exciting, hard to replicate, and will cause people and the industry to talk about it.[6]
3. There is a collective consensus that the timing (data/intuition) is right.
4. There is consensus that the human resource strategy is aligned with each operating discipline. The right people are in the right spots.
5. The risks with the right countermeasures have been identified.
6. There is a proper allocation of resources (people, plants, money, etc.)

Disciplined Preparation: Pre-Launch/Launch

This is a big area of failure for most firms. It is a lot of work, and you must be different to be successful and stand out. A lot of firms do not prepare or do not have a proper plan in place to address their pre-launch or launch strategies. To reference the Accenture study, very few executives admitted they don't have the proper planning in place to be successful innovating.

Pre-launch disciplined preparation should involve determining which channels of distribution are best, what media sources the target market uses, how much the product will cost, what type of warranty it will carry, if a pull or push strategy should be attempted, and so on. In addition to the marketing and supply chain questions, other areas must be thought out, such as manufacturing, accounting, and finance, to have a plan in place once the product is produced or designed and then launched.

A disciplined launch approach is the plan the firm has once the product is introduced in the market. This includes monitoring the product to determine if it is functioning properly, there are any changes or tweaks that are needed, what its sales are, if there are any problems meeting demand, how the advertising strategy is working, and so on. All aspects of what happens when the product is launched should be thought out and addressed with contingency plans in place to avoid a delay in the event if something is not right.

---

6   Seth Godin, *Purple Cow: Transform Your Business by Being Remarkable, new edition (New York: Penguin, 2009).*

Disciplined Preparation: Operating Discipline

The first area to note and bring a special focus to is that as a firm goes through the disciplined preparation process, everything picks up speed. The outcome of this is when the go-live event takes place and all operational disciplines are operating at optimum speed and capacity. Too often organizations don't start working until the go-live event, which is wrong. This will be discussed in greater detail in the next section, but it is key to provide the proper context, here. Listed are the major operational disciplines that must be addressed relative to an effective product launch/go-live event. The importance of knowing the impact of each initiative even though it may not be your core competency is critical to the success of the organization and your own personal growth. Too often people are very knowledgeable about their core skill set but know very little about the other operational disciplines. The result is that they look at situations and initiatives without the proper perspective.

A common departmental job rotation for key leaders is human resources, manufacturing, and advanced research and development (R&D). A rotation in human resources helps leaders understand the importance of culture and aligning people with the strategy, developing the right talent, and retaining employees. Nothing happens without the right people aligned in positions that fit their individual skill sets.

Manufacturing is another prime rotational area because if one is in the business of building things, being on the factory floor is very enlightening. For the factory to build high-quality products on time, every operational discipline must run right. If not, the mess typically shows up on the factory floor. Therefore, understanding the manufacturing process helps improve efficiency and can provide the knowledge needed to fixed minor problems that may arise.

Advanced R&D is understanding the importance of innovation and being a next practice organization. *Next practice organizations* are those that improve their best practices to develop new business models that improve the firm versus doing what works best. In addition, advanced R&D ensures that everything is done properly so that when the product is produced, everything runs smoothly. Knowing a little about each discipline will ensure a more effective and innovative GT-MAP process.

Acceleration of Everything

Great organizations do the right things, the right way, all while increasing speed or acceleration. *Acceleration* in innovation is the act increasing the speed or velocity of the product to gain a competitive advantage, prevent competitors from copying, and recouping research and development dollars faster.

A term that is synonymous with acceleration is kaizen. *Kaizen* is a business philosophy or system that is based on making continuous positive changes on a regular basis to improve productivity. Kaizen is a Japanese word that means "change (kai) for the better (Zen)." It focuses on continuous improvement/increased speed over time to create improvements for the company. Key objectives of kaizen include waste reduction, better quality control, just-in-time delivery, work standardization, and efficient use of equipment.[7]

As simply one of the most successful investors of all time, Warren Buffett knows the value of kaizen and the idea of continuous improvements each day. He reads a reported five hundred pages a day on topics that helps support his empire. If you want to be as successful, practice continuous improvement every day. Start out reading five minutes a day on investing and increase this daily. This is practicing kaizen, and hopefully you could be as successful as Warren Buffett.[8]

Also, within the area of acceleration, aura is the second key component. *Aura* a distinctive and pervasive quality or character or air, an atmosphere that helps firms to gain the attention of customers. Aura creates the atmosphere, motivation, and the excitement of everyone involved. Within the global marketplace there are 12 key stakeholder groups:

1. Associates/employees
2. Suppliers
3. Distribution
4. Consumers
5. OEMs (original equipment manufacturers)
6. Transportation
7. Partners
8. Politicians
9. Media
10. Communities in which business operates
11. Shareholders
12. Observers

Apple is one of the best aura examples in the last five years, as people would line up the day before their newest i Phones were available to buy it. While it was the consumer who was lining up, it was the other 11 stakeholder groups that were talking and writing about the innovation, thus creating the aura. In 2017, Apple was the most valuable brand according to Forbes, the eighth year in a row.[9]

Kaizen and aura are intertwined as they are both a key part of innovation and the GT-MAP. Steve Jobs and Tim Cook as CEOs of Apple over the past eight years, during which Apple was

---

7   Will Kenton, "Kaizen," Investopedia, July 26, 2018, https://www.investopedia.com/terms/k/kaizen.asp?partner=asksa.

8   Ankit Shah, "The Japanese Formula for Buffet-Like Success," Common Sense Living Newsletter, August 18, 2015, https://www.commonsenseliving.co.in/common-sense-living-letters/detail.aspx?date=08/18/2015&story=433&title=The-Japanese-Formula-for-Buffett-like-Success.

9   Kurt Badenhausen, "The World's Most Valuable Brands, 2018," *Forbes,* May 23, 2018, https://www.forbes.com/sites/kurtbadenhausen/2018/05/23/the-worlds-most-valuable-brands-2018/#e4e3b71610c1.

the top brand, indicates that team, not talent, is vital. Preparation, not talent, wins. Therefore, disciplined preparation, continuous improvement, aura, and kaizen are ways companies can accelerate in the market to innovate properly and have greater success.

In addition to mentioned ways companies can accelerate, firms can also focus on four key areas to help it accelerate in innovation:[10]

1. Focus
2. Agility
3. Motivation
4. Efficiency

Focus

In the context of innovation, *focus* is the speed needed for getting to market quicker. A focused approach allows firms to stay on track with their innovation and not get off path, thus slowing them down. Some ways to stay focused include not changing the product once it is agreed on and doing marketing research early to discover what the customer wants versus in the middle of the process. Having information on how to satisfy the customer at the beginning sets the stage for how the product will be developed and what the roles of the innovation team members are. Finally, determine a pathway for innovation with measurable objectives that can be used to judge how the innovation is progressing throughout the process.

Agility

If focus is the speed, agility is the accelerator. *Agility* is the accelerator because it allows firms to change the direction they are traveling if they run into issues and allows for open communication between team members to solve problems quickly and keep going. Feedback and open communication are the keys to agility by having the diverse innovation team utilize their skills and experience to talk through the process of building, measuring data, and learning through brainstorming ways to overcome any obstacles.

Motivation

Motivation is the energy needed to accelerate in innovation. Motivation can be propelled by people and the corporate culture that delivers this valuable attribute to accelerate. It starts with top management creating a culture that appreciates its employees, is open to suggestions, and frequently has whiteboard sessions to bring people together to discuss ways to improve. Motivation can also be started by hiring the right people who bring a sense of excitement and energy to the company. All these things put together help to create the energy the excites everyone within a firm and drives innovation.

---

10   Kristin Zietlow, "4 Key Ways to Accelerate Your Speed to Market," Disher, March 6, 2018, https://disher.com/2018/03/06/4-keys-accelerate-your-speed-to-market/.

Efficiency

Efficiency accelerates innovation by having processes in place that have been proven. The processes don't waste time and are simple. Efficient processes are a product of benchmarking best practices and a reflection of previous innovation to discover ways firms succeeded or didn't, and then learn by these for future work.

Acceleration of innovation is essential for many reasons that are stated throughout this text. This past section has offered reasons and techniques to increase the acceleration of innovation to gain an advantage in the market and to build from the firm's experiences to refine the processes and allow for greater acceleration. It is essential that ways to accelerate are always being reviewed and communication among the team is open and honest. This will ensure that the team is operating in the most efficient manner and acceleration is guaranteed.

Teamwork Makes the "Dreamwork!"

Behind every great team of people, and when teams are measured against desirable traits and each member is trained to perform the necessary disciplined activities for a successful launch, achieving this goal is all but guaranteed.

Following are a few character traits of exceptional teams:

1. Leadership
2. Trust
3. Heart
4. Preparation
5. Kaizen/next practices
6. Focus
7. Accountability
8. Continuous learning
9. Perspective
10. Excellence

During the launch stage, utilizing the GT-MAP, within the organization, operating disciplines, and even external organizations, these ten character traits should be seen and experienced. If not, the traits that are missing should be identified. The resulting action should be either to change your employees' mind-sets or attitudes or switching who is on the team. This should be done until all ten traits are "checked off." Different organizations will have different top ten characteristics of a great team, but the reality is very few take the time to do it. The process to determine the right people for the teams is simple; keeping them focused and aligned is simple. All it takes is disciplined preparation. The process for accomplishing this is presented as follows:

1. The right teammates (people)
   - Determine the top five demonstrated skill sets needed.
   - Determine the top five demonstrated characteristics.

2. The right team
   - Determine the appropriate roles/responsibilities.
   - Ensure all operating disciplines are represented, both within the organization and outside the organization. Most often, the "outside" firms are left off the teams.
3. Focused and Aligned
   - The vision and plan must be mutually agreed on per the top five criteria previously discussed.
   - Objectives, responsibilities, date of completion, status defined, and communication must be established.

If these are done on a regular basis, and the status of each one is updated frequently, firms will experience success. This update can be accomplished by using the following coding system: Green means on track, red means not on track and needs to be addressed, "C" stands for completed, and "NLA" stands for no longer applicable. Red's should always be addressed first and ideally should not remain red for long.

Hourly, daily, weekly, and monthly communication should be performed all the way through the process to ensure the red issues are being addressed, and the timing and duration should be adjusted as needed.

As previously stated, time is the most precious resource. If the project is behind, accelerate the frequency of meetings to focus on the red's. Many companies overcomplicate matters by developing the right team and the right execution rather than simply following the aforementioned steps.

Using Marketplace Feedback for R&R: Adjust, Evolve, and Lead Discussions

Everything ultimately revolves around the consumer. Today, more than ever, feedback is key during the launch. A tremendous amount of time and money has gone into launching the product. Regardless of the team's preparation, there will be things that will go wrong, and thus adjustments must be made quickly. It is recommended to meet regularly to discuss the following:

1. What is working
2. What is not working
3. What was missed
4. How is the competition reacting
5. Are their any significant macro/global events

Any one of the five items could be a surprise challenge. Too often the product goes live, then the euphoria disappears, and people move on. However, significant investments have been made, and the firms who have an effective R&R process, make the appropriate adjustments, and evolve will typically become leaders in the marketplace. What products have you purchased lately knowing the manufacturer adjusted since the initial introduction of the product? This post go-live-launch methodology is critical to continuing leadership. This is a common methodology among great companies. When issues are found while monitoring the product's performance post-launch, the issue must be resolved quickly to stop the possibility of damaging the reputation of the new product.

Execution delivers everything, and too many great innovations and ideas never realize their full potential due to poor execution. It is key for each team member to evaluate, appreciate, and understand the interconnected operating principles presented in this chapter. Execution takes hard work, and the more you and your team practice these methods, the greater the chance of your new product's success.

Review Questions

1. What is a disciplined approach?
2. What are the six steps suggested to follow a disciplined approach?
3. What are four specialized areas found within the firm?
4. What are four areas that are usually outsourced when going outside the firm?
5. What are the six keys or indicators the firm is following the right plan?
6. How are pre-launch and launch disciplined approaches different?
7. What are the three areas executives usually study during job rotation?
8. What is acceleration? What is the relationship between kaizen and acceleration?
9. What are five traits of a great team?
10. What are four questions innovators should ask during an R&R discussion?

Discussion Questions

1. Discuss additional ways firms could practice a discipline approach. Why did you select these methods?
2. Share with a classmate the importance of specialized areas within and outside the firm. Do you feel they lead to a more efficient organization? Why?
3. Offer additional ideas for indicators firms can use to determine if they have the right plan. Share with a classmate why you selected these.
4. Discuss with a classmate other items not discussed in the text regrading pre-launch and launch discipline approaches.
5. Share with a classmate some additional areas in which you feel executives should participate in a job rotation. Why do you feel these areas are important?
6. Offer for discussion additional ways firms can accelerate. Share your rationale.
7. Share with a friend some great teams you have been a part of. Did they possess the traits indicated in the chapter?
8. Do you feel R&R sessions can be helpful? Share with a classmate why you feel this way.

Extension Activity

Today, what major initiative or event do you have coming up within the next ten days? It could be a test, interview, presentation, date, or sporting event. List your desired outcomes, including the result and objective. Then, write a simple, one-page ten-step plan. Take no more than 15 minutes, then GO!

BIBLIOGRAPHY

"Manage Innovation Risk with a Disciplined Approach," Innovategov, http://innovategov. org/2013/11/27/manage-innovation-risk-with-a-disciplined-approach/.

Zimmerman, Tamara, Gardiner, Stephen, and Wallis, Jodie. "A Guide to Self-Disruption: Driving Growth Through Enterprise Innovation Strategies in the Digital Age." Reviewed June 6, 2019. https://www.accenture.com/_acnmedia/Accenture/Conversion-Assets/Microsites/Documents21/Accenture-Self-Disruption-Enterprise-Innovation-Strategies-Digital-Age.pdf.

"Successful Innovation—A Disciplined Approach," Dentons, October 22, 2013, https://www.dentons.com/en/insights/articles/2013/october/22/successful-innovation---a-disciplined-approach.

Duckworth, Angela, *Grit: The Power of Passion and Perseverance*. New York: Scribner, 2016.

"Lincoln Never Quits," http://www.rogerknapp.com/inspire/lincoln.htm.

Godin, Seth. *Purple Cow: Transform Your Business by Being Remarkable, new edition (New York: Penguin, 2009)*.

Kenton, Will. "Kaizen," Investopedia, July 26, 2018, https://www.investopedia.com/terms/k/kaizen.asp?partner=asksa.

Shah, Ankit. "The Japanese Formula for Buffet-Like Success," Common Sense Living Newsletter, August 18, 2015, https://www.commonsenseliving.co.in/common-sense-living-letters/detail.aspx?date=08/18/2015&story=433&title=The-Japanese-Formula-for-Buffett-like-Success.

Badenhausen, Kurt. "The World's Most Valuable Brands, 2018," *Forbes*, May 23, 2018, https://www.forbes.com/sites/kurtbadenhausen/2018/05/23/the-worlds-most-valuable-brands-2018/#e4e3b71610cl.

Zietlow, Kristin. "4 Key Ways to Accelerate Your Speed to Market," Disher, March 6, 2018, https://disher.com/2018/03/06/4-keys-accelerate-your-speed-to-market/.

Assessing the Product's Performance and Applying Adjustments to Increase Success

CHAPTER EIGHTEEN

What's Working, What's Not, and What We Missed

INTRODUCTION

As previously discussed, firms should be highly motivated to introduce products as quickly as possible to recoup R&D dollars, prevent competitors from stealing their ideas, and increase sales and profits. This rapid introduction may require firms to make changes to their products after their introduction. Firms must monitor customer feedback and sales to see if the target market is accepting of their innovation. Making changes to products once they are introduced should be done subtly and without recall if possible. We refer to this as "adjust, evolve, and lead," which simply means to make small adjustments once introduced. Firms should adjust their products if they possess harm to the user, are of poor quality, are too expensive to manufacture, or if consumer preferences change. In any event, going to market fast is the key to innovation.

A firm should also regularly analyze its supply chain network to recognize and implement any additional adjustments. Correcting inefficiencies in a firm's supply chain helps to get the product to more people, increases profits, and controls the process to benefit from customer feedback. Firms can perform their demand planning at the end of a cycle versus the beginning, offer same-day delivery, expand globally, evaluate new markets based on competition and price pressure, and offer products directly to consumers. These few tactics can help firms to improve their supply chain efforts and increase sales and profits.

Firms should also continuously seek to discover new users. Many times the intended target market may not be the only one that adopts the product, so firms must be aware of new markets and adapt the product to satisfy the needs of a new group of customers. Also, changes may be required in the GT-MAP. Too many firms think a website will satisfy all their needs, and it will not. Firms must be fluid (ever changing) and find ways to attract new customers and build a community of current ones. This is where aura comes in as it accelerates customer attraction. Also, firms must change the GT-MAP to suit their firm's individual needs, as this proven framework is a solid foundation for success but requires adjustments for various businesses. Last, adjustments may be required weekly and at the end of the quarter for the GT-MAP. Continuous evaluation helps address short-term problems and opportunities that arise and ensures the firm will achieve its goal. Reflection is vital to adjustments as it gives managers time to shut out the world and think about how the GT-MAP is performing.

Learning Objectives

In this chapter students will learn about the following:
- Why quick product introduction is important
- How firms can adjust after product introduction
- Why firms should adjust products before and when introduced
- How to adjust the supply chain of a firm to increase revenue
- How to adjust products to cater to an unintended market
- Why the GT-MAP should be evaluated and changed
- The importance of making changes at the end of the quarter

Learning Outcomes

By the end of this chapter students will be able to do the following:
- Identify when to introduce a product and when to make changes
- Identify changes firms can use to make their supply efforts more effective
- Create a supply chain strategy to increase efficiency and revenue
- Learn to scan the external environment to identify potential new customers
- Develop a strategy to improve the GT-MAP
- Understand why adjusting at the end of the quarter is more beneficial than at the beginning

Key Terms

New product development: The process where an innovation is thought of and then developed to launch in a specified market

Product recall: A process where a company's product is found to fail or cause harm to the end user, thus requiring the customer to return the product for repair or replacement

Public relation: Information provided by a company to the public typically telling of good it is doing with the hope to gain awareness

Alternative materials: Use of a substitute material than the original to reduce cost or weight or to increase recyclability

Cumulative volume discounts: Exist when a firm buys products over a period and receives a rebate for its purchases

Non-cumulative volume discounts: Discount for a one-time purchase

Co-op (cooperative): Group that is formed to share in expenses or reduce costs

Nearshoring: Having a good or service manufactured or developed in another country that is near the host country

Offshoring: When products or services are manufactured or developed in countries that are not near the host country

Efficient design: Design of a product or service that minimizes waste and is easy to manufacture

Cellular manufacturing: Assembly of a product at one location using multiple stations to assemble, reducing time and distance traveled to produce a finished product

Robotics: Computer-controlled robots typically used in assembly lines to perform routine tasks

Packaging: Material that protects, informs, sells, and attracts consumers to a product

Supply chain network: Stakeholders that provide the raw material; produce the products, wholesale, or warehouse goods; and deliver them to retailers for sale or to the final customer

Exchange rates: Comparison of currency value in relation to another from a different country if exchanged

Shipping costs: Costs associated with transporting raw material and finished goods to be sold to the final consumer

Tariffs: Costs or fees associated with imports by governments to raise the price to discourage the purchase of the good

Wholesaler fees: Profits wholesalers make when marking up products to be sold to retailers

Returns: Taking back a good due to warranty issues, malfunction, or recall

Infrastructure: Foundation of a nation regarding communication, roads, utilities, housing, and so on that allows for commercialization

Direct channels: Selling a product directly to the final consumer and not utilizing a broker or wholesaler

INNOVATION, PRODUCT DEVELOPMENT, AND THE WHOLE PROCESS

This chapter reviews the ways we innovate, how and why we developed the products we did, and what are the good and bad results regarding our process. When we identify innovation, we must step back and ask a few simple questions. First, does the innovation support the mission and vision of the company? Second, will the target market want the product we are about to create? Third, will they buy it and what will they pay for it? Fourth, does the product contribute to the firm's product portfolio? Finally, will the product bring increased profits and greater market share? Firms must reflect and answer these questions honestly to be successful.

Companies that do not put forth the effort to be original and authentic with their offerings and do not add value to society often find themselves competing on price, instead of the attributes and solutions that consumers truly appreciate. Innovations must be carefully thought out and research must be conducted to determine the real value the product brings to the target market.

Product development is a seemingly simple process, but the best firms know how to maximize their resources to produce optimal results. The development of products requires a financial and resource commitment that most firms fail to comprehend. For instance, does the innovation require additional machinery, labor, raw materials, or a different distribution channel? All these factors signify a commitment of resources that firms must analyze on a return on investment (ROI) and market share perspective. Ideal innovations can be developed with existing machinery and are part of a platform process. Remember, a platform is like a pizza where the dough, sauce, and cheese make up the platform and customers tailor it to their liking. Adopting product development with existing resources helps to minimize the loss in the event the product fails. Therefore, firms must analyze what they currently have and what they can do with these assets.

The entire innovation process is a work in progress. Companies must continuously evaluate their successes and failures and learn from these. Benchmarking best practices is a sign of superior innovative companies. They analyze what makes them successful and then repeat these practices in future innovations. As discussed in previous chapters, your study habits have probably changed since you started in college based on what works for you to get the best grades. This practice is also used by companies as it helps them be successful and minimize losses.

By adjusting, evolving, and leading, firms can quickly develop and release their products to the market to avoid competitors stealing the innovation and recoup R&D expenses. The premise of adjusting on the fly is to introduce the product and then monitor its use by consumers to make any changes deemed necessary for it to be successful. Consumers can be surveyed and social media can be monitored to gain a perspective on the benefits provided to consumers. The gamble for firms is that the innovation should be tested enough to ensure it will not fail or need to be recalled. Innovations should be tested to determine safety and satisfaction of consumer needs. If those tests go well, then using existing or established distribution channels can be utilized to get the product into the market. Consumer response is then used to adjust the product while continually selling it in the market.

Many times, adjustments to products are made behind the scenes without consumers having knowledge of these changes, while it is the massive recalls that most often draw ire from consumers regarding product deficiencies, creating negative press for firms. The key is to test and distribute the innovation as fast as you can to gain an advantage and provide additional resources for firms. The ability to quickly launch products is also affected by the type of product. For example, pharmaceuticals require many years of testing, while a new flavor of candy does not. Firms must be aware of the type of product and if prolonged testing is required; a patent should be filed to protect the typical R&D funding that is required.

Product Corrections

As discussed, innovators run the risk of losing the competitive advantage their product may bring if they hesitate too long. There is a fine line that determines when a product can be launched and when to wait to make corrections to the product. There are some parameters that innovators should use to determine when to make product corrections:

1. The prototype does not function within the guidelines established by the innovation team in alpha and beta testing.
2. The safety of the user is of concern.
3. The intended level of quality is not met.
4. The product is too expensive to manufacture in its current form.
5. Customer preferences changed.

The Prototype Does Not Function within the Guidelines Established by the Innovation Team in Alpha and Beta Testing

Innovations are conceived early in the new product development process. *New product development* is the process where an innovation is thought of and then developed to launch in a specified market. The reason for the innovation is to fill a consumer's needs and provide profits to the firm. As discussed earlier, most firms early on create a document or charter that defines in quantifiable terms what the new product will do, how much it costs to produce, the anticipated sales (units and volume), and the expected profits. This document or charter should act as the measurable goals in driving the development of the product. If the results of alpha and beta prototype testing fall short, the product needs to be modified or potentially canceled. Once changes are made and the product is tested once again to determine if it will satisfy the goal of the innovation, it can then be considered for launch.

The Safety of the User is of Concern

Products that pose a potential danger to the user must be evaluated on how to make the product safer. A potentially dangerous product should also provide warning labels to let anyone who uses the product know of the potential threats. Many products are bought and sold; therefore, manufacturers must provide warnings to anyone who may use the product now and in the future. Another issue with product safety is that potential lawsuits that may occur from selling a product that causes harm. Lawsuits not only cost firms large sums of money, but they also cast the company in a poor light in the eyes of consumers. Therefore, product safety is a key component driving product change.

Firms can test their products in simulated conditions to ensure the product performs as expect with no threat of harm. If a product is in the market for some time and fails, firms must be prepared to issue a product recall. *Product recall* is a process where a company's product is found to fail or cause harm to the end user, thus requiring the customer to return the product for repair or replacement. The following are suggestions firms can take to prepare for a product recall:

1. *Prepare for the recall*. This includes determining how dangerous the product is in the market. If the product is failing and causing death, there should be warnings issued to the public immediately. If the product has a slight chance of failing, firms have more time to deal with a solution. Firms should establish a designated hotline that is manned with employees who can answer questions and provide information. In addition, a link should be provided online to allow customers to report problems and provide them with information and details about how the recall will work. Moreover, a solution to the product failure must be designed and available for consumers.

2. *Announce the recall*. It would be effective for large firms with more resources to hire a reputable spokesperson to announce the recall. The announcement should tell the public the level of danger and why the recall is being done, reference the hotline and links, and explain how to get the product fixed. In addition, periodic updates are beneficial to show the firm's level of responsibility and care for the affected consumers.

3. *After the recall is complete*. Firms can report ways it corrected the problem through public relations. *Public relations* is information provided by a company to the public typically telling of good they are doing with the hope to gain awareness. Firms would provide information to various agencies in the hope the controlled message will boost the company's image. Firms must also monitor the solution used to be sure it corrected the problem. Finally, in rare cases, firms can sponsor some worthwhile event or cause to boost its image.

HOW DO YOU TAKE THIS FROM THEORY TO PRACTICE?

In September of 1982, Johnson and Johnson's (J&J) brand Tylenol was found to cause the death of seven people in Chicago. Someone had laced the extra-strength pain reliever with cyanide because the bottles were not tamper proof. J&J did not hesitate and ordered the immediate pulling of every bottle of Tylenol from store shelves. This action would have a drastic effect on sales as Tylenol accounted for 17 percent of J&Js sales in 1981. The result was a drop in market share from 37 percent to 7 percent.

Within two months of the lacing of Tylenol, a new tamper-proof bottle and packaging was introduced. Due to the responsible actions of J&J and its CEO James Burke, sales soared. Tylenol regained 30 percent of the painkiller market share and stocks hit a 52-week high. The actions of J&J and Mr. Burke were the start to product recalls. Traditionally, products at that time were not recalled, but due to the deaths of users of Tylenol, J&J made the right decision to issue a massive recall. As a result, J&J was rewarded for the responsiveness by consumers.

The Intended Level of Quality is Not Met

As mentioned in previous chapters, price is a surrogate for quality. When the product is conceived, a certain level of quality is built into the product as reflected in its price. For example, when you buy a Craftsman hand tool, it is warranted for life if you have the receipt and didn't misuse the tool. You will pay a premium for this tool because of the warranty. If you purchase a similar tool at a Dollar General, it will not have a lifetime warranty, and at the same time, you will not be asked to pay a premium for it. This same holds true for products being innovated. Price often reflects quality. If there is a deficiency in this relationship, the product must be changed.

On rare occasion a product may be offered that is perceived to be high quality at a lower price point. Consumers call these products a bargain. This scenario is rarely found as companies that offer lower-priced items tend to not build higher levels of quality into the products or offer fewer attributes to keep price low and compete on value.

The Product is Too Expensive to Manufacture in Its Current Form

When companies operate in cross functional groups, all areas of the company are involved in the innovation process. This tends to allow the firm to predict the costs and capabilities more accurately to manufacture or develop the product. If companies find their manufacturing costs are too high, they have a couple of options including outsourcing and increasing efficiency (just in time manufacturing and six sigma). In addition, other ways to reduce manufacturing costs include using alternative materials, decreasing raw material costs, near or off shoring, efficient design, recycling, use of robotics, and reduced packaging.

Alternative Materials

Alternative materials are substitute materials slightly modified from the original to reduce cost or weight or to increase recyclability. Firms seek ways to reduce costs by seeking out alternative materials. This is evidenced by soda manufacturers switching from all glass to plastic bottles, replacing steel car bodies with plastic to reduce weight and increase fuel efficiency, substituting gasoline with ethanol, and replacing paper grocery bags with plastic. Firms are constantly seeking alternative means to reduce costs and increase profits. By effectively finding a suitable alternative, firms may be able to reduce their costs of manufacturing.

Decreased Raw Material Costs

Decreasing raw material costs is achieved by tough negotiations with suppliers or by joining a co-op, which increases buying power through numbers. A *co-op (cooperative)* is a group that is formed to share in expenses or reduce costs. Firms join a co-op to increase their buying power for a small administrative fee, which is offset by the savings they realize.

Firms can also seek cumulative and non-cumulative volume discounts for purchases. *Cumulative volume discounts* exist when a firm buys product over a specified period and receives a rebate for its purchases. *Non-cumulative volume discounts* include a discount for a one-time purchase. Both encourage companies to purchase large volumes to decrease their costs. The savings realized by firms helps reduce their manufacturing costs and gives them both a competitive advantage and increased profits. Typically, firms are offered a discount on a manufacturer's bill if they pay early. A common discount is 2/10 net 30, meaning a 2 percent discount if the bill is paid by the 10th of the month, or the balance is due in full after 30 days. However a firm wishes to seek a discount, it is a good manufacturing practice to reduce costs.

Near or Offshoring

Another means to reduce manufacturing costs is to have products produced or developed in countries outside of the United States that have lower labor rates. *Nearshoring* is having a good or service manufactured or developed in another country that is near the host country. This practice is widely used by the US auto industry where cars are produced in Mexico due to lower labor rates than what is being paid to union workers. *Offshoring* is when products or services are manufactured or developed in countries that are not near the host country. This practice is widely used by clothing manufacturers where clothes are made in Vietnam, Malaysia, and so on due to lower labor costs and then are shipped to the US for sale. Firms have effectively used these two methods to reduce costs but are subject to political and consumer pressure to return jobs back to the US. Many service centers were established in the other countries (e.g., India) to handle customer complaints and to take orders. The US has seen many of these jobs return to the US to satisfy the wishes of their stakeholders.

Efficient Design and Recycling

Products that are designed well and easy to manufacture reduce waste, which helps reduce costs. In addition, scrap that can be recycled helps offset the cost of material, which minimizes loss. *Efficient design* is the design of a product or service that minimizes waste and is easy to manufacture. Eliminating steps in the manufacturing process helps increase volume and reduce costs. This is shown in cellular manufacturing where a finished product is assembled in one work station. *Cellular manufacturing* is the assembly of a product at one location using multiple stations, thus reducing time and distance traveled to produce a finished product. Unlike an assembly line where products are slowly produced over multiple points of contact, cellular manufacturing produces products in close proximity to the assemblers, so this method reduces floor space, time, and labor needed to assemble a product.

    Recycling of waste is way firms can be socially responsible and recover cost of raw materials. Consumers have been shown to support companies that demonstrate corporate social responsibility, so recycling is an easy way to demonstrate this.

Use of Robotics

Robotics are computer-controlled robots that are typically used in assembly lines to perform routine tasks. While robots make up a small percentage of the workforce, their increased adaptation for the future will have a drastic impact on full-time employees. A report by McKinsey & Company found that by 2030 there will be a potential loss of full-time employment by 400 to 800 million jobs due to robots or technology. This will result in 75 to 300 million people having to seek another job or a new occupation category.[1] We are currently

---

1   James Manyika et al., "Jobs Lost, Jobs Gained: What the Future of Work Will Mean for Jobs, Skills, and Wages," McKinsey & Company, November 2017, https://www.mckinsey.com/featured-insights/

seeing some of the early starts to this phenomenon with self-checkout retail registers, online ordering, increased robots in manufacturing, self-driving cars, and Amazon using Alexa (artificial intelligence) to help consumers. Overall, technology will be adapted more to the landscape of business, thus driving down wages, injury due to fatigue, reduced benefits, pay outs, and so on.

Reduced Packaging

Packaging is the material that protects, informs, sells, and attracts consumers to a product. A common tactic used by companies is to make the packaging look large in comparison to the product to give the impression consumers are getting more. This is used predominantly in the food industry. Recently, consumers have demanded reduced packaging due to the tremendous amount of waste that is generated by companies.

Packaging should also be recyclable. This will allow the packaging to be repurposed and show a sense of CSR, like scrapping unused raw materials discussed in efficient design. Whatever firms choose to do with regards to packaging, these product changes will reduce the material used to cut costs and show they are good stewards to the environment.

Customer Preferences Changed

The final area that may constitute a product change is that *consumer preferences* may have shifted from when the original design was conceived. As we have emphasized in this text, innovation must have the consumer at its heart to sell products. Therefore, firms must continuously monitor industry trends, competitors' products, and customer feedback to get a pulse on what consumers want in the products they buy.

THINK ABOUT THIS!

Henry Ford changed the modern way of manufacturing through his innovative use of the assembly line, which allowed Ford Motor Company to produce the famous Model T faster than any other automobile manufacturer at a fraction of the cost. By 1921, the Model T accounted for half the automobiles on the road with a price tag of $415. However, within a few years, consumer preferences began to change from wanting a pleasure car to a passenger car. Consumers also wanted their cars to be more stylish than what the Model T offered. To compound the issue, Henry Ford saw no reason to keep up with his competitors who began offering features such as an electric start, hydraulic brakes, windshield wipers, and more attractive interiors. As a result, sales of the Model T slipping by the mid-1920s and in 1927 Ford shut down the assembly line producing the Model T and began manufacturing the Model A.[2]

---

future-of-organizations-and-work/what-the-future-of-work-will-mean-for-jobs-skills-and-wages.

2 "Henry Ford and Innovation," The Henry Ford, https://www.thehenryford.org/docs/default-source/default-document-library/default-document-library/henryfordandinnovation.pdf/?sfvrsn=0.

Based on the example of Henry Ford and the success he had from innovating and then failing to recognize changing consumer preferences, it is important that firms stay in contact with customers and scan the external competitive environment to see what consumers want and what the competition is doing to gain their business. Therefore, firms should always strive to be vigilant at identifying new trends and continuously satisfy ever-changing consumer preferences to retain and grow their business.

Supply Chain Corrections

Firms must continuously monitor the efficiency of their supply chain network to achieve profitability and efficiency. *Supply chain networks* are the stakeholders that provide the raw material; produce the products, wholesale, or warehouse goods; and deliver them to retailers for sale or to the final customer. When a product is conceived, the proper means to distribute the product in the market may not by the most beneficial to the firm. Firms may choose to distribute the product through traditional retail channels but fail to place the product in the proper locations frequented by the target market. Another scenario may include failing to address the need for online sales or trying to service markets that are geographically too wide, thus potentially decreasing the level of service. These are just a few examples of deficiencies in the supply chain channels that firms must monitor to increase profits and level of service and to improve efficiency.

While there are several corrections firms can pursue to make their supply chain system more efficient, we will focus on the following:

1. Demand planning at the end of the cycle
2. Same-day delivery
3. Globalization.
4. Increased competition and price pressure
5. More direct channels to improve service and monitor consumer inputs

Demand Planning at the End of the Cycle

Many times, firms initially plan their product demand at the beginning of the product life cycle. While this is needed for the initial production run, a more accurate way to predict future sales is by using the most current data to predict future needs at the end of the distribution cycle. By planning at the end of the end of the distribution cycle firms can more accurately predict real-time demand for their products. It also gives firms the ability to account for changes in the external environment, which can have a drastic impact on the sales and profits of the company, if not accounted for. Real-time data often helps firms be more responsive to changes in the marketplace.

Same-Day Delivery

To increase level of service, firms that cater to local customers are offering same-day delivery, such as RUSH, Shipt, and UberEats. Firms near their customers are taking advantage of this to increase the level of sales and service by offering same-day delivery. Society is becoming more motivated by instant gratification and immediate response. The days of leaving a message and waiting for a response are long gone. Society sends text messages, emails, and instant messages and orders products with free next-day delivery to satisfy their need for immediacy. Therefore, finding ways to satisfy immediate consumer needs will help firms increase their market share.

Globalization

Some of the greatest opportunities and challenges facing supply chain are in globalization. By using a globalization strategy, companies can service a bigger market, source cheaper raw materials, and have the potential to save money. While these broad examples of the benefits of globalization help firms, these subject warrants further investigation.

Globalization provides firms the ability to reach a wider audience and grow new markets. If sales in an existing market are not what a firm predicted, it has the option of expanding to other markets that have a need for its products. As discussed in previous chapters, standardizing a product is important to reduce costs and to achieve economies of scale. In addition, if a firm is already selling products in an existing market, it makes sense to utilize the supply chain channels to be more efficient, especially when a shipping container or semi-load of goods are going to certain markets and may have room to send more goods. Therefore, firms must analyze the potential that globalization may bring them and determine if it is a viable option.

Another benefit of globalization is the ability to source cheaper materials, labor, and products. As previously discussed, firms can offset higher shipping costs by reducing their labor expenses. Also, firms can take advantage of cheaper raw materials or products purchased in other countries. This cost savings can be realized by a better exchange rate on currency, or by finding these items at a reduced price.

Challenges facing firms utilizing a global strategy include cost, poor infrastructure, and governments. The cost of doing business globally can be offset by the savings incurred, as described. However, the total costs associated with a global strategy must be analyzed. Firms must determine loss on exchange rates, shipping costs, tariffs, wholesaler fees, and returns. *Exchange rates* are the comparison of currency value in relation to another from a different country if exchanged. Firms in countries with a favorable exchange rate over another firm located in a less-favorable exchange can purchase more goods with less money. This helps reduce costs and increase profits. Exchange rates must also be analyzed when sending currency back into the host country to find a rate that will minimize loss. **Shipping costs** are the costs associated with transporting raw material and finished goods to be sold to the final consumer. Shipping costs can be very expensive, so firms seek ways to reduce these costs including negotiating with suppliers to pay all or some of the expense, seeking a discount for bulk or quantity, and locating warehouses close to major accounts. *Tariffs* are costs or fees associated with imports by governments to raise the price to discourage the purchase of the good. Governments try to protect certain industries by placing a tariff on goods that come into their country that can pose a threat to taking sales away from them. Historically, the US imposed few tariffs on other countries as it believes in a capitalistic society; however, President Trump has imposed a record number of tariffs on China to curve the trade deficit. Bangladesh, for example, imposes a lot of tariffs in the Asian-Pacific Rim countries with Bangladesh imposing the highest to protect their apparel industry. Countries that impose the highest tariffs on imports include the Bahamas, Gabon, and Chad.[3] *Wholesaler fees* are profits wholesalers make when marking up products to be sold to retailers. One way firms counter wholesaler fees is to sell directly to the final consumer. This strategy allows for higher profits and controls the supply chain. In most cases, it is not feasible or profitable enough to not use wholesalers. Wholesalers have a network of retailers that offer a firm's products to the final consumer. It is not worth the time and expense for manufacturers to establish this network as they seek to maximize sales and can do so by using wholesalers. Therefore, utilizing wholesalers is a better alternative to direct sales. *Returns* are taking back a good due to warranty issues, malfunction, or recall. There is a cost to having a return policy and many firms simply reduce their costs by giving a retailer credit for a good and then having their sales team audit and recycle the return. Depending on the item and its cost, it is not worth firms to take back goods that are returned.

Poor infrastructure can also impact the efficiency of supply chain efforts globally. *Infrastructure* is the foundation of a nation regarding communication, roads, utilities, housing, and so on that allows for commercialization (a review from Chapter 7). If the roads or ports are not acceptable, firms will have a difficult time trying to sell their products. Good infrastructure benefits firms in many ways. First, shippers can take advantage of good roads to get products to customers quicker and with minimal damage to their vehicles (i.e., normal wear and tear). Shippers can also choose routes that are shorter and have minimal stoppages when their choices are greater. Second, strong infrastructure allows firms to reduce their fleet, warehousing expenses, and inventory costs. Accessible warehouses located close to the largest customers help improve service, reduce stockouts, and use less fuel. It also allows for fewer miles driven so it is better for the environment. Finally, it helps increase profits. Reducing expenses, stockouts, and having shorter routes help reduce the amount of time spent to service customers who are remote. Therefore, infrastructure plays a critical role for firms when servicing customers.

Governments have a huge impact on globalization as a strategy due to the level of stability and turmoil present, as we previously discussed with entry-mode strategies, which are the ways firms can enter a country to minimize their level of risk. These strategies must be evaluated when expanding globally to increase revenue while maintaining an acceptable level of risk. Governments can also make doing business in their country difficult for foreign companies. China and India for example, will not allow foreign firms to operate solely in

3   Sarah Hansen, "Which Countries Have the Highest Tariffs?" Investopedia, May 8, 2019, https://www.investopedia.com/ask/answers/040115/which-countries-have-highest-tariffs.asp.

their country and require firms to have a host company as a business partner. Other items to consider include the historical stability of the country to which firms are expanding and any laws that are in place to block revenue back to the US or requirements for employing domestic workers. Finally, firms must consider the costs associated with doing business in a new country and the impact it has on profits and sales.[4]

Increased Competition and Price Pressure

Firms need at assess the competitive reaction to increased availability of their products and the level of resources it has available to compete. If expansion into a new market in which a competitor is deeply entrenched is the strategy, a firm must utilize many assets to gain awareness and to compete. The ROI for each expansion should be analyzed to determine if it is worth the investment being contemplated. Sometimes an alternative strategy can be utilized for the expansion including selling products in smaller markets with fewer competitors or directly to the customer. Whatever the strategy employed, firms must seek ways to minimize their expenses and increase their profits through expansion.

In addition to increased competition, price pressure must also be assessed when expanding to a new market. Larger metropolitan areas will have greater pricing pressures due to the higher levels of competition, which typically use price to compete. Therefore, profits will be reduced due to price pressure to compete. Firms must find ways to alleviate pricing pressure and increase profits. One way is to seek ways to lower overall costs like those described in the globalization section. Also, firms can use pricing strategies such as offering rebates, which attract customers seeking a lower price, but with a low redemption rate. The scenario of lowering price can offer three strategies for a firm. First, the firm can discount the price and make up the lowered profits in volume. Second, the firm can seek out markets that have fewer competitors and thus lower price pressure. Third, firms can use a blended approach that offsets lower profits by competition in areas with low and high price pressure and then evaluate the net profits using this approach. Whichever they decide, an analysis must be conducted and the best solution must be undertaken.

More Direct Channels to Improve Service and Monitor Consumer Inputs

We touched on supply chains utilizing direct channels in wholesaler fees and price pressure. *Direct channels* are selling a product directly to the final consumer and not utilizing a broker or wholesaler. Let's take a more in depth look at this way to increase profits and obtain feedback for future innovation. A supply chain servicing direct channels has its advantages and disadvantages. The advantages include reduced costs by not having to compensate a wholesaler, more control over the logistics, and establishing a direct relationship with the customer.

Selling directly to the final consumer helps eliminate fees collected by wholesalers and brokers. This cost savings can improve the overall profitability of the firm and help maintain

---

4   Mike Collins. "The Pros and Cons of Globalization." Forbes. May 6, 2015. https://www.forbes.com/sites/mikecollins/2015/05/06/the-pros-and-cons-of-globalization/#391a26edccce.

the price point found from focus groups or surveys. Wholesalers and brokers must upcharge a product to be profitable. Firms can sell a product at a slightly lower cost than what would be charged in the distribution channel, which increases their profit margins and reduces price pressure in the market.

Logistical control can also be sought by taking the order, ensuring the desired delivery method and terms are met, and then monitoring the product's arrival to the final customer. When firms sell products to wholesalers, they lose this level of assurance. If the wholesaler doesn't initiate a reorder or it has poor shipping practices, the firm will typically pay the price in terms of reputation and service and will lose customers. Therefore, the firm taking logistic control can eliminate these potential problems.

Selling directly to the final customer also helps firms establish relationships with their clients. Firms can make direct offers, encourage more use, address issues that may arise, and answer questions clients have on use and performance. Having direct contact helps ensure a consistent level of service and to address any service failures that may arise.

While there are several advantages that are a result of directly servicing customers, there are also some disadvantages. Disadvantages include an insufficient distribution network, increased shipping costs, and lack of control in the supply chain. Firms must weigh the benefits and challenges of direct channels to determine which is better to use, which gives the firm the maximum profit opportunity.

Insufficient distribution networks can be a serious detriment to firms that have no established networks in place. The advantage wholesalers and brokers bring to supply chains are established networks that can be used to distribute products to the desired target market and do so in the most efficient manner. Firms that select to use a direct approach must figure out the right channels to distribute products and how the channels operate. This can slow the introduction of products in the market and cost firms the ability to recoup R&D dollars and slow profit realization and gains in market share.

When firms distribute their own products to the final customer, they typically need to account for increased shipping costs. Firms lack the means to distribute their own products via company-owned transportation, so utilizing third-party logistics is essential. This can add to the cost of distribution of products to customers and increase the expense of delivery, thus reducing profits.

Finally, utilizing a direct distribution network can create a lack of control. Giving outside firms the ability to distribute products affects the service levels, reputation, and quality of a firm. Firms must seek companies that can provide the level of service they seek and work with these firms to ensure the service is maintained consistently. While third-party logistics and direct shippers provide tools for companies to be successful (i.e., tracking orders and anticipated delivery dates), this level of service must be maintained to increase the reputation and loyalty of a firm's customers.

Intended User Corrections

Innovators predict the intended target market based on focus groups, survey data, and previous market performance in the initial phases of innovation. These techniques for discovering a firm's target market are essential for developing a product that has features and attributes desired by the targeted customer. Sometimes firms can attract a target market not thought of in the initial ideation process. Examples of this include text messaging (which was created for cell companies to communicate with their clients), Kleenex (developed for woman to remove their make-up), Rogaine (the original purpose was to reduce high blood pressure), and Bag Balm (developed for cows utters, but farmers' wives found it softens their husbands' hands).[5] Other areas we see unintended markets adopt products include music, fashion, and food. Firms can increase the sales by making changes to whom they sell their products to as well. It is important that firms scan the external environment to identify potential new clients to sell their products to based on trends, social media, and feedback.

GT-MAP Corrections

While the Go-To Market Aura Plan (GT-MAP) is a proven framework, devised by John Sztykiel from his experience as CEO of Spartan Motors for over 28 years, it is intended to provide guidance to firms during the innovation process, certain areas will need to be adjusted, corrected, or defined based on each individual firm's needs. These areas include the following:

1. **Focusing too much on the website**. Firms fail into the trap of thinking their website does all the marketing they need to be successful. Firms need to be fluid, meaning ever changing, and this should be reflective in their website and marketing efforts. Google changes the Doodles seen on the homepage daily, which has created a community of Doodlers who seek the changes, thus creating more exposure for Google.[6] This has also helped build the aura around the Doodles, a concept we focused on in several chapters as it is a key part of the GT-MAP. Aura is the accelerator that gains people's attention and creates a community as seen with the Google Doodles.

2. **The mission and vision of the firm**. The mission and vision for every firm is unique. The mission of the firm is the purpose for the company's existence and guides its actions and decisions. The vision describes where the company is going and what it seeks to accomplish. It is obvious from these descriptions that the purpose and accomplishments of a firm is unique to that organization. Nonprofits seek to support a cause or society, while for-profit corporations seek to acquire wealth and provide a return for shareholders. Therefore, while the GT-MAP works well for any organization, changes must take place to support the mission and vision.

---

5 "9 Stellar Examples of the Unintended Use of Products," Printwand, January 5, 2012, https://www.printwand.com/blog/9-stellar-examples-of-the-unintended-use-of-products.

6 "Doodles," Google, https://www.google.com/doodles/about.

3. **Environmental scanning to determine where the firm has advantages and disadvantages**. In order to be competitive, firms must routinely scan the external environment to see where opportunities and threats exist. Environmental scanning was described as the external factors that affect the firm including economic, political, social, and technical factors. These external factors will affect firms differently and should be accounted for when devising the GT-MAP framework to guide innovation. For instance, as economic conditions affect how firms do business, if a producer of expensive products is caught in a recession, it may wish to start a new line of products that carry a different brand and offer products at a reduced price point.

   Political decisions also affect innovation. Nonprofits in 2018 were affected by the US government increasing the standard deduction, thus making charitable contributions for the majority of US taxpayers non-existent.[7] Social factors also impact firms. As millennials become the dominate consumer group there will be a shift toward products that are more technologically driven and environmentally friendly, so firms must consider these when innovating.[8]

   Finally, technical factors are unique to firms and the need they have for innovation. Technical factors play a multi-faceted role from manufacturing, how the product functions, how they are offered for sale, and the way firms communicate with customers. These factors are different for every firm, so the GT-MAP will be adjusted to reflect how external factors affect the firm's innovation efforts.

4. **Opportunities for the firm**. Every firm seeks different opportunities, so the way it conducts business will also vary. This will make using a universal framework helpful, but not recommended, as it should be changed to support the opportunities a firm seeks. Examples may be firms wanting to enter a new market, increase market share, improve sales, acquire another firm, and so on. The GT-MAP will give the firm an overall framework that it will customize to support the opportunities sought.

5. **Who are the target markets?** Firms also have various target markets that require customizing the GT-MAP to work. Remember, the innovation must satisfy the needs of the target market while providing value to both the firm and its customers; therefore, defining who the target market is and how it relates to the GT-MAP will help ensure future success. In addition, secondary markets must also be identified, and this means the GT-MAP will require further adjustments (more on this in the next section). Different target markets can be reached in different ways due to the various

---

7   "Charitable Giving to Take a Hit from Tax Law," *CBS News*, December 28, 2017, https://www.cbsnews.com/news/charitable-giving-to-take-a-hit-from-the-tax-law/.

8   "Green Generation: Millennials Say Sustainability Is a Shopping Priority," Nielsen, November 5, 2015, https://www.nielsen.com/us/en/insights/news/2015/green-generation-millennials-say-sustainability-is-a-shopping-priority.html.

media outlets, activities they participate in, and behaviors they exhibit. Therefore, adjusting the GT-MAP to address various target markets is crucial.

6. **Selecting the market to provide the innovation.** Just as we recommend adjusting the GT-MAP for target markets, when a firm identifies a new market in which the firm wishes to compete, the GT-MAP will require an additional adjustment to reflect the newly identified market, as it will be unique for the new product being developed and sold. Just as Ferrari does not build luxury high-performance automobiles and sell them to the same market looking to buy a Chevrolet, if it were to adjust its cars for an entirely different market, it would need to adjust its GT-MAP to accommodate the unique market that it wants to pursue. In any market, the distribution channels and ways products are sold may vary, and seeking ways to trial and sell products may also be different. For example, selling a new app will likely require a different approach than selling a new kind of health food; therefore, adjusting the framework to best address the markets sought is essential and unique for organizations.

Adjust the GT-MAP Weekly and at the End of Each Quarter

Now that we have discussed the need to take the GT-MAP and customize it to the firm's goals and objectives, organizations must use it as a barometer to gauge their success. The work the firm puts in must not be taken and then put in a drawer only to be looked at again at year end. The GT-MAP should be reviewed weekly to stay on track, and then quarterly to seek the bigger picture, answering the question "How are we doing?"

Weekly reviews help the firm act on competitive threats and operational problems that come up from unsuspecting events. For example, if a firm is suddenly no longer able to provide the raw materials that they rely on to produce their products, they must act quickly to find a new source. Waiting for a quarterly review will not help them in this situation. Weekly or even hourly reviews will help to make small changes to the GT-MAP if problems or opportunities arise.

Quarterly reviews help teams see the big picture and judge how they are doing to reach the company's broader goals. Adjustments to the GT-MAP on a quarterly basis helps achieve the yearly goal established and gives the weekly changes time to play out and then to evaluate their success. It also helps to give decision makers time for reflection and analysis of the GT-MAP to determine if they are missing something or if they are doing what is necessary to be successful. Reflection is the theme of chapter 21 and is an important part of achieving long-term goals. Not every good thought or plan is conceived in one sitting. Reflection helps to drown out the noise of the world and gives us time to ensure we are taking the best course of action.

Review Questions

1. What are five things innovative companies must reflect on?
2. What does "adjust, evolve, and lead" mean?
3. What parameters can firms use to make product corrections?
4. What steps should firms use if they must recall a product? What else would you suggest?
5. Identify ways firms can reduce their manufacturing costs.
6. What corrections can firms make to their supply chain? What other suggestions would you include?
7. Why is it important to find unintended users?
8. What are adjustments, corrections, or refinements individual firms can make when it goes to the GT-MAP? Give three examples not included in the text.
9. Name the two types of adjustments that occur in the GT-MAP. Do you feel this is too much or not enough? Why?

Discussion Questions

1. Think of a time in your life when you had to adjust the way you were doing something. Could your changes be related to a company? How?
2. Share other ways you would make product corrections not listed in the text. Why did you list these?
3. Do you feel adjusting, evolving, and leading is important or would you rather test a product to the point it has no chance of failure? Share your rationale.
4. What are some other ways firms can make their supply chain more efficient? Provide some examples for your suggestions.
5. Provide three examples of products that were adopted by unintended users. Did the firm change the product to cater to this market? What other changes would you make for your examples?
6. Review the table of contents, which is the GT-MAP. Of the contents listed, what are other parts of this framework that could be corrected?
7. Share with a classmate or your professor a time you reflected on a situation and found a good solution (please do not share anything of a highly personal nature that may be perceived as inappropriate). Did you go to a quiet place or did you work with someone to reflect?
8. Should the GT-MAP do monthly reflections and adjustments? Discuss why you feel this way.

Extension Activity

1. Form a small group and think about ideas you have had for innovative products. Now that you have an extended knowledge of innovation, what ones do you feel would be

successful? Why do you feel this way? (Keep in mind the product should be hard to duplicate and unique, and you should be passionate about it).

2. Think of a product that in its current state could be used by another unintended target market. Why do you think this is?

BIBLIOGRAPHY

Manyika, James, et al., "Jobs Lost, Jobs Gained: What the Future of Work Will Mean for Jobs, Skills, and Wages," McKinsey & Company, November 2017, https://www.mckinsey.com/featured-insights/future-of-organizations-and-work/what-the-future-of-work-will-mean-for-jobs-skills-and-wages.

"Henry Ford and Innovation," The Henry Ford, https://www.thehenryford.org/docs/default-source/default-document-library/default-document-library/henryfordandinnovation.pdf/?sfvrsn=0.

Hansen, Sarah, "Which Countries Have the Highest Tariffs?" Investopedia, May 8, 2019, https://www.investopedia.com/ask/answers/040115/which-countries-have-highest-tariffs.asp.

Collins, Mike. "The Pros and Cons of Globalization." Forbes. May 6, 2015. https://www.forbes.com/sites/mikecollins/2015/05/06/the-pros-and-cons-of-globalization/#391a26edccce .

"9 Stellar Examples of the Unintended Use of Products," Printwand, January 5, 2012, https://www.printwand.com/blog/9-stellar-examples-of-the-unintended-use-of-products.

"Doodles," Google, https://www.google.com/doodles/about.

"Charitable Giving to Take a Hit from Tax Law," CBS News, December 28, 2017, https://www.cbsnews.com/news/charitable-giving-to-take-a-hit-from-the-tax-law/.

"Green Generation: Millennials Say Sustainability Is a Shopping Priority," Nielsen, November 5, 2015, https://www.nielsen.com/us/en/insights/news/2015/green-generation-millennials-say-sustainability-is-a-shopping-priority.html.

CHAPTER NINETEEN

Are We on Track?
What Did We Learn?

INTRODUCTION

Firms often measure innovation success by analyzing data from three primary areas: financial, processes, and adoption. While assessing the overall financial performance of an innovation is meaningful for employees, stakeholders, and investors alike, assessing data from the firm's processes is an *internal* measurement that is most meaningful to the teams and their leaders as the results specifically target their internal performance, as opposed to data regarding the innovation's adoption, which is a measurement of how well the innovation is performing *externally* in the market.

When executed well, these three areas provide a comprehensive snapshot of how well the innovation is performing, and teams can use that information to determine what changes would be advantageous to adopt. Proposed changes should always be measured against a firm's organizational capabilities and leadership metrics to determine its strengths and weaknesses, along with the probability of success.

For a firm to address these data with a consistent and controlled bias toward action, there are three strategic activities that can help firms increase their success: planning, monitoring, and learning. Additionally, there are five best practices that firms can use to improve their operations and help ensure future competitiveness, which are creative thinking, the management of chaos, adoption of new technology, practicing empathy for employees and identifying new ways to retain them, and continuously developing improved systems and processes that support the firm.

This chapter also identifies ways to accelerate a product launch faster than what has been discussed previously. Speed to market is crucial, and firms that strive to shorten the length of time to release new, compelling products have a competitive advantage over everyone else. Finally, we will identify six common failures that firms commit along with proven solutions that firms can implement to overcome these failures.

Learning Objectives

In this chapter students will learn about the following:

- Traditional financial measures used to determine innovation effectiveness
- How firms use processes to gauge their effectiveness with innovation
- Why organizational capabilities and leadership metric inputs and outputs are a useful tool to judge effectiveness
- Three key areas that help support a firm's strategic thinking
- Seven ways firms can accelerate their launch over traditional methods
- Six common failures and solutions firms commit

Learning Outcomes

By the end of this chapter students will be able to do the following:

- Understand way firms use financial measures to determine innovation success
- What processes are and how they are used to tell if the innovation efforts are successful
- How to identify the firm's capabilities and use their leadership to gain an advantage
- Considerations used for developing strategy
- Ways to identify failures and take corrective action to overcome them

Key Terms

Return on investment: The amount of money made or lost relative to the money invested

Sales increase: The growth of sales measured in a quantifiable manner for a specified period

Average margin rate (or gross profit margin): The percentage of profit generated from sales

Patent: Legal form of protection issued by a government to a firm to allow it to design, develop, and sell a product for a specified period

Active projects: Those that are in some stage of the innovation process but are not yet launched

Organizational capabilities: Concentration on a firm's infrastructure and the innovation process to ensure it is developing an approach that is repeatable and sustainable toward future innovation

Leadership metrics: Identification of the behavior senior managers must provide to support a culture of innovation and provide future growth

Strategic planning: Systematic approach to obtain a desired goal by developing plans and objectives in a sequence that allows realization

Monitoring: The ongoing evaluation of an innovation's progress toward achieving a set of specific goals and performance objectives

Learning: A continuous process where firms assess progress, engage key stakeholders, and identify new opportunities to support the firm's mission, vision, goals, and objectives

Accountability: The ability for leaders to be responsible for their actions

Transparency: Operating in a manner that is open for all to see what the goals and objectives are without having a hidden agenda

Fairness: The act of treating everyone n the firm in a manner that is just and void of favoritism

Honesty: The practice of always telling the truth and following through on promises

REVIEW THE EFFICACY OF THE PROCESS AND STRATEGY

Reviewing the effectiveness of the innovation process has traditionally focused on financial, process, and adoption measures. More specifically, the following are the traditional types of measures used by most firms.

Financial

1. **Return on investment (ROI)** is the amount of money made or lost relative to the money invested. Firms use ROI as a primary metric to see how profitable their innovation was. ROI is calculated by the following: (net profit/cost of the investment) x 100. ROI should also be clarified by the period it is being measured to compare its results (i.e., one year versus two years). An average return of 15 percent per year is more desirable than a total return of 15 percent over two years). In addition, firms must also factor in any other expenses that could impact the ROI result (e.g., taxes, expenses, etc.).

2. Sales increase over a specified period (measured in percentage or dollars) can be used assess financial performance. **Sales increase** is the growth of sales measured in a quantifiable manner for a specified period. If firms fail to specify what their desired increase will be it is hard to judge how effective the innovation is. For example, if a firm says it wants to increase sales next year and does so by .01 percent, did it not achieve its goal? Therefore, firms must quantify the sales increase and period. For example, a firm wishes to achieve a 5 percent sales increase or an increase in sales of $1 million from January 1 to December 31. In this example, the amount and period are given to provide a measurable result.

3. **Average margin rate (or gross profit margin)** is the percentage of profit generated from sales. The formula to calculate the gross profit margin is sales/cost of goods sold. The higher the margin the more it benefits the firm by providing surplus cash. Firms can use gross profit margins to determine the level of competition and estimate if the sales price is too low or if they are paying too much for their goods.

HOW DO YOU TAKE THIS FROM THEORY TO PRACTICE?

How does gross profit percentage affect profitability? Are all industry gross margins the same? Why is a higher gross profit margin the key to profitability?

Before entering the world of higher education, one of Professor Ferguson's business ventures was owning multiple retail liquor stores for over twenty years in Michigan. The liquor industry pricing and gross profit percentage is controlled by the state. Retail liquor stores earn 17 percent gross margin on the sale of liquor. Retailers can increase the price to improve their gross profit margins but are subject to competition. In addition, retailers make more money on the sale of beer, wine, snacks, and soda. Professor Ferguson tried to balance the lower margins on liquor by selling higher margin products to improve net profits.

A bar in the Michigan purchases liquor at a lower cost than a retail liquor store, but it can sell it in the drink form for extremely higher margins. For example, a bottle of liquor may cost a retail store $10 and profits only $1.70. A bar buys it for $9.00 and can get 25 drinks at $4.00/drink, generating $100 in sales or netting $91.00. You can see by this example that $1.70 versus $91 is not good. In addition, net profits are calculated by deducting expenses from gross profits; therefore, bars earn more net profits than a retail liquor store.

Process

Some process measures firms can use to determine the success of their innovations include the following:

1. A *patent* is a legal form of protection issued by a government to a firm to allow it to design, develop, and sell a product for a specified period. Firms seek patents to lock in a competitive advantage over their competitors as they seek to recoup R&D dollars while simultaneously gaining market share. The more patents a company receives the greater the opportunity the company could receive royalties for the use of the patent from its competitors. Therefore, patents provide firms an advantage in profits and market share, while also reducing a competitive threat.

THINK ABOUT THIS!

Milwaukee Power Tools holds a patent for lithium-ion batteries used for their power tool line. In 2014 they filed a lawsuit against rival Snap-On Tools for patent infringements. The case was settled in court on October 26, 2017, where a judge awarded Milwaukee $27.8 million for royalties not paid by Snap-On for using lithium-ion technology.

Lithium-ion batteries are the standard used by power tool manufacturers and Milwaukee receives a royalty from each manufacture that wishes to use technology. Therefore, Milwaukee earns profits from the sales of their tools and a royalty from their competition, thus increasing their profitability.

2. *Active projects* are those that are in some stage of the innovation process but are not yet launched. Active projects give firms options to pursue or cancel a project based on its potential. It is more advantageous for firms to have many active projects in the conceptual or development stage rather than very few. There are times when a brief strategic window may open for a firm to capitalize on an opportunity. If it has an active project in place, this can cut development time and allow it to respond more quickly to the opportunity; therefore, it is highly desirable for firms to manage the development of several active projects simultaneously.

3. Like active projects, *ideas* are the initial seeds that are planted to conceptualize an innovation. Yet, the source of all new ideas is creativity and firms must be not only be open to suggestions, but invite and reward creative suggestions by employees and teams to continue delivering innovations to the market. The common reasons why most ideas are shelved or eliminated is because they fail to support the mission and vision of the firm, do not add value to a firm's portfolio, are considered too expensive to develop, the firm is not currently capable of manufacturing the product, or the firm lacks the expertise to develop the technology.

The popular analogy used to depict how firms receive and process ideas is through visualizing a funnel, where many ideas enter the wide end and very few exit the narrow end; therefore, firms that leverage this analogy should encourage as much ideation as possible to identify and capitalize on the very best ideas. One company well known for helping existing firms improve their innovation process is IDEO, who has developed a seven-step process to generate as many ideas as possible rather than one "perfect idea": (1) defer judgement, (2) encourage wild ideas, (3) build on the ideas of others, (4) stay focused on the topic, (5) have one conversation at a time, (6) be visual, and (7) go for quantity. The metric IDEO uses to determine if they have nurtured a productive brainstorming session is if one hundred ideas were generated in sixty minutes.[1]

Adoption

Firms can also assess the adoption rates of their innovations to determine their success. As we discussed adoption rates in detail earlier, this section is a quick review of this topic. When firms launch a product, the rate of adoption by consumers will vary. Firms can use adoption rates to determine if they have successfully addressed the needs of their target market while also determining if there is a segment that has yet to be considered with future adopters who have unmet needs. Firms can also monitor adoption rates to determine best practices for product launch for future innovations.

The prior section provided a review of how firms have traditionally evaluated innovations' successes. While these same measures are still used today and are helpful in predicting future success, there are other, newer measurements firms use to assess their innovation success, which incorporates organizational capability and leadership metrics. Firms must assess their capabilities to provide a consistent process, yet they must also strive to continuously improve with active support from top management. Without top management's support, firms would never have the budget or approval to innovate; therefore, it is important that top managers actively stand behind their innovation teams while providing positive guidance and openly communicate their support to the firm's internal community.

---

1   "Brainstorm Rules," Design Kit, www.designkit.org/methods/28.

Organizational Capabilities

Organizational capabilities concentrate on a firm's infrastructure and the innovation process to ensure they are continuously refining an approach that is both repeatable and sustainable, which include input and output metrics. Examples of input metrics are the following:

1. Training and robust support for employees who are responsible to innovate for the firm.
2. A formal structure and procedure that supports the firm's innovation efforts. This should be communicated through the organizational chart to depict who reports to who, the chain of command, as well as documentation regarding the training, policies, and procedures for teams focused on innovation.
3. The continuous documentation and monitoring of each team member's specialized skills. (The concept of charging HR with the task of tracking the specializations that employees possess was covered earlier in the text.)

Output metrics include the following:

1. The number of innovations that have been launched or are in development. This helps document the firm's success as well as identify its strengths; however, this information should also be used to evaluate the firm's process toward continuous improvement.
2. Identification of the firm's new capabilities as it informs new, potential outputs are important. Firms that regularly evaluate their capabilities are more likely to identify new opportunities, which can give them a distinct, competitive advantage. This philosophy follows the platform approach covered in previous chapters, as firms use a successful platform to launch new products.

Leadership Metrics

Leadership metrics identify the behavior of senior managers, who must actively and vocally support a culture of innovation to ensure future growth. As with any company, senior leadership is often the guiding force that leads an organization to success or failure. There are three inputs that senior leadership should provide to their firms, and these inputs should be used to measure their involvement, as well as their investment in the firm's innovation community. These include the following:

1. The time spent with daily operations versus guiding or supporting innovation efforts. There is a direct correlation between time spent guiding or supporting the firm's innovation process and its success. Top-level managers must invest in the innovation process in a way that stimulates the work of the teams. Managers who try to take over the process and impose an authoritarian mentality often stifle the work of the

innovators, which usually results in the project's failure; therefore, managers must encourage, guide, and support the teams so they are motivated to succeed.

2. Managers must possess the tools necessary to lead for success. Just because a manager is appointed a senior position, doesn't mean he or she is an expert at everything, especially innovation. There are many instances where firms hire the wrong person to run the organization. Their hiring is usually driven by reputation or past success. Firms hiring senior-level managers should do their homework to see what skill sets they bring to the company. If they have no background in product innovation, their assistance will not be driven by experience and success. Any advice offered will likely be based on past experiences that may resemble a similar scenario to what the innovation team is facing; therefore, innovative firms need to hire top managers experienced with guiding and supporting innovation teams.

3. Firms need to assign responsibility to senior managers for their innovation projects. By hiring top managers and assigning them to specific projects, firms can take advantage of the senior manager buying into the concept and guiding it from day one. This will help ensure the innovation is fully funded and supported from the conceptual phase to the launch. The downside to this philosophy is that top managers may believe in the project so much that when it is obvious it is not a good fit or is not feasible, they may not be objective or pragmatic enough to cancel it. Top managers should guide at an arm's length so that they are more likely to make sound decisions, such as shelving a project before valuable resources are squandered.

There is one primary output regarding leadership metrics, which is that team leaders who successfully lead innovation projects should be promoted to senior management. Promoting team leaders to top leadership roles is not only a good idea, it is a best practice among the world's most innovative companies. Promoting from within boosts morale and strengthens the former team leader's commitment to the firm, while helping to ensure that the firm is less likely to lose the knowledge, skills, and abilities to the firm's competition. Successful team leaders know the firm's capabilities, best practices, mission and vision, and the internal assets necessary to innovate. Many firms hire from outside the firm and lose their top talent when their best interest is to support a culture of hard work and commitment and to reward top performers with promotions.

ASSESSING THE STRATEGY

While assessing the success of an innovation is crucial, it is also important to be strategic when assessing how efficiently the innovation processes are executed. The three main areas to address how innovation teams supports the strategy of a firm are planning, monitoring, and learning. However, before we delve into these three areas, it is important to note that key stakeholders should be invited to engage in all the firm's strategic efforts per their knowledge, skills, and abilities to help ensure an innovation's success. Key stakeholders, like senior management, should also not only guide and support the innovation efforts, but they should help establish the metrics used to determine the innovation's success, and they should be provided with open and unfettered access to the resulting data. In addition, continuous feedback and learning loops must be established and monitored to determine success and failure. It is impossible to determine what key stakeholders' value when we do not communicate with them or monitor their reaction to the performance of a firm's innovation. Finally, the metrics we use to monitor the reaction of key stakeholders are not an end in themselves, but a guiding force for the entire organization to ensure everyone is providing value and satisfying the needs of these stakeholders.

Strategic planning is systematic approach to reach a desired goal by developing plans and objectives in a sequence. Unlike long-term planning, which begins at a firm's current position and works forward, strategic planning begins at the desired goal and objective and works backward. Strategic plans are designed to be longer in duration than tactical plans and must support the mission and vison and satisfy the needs of the key stakeholders to be successful. They must also include environmental scanning (internal and external) and the allocation of resources to support the plans. Top managers devise the strategic plans, then these plans trickle to each level of the organization as goals or targets for teams to achieve; therefore, strategic planning is a comprehensive process that affects everyone at every level in the organization and is intended to support the success of all future innovations.

Monitoring is the ongoing evaluation of an innovation's progress toward achieving a set of specific goals and performance objectives. Ideally, monitoring should be executed in real-time against pre-established metrics and milestones within a defined timeline. Leaders who regard monitoring as a passive activity, like watching a sports event, jeopardize the valuable opportunities that will invariably unveil themselves to the actively engaged manager to apply adjustments quickly and confidently, which can greatly impact the success of an innovation. Regardless of whether an adjustment is warranted, monitoring helps firms document an innovation's performance via cause and effect, which also helps inform leaders as to how they can improve their monitoring and adjustment processes in the future.

It is common that some goals and objectives are simply too optimistic and not in line with reality. Leaders who are actively engaged in monitoring process are always the first to discover what is or is not in line with reality; therefore, these leaders should be empowered to make the appropriate adjustments, as quickly as possible. Recall in the prior chapter where we described the need for firms to continuously adjust, evolve, and lead. Monitoring is critical to helping firms adjust and evolve their strategy based on stakeholder and market needs and then lead the organization toward taking the necessary steps to gain a competitive advantage.

Learning is a continuous process where firms assess progress, actively communicate with key stakeholders, and identify new opportunities to support the firm's mission, vision, goals, and objectives. Learning requires continuous feedback from stakeholders, monitoring of social media, addressing consumer complaints, and conducting focus groups to keep a pulse on what is important to a firm's target market. Like monitoring, the world of business is constantly changing, so learning is key to being aware of the trends that present new and unique opportunities, shifts in the desires of targeted customers, and alternative ways to make key stakeholders happy.

Leaders who set forth strategic plans with a "fire-and-forget" methodology do so to the determent of the innovation and the firm. Top managers must lead the charge to be strategic and communicate with the entire organization to ensure the goals and objectives for the future are clear. The entire organization must be incentivized to listen, communicate, and seek feedback from key stakeholders to be sure it is delivering what its customers want as it often uncovers new pathways for future innovations.[2]

WHAT IMPROVEMENTS SHOULD BE CONSIDERED FOR FUTURE DEVELOPMENT?

Traditional leadership in a global world is obsolete. Firms today will not enjoy the same competitive advantages they did forty to fifty years ago. Today's companies are faced with not only changing consumer tastes, but also stiff competition from start-ups and new business models. It is common to find companies that enjoyed a competitive advantage out of business in less than a year or two. There are five ways firms can improve the way they do business to ensure their success in the future:

1. **Have the ability to think creatively**. Traditional leaders often rely on past success when leading a company; however, companies today face increasingly stiff competition not only domestically, but internationally. Therefore, leaders must take advantage of disruptive technologies and embrace the fact that business changes very quickly and sporadically when compared to how market changes unfolded in past decades. Leaders who can anticipate these changes will ensure their firm will be ready for new challenges to thrive in a competitive world.

2. **Manage chaos while being successful**. Leaders must navigate the chaos of an ever-changing business world and identify new ways to remain competitive. It is illogical to conduct business the same way it has been done in the past when the competition is finding new ways to compete and gain market share.

3. **Identify new technologies that can provide advantages to the firm**. Top leaders are typically older, and their adoption of technology may be slower than younger employees. It is essential that top managers understand and use technology to remain competitive, as well as introduce new ways to harness technology to

---

2   Soren Kaplan, "The Complete Guide to Innovation Metrics—How to Measure for Business Growth," Innovation Point, May 21, 2018, http://www.innovation-point.com/innovationmetrics.htm.

improve their position in the market. Remember how Kodak refused to adopt digital technology, despite owning several patents?

4. **Practice empathy toward your employees**. Employees today are faced with the realization that most are employed to do a specific job with little reward. The days of employee bonuses, stock options, and pensions are over, while many executives seek ways to increase profits to enhance their own personal bonuses. These cuts typically involve firing employees, outsourcing work, and adding technology to replace humans. Firms would do better by investing in their workforce to deliver the highest quality goods, which would also likely increase their employees' morale and commitment to their work.

Leaders need to focus on four areas to increase employee retention:

- *Accountability* is the ability for leaders to be responsible for their actions. Leaders must be willing to step up and assume responsibility for the decisions they make without fear of portraying themselves as inferior.

- *Transparency* is operating in a manner that is open for all to see what the goals and objectives are without having a hidden agenda. Transparency has become a major topic, as many stakeholders are expecting, and in some cases demanding, for corporations to reveal how they operate their business. Stakeholders believe they have a "right to know," and through transparency, firms can deliver this value to them.

- *Fairness* is the act of treating everyone within the firm in a manner that is just and void of favoritism. Managers who treat employees differently create an atmosphere of unfairness, which can be detrimental to the organization. Issues such as the gender gap of females in C-suite roles, pay inequality, and nepotism are just a few examples of how not being fair in the workplace has created situations that are being vocalized by employees and action groups. Top managers should treat all employees the same when it gives considerations for raises, promotions, and assignments. This is not only fair but reduces the possibility of a discrimination lawsuit.

- *Honesty* is the practice of always telling the truth and following through on promises. Nothing soils the moral fabric of a leader more than dishonesty. Dishonesty creates an atmosphere of distrust and fear. Leaders who are honest often find themselves surrounded by the best talent as people want to work for honest, trustworthy leaders.

- **The ability to design systems and processes that are acceptable to employees** is important for strong leaders to understand the capabilities of their employees and how to harness technology. They can blend these two to create systems and processes that give the firm a strategic and competitive advantage. A good leader recognizes his or her weaknesses and hires talent whose strengths offset his or her deficits. Top leaders have many years of business experience, but few are experts in all fields; therefore, it is important to construct a team that is capable in all areas to operate a business.

As the baby boomer generation is replaced as the dominate consumer group, Generation X, Y, and Z will demand more products that are technology based. These next generations of consumers will use more services and apps than past generations, so firms must be ready, willing, and able to deliver. Also, technology often helps increase efficiencies. The ability to incorporate such things as rapid manufacturing and online ordering are just two of the ways technology has changed the landscape of how business is conducted. Therefore, older managers must learn to combine the most capable talent with technology to survive in the future.[3]

HOW DO WE ACCELERATE EVEN FASTER?

Accelerating a firm's innovation efforts is not a fad or a passing thought; it is a necessity in a highly competitive business environment where great ideas that yielded incredible profits can vanish in a matter of months. We have discussed ways to accelerate innovation through adjusting, evolving, and leading, but let's take some time to dive a little deeper into this subject to get a clearer understanding on how innovation can be accelerated.

1. **Refine processes and develop mastery with existing technology and manufacturing capabilities**. Remember, we discussed the learning curve in the context of how Boeing assembles a new aircraft design. The first five planes require the most time to assemble while the last five require the least. This also holds true in residential construction for builders who only construct speculative homes of the same design. What do these two examples have in common? The answer is in the learning curve. Boeing employees and speculative builders assemble the same design repetitively and by doing so they devise short cuts to accelerate production, sometimes to their detriment. Consider the multi-billion-dollar hit Boeing took when Indonesian airline Garuda canceled their order for 49 of the 737 Max 8 after two conspicuously similar crashes killed hundreds of people just months apart.[4]

2. **Another way to accelerate innovation is to make small attribute changes to existing products**. As described in the first example, attribute changes do not affect the production of the new products. The same machinery, people, and raw materials are used to produce a slightly different version of the same product. What is the difference between Cherry Coca-Cola and the original Coca-Cola? The answer is obviously the cherry flavoring. The base product is still in place, but the flavor has been altered. Coca-Cola achieves economies of scale through mass production, and

3   Jared Linzdon, "Five Skills You'll Need to Lead the Company of the Future," Fast Company, May 17, 2017, https://www.fastcompany.com/40420957/five-skills-youll-need-to-lead-the-company-of-the-future.

4   David Meyer, "Passengers Have Lost Trust: Boeing Suffers Its First 737 Max Order Cancellation after Deadly Crashes," *Fortune*, March 22, 2019, http://fortune.com/2019/03/22/boeing-737-max-order-cancel/.

the only thing that has changed is the flavor added to the mixture; therefore, attribute changes help firms better utilize their manufacturing capacity and reduce the expense of developing a new product.

3. **Use the same innovation team to produce similar products**. Much like the advantages that are afforded to firms that work their way through learning curves, using the same innovation team can help accomplish the same results. A well-organized and results-focused innovation team can recreate similar results, especially if it is a slight attribute change to an existing product. It will be able to identify pitfalls in the process and avoid delays in design as it has requisite experience.

4. **Stay lean and avoid bureaucracy**. The current preference with organizational structures is horizontal versus the traditional vertical design. A classic, vertical organizational structure makes it hard to communicate with key managers. Conversely, horizontal structures allow much easier access to key people and information. In addition, decisions made within horizontal organizations are often faster, which is a bonus when firms seek way to accelerate their innovation process.

5. **Create a sense of urgency**. A sense of urgency is a fantastic motivator. In sales, it will motivate consumers to buy because they believe the product may not be available if they delay their purchase. Urgency also works to motivate employees to perform when there is a time crunch, and it is wise for firms to hire employees who thrive under the pressure of a deadline; however, managers should gauge which of their employees are able to perform well under pressure and those who may have a difficult time dealing with pressure and who will not respond well to urgency.

6. **Open the innovation team to interested employees**. Innovation teams require new members who possess fresh, diverse thinking along with the energy and motivation to succeed. It would benefit a firm to have the outgoing members train incoming members to acclimate the new member to the team as quickly as possible. Accelerated innovation requires a tremendous amount of energy, and new members are a great source for excitement and enthusiasm.

7. **Innovate throughout the company, like social innovation**. Another way to accelerate innovation is to open the opportunity for innovation to all employees versus a cross-functional team. This concept is representative of social innovation where an idea is introduced to the public, who then contributes to the development of the idea. This method is often very successful as it provides unique, diverse thinking and the expertise of countless people who are eager to contribute to an innovation versus a much smaller number of employees within a single team. Firms can mimic this within the organization and tap the talents of current employees for contribution. Sometimes employees are shy or reluctant to volunteer for a position on a cross-functional team. If their contributions are voluntary, they may be more willing to participate in the innovation process; therefore, firms can extend the innovation opportunities to more

people and thus utilize the talents of a larger number of people, which can accelerate the innovation process.

The process of rapid acceleration requires firms be lean, agile, and fearless in their pursuit toward following untraditional business strategies while supporting inclusivity by opening the innovation process to everyone who wants to contribute. Many firms fall victim to their own legacy-based processes, strictly practicing the same methods they always have in the past. Firms must be willing to try new ways to innovate, learn from other successful firms, and benchmark what has made them successful to compete. Firms must capitalize on their past success, innovate using proven processes regarding development and production of new products by repurposing the most successful teams to focus on redeveloping similar innovations, and create a sense of urgency while encouraging the inclusion of new ideas and efforts from all interested employees. Moreover, these teams should be incentivized to create a sense of urgency among a larger community of employees to contribute to the company's innovations and to be inclusive in developing new, diverse talent. The goal is to incorporate the very best ideas from any employee as the new product moves through the innovation process, ultimately providing consumers with a new, highly desirable product at the right time. When firms accomplish this, it is often accompanied with great success.

REVIEW GOAL AND OBJECTIVE ATTAINMENT

A firm that doesn't review its goals and objectives is like a person who writes checks from a checkbook but has no idea if there are funds to cover them. Companies face a similar dilemma when they set goals but fail to review the performance measures they established to see if their goals and objectives were met. Firms that set goals and then do not set up measurable results are destined for disaster. It is easy to reach a goal when you vaguely define what you want to accomplish. Firms must review their measurable goals and determine if they achieved the desired results. If they didn't reach their goals, they must re-evaluate why the strategies they used did not perform as expected and make the necessary changes. This process is continuous; constant adjustments must be made to ensure that the goals and objectives that are sought are being realized and met.

Why Firms Didn't Obtain Their Goals

There are several reasons why firms fall short of their goals. These reasons may be specific to the firm or they may be due to some extraordinary circumstances, such as a catastrophic weather event. We will focus on six common reasons why firms fail to meet their goals and what they can do to correct this. What is important to remember is that failing to meet a company's goal can always be changed by constant monitoring and adjustment. If a firm is not on track to obtain the goals and objectives it seeks, changes can be made to make this a reality. However, this requires frequent, disciplined review and tightening of the firm's feedback loops.

The six common failures and suggested solutions to meet their goals include the following:

1. **Setting unrealistic goals**. Goals set by a firm must be obtainable and realistic. If a firm's sales were $1 million last year, setting a goal of $10 million the following year would not be realistic. Goals must reflect the true capability of the company. Often, unrealistic goals are set to satisfy the desire of stakeholders, but once the actual numbers are tabulated, investors may shy away due the company's irrational exuberance; therefore, the best bet is to be realistic when setting goals for the firm. Look historically and see what your reality may be. Set goals based on historical data and account for pending business that may transpire in the new fiscal year. It benefits a firm to account for larger-than-normal sales, especially for public companies. Stakeholders desire stability, so accounting for a large sale can help ease future expectations and limit the risk of investing in a firm's stock.

    When a company sets unrealistic goals, employee morale decreases while frustration rises within the ranks. Employees who recognize that their goals are obtainable are much more motivated to achieve the desired results, especially if they know they will be rewarded.

2. **Goals that ignore customer data**. Data collected on customer activity with a firm is a valuable part of developing goals. Firms must always remember that it is the customer who drives their business. It is good to have an effective way to capture customer feedback, such as a web forum or a suggestion box. Do everything you can to engage your customers in ways that they will recognize are responsive, sincere, helpful, and productive. Identify their concerns and seek out their suggestions about what steps you could take to improve your business. By establishing multiple ways of communicating with your customers, you can more accurately predict what they want and then provide it to them. This will also serve to help you meet your goals and increase customer loyalty.

3. **Failing to communicate the goals to the team**. Very few executives effectively communicate the firm's plans and objectives they have promised to shareholders or investors with the rest of the organization. What's worse, very few departments have an idea what other departments must accomplish in the coming year, which often creates a state of uncertainty within departments as to how the organization expects them to perform. The logical choice is to present the strategic plans and objectives to the entire organization, as well as at department-level meetings, to communicate what the firm is trying to accomplish and how everyone can work together to make the goals a new reality. Communication is critical to success; therefore, top managers must make everyone aware of what is expected in the coming year and how their efforts will help the organization reach its goals.

4. **Firms that lack the KSAs (knowledge, skills, and abilities) necessary to accomplish its goals and objectives**. We have previously discussed the need for the Human

Resources department to maintain an inventory of its employees' skill sets. Firms that are determined to achieve their goals must have employees with the knowledge, skills, and abilities to do so. If a firm is lacking talent in an area that is needed to reach a goal, it must either hire someone from the outside or identify a promising candidate to develop from within. Firms who are not effective at planning usually attempt to move forward without the right people in place for an extended period, which wastes time and resources, as well as demoralizes employees. Therefore, before firms devise their annual planning, they should define what specialized knowledge, skills, and abilities will be necessary and determine if these attributes already exist within the organization. If not, top managers must recruit the right people and have them trained and oriented before the plans are executed.

5. **Lack of a realistic budget to reach your goals.** There is an adage in business that states "You must spend money to make money!" This holds true when companies devise plans that affect departments. If there is to be an increase in the marketing efforts, then money must be allocated to support this goal. If the resources are not available to support the goal or objective, then it will likely fail. This isn't to say that firms should allocate money and then spend it blindly to accomplish their goals. Businesses must seek the most efficient and effective means possible to achieve their goals while spending as little as possible.

6. **There is a hole in the dike.** "A hole in a dike," otherwise referred to as the weakest link, is an identified vulnerability in the organization that can jeopardize its ability to do business as intended. Whether the weakness is associated with a faulty assumption, person, process, product, or relationship, "a hole in the dike" creates a situation that must be dealt with to strengthen the organization. In this way, business is like nature; the market is an environment that favors not only the fittest, but the most adaptive, and it is no surprise that the strongest firms often have the most talent, resources, and strategic plans in place to give them a distinct advantage over their competition. Therefore, innovative firms dedicate time and effort to identify the spots that need to be addressed and then correct the problems to be successful.[5]

Firms must be honest and open about what is holding them back from accomplishing their goals and what they can do to overcome these issues. Planning is a continuous process; therefore, firms must be at the ready to make small changes as situations arise and learn to be as dynamic as possible. It is important that they focus on the yearly goals and objectives within short-term periods. Firms must have a concise vision and try to anticipate problems that may arise before they cause problems that hinder them from achieving their goals. This

---

5   Eyal Katz, "6 Reasons Your Business Fails to Meet Strategic Goals (and What to Do about It)," BPlans, May 23, 2018, https://articles.bplans.com/6-reasons-your-business-fails-to-meet-your-strategic-goals-and-what-to-do-about-it/.

will improve their abilities to take regular, corrective actions rather than the alternative: fewer, more disruptive actions, as they attempt to make their long-term vision a reality.

Review Questions

1. What are traditional financial measures used to determine firm effectiveness? Briefly explain each.
2. What are processes firms use to determine effectiveness? Briefly explain each.
3. What are organizational capabilities? What metrics can be used to determine success?
4. What are leadership metrics? Briefly describe inputs and outputs.
5. What three areas support the strategy of a firm? Give a short description of each.
6. What are five ways firms improve the way they do business to survive? Describe each.
7. What are seven ways firms can accelerate a launch?
8. What are the six common failures firms commit when meeting their goals and objectives? Describe each.
9. How can firms overcome these failures listed in question 8? Explain.

Discussion Questions

1. What are other financial measures not listed in the text that firms can use to determine success? Why do you feel they are important?
2. Share your thoughts with your professor on other processes that firms can use to be more successful. Why did you list these?
3. Share three additional organizational capabilities not listed in the text that you feel could be used to determine the success of the organization. Why did you list these?
4. Select a leader you know and share the inputs and outputs that fit his or her style.
5. What are other ways firms can support their strategy? Share with your professor your thoughts and describe each to them.
6. Select three of the ways firms can accelerate. Describe why you feel these are important.
7. What are additional failures you feel firms commit when trying to meet their goals and objectives?
8. Describe a time when a job, organization, or group committed some of these failures. How did they recover from that?

Extension Activity

Compare two companies, one that is successful at innovation and the other, not successful. Using the seven items in the section "How Do We Accelerate Faster?" what did the successful firm do right and what did the less successful one fail to do?

BIBLIOGRAPHY

"Brainstorm Rules," Design Kit, www.designkit.org/methods/28.

Kaplan, Soren. "The Complete Guide to Innovation Metrics—How to Measure for Business Growth," Innovation Point, May 21, 2018, http://www.innovation-point.com/innovationmetrics.htm.

Linzdon, Jared. "Five Skills You'll Need to Lead the Company of the Future," Fast Company, May 17, 2017, https://www.fastcompany.com/40420957/five-skills-youll-need-to-lead-the-company-of-the-future.

Meyer, David. "Passengers Have Lost Trust: Boeing Suffers Its First 737 Max Order Cancellation after Deadly Crashes," *Fortune*, March 22, 2019, http://fortune.com/2019/03/22/boeing-737-max-order-cancel/.

Katz, Eval. "6 Reasons Your Business Fails to Meet Strategic Goals (and What to Do about It)," BPlans, May 23, 2018, https://articles.bplans.com/6-reasons-your-business-fails-to-meet-your-strategic-goals-and-what-to-do-about-it/.

CHAPTER TWENTY

What's Next and What Decisions Must Be Evaluated?

INTRODUCTION

Firms should measure success beyond the financial, process, and adoption rates of the innovation. They must also identify if the innovation continues to support the company's mission and vision, positively contribute to the product portfolio, increase customer perception and service, improve sales and market share, and determine if the firm is leveraging its resources as efficiently as possible.

Once an innovation satisfies these parameters, the next logical step is for a firm to consider line extensions to continue the success of the innovation. Line extensions can manifest as simple attribute changes (horizontal) or they can be more complex and break a product down by offering extensions in a variety of prices and qualities, creating different versions using an established platform (vertical). This chapter offers several questions that are used to help determine if the extension is worth the firm's investment and additional effort.

When firms judge the success of their product launch, they must redefine the target market, justify the reason for the launch, understand the target market's purchasing behavior, and then identify new, additional ways for consumers to purchase the innovation, while ensuring that the new products are significantly unique from what the firm's competitors offer. Moreover, there are distinct advantages to the firm that also provide trialability and offer easier methods to repurchase products, such as a subscription that automates and ensures future transactions and identifies improved ways to launch the new line extensions as quickly as possible. Firms should also strive to create aura for the extensions, which is a critical element of the GT-MAP. Finally, the line extensions must be evaluated against the GT-MAP to determine the target market's need and the value it will provide to the consumer and the firm.

Learning Objectives

In this chapter students will learn about the following:

- How to judge the success of a firm's innovation
- Why firms use line extensions and two types that are used
- How firms evaluate the market for successful product launch
- Why creating aura around the line extensions is beneficial
- How to use the GT-MAP to evaluate line extensions

Learning Outcomes

By the end of this chapter students will be able to do the following:

- Use the criteria provided to judge the success of an innovation and make suggestions for improvement
- Understand what a line extension is and which of the two types indicated are best to use
- Recommend to a firm why it should utilize a line extension strategy and ways to measure the impact
- Provide to top managers reasons when and why it is best to launch an innovation based on market conditions
- Know strategies to create aura around a line extension and why it is important
- Use the GT-MAP to evaluate the effectiveness of a line extension

Key Terms

Sunk costs: Money that is permanently lost and cannot be recovered

R&D costs: Costs that are incurred initially that can be recovered through the sale of the innovation

Countertrading: When goods are purchased by one firm by trading its goods for another firm's goods versus exchanging cash

Line extension: The use of an existing product brand name to introduce a new product that is slightly different

Horizontal line extensions: Extensions that retain the same pricing and quality as the original product line, but change the features of the product (i.e., color, flavor, or scent)

Vertical line extensions: Those that increase or decrease the product price or quality to create various categories of products

Category impact: Identifies the impact the extension will have on the entire product category

Brand portfolio impact: Measures the added value the extension contributes to the brand name

Parent brand impact: The added value the extension contributes to the parent brand

Variant impact: The volume change that is created by the new extension

HOW IS THE INNOVATION PERFORMING AND WHAT ARE THE NEXT STEPS?

Earlier, we discussed four ways to evaluate the success of an innovation including financial, process, adoption measures, and strategy. While these measures are vital in determining how to measure success, we must look at other factors that affect the success of our innovation. Firms must ask "How is the innovation performing and what is next?" Ultimately, firms need to determine if the innovation has met the organization's goals and if they should continue offering the product.

This next section will identify other ways to determine success on a deeper level for the firm. While these additions to the previous measures outlined in the text will give the reader a better understanding of how to measure success, they should also serve as topics to stimulate thoughts regarding how important monitoring the success of an innovation success is. As success does not occur in a vacuum, measurable parameters must be established and evaluated at various levels of the firm to determine if the innovation is providing value to the firm and if it is worth the organization's efforts to continue providing the product despite consumer demand.

Others criteria firms can use to determine success of the innovation include the following:

1. Does it support the firm's mission and vision?
2. Does it add value to the product portfolio?
3. Has consumer perception of the firm increased?
4. Did the innovation deliver the firm's promise for high levels of customer satisfaction?
5. Is the innovation allowing firms to use their resources efficiently?
   - Financial
   - Equipment utilization
   - Reduced costs
     - ☒ Achievement of economies of scale
     - ☒ Component part and raw material discounts
     - ☒ Reduced waste
   - Increased productivity
6. Is there an increase sales and market share?

Does the Product Support the Firm's Mission and Vision?

Earlier, we discussed in detail what the mission and vision of the firm is and what it means as a guiding force to its operations. As a refresher, the mission is the purpose of the company's existence and serves to guide actions and decision making. The vision guides where the firm is going and what it seeks to accomplish. Every innovation should satisfy the needs of a customer, add value to the firm, and support the firm's mission and vision. It is important that these factors are considered when the initial development begins. If the innovation fails to satisfy these factors, it should be reconsidered or developed in a way to accomplish these criteria.

Does It Add Value to the Product Portfolio?

Throughout the text we have discussed the importance of having a portfolio of products that are complementary to one another while accomplishing the mission and vison of the firm. Some firms' missions and visions include supporting a diverse portfolio, such as a conglomerate, where they use a wide array of products to add value; however, most firms tend to offer or develop products that improve efficiencies, elevate the firm's image, and fully utilize the manufacturing capacity they possess, such as Apple and Dell. A firm's product portfolio is an important way for a firm to increase equity and ensure success of future products.

Has Consumer Perception of the Firm Increased?

As previously discussed, the use of a perceptual map help firms visualize their performance in relation to a competitor's based on two factors, price and quality. A firm's innovation should help it increase customer perception as this will help a firm establish a desired level of pricing, brand image, quality, and reputation. Keep in mind, the brand of a firm or product is intimately associated with a consumer's expectations; therefore, the innovation should support the perceptions the firm seeks from the product's target market. Consider Honda Corporation and the brand perception associated Honda's vehicles versus Acura's vehicles. Even though both lines of vehicles are constructed from the same platform, Acura carries a much higher price point and offers more luxurious features; therefore, a firm's innovation should support the level of perception its customers have come to expect, or the result will be a negative impact on sales.

Did the Innovation Deliver the Firm's Promise of Exceptional Customer Satisfaction?

Like perceptions, the level or quality of a firm's customer service has a major impact on the success of an innovation. If the service levels are below what customers expect, they will be reluctant to repeat their purchase and they will probably not provide positive word of mouth about the product. If the service is better, it can increase the satisfaction they feel for the company and encourage increased purchases. The double-edged sword is that increased service levels are then expected across all products offered by the firm, so increasing the level of service should be consistent to prevent backlash. Like offering various brands to meet different perceptions and expectations, this strategy also works for customer service. For example, the Hilton Corporation offers several brands at different levels of service with the Waldorf Astoria Hotel and Resort at the highest level, followed by Hilton as its higher upscale brand, then Double Tree as upscale, and finally Hampton as its midscale brand.

Another aspect of customer service is the effect it has on expenses and profits. Firms that provide a "concierge level" of customer service will incur a greater percent of labor expense over ones that do not. This will have an impact on profits, so firms try to reduce this by charging higher prices for providing excellent customer service. Also, higher levels of customer service require more training and formal rules to be put into place. High levels of customer service require service providers throughout the firm to be consistent. Consider Walt Disney theme parks, where employees are trained to provide a high level of customer service to all their guests, and the customer loyalty that this establishes, including repeat purchases and greater assurance of future success through what will be discussed later in this chapter, line extensions.

Is the Firm Using Its Resources Efficiently in Its Support of the Innovation?

Innovations that require different processes and specialized raw materials may derail a firm's ability to be efficient. As discussed earlier, firms should examine ways to utilize current machinery, raw materials, processes, and existing space and fill remaining manufacturing capacity to support the innovation as efficiently as possible because efficiencies produce less waste, increases profits, reduce labor expenses, and overall, allow firms to do more with less. The following list outlines different ways for firms to efficiently use their existing resources to continue supporting their innovations while increasing sales and profits.

Financial

Certainly, firms with greater financial resources than their competitors have a distinct advantage; however, the firm that most efficiently uses its resources, such as its finances, will create new opportunities to purchase new equipment, invest in top talent, enter markets where competition is intense, purchase larger quantities of materials to receive deeper discounts, or even buy out the very competitors who ran their business inefficiently for too long and decided to sell.

Firms that are financially strapped have the opposite set of circumstances. They may have to take on heavy debt to buy new equipment, accept workers who top firms rejected, enter smaller markets with less competition and thus less sales, negotiate harder for discounts, and be subject to unfavorable stakeholder support. The adage "cash is king" is very true in business. Financially sound companies have many more advantages than those that are not; therefore, establishing disciplined financial practices will help firms compete and survive. Firms must determine if the innovation has helped the financial success of the company and, if so, then proceed. If not, the firm must identify how to rise above the current financial predicament, and discovering new efficiencies is an effective method to accomplish this.

Equipment Utilization

Equipment that provides firms with options in manufacturing helps reduce space and increase flexibility. Identifying how the equipment is used also helps increase efficiency. Equipment should be designed to perform multiple processes, if possible. This will decrease the size of the equipment's footprint while increasing the speed of manufacturing. In turn, this increases the units available to be sold and reduces costs by operating within a smaller space. Firms must ask if the innovation is utilizing the equipment to its fullest extent and if it is contributing to the overall performance and profitability of the company.

Firms that utilize old equipment may believe they are saving money because they own it; however, older equipment lacks the ability to rapidly manufacture products and is more likely to fail or break down in comparison to new, more modern equipment. Firms must constantly evaluate the efficiencies they are receiving and convert this into the profit potential they are losing by integrating up-to-date equipment. Profitable firms tend to consistently investment in new equipment that offers advantages associated with greater efficiencies as well as increased sales and profits.

Reduced Costs

Firms must analyze if their innovation has increased or reduced costs. Costs are outside of sunk costs or research and development (R&D). **Sunk costs** are money that is permanently lost and cannot be recovered. All firms experience sunk costs as all firms must purchase items upfront that are needed to produce the innovation. **R&D costs** are costs that are incurred initially but that can be recovered through the sale of the innovation; therefore, firms must spend money to make more, which is especially true for expenses associated with research and development. Money spent innovating a new product is a risk that firms must take to increase their profits, sales, and market share, and ideally to thrive. Successful firms seek new opportunities to invest their financial resources into products that are most likely to generate increased profits and ensure long-term success of the company.

Another way firms can reduce costs is by increasing the frequency of deliveries of raw materials and component parts. Firms that buy large quantities of raw material may hurt their profitability in a few ways. First, buying in large quantities often ties up financial resources that could be used to support production (i.e., holding costs). As covered earlier, holding costs are associated with buying merchandise or components that a firm then stores in its inventory until those items are sold to recoup the firm's investment; therefore, ordering large quantities of items increases a firm's holding costs. By ordering smaller quantities of items more frequently, firms can use their financial assets for other aspects of operating the business. Second, if discounts are negotiated into the amount of raw materials purchased, running out of one raw material may trigger a reorder and adversely affect a volume discount, resulting in increased costs and reduced profits. Finally, in our highly competitive global market, there is an increased opportunity for substituting lower-cost items used to produce a firm's final product. If the substitution doesn't affect the appearance or performance or cause harm to the user, this is a good strategy to reduce costs and increase profits.

THINK ABOUT THIS!

How could Professor Ferguson have increased his profits from building decks by substituting items to reduce costs?

When Professor Ferguson owned and operated a construction company, he built decks for customers. While he prided himself on using 4-by-6 treated posts to support the structure with 2-by-12 joists, spindles spaced at 3 3/4 inches for the deck, in hindsight his choice of materials increased his costs and reduced profits. Structurally, he could have used 4-by-4 posts with 2-by-8 floor joists, spacing the spindles at 4 inches. These changes would have provided his customers with a high-quality deck that was code compliant and safe, yet it would have drastically reduced his material costs and supplemental costs, such as with joist hangers, nails, and carriage bolts, while increasing profits.

Eliminating product attributes that customers do not want or need is another way to reduce costs. Many times, firms add attributes to a product to make it superior to what their competition offers but these attributes are neither used nor appreciated. Think of how many people you know who disable most or all the driver alerts that are offered in most newer vehicles. While the reason for developing those types of technologies is likely well intended and well warranted, many people find these features annoying and turn them off. Therefore, firms should always strive to improve their communication with target markets to accurately identify which attributes are desirable and which ones can or should be eliminated.

Countertrading is another way to reduce costs. *Countertrading* is when one firm's goods are exchanged for another's, and instead of a transaction based on cash, the transaction is based on what is considered a fair swap between two parties, and it is a very common practice for firms to exchange finished goods, warehouse space, or services in order to reduce costs. Countertrading works especially well for firms that have a higher gross profit margin than the company with which they are countertrading, which is like receiving a favorable foreign exchange rate on domestic currency. In this case, higher profitability means a firm can receive more for its investment.

Firms must constantly identify new ways to reduce the costs they incur and spend their money as wisely as possible to be successful. Reduced costs can be realized through various ways, as further outlined next.

Leveraging Economies of Scale
Achieving economies of scale has been discussed throughout the text, but as a refresher, achieving economies of scale means spreading your fixed costs among several units produced, thus reducing costs and increasing profits. Firms must always seek new ways to achieve this. There are several strategies to do so, and many are discussed in this chapter. Firms can use continuous innovation (changing attributes without changing behavior) to increase the sale of products and achieve economies of scale. Firms can also find ways to increase frequency of use or find new markets where they can sell the same products to increase production.

Finding new markets for a product has also been discussed in several chapters. Recall how Arm & Hammer was originally marketed as baking product, but it is now also marketed as a popular and effective deodorizer. Tyvek was originally developed as a house wrap by DuPont, but it is now used to keep a wide variety of items dry, such as clothing during shipping. Innovators would do well to follow suit with their products by exploring unmet needs in different markets, thereby increasing the number of units sold and achieving new economies of scale. This strategy has worked for CNN to increase its viewership; Dawn dish soap, which is also used as a mosquito repellent; and fast food restaurants that offer lunch-only items, happy hour specials, limited-time dinner entrees, and late-night snacks along with all-day breakfasts. Finding new markets is a very effective way to reduce costs and increase profits, as shown by these examples, and is a successful strategy used by many companies.

Component Parts and Raw Material Discounts

We discussed obtaining discounts either by pursuing cumulative or non-cumulative credit to purchase products. We also discussed paying within 10 days to obtain a discount (e.g., 2/10, net 30). Finally, we noted that firms can negotiate to receive discounts from vendors. Whatever the firm's preferred method of pursuing a discount is, it should explore all its options to reduce costs and increase profits.

What are other methods to obtain discounts on components and raw materials used to produce a final product? Becoming a member of a buying group is another way to reduce costs. A group is formed typically by a third party, and the members' buying power is then leveraged to negotiate deeper discounts. A fee is typically associated with being a member of a buying group, but the fee is usually offset through the savings the firm receives; therefore, this has become a very popular option for firms seeking to reduce their costs.

A final way to reduce component and raw material costs is to negotiate discounts based on the products produced as defined by a specific contract. For example, consider a builder who is under contract to build thirty homes in one year, who then approaches his or her subcontractors for a reduced rate due the volume of work associated with building thirty homes versus five or less. In turn, the subcontractors can and should negotiate with their suppliers based on the volume associated with helping construct thirty homes. In this model, everyone receives deeper discounts and the cost of materials is less, thereby increasing profits.

Reducing Waste

Reducing waste is a simple way to cut costs. Less waste translates into less cost associated with items such as raw materials since less is needed to produce the firm's finished goods. Improved product design, manufacturing methods, and quality control help to ensure minimal waste is created. Finally, firms may also identify ways to sell the byproducts of their operation. For instance, Styrofoam was originally a byproduct of a process used by Dow Chemical until it was discovered to be an excellent insulator. Ford Motor Company often produces an excess of electricity at its Rouge plant, which it then sells what it doesn't need to regional municipalities. These are all effective means by which firms reduce their costs by reducing waste.

Increasing Productivity

Any efforts that result in an increased capacity of work are increases in productivity, and today one of the most common ways firms achieve increased productivity is through automation. As leaders consider all the resources and operations that are required to support producing an innovation, they should identify which ones would be the easiest and most cost effective to automate. Two of the most innovative forms of automation are machine learning and artificial intelligence, which is being leveraged with remarkable success by firms around the world. J. P. Morgan was desperate to solve its ever-increasing backlog of new and expiring commercial loan agreements to either negotiate, renegotiate, or terminate. The bank estimated that they had hundreds of thousands of hours of work, which could only be accomplished by teams of lawyers and loan officers with at least ten years of experience. In order to increase the firm's capacity to complete the work, they used artificial intelligence to read and assess the risk of every loan agreement and determine the best course of action, as would any well-paid, experienced member of J. P. Morgan's legal team, except rather than it taking 360,000 hours, it only took a few seconds.[1]

Is There an Increase in Sales and Market Share?

Two key components in determining how the innovation is performing is to evaluate sales and market share as compared to the original goals established by the firm to determine if the innovation is successful. Increasing sales and market share indicates several results, such as an increased rate of adoption, how well you are recovering R&D dollars (which should ideally be earmarked for the next innovation), how well your customers' needs are being satisfied, how many repeat purchases are occurring, if the aura worked, if advertising is being properly directed to the target market, and so on. Comparing current sales and market share to the goals established by the cross-functional teams gives firms the ability to predict profitability and to increase production and prevent out-of-stocks. Sales and market share figures can also be used to determine if the workforce needs to be increased and how much raw materials are needed to sustain production. Sales and market share are an important component in determining the level of success of the innovation and helps managers determine when to innovate again using a similar platform or to create a new product.

WHAT LINE EXTENSIONS ARE WE CONSIDERING AND WHY?

Line extensions are a natural way for firms to extend their product offerings using an existing product. *Line extension* is the use of an existing product brand name to introduce a new product that is slightly different. Using an example of

---

1 Hugh Son, "J. P. Morgan Software Does in Seconds What Took Lawyers 360,000 Hours," Bloomberg, February 28, 2017, https://www.bloomberg.com/news/articles/2017-02-28/jpmorgan-marshals-an-army -of-developers-to-automate-high-finance.

line extensions, such as Diet Coke, and Diet Caffeine-Free Coke, most consumers are well-aware that the core brand is Coke, but that these other related products are the result of the firm changing minor attributes in comparison to the original product. As described in previous chapters, this is a common method of innovation: Firms leverage the success of an existing product and extend the offering in other ways to encourage new and existing customers to build loyalty while buying the product line and increasing sales.

Line extension come in two types. *Horizontal line extensions* are extensions that retain the same pricing and quality as the original product line but change the features of the product (i.e., color, flavor, or scent). The other type of line extension is the *vertical line extension*, which either increases or decreases the product price or quality to create various categories of products. Examples of vertical line extension include Toyota and Lexus or Nissan and Infiniti. These two automobile manufacturers offer various models at distinctly different price points. The automobiles also use the same platform regardless of brand, so it is cost effective for them to pursue this strategy. By altering the price and quality, firms can offer consumers many different product lines from one parent company.

Firms create line extensions for the following reasons:

1. To increase the parent brand's revenue.
2. To address changing consumers' needs and tastes.
3. To take advantage of the success associated with the original product line.
4. If the risk of extending the line is low.
5. If the line extension provides additional ways to compete.
6. If the line extension fills a void in the marketplace.
7. If extending the line will increase sales and profits.
8. If the line extension will improve efficiency and maximize the firm's capacity.
9. If the line extension will helps achieve economies of scale.

Regardless of which reasons a firm chooses to justify extending a line, the line extension must provide a benefit to both consumers and the firm who creates it, or it will not be worth the firm's investment. As a firm decides to move forward with creating a line extension, it must assess the impact it will have in four areas.

1. Category impact
2. Brand portfolio impact
3. Parent brand impact
4. Variant impact

Category Impact

Category impact identifies the impact the extension will have on the entire product category. If the extension will only increase sales by a marginal amount, it may not be worth pursuing. Many companies pursue this type of strategy to test new products. For example, Pepsi used to test many flavors of Mountain Dew trying to determine which would be most popular. Philip-Morris, now Altria, used to test many brands of cigarettes while simultaneously strengthening its parent brand of Marlboro. Many firms attempt to extend lines that could add value to the parent brand resulting in increased sales, profits, and market share.

Brand Portfolio Impact

Brand portfolio impact measures the added value the extension contributes to the brand name. Firms want to create a powerful brand to compete in the market place. A strong brand does many things for a company: increases the brand equity, gives customers a better perception of the brand, helps decrease the need for advertisement, and gives consumers a clear expectation of what the brand will do for them. If an extension can help the firm accomplish these variables, it should add it. The brand portfolio is an important tool for firms, and this should ultimately support the mission and vision of the company.

Parent Brand Impact

Parent brand impact is the added value the extension contributes to the parent brand. The parent brand is the one firms most often rely on to promote their products, such as Coca-Cola, Kellogg, and Ford. If a new extension is perceived in any way as a potential threat to the parent brand, then it must not be introduced. For example, if Diet Coke cannibalized the sale of Coke, then it would likely jeopardize the health and well-being of the firm; therefore, it would need to be phased out. Firms must determine what impact an extension could have on the parent brand and assess if it is worth the risk of introducing it.

Variant Impact

Variant impact is the volume change that is created by the new extension. Firms must be aware of the impact the extension will have on the existing bestsellers of the product line. They must determine what impact the extension will have on the overall line and if it adds value to it. Without adding value, the extension is not worthy of introduction. Therefore, firms must assess if the extension limits cannibalism and adds value to the entire product line.[2]

Evaluation of the Market for a Successful Launch of Product Extensions

Once a firm determines which lines to extend, it must evaluate the opportunities that are available to ensure a successful launch its products. In previous chapters we discussed in detail the need to bring the innovation to market with speed. This section will serve as both a review and introduction of new insights on what a firm needs to launch an extension of a product. The items to address to launch the extension include the following:

---

2   Lee Markowitz, "Are You Confident Your Line Extension Will Pay Out?" Ipsos, June 1, 2011, https://www.ipsos.com/en-us/are-you-confident-your-line-extension-will-pay-out-0.

1. **Identify the target market**. The target market has been discussed in several chapters of this text, but it is worth reinforcing that the target market is the group of consumers that the firm focuses on to sell the innovation to because the product will likely satisfy consumers' wants or needs. Innovators need to assess if the extension reaches the same target market or if they can broaden their target market to reach new customers. We have discussed in detail the need to provide the target market with innovations that will satisfy consumers, thereby providing a market of buyers.

2. **Identify how the target market prefers to process information**. Each target market has a distinct way it seeks and consumes information. It is up to the firm to discover the most frequent means the target uses to seek information so its advertisement about the product is seen and placed into memory. Digital marketing has helped marketers pinpoint their advertising efforts to find the target market and provide the information necessary for them to make a buying decision.

3. **Define the problem you are addressing**. Firms can use marketing research to identify how the extension can satisfy the needs of the target market. However, a common problem of marketing research is not defining the problem you are trying to identify correctly. Firms must conduct focus groups, perform surveys, and communicate with the target market to identify what they want, how they want it, and why, including a clear understanding of what will prompt them to buy the product. Discovering customer needs is essential for every innovation. It has been stated several times in this text that consumers buy products based on what will satisfy their needs and wants. Therefore, firms must determine what their target market needs to solve their problems, and then offer it to them in a way that is most compelling.

4. **Understand the consumer's buying process**. Firms must first identify who the target market is, determine what ways they obtain information to make a purchase, figure out what they are willing to pay for a product, and then what will stimulate them to buy. If a firm has no idea what this entails for the extension, they will likely perform poorly in the market. As we have discussed in previous chapters, firms must realize what the process is to compel the target market to buy their products. If they lack this information, their sales will suffer greatly. Therefore, marketing must conduct research to determine who the target is, why they will purchase the innovation, how much they will pay, how often they will repurchase the product, and how likely they are to be satisfied.

5. **Provide a seamless, online purchasing experience**. With the ever-expanding options to purchase items online that consumers experience every day, a poorly constructed website or purchasing process will result in poor sales. If the extension is offered to the same customers through the same channels, this will enhance the online experience. When a new target market is addressed, but the new target market does not have any experience doing business with the firm, it becomes

the firm's responsibility to make this experience as positive as possible in order to stimulate initial and repeat purchases. In many instances, consumers can shop for the same product from multiple channels. Firms that provide the best experiences will retain online shoppers, and as a result, shoppers are more likely to return to make additional purchases. Firms achieve this by providing an easy-to-navigate website. In addition, the site must be easy to search, offer the choice to speak with a human being, and be a safe and secure way to purchase the products. If a firm cannot provide these basic utilitarian expectations, its sales will suffer.

6. **Validate the product.** To get the product extension noticed in the market, it must sell. The sales of products help to validate it as a worthwhile purchase, but if consumers do not buy the product, it will trigger concern from other consumers, and they will likely intuit that there is something wrong or that the product does not perform as promised. Therefore, firms must execute a comprehensive marketing plan that will promote the product to generate sales. This must be a well-thought-out plan that addresses who the target market is, which markets the product will be sold in, the price point, distribution channels, and more. A comprehensive marketing plan should help validate the product and bolster the success of the innovation.

7. **Differentiate yourself from your competitors**. In this text we have repeatedly discussed the importance of being distinctly different from your competitors. We shared with you three things that an innovation should satisfy to give a firm a strategic advantage. It should be hard to duplicate and support the mission and vision of the organization, and firms should be passionate about it. If your product is like your competitors, the natural way to compete is through price. Price is not a good way to build loyal customers, and worse, it is a practice that erodes profits. Firms should make their innovations unique and offer customers something that will satisfy their needs. A unique product doesn't have to compete on price because there is nothing else like it in the market. This creates an opportunity for companies and the firms that sell the products. Ideally, customers will seek out the firm's products and consumer demand will drive the sales, rather than the price point.

8. **Be original**. Beyond a firm's attempt to differentiate itself from its competition, the best way to stand out is to be both truly original and authentic. This is much easier said than done as it requires a firm to intimately understand why it is original from any other organization and why the firm adheres to the fundamental concepts that make it original, as well as provide a compelling invitation to its loyal consumers as to why they should associate their own personal identity with the firm's brand. Keep in mind that there is often a direct correlation between a consumer's perception of the company's originality and the level to which the company actively "stands" for something greater than itself, and as a result creates meaning for its customers. Let's take a moment to test this.

While this exercise is entirely subjective, avoid answering the following questions based on your own opinion, but rather practice empathy for how you believe large groups of people may feel about the following companies and their brands. In each row of the following table, identify one or more companies that (1) are distinctly original, (2) stand for something greater than themselves, (3) create meaning for their customers, and (4) compel their loyal customers to associate their own personal identity with the company's brand.

TABLE 20.1   *Company Authenticity Exercise*

Folgers	Maxwell House	Starbucks
Este Lauder	Maybelline	Revlon
Harley-Davidson	Honda	Kawasaki
Land's End	L.L. Bean	Eddie Bauer
Burger King	McDonald's	Wendy's
Adidas	New Balance	Nike
AT&T	T-Mobile	Verizon
Ford	GM	Tesla

Were there any rows where you struggled to identify one company that truly stood out as original and authentic? Take another look at those choices and ask this last question: Which of the three companies you chose would cause its customers to mourn the most if it were to announce that it would no longer exist?

9. **Get the customer to try the product extension**. A common way to get a customer to try a firm's new product is to extend an offer or demonstrate its value. Firms often give consumers coupons, rebates, or free samples to stimulate a trial. Firms should plan a demonstration if the product is dangerous or large. Many technology-based products give a free trial for a specified number of days so that the customer can assess the product firsthand before buying it. The key to repeat purchases is to compel the consumer to try the product.

    Demonstrations, incentives, and sampling are proven methods to entice consumers to try a product. Customers who shop at Sam's Club or Costco on weekends could literally receive a free lunch when considering all the samples that they are encouraged to try while walking through the store. Companies wouldn't give their product away for free if it wasn't an effective method to motivate people to buy the product. So, what happens? A customer tries a slice of pizza and then the employee is trained to say something like, "Isn't that so good?" Conveniently, behind the employee's demonstration table is a freezer full of pizzas to encourage an immediate sale.

10. **Develop strategic and tactical plans**. Strategic planning is devised by top managers and is meant to guide the company for many years. Tactical planning focuses on a shorter timeframe and supports the strategic plan. Firms must have both in place

when they are launching a product extension. In addition, a comprehensive analysis must be conducted to identify competitive threats and the ways in which a firm can take advantage of its resources when launching the product. This is an ideal time to perform a SWOT analysis. Other items to address include marketing plans, distribution channels, and a specific list of retailers that would be best to sell the products. We have discussed these items in detail throughout the text, but launching a product must be a calculated event, and having a solid plan in place helps firms ensure success.

11. **Communicate the plan to the entire firm**. All the planning in the world will not yield any results unless the top managers effectively communicate the organization's plan. Leaders at successful firms share the organization's plans with the entire company as they understand every employee is responsible for its success. Like a football team that emerges from a huddle, every player on the field is expected to know what he or she needs to do to make the play work, and firms would do well to do the same. Employees should understand why the firm is launching the extension and what benefits it seeks. The other benefit of sharing the plan company-wide is that it can (and should) generate enthusiasm and strong commitment among its employees. (If it doesn't, leaders should revise the plan until it reinvigorates its workforce.)

12. **Create aura**. Aura is the buzz that gains attention and creates excitement. Firms can use this to their advantage to create a sense of urgency regarding the purchasing and availability of the product and to encourage preordering. We will discuss this in greater detail in the next section.

13. **Perform testing and gain customer feedback**. Earlier, we discussed the need to evolve, adjust, and lead. Firms must test their products before launch to make any necessary changes to encourage a products' success in the market, but also monitor consumers' responses to the launch. Adjusting the product extension after launch should be firmly based on customer feedback as it is a way to take advantage consumers' firsthand knowledge about any issues or shortcomings and ensure that subsequent buyers will have a better initial experience with the product.

14. **Predict the unknown**. Many companies are good at most things, but they often lack talent in certain areas. This means firms must do their best to predict any issue that may inhibit a successful launch. Benchmarking is important in this situation as firms that document successful launches can build on past experiences to ensure subsequent launches are as successful as possible.

15. **Tell a consistent story**. Public relations are great at sharing consistent messaging with the public about the firm's products, but employees should be encouraged to do the same. Consistent storytelling spread by all employees can help build aura among stakeholders regarding the extension and is likely to lead to customers hearing the story, and in turn, share it with others. Recall a time when you prepared for a series of job interviews. Did you notice that over time your responses became consistent and more refined as you answered predictable questions? The same holds true for telling

the product's story. Be consistent and create excitement among stakeholders and you will gain attention.

16. **Reflect on the experience**. Once the process is complete, it is time to reflect on the positives and negatives of the process. Did the teams perform well? Was the testing enough? What can we do to use elements of the innovation for the future? By consistently learning from our mistakes, we can improve on our future as it unfolds. Firms must evaluate the entire process and decide what should be used for benchmarking the future to ensure the product extension launch process is as successful as the original product or the one that superseded it.[3]

Create Aura for Line Extensions

Earlier, we discussed the need to create aura. Aura is the buzz that a firm purposely creates around a product to gain consumer attention. With over three thousand marketing messages a day being targeted at us, aura helps to break through the selective attention we have and generates consumers' interest. While this is important for the innovation in development, it is also important for any future extensions as well. The success of the innovation and the subsequent line extension warrants telling customers about the horizontal or vertical extensions. If a consumer has a positive experience with the original product, there is a good chance he or she will purchase the extension.

As the consumer already has direct knowledge and expectations of the brand, he or she is a promising target for the extension. Again, perhaps more than any other movie franchise, *Star Wars* successfully leverages aura as consumers are exposed to a variety of promotions associated with the upcoming movie months in advance. Firms that create aura around extensions often stimulate pull demand (i.e., getting consumers to demand the product versus stocking it and hoping it sells), which usually yields strong initial sales and continues far longer than what many analysts would predict. So, what are some ways to create aura around the line extension? There are several methods that can be used to accomplish this:

1. **Create a waiting list or set a release date**. As previously discussed, one of the most effective methods of selling is to create a sense of urgency. By offering a waiting list or setting a release date for the launch of a new product, consumers are more likely to feel that it is important to them to be one of the first to purchase the new extension. Apple uses this strategy very well when it launches a new product. When they set a release date, early adopters will often camp out for days in front of their stores to be one of the first to own the product. Waiting lists are equally effective because they give customers a sense of hope that they will be one of the many selected to get the

---

3   Forbes Agency Council, "17 Steps to Take before You Launch a Product or Service," *Forbes*, October 24, 2017, https://www.forbes.com/sites/forbesagencycouncil/2017/10/24/18-steps-to-take-before-you-launch-a-product-or-service/2/#28af8cb571f2.

new product. The sense of exclusivity gives customers the feeling they are special if they are selected.

2. **Use public relations to create teasers and inspire mystery**. This highly effective strategy is used all the time to promote many types of products through movie trailers, product previews, and obscured images of products like cars. All of this serves to build a story, and it is very effective because the company controls it, so everything that is revealed should be according to plan. While this strategy can backfire if an internal person releases unapproved information to the public, it is successfully used today by many market segments and is highly effective at creating aura for extensions.

3. **Use social media to connect with current customers and attract new ones**. In the digital age in which we live, social media should play a strong role in any marketing campaign. There are more people on social media than not, and many firms use social media to inform customers of recent company events, attract new customers, and monitor consumer responses regarding the firm's performance; therefore, it is only expected that social media is an excellent way to create aura around line extensions as well. The majority of a firm's customers may follow its official social media sites, so firms should release teasers regarding line extensions, deliver exclusive offers, encourage followers to invite others, or upload their own personal video of the new extension. Social media is a highly effective tool because firms can specifically target current customers. This saves on the cost of advertisement and firms can use cookies to make personalized offers.

4. **Launch the product at an event**. Creating aura around a line extension should be big news rather than a soft roll-out. Firms need to make the launch of the extension an event. Apple does this very well. Automobile companies do this at the International Auto Show in Detroit. The NFL does an excellent job with this during the draft of its players. What do these three examples have in common? They create an event out of the launch, and this draws attention on the part of the firm's stakeholders.

5. **Advertise the extension with the original product to establish the connection**. The reason the original brand has an extension is largely due to its sustained success. Firms should not extend a new line for a product associated with marginal success. Remember, line extensions should add value, increase sales, improve profits, and support the mission and vision of the organization; therefore, it makes good sense to market both together to make the association for the consumer and give the extension the same expectation on behalf of customers. This strategy works extremely well for horizontal line extensions as the new product typically carries similar price points, quality, and benefits as the original. By associating the two, the extension often receives instant

recognition and credibility. What's more, consumers' expectations of the extension are answered automatically, again, due to the association with the original product.[4]

Creating aura around the line extension is a highly effective strategy to ensure its success. If you stop and think about the way firms market line extensions, you will see how the strategies provided are used consistently throughout many market segments. Consumers can't wait to get the newest iPhone, the latest model year for cars, a new type of hamburger, or a new type of beverage. It is up to the firm to gain the consumer's attention to the new line extension to stimulate sales. Aura is a highly effective way to accomplish this.

Evaluate New Extensions within the GT-MAP

Firms should evaluate the line extension based on the GT-MAP to see if it fits the product portfolio, improves the operations of the firm, and fits the mission and vision and then determine if it will likely provide new value to customers and the organization. When using the GT-MAP, it starts by addressing market needs and continues through concept generation, product development, launch, evaluation, and revision, while also assessing future innovation opportunities. It is a comprehensive framework that measures the worthiness of all innovation. Many firms fall victim to thinking that because the original product did well, the extension will be equally successful. While this may seem logical, overextending a brand can cause problems, as witnessed by Starbucks, or firms fail to test the extension with consumers and are left wondering why it wasn't accepted. Firms must ensure that they are producing an extension that will satisfy the criteria of the GT-MAP.

Recall that horizontal line extensions are the easiest form of innovation to pursue as they involve minor changes and use anticipated expectations from consumers, while vertical line extensions are more difficult as they are quite different from what consumers are most familiar with since vertical extensions do not typically use the same branding, but instead leverage the same platform. Therefore, the challenge is to inform consumers that the vertical extension is part of the original brand, yet certain variables have changed (e.g., price and quality). Vertical line extensions also take more time and resources since they are more like developing a new product than modifying an existing product.

Using the GT-MAP framework, firms must evaluate the following:

1. **Market need**. As we have discussed many times, if there is no need for a product, consumers will not buy it. This is particularly true for consumer goods where companies create so many extensions the consumer becomes confused or overwhelmed by so many choices. The craft beer industry has reached a saturation point that new additions are met with reduced enthusiasm. The soft drink industry has been victim to this by using a parent brand and introducing extensions that were later discovered

---

4   Jayson DeMers, "7 Cheap Ways to Generate Buzz for Your Business," *Forbes,* May 21, 2015, https://www.forbes.com/sites/jaysondemers/2015/05/21/7-cheap-ways-to-generate-buzz-for-your-business/#54d69b4f52a9.

to be unwanted; examples include Pepsi Kona, Pepsi Clear, and various flavors of Mountain Dew. Ensuring that there is a want or need before proceeding with the extension is an important step.

2. **Concept generation**. Concept generation for horizontal extensions are usually much easier and straightforward than vertical extensions. Horizontal extensions, as previously indicated, are additions to a current product (e.g., Coke Zero, Bud Light, hazelnut-flavored Maxwell House coffee, etc.). If the concept satisfies the market need, a firm is off to a good start. If it is a vertical extension (e.g., Honda and Acura), this poses some additional challenges. While the platforms are usually the same, the vertical extension will offer varying price points and quality differences. Firms must determine what is expected and acceptable to the target market for which they will offer the products. While firms will use the same platforms, the concept will change regarding the overall concept. Firms need to treat vertical extensions as new innovations and seek consumer feedback and work in their functional groups to develop the new extension.

3. **Product development**. When market needs and concept generation have been determined, it is time for the firm to develop the product. These two elements will guide the development of the product. Again, based on which type of extension is chosen (vertical or horizontal), the amount of time to develop and launch will vary greatly. Horizontal is the easiest way to develop an extension as it involves the least amount of effort. Firms have the technology and machinery already in place to develop these products, so most firms tend to pursue this strategy. For a vertical extension, this process is more intense, requiring firms to develop, test, and plan for alternative distribution channels, and they may even need to target a new consumer group. For example, the target market for Honda is not the same market as Acura. New consumer behavior, ways to advertise, expectations, and motives for buying must be determined. This will slow the development of the extension, but it can create significant opportunities for the firm.

4. **Launch**. Launch for a horizontal extension is easiest as it will typically utilize the same distribution channels, be offered in a similar fashion as the original, and use the same advertising channels. Launch for a vertical extension could require all new distribution channels or perhaps similar channels but different selling venues. If a vertical extension is increased luxury, the sales outlet should be located near the target market. Schedule a launch event to gain attention and create aura that will attract as much interest as possible to make the target market aware of the new product.

In addition, the launch will be slower for vertical extensions versus horizontal due to the amount of testing that needs to take place, as well as the involvement of the cross-functional teams. A vertical extension can be compared to developing an innovation, but it doesn't require a new platform on which to deliver the extension, so this will help expedite the launch overdeveloping an entirely new product.

5. **Evaluate**. This is one area where horizontal and vertical line extensions are very similar. The evaluation methods previously covered, which are commonly used to measure the financial, process, adoption, and strategy performance of the innovation, must be assessed. If the extension does not significantly contribute to these three areas, a strong argument must be presented to justify its continued existence. For instance, sometime firms will argue to keep the extension as it helps to fill the breath of a product category, but the extension should be eliminated it if fails adds value to the firm. The top-level managers must make these decisions while considering the overall well-being of the firm.

6. **Revise**. Revising a line extension is more prevalent for vertical extension that horizontal. Horizontal extensions are typically eliminated if they need to be revised because they are an extension of an original brand. A common strategy is to introduce a new extension to replace one that did not perform well. Vertical extensions require the same strategy of adjust, evolve, and lead, as laid out in an earlier chapters, but they are usually associated with a much longer period before launch. Monitoring a product's sales performance, consumer feedback, social media, and blog posts, as well as its profitability will help to determine how the success of the vertical extension. Consider the vertical extensions offered by Infiniti, Acura, and Lexus as they provide more luxury and styling over their original launch products.

7. **Evaluate for future extension**. Line extensions also provide future opportunities for firms. Original products can be extended several times, and firms should set a goal to continually monitor what consumers seek to satisfy their needs and wants when considering another extension. Firms must also benchmark their best practices used when launching previous line extensions, perfect their methods, and learn from their mistakes. The most successful firms will often develop several extensions simultaneously, introducing them when market conditions appear most favorable. This is especially true for horizontal extensions as vertical extensions pose more challenges, but developing an extension based on a current product is one way to ensure that future line extensions are viable.

Review Questions

1. Identify ways to determine how to judge the success of the innovation.
2. What is a line extension?
3. Name two types of line extensions and provide three examples of each that are not found in the text.
4. List five reasons why firms use line extensions. Which do you feel is most effective?

5. What are four ways to measure the impact of line extensions? Provide an example for each.
6. How do firms evaluate the market for a successful launch?
7. What are ways companies can create aura for their line extensions?
8. What items in the GT-MAP framework can be used to evaluate extensions?
9. Select an existing line extension and, using the GT-MAP, evaluate it and provide your thoughts on its success.

Discussion Questions

1. Prepare for your professor an evaluation of the success of an innovation currently introduced. What did the firm do correctly? What could they improve on?
2. XYZ, Inc. currently sells hamburgers and fries as their original product. Share two ways XYZ can perform a horizontal and vertical line extension of their original product.
3. Share your thoughts on other reasons why firms use line extensions. Discuss why you listed these reasons.
4. Share one additional impact you feel an extension has on a product category. Why did you list this?
5. Using the items listed in ways to evaluate the market for a successful launch, select a product and discuss how a company can use this information to launch a product.
6. Do you feel aura is important? Share a product that did an effective job gaining your attention or not gaining your attention. Why did you indicate these things?
7. Discuss what additional items you feel can be added to the GT-MAP. Why did you indicate this?

Extension Activity

1. Gather in small groups and list products that firms have performed line extensions for, giving examples of both horizontal and vertical extensions. Were they successful? Share the findings with the class.
2. Pair up with a classmate and discuss other criterion to determine success and logical next steps for firms to address in relation to what was discussed in the first section, "How Is the Innovation Performing and What Are the Next Steps?".

BIBLIOGRAPHY

Son, Hugh. "J. P. Morgan Software Does in Seconds What Took Lawyers 360,000 Hours," *Bloomberg*, February 28, 2017, https://www.bloomberg.com/news/articles/2017-02-28/jpmorgan-marshals-an-army-of-developers-to-automate-high-finance.

Markowitz, Lee. "Are You Confident Your Line Extension Will Pay Out?" Ipsos, June 1, 2011, https://www.ipsos.com/en-us/are-you-confident-your-line-extension-will-pay-out-0.

Forbes Agency Council, "17 Steps to Take before You Launch a Product or Service," *Forbes*, October 24, 2017, https://www.forbes.com/sites/forbesagencycouncil/2017/10/24/18-steps-to-take-before-you-launch-a-product-or-service/2/#28af8cb571f2.

DeMers, Jayson. "7 Cheap Ways to Generate Buzz for Your Business," *Forbes,* May 21, 2015, https://www.forbes.com/sites/jaysondemers/2015/05/21/7-cheap-ways-to-generate-buzz-for-your-business/#54d69b4f52a9.

CHAPTER TWENTY ONE

Why is R&R (Reflect and Review) Important?

INTRODUCTION

As the innovation process winds down, firms must use the lessons learned, both good and bad, to reflect on what they found and to make the next innovation more successful. This chapter discusses using reflection and review (R&R) as a necessary way to benchmark what contributed to the innovation's success to next practices. We will discuss six steps to reflection and how change accelerates the importance of R&R. The concepts of best practices and next practices are also discussed and how best practices limit firms, while next practices encourage continuous improvement and innovation. Finally, John Sztykiel will provide his closing thoughts as to what we hope for you was a great experience filled with lots of learning about the world of innovation.

Learning Objectives

In this chapter students will learn about the following:

- Why R&R is the key to innovation
- How change accelerates and the importance of R&R grows
- The differences between best practices and next practices

Learning Outcomes

By the end of this chapter students will be able to do the following:

- Reflect and review on how the innovation process was conducted, taking away next practices and benchmarking what made it successful
- Know how to use the foundational points of innovation while adding concepts of the GT-MAP to accelerate change
- Create an innovation plan

Key Terms

Reflection: Thought, thinking, consideration, or dwelling on something

Review: Think or talk about something in the past

Best: The practice or process of becoming number one within the known parameters

Best practice: Procedure that is standardized within a firm or industry to accomplish a task

Next practice: The ability to stimulate, devise, and accelerate innovation based on consumer needs

REFLECT AND REVIEW (R&R) AND ITS IMPORTANCE

Any time a firm undertakes the scope and magnitude of work as indicated throughout this book, it is crucial that all teams take time to reflect and review all aspects of what has occurred. It is important to note that this should not be considered optional. It is imperative, when continuing striving for improvement and growth, both of which depend upon developing next practices, that teams reflect and review so that the next innovation can provide both the firm and its customers greater value and more impactful results.

Reflection

Reflection is thought, thinking, consideration, or dwelling on something. Reflection is an important part of the innovation process. Without taking the to time to reflect on what we did right or wrong and ways to improve on these, firms are wasting their efforts. Reflecting on the lessons from the text should reveal that reflection helps provide Kaizen or continuous improvement for the firm as it seeks ways to innovate with speed and efficiency. A research paper conducted by Somech[1] (2006) revealed that reflection plays a key role in innovation by increasing individual skills, building a collective culture, and serving as a way for top leaders to participate. Reflection is also a great tool to enhance learning through self-improvement.[2]

Reflection forces us to set aside time to analyze our actions and plans and really decide if we are on the right track. In the busy world in which we live, there is little time to reflect, so incorporating this plan into the innovation process is a great way to open communication and think about if we are doing what is best to provide a future framework for firms to survive and maximize both profits and possibilities.

In an interesting article by Umair Haque entitled *"Making Room for Reflection Is a Strategic Imperative"* the author pointed out that most companies are trained to do but not reflect. Dr. Haque points out that while the "doing/reflecting ratio" is disproportionate, there needs to be a

---

1   Anit Somech. "The Effects of Leadership Style and Team Process On Performance and Innovation In Functionally Heterogeneous Teams." *Journal of Management,* no. 1 (2006): 132–157. https://doi.org/10.1177/0149206305277799

2   Life LeGeros, "R is for REAL Reflection," Tarrant Institute for Innovative Education, September 25, 2015, http://tiie.w3.uvm.edu/blog/getting-real-about-student-reflection/#.W00NYdJKjIU.

greater emphasis placed on reflection on the part of firms.[3] Reflection gives the firm the ability to be motivated to experiment, provides for a higher level of innovation, gives the spark of deeper meaning, and gives a sense of purpose. Most firms do not know how to reflect, and this leads them to be just another "me too" company. The article gives six steps to guide reflection:

1. *Why.* The "do" mentality typically asks how, as in "How can we sell more products?" Why gives a sense of purpose and asks the bigger question "Why are we in business?" It answers the question of what the higher purpose is that drives innovation. Reflecting on the mission and vision of the firm should help to answer this question and answer the why.

2. *What.* What asks firms to reflect on the competencies they possess to be able to achieve or achieve the "why." It asks firms to reflect on this question: "Does the current 'what' support the 'why'?"

3. *Which.* Which helps to ask firms which goods, services, stakeholders, and resources they currently have help to bring the competencies to fruition. This takes reflection to think about and to analyze the current state of the firm.

4. *Primarify.* Many firms fall into the trap of using data that is very old to guide their reflection. Better reflection requires using primary data (i.e., data collected face to face) to get the most current thoughts, impressions, and so on from their customers.

5. *Qualify.* Reflection doesn't seek what is happening; it seeks why things are happening and how they impact society. Reflection requires useful qualitative data that gives firms perspectives from human experiences.

6. *Simplify.* Reflection should provide concepts that aren't influenced by the boardroom, but by the ability to do a greater good. It should be thoughtful and simplistic in its approach, while giving purpose to the firm.

While these six steps may seem easy to do, they are lacking it today's fast-paced world. Think about the last time you were free from distractions and had time to reflect on your schooling, life, future, and so on. Reflection is not something that happens immediately but must be part of your life or the agenda of firms seeking to innovate at a higher level.

Review

To review is to think or talk about something in the past. Reviewing helps firms analyze what they have done to determine if the results were as expected and if they accomplished their goals. If they did well and it was very successful, firms should benchmark these practices. If they didn't perform well or had problems, these should be noted as well. Reviewing forces

---

3   Umair Haque, "Making Room for Reflection Is a Strategic Imperative," *Harvard Business Review,* November 24, 2010, https://hbr.org/2010/11/reflection-items-not-action-it.

firms to look back at the evidence of their innovation processes and determine if they need to change anything for future innovation.

The firm's ability to review is sometimes hindered by things such as poor performance, laziness, success, or just not making it part of the planning process. Firms need to constantly review their GT-MAP to see how they are doing and to adjust for any threats or opportunities they see. It is only by reviewing and taking the time to reflect that the best firms perform at a higher level and achieve greatness.

AS CHANGE ACCELERATES, THE IMPORTANCE OF R&R GROWS

Today speed not only matters, it is key. With all this speed, one forgets about the importance to think and reflect on what is working and what is not. Think about the changes and data we are seeing and what we are not. People often wonder why the same mistakes are made on a continuous basis; it is due to the lack of reflection and review.

In an interesting article by Paul Hobcraft identifying the changing landscape of innovation, he points out that innovation today is rapidly changing, and the basics are being replaced by new and creative frameworks.[4] The basics of innovation on a corporate level include building engagement, leadership, and participation by all stakeholders. In addition, innovation helps to create a culture, climate, and community that helps innovation evolve and thrive. On the consumer side, the basics include understanding consumer needs, building new business models to better serve the target market, and monitoring consumer comments to gain a better feel for what they seek. The article goes on to indicate that while the need to be innovative is essential for survival, many firms are frustrated and disappointed by their lack of truly understanding how it works. A big part of this stems from the lack of reflection and reviewing what firms do right and wrong.

The new and creative frameworks, while not mentioned in the article, can include the GT-MAP, which is a new concept of innovating with speed, creating aura, building on efficiencies, and having a plan in place, to name a few key concepts. Without taking the time to move past the basics and adopting this new framework, firms would be hard pressed to succeed as they would not fully understand how it works and how it can benefit the firm. Therefore, as innovation fades from being a growing trend for businesses to more mainstream, firms need to review and reflect to keep up with these changes.

---

4   Paul Hobcraft, "Reflecting on Our Innovation Practices," Innovation Excellence, https://www.innovationexcellence.com/blog/2018/03/13/reflecting-on-our-innovation-practices/.

BEST PRACTICE VERSUS NEXT PRACTICE

American business has historically discussed using best practices to improve operations; however, there is new thinking helps ensure innovation through continuous improvement and it is called "next practices". Best practices use established ways of operating without improving, but this often slows down the innovation process and can have negative effects on the company's performance. Next practices are ways firms capitalize on what they are doing right and improving those processes to make their firm more efficient and profitable. This next section will identify the differences between the two terms and why next practices are useful for innovators.

Best Practices

The term *best practice* started to become popular in the 1970s. The definition of *best* is "the practice or process of becoming number one within the known parameters." This is the number-one issue, as *best practice* is an outdated term in today's world, because it centers around the known. ***Best practice*** is a procedure that is standardized within a firm or industry to accomplish a task. Innovation is about the unknown. Today when change is happening as fast as it is, what is known could be irrelevant within 24 hours.

If firms were to use only best practices, we would never move forward with innovation because we would cling to the past practices that brought success. This is common of firms that fail to innovate and just do what they have perfected without changing. Thirty years ago, the term *value* meant high quality. Today it means average commodity, the opposite of thirty years ago. Today we are in an "experiential" world, not a "value" world. This is not surprising in many respects as life is short and one should experience life, not value it. There is a big difference between value and experience. This is a deep thought, one to reflect on: Suppose someone does nothing with his or her whole life except live in a small room. He or she would eat the right number of meals per day and exercise regularly, essentially live in a very small area where all is provided and a schedule is set. The risk of injury, accidents, and stress is reduced dramatically. One could say that this person values life so much that he or she will reduce all opportunities for a negative event.

This is a prison, state or federal, and few people desire to live their whole life in a prison. This also supports the growing trend of realism/reality in all marketing. The world is becoming more experienced oriented, as are people.

Sergio Marchionne, the CEO of FCA (Fiat Chrysler Automotive) earned his degree in philosophy and law. Mark Cuban has said more than once that tomorrow's leaders will have a liberal arts background. All of this is based on the premise that humans are consumers and while humans think with their head, ultimately what drives their decision making is the heart, or as we identified in chapter 1, the limbic brain. The heart is often known as the "wellspring of all emotion." Too often people look at the data and perceive that people think in a logical way and base all the innovation and the GT-MAP on logic. Again, as we identified in chapter

1, the reality is the limbic brain rules, driven by all of its emotions and passion, as that is where all of our decisions are made.

Next Practices

In today and tomorrow's world, do you desire to be the "best of the best" or to be viewed as "next," the leader of not just today but tomorrow as well? Once you become known as "best," people become complacent or comfortable. The passion and the drive to be "next" is no longer as strong and soon you are no longer best. Jim Collins said, "Good is the enemy of great."

Next practice is the ability to stimulate, devise, and accelerate innovation based on consumer needs. Next practices give innovators the motivation to create products and processes, but before they can bask in the glow in the success, are forced to start again. It is a way to provide motivation and prohibit complacency. Kaizen is a form of next practice as it strives to seek continuous improvement. Authors Brian Moran and Michael Lennington wrote a bestselling book, *The 12-Week Year*: *Get More Done In 12 Weeks Than Others Do In 12 Months*.[5] The underlying themes of the book are as follows:

1. Discipline
2. Change happens so fast one should look at their year in 12-week increments
3. Reflect and review … thinking time

Moran and Lennington discuss the importance of thinking time and how it improves results. To become a next practice individual, people must first implement R&R in their personal lives. It has often been asked, "Do you ever think about what you are thinking about?" Everyone thinks many thoughts per day, but too often we do not spend focused time thinking or reflecting on our most important thoughts. Not only will this help your personal life, but this R&R mentality will also move over into your business life. In business it is simple; just insert time to reflect and review on the projects and the organization's structure and culture. People simply make time to think and discuss without feeling the pressure to decide. In reality, it's not hard; we just must have the mental conviction to do it.

R&R ON THIS TEXT

Over the course of this semester you have been exposed to many terms and concepts you may have never heard or thought about. Our goal when we started this text was to provide a tool kit of ways to innovate using the proven GT-MAP. It was our hope to provide a more realistic view of innovation than the current textbooks on the market today.

---

5   Brain P. Moran, and Michael Lennington. "*The 12 Week Year: Get More Done In 12 Weeks Than Others Do In 12 Months.*" New Jersey: John Wiley & Sons, 2013.

Closing Thoughts

The importance of R&R, both personally and from a business perspective is paramount as sports coaches use the term, "tale of the tape," or reviewing the team or an individual's game performance on film where there is no emotion and no time constraints, and this is critical to improved execution. This is important methodology and needs to be adopted first by yourself.

Second, focus on people's hearts, not their brains and you will be amazed at the success you will have. Next practices, never settle at best; be known as next, not just once but on a continuous basis. The enemy of next is best as one becomes complacent.

Innovation is about going where no one has been before, where perception becomes reality, and where tomorrow becomes today. Without faith, the belief that we have yet to see all that man and this world has to offer, the future will never happen. Last, attitude, our "heart" through our mind, drives everything.

The following are 10 things that have changed the landscape of business over the past 115 years. As you review them, think of how far we have come and where we can go to make the world a better place. How can you as a innovator make the difference toward this change using the tools you have learned using this text[6]?

1. Business Is about More Than Profit, 1908

At a time when success in business was equated with ruthlessness, Harvard President Charles Eliot launched a graduate school to teach executives to be moral actors in society.

The impact: The Harvard MBA remains a pinnacle achievement in higher education and doing good is now widely considered good business.

2. The Five-Dollar Workday, 1914

Henry Ford doubled his employees' pay in the hope that other mass producers would follow, establishing a class of consumers who could afford Ford cars and other goods.

The impact: Ford helped create the middle class, but globalization and stagnant wages have since stalled the American flywheel of success.

3. Comprehensive Employee Benefits, 1928

Kodak CEO George Eastman adopted "welfare capitalism," granting benefits that were lavish for the era, such as life insurance, profit sharing, tuition assistance, and a retirement annuity.

The impact: As happy employees helped Kodak thrive, its HR innovations spread and still influence the likes of Whole Foods and Starbucks.

4. The Innovation Lab, 1944

In an old dairy, 3M Management set up the Products Fabrication Laboratory (colloquially known as the "funny farm") for lab technicians to dream big without constraints.

---

6   David Lidsky, "10 Big Bets on Optimism That Changed the Business World," Fast Company, January 15, 2018, https://www.fastcompany.com/40509052/10-big-bets-on-optimism-that-changed-the-business-world.

The impact: 3M's misfits of science invented such breakthroughs as surgical tape. Xerox PARC and Google X's moonshot labs owe 3M a debt.

5. *Managing by Walking Around, 1957*
William Hewlett and David Packard wrote down their company's approach to leadership, which encouraged executives to interact directly with line workers, so each could learn from the other.

The impact: "The HP Way" became the leading Silicon Valley management style; even non-tech firms have embraced its flattening of hierarchies.

6. *Putting Customers First, 1975*
John Bogle refused outside investment when starting his mutual fund company, Vanguard, which let him focus on saving clients' money rather than goosing profits for his backers.

The impact: Competitors have had to lower fees as Vanguard has amassed $4 trillion in assets. Jeff Bezos is Bogle's modern-day customer obsessive.

7. *Flexible Workplaces, 1993*
When advertising legend Jay Chiat opened the new Chiat/Day offices, he sought to boost creativity by banishing assigned desks in favor of using laptops and cell phones to work anywhere.

The impact: Ad folks rebelled against the set up, which was too radical for its time, but Chiat's idea lives on at WeWork and other coworking spaces.

8. *Domestic-Partner Benefits, 1996*
In the same month that Congress banned gay marriage, IBM extended healthcare benefits to its employees' gay and lesbian partners.

The impact: Corporations helped mainstream LGBTQ rights; in 2015, 379 firms, from Apple to Disney to Target, formally urged the Supreme Court to reverse the Defense of Marriage Act.

9. *Going Green, 2005*
When GE introduced Ecomagination, a suite of environmentally friendly products, it seemed like a joke from the once-notorious polluter.

The impact: GE has generated $270 billion in revenue from products such as windmills; cut greenhouse-gas emissions; and inspired Walmart, PepsiCo, and other giants to be more sustainable.

10. *Calling Out Sexual Harassment, 2017*
Beleaguered by assault and abuse in the workplace, women are using social media and other platforms to shine a light on wrongdoing.

The impact: Prominent serial predators and bullies have lost their jobs, and enlightened businesses have begun to wrestle with systemic misogyny and long-standing power dynamics.

Innovation, the GT-MAP, the fact that you have just one life so make the best of it. Don't be the person who says, "I wish I would have … !" Be the person who did what you wished for. You now have been given some great tools. Move; make it happen!

Review Questions

1. What is reflection and why is it essential for innovation?
2. Why is reviewing an innovation process crucial for firms?
3. What are the six steps to reflection?
4. Is innovation changing? How does the GT-MAP framework give firms an advantage over basic innovation principles?
5. Compare best practices and next practices.
6. What was your number-one take away from R&R on this text?

Discussion Questions

1. Why are we an "experiential" world today versus a "value" world?
2. What type of world will we be in in twenty years? Will it be an artificial one with the growth of AI? What else?
3. What is the difference between "valuing" life and "experiencing life"? How does this relate to innovation, the GT-MAP?
4. How does a firm's aura grow when it becomes known as a next practice organization?
5. Today, what innovations or GT-MAPs do you see that are a result of focusing on the heart?
6. Why do people struggle with review and reflect?
7. Why do organizations struggle with review and reflect?

BIBLIOGRAPHY

Somech, Anit. "The Effects of Leadership Style and Team Process On Performance and Innovation In Functionally Heterogeneous Teams." *Journal of Management,* no. 1 (2006): 132–157. https://doi.org/10.1177/0149206305277799

Life LeGeros, "R is for REAL Reflection," Tarrant Institute for Innovative Education, September 25, 2015, http://tiie.w3.uvm.edu/blog/getting-real-about-student-reflection/#.W00NYdJKjIU.

Haque, Umair. "Making Room for Reflection Is a Strategic Imperative," *Harvard Business Review,* November 24, 2010, https://hbr.org/2010/11/reflection-items-not-action-it.

Hobcraft, Paul. "Reflecting on Our Innovation Practices," Innovation Excellence, https://www.innovationexcellence.com/blog/2018/03/13/reflecting-on-our-innovation-practices/.

Moran, Brain P. and Lennington, Michael. "*The 12 Week Year: Get More Done In 12 Weeks Than Others Do In 12 Months.*" New Jersey: John Wiley & Sons, 2013.

Lidsky, David. "10 Big Bets on Optimism That Changed the Business World," Fast Company, January 15, 2018, https://www.fastcompany.com/40509052/10-big-bets-on-optimism-that-changed-the-business-world.

Acknowledgments

This text could not have been possible without the help of some important people. I want to first acknowledge my co-authors. John Sztykiel, who helped me realize the importance of innovation while I taught at Michigan State which I am grateful. Next, Moss Ingram has been a breath of fresh air to this project and a man who is utterly amazing in his knowledge and understanding of this topic. I thank you both!

Next, I want to acknowledge Michael Brady, my department chair at Florida State, and our Dean, Michael Hartline, for their encouragement in helping me bring innovation back to the College of Business. Their realization of the importance this topic is appreciated by me and future Seminole innovators.

I would also like to acknowledge my parents who have always been my biggest fans and support. Thank you for the encouragement to always be my best and pursue my dreams no matter how lofty they may seem.

Finally, I want to acknowledge the grace that God has given me and the ability to achieve all the things I have done in my life. I did not do these things by chance, and I know He has been instrumental in my success.

—Keith E. Ferguson

This book and so many other optimal experiences in my life would not have been possible without the recognition, foresight, and wellspring of encouragement from my dear friend Dr. Gilda Gely. I am forever grateful for her support.

I would like to thank my friend Dr. Keith Ferguson for inviting me to collaborate on this project, as well as John Sztykiel for his vision and entrepreneurial drive, and to our family at Cognella, with very special thanks to Jennifer Codner, Michelle Piehl, and Abbey Hastings.

Thank you to my early innovation mentors Bill Guest and Eric Heller, whose introduction to innovation changed my life.

Thank you to my fellow core innovation teammates, Becky Yoder and Ann Sandberg, for all their inspiration and ideation.

Thank you to my friend Dr. Anne Mulder for her contagious passion and enlightened understanding.

Many thanks to Birgit Klohs and The Right Place, whose strategic and sustainable economic development has transformed a region and improved the lives and opportunities for everyone who lives within it.

I would also like to thank Judy Stark, Deb Dewent, Linda Chamberlain, Juan Oliverez, Misty McClure, George Waite, Penni Wenninger, Patti Trepkowski, Mary Brown, Kevin Budelmann, Mark Champion, Mindy Firlan, Michael Schavey, Pat Ingersoll, Felix Pereiro, Chris Arnold, Donna Kragt, Fiona Hert, Mike Vargo, Greg Northup, Jennifer Smith, Rachael Bower, Jan Ensing, Laurie Schaut, Juan Heredia, Peggy Gorno, Tina Hoxie, John Cowles, Ric Underhile, Eric Kunnen, Casey DuBois, Jason Sosa, Klass Kwant, and Elly Bainbridge for their support and engagement in the innovation process.

I would also like to thank my colleagues Julie Parks, Scott Mattson, Deb Stout, Vicki Maxa, Dan Keyes, Bill Pink, Amy Mansfield, Jimmie Baber, Pamela Miller, Frank Conner, Mike Klawitter, Nan Schichtel, Kathy Mullins, Deb Bailey, Greg Forbes, Steve Abid, Eric Mullins, Robert Hendershot, Katie Kalisz, Maryann Lesert, Nora Neill, Fred van Hartesveldt, Jeff Spoelman, Rachael Jungblut, Erin Rozek, David Selmon, John VanElst, Cheryl Cole, Gayl Beals, Kyle Lacksheide, John Doane, Nate Haney, Ben Smith, Drew Rozema, Kevin Dobreff, Mansfield Matthewson, Jane Ann Benson, Keith St. Clair, and John Doneth for their support in design thinking and innovation, especially in the context of teaching and writing.

Thank you to Mark Dodd and Kwasi Joseph—without their coverage, this work would not have been possible.

Many thanks and appreciation to Fred Leebron, Michael Schumacher, Elissa Schappell, David Payne, Pinkney Benedict, Robert Polito, Khris Baxter, Chuck Wendig, Michael Kobre, Andrew McLean and Dawn Kresan for opening doors for me to become a better writer.

Additionally, many thanks and appreciation to Gayle DeBryn, Nate Young, Michael Dillane, Ken Krayer, Lloyd Walker, and Thomas Newhouse for helping me become a better designer and innovator.

Also, many thanks and appreciation to Laura Magnussen Linares, Carrie Wing, Michelle Powell, Jill Olszak, Diane Artel, Mae DiBenedetto, Loie Yaeger, Tricia Heersink, Pam Bernard and Tim Preheim for the opportunity to be a part of one of the best teams to edit and write IT-based training books for industry.

I would also like to thank my parents, Bill and Laurel Ingram, who taught me much about ideation, hard work, and prototyping, as well as many thanks to my brother, Grant, whose exceptional innovations have benefited thousands of people world-wide.

Thank you to Margaret Atwood, not only for continuing to engage in the time-old tradition of teaching and mentoring new artists, but for demonstrating that working writers are also entrepreneurs, innovators, and designers, and for developing products in addition to poems, short stories, and novels.

Most of all, thank you to my wife Genevieve and our two innovation designers, Nora and August, for their love, support, brilliance, and light.

—Moss Ingram